From Sight to Insight

. . . both sight and insight derive from fierce consciousness, whether it begins in looking at a small object or in paying attention to all of the implications and resonances of an idea or image.

MARVIN BELL

From Sight to Insight

Stages in the Writing Process

FOURTH EDITION

Jeff Rackham
The University of North Carolina, Asheville

Olivia Bertagnolli
The University of North Carolina, Asheville

Holt, Rinehart and Winston, Inc.

Fort Worth   Chicago   San Francisco   Philadelphia
Montreal   Toronto   London   Sydney   Tokyo

Acquisitions Editor	Michael Rosenberg
Developmental Editor	Leslie Taggart
Project Editorial	Impressions Publishing Services
Production Manager	Kathleen Ferguson
Art & Design Supervisor	Serena Barnett
Text Design	Impressions Publishing Services
Cover Design	Karin Clare

Library of Congress Cataloging-in-Publication Data

Rackham, Jeff
   From sight to insight : stages in the writing process / Jeff Rackham, Olivia
Bertagnolli. — 4th ed.
     p.   cm.

   Includes index.

ISBN 0-03-052208-0 (paperback)

   1. English language—Rhetoric. I. Bertagnolli, Olivia. II. Title
  PE1408.R13   1991
  808'.0427   90-40434
                                                     CIP

Address for editorial correspondence: Holt, Rinehart and Winston, Inc., 301 Commerce Street, Suite 3700, Fort Worth, TX 76102.

Address for orders: Holt, Rinehart and Winston, Inc., 6277 Sea Harbor Drive, Orlando, Florida 32887. 1-800-782-4479, or 1-800-433-0001 (in Florida).

Printed in the United States of America

1 2 3 4 090 9 8 7 6 5 4 3 2 1

Holt, Rinehart and Winston, Inc.
The Dryden Press
Saunders College Publishing

Preface

This fourth edition builds on the suggestions of instructors who have used *From Sight to Insight* in more than 150 colleges and universities. Drawing on their advice, I have doubled the number of student essays in each unit and replaced more than half the professional essays and stories throughout the text with new works, usually by noted authors. In keeping with the original philosophy of *From Sight to Insight*, I've attempted to choose both student and professional works that are easily imitable, rather than those that, for all their quality or fame, often seem inhibiting to the aspirations of average college freshmen. In addition, the unit on "Writing about Ideas, Issues, and Values" has been significantly expanded first by more fully developing a discussion of how rhetorical modes contribute both to seeing a subject and to understanding it, and second, by creating an all new chapter on "The Analytical Mind." Numerous student examples enrich both chapters, and four new professional essays illustrate how formal rhetorical patterns have been used successfully, either separately or in combination.

    The third edition's emphasis on journal activity has been retained because of its popularity and success. Recent studies continue to show that journal writing is an essential activity, not only for student writers but also for scientists, historians, mathematicians, artists, psychologists—for anyone whose profession involves thinking or creative activity—not only in the preparation stages but throughout the whole process by which ideas and language develop. We now know that such individuals use journals as part of an ongoing activity, sometimes independent of formal work, at other times as a direct or indirect resource to any given phase of writing. "Journal Practice" is therefore included throughout the text to show the variety and levels of writing that journals contribute to. For those instructors who don't use journals, all "Journal Practice" assignments can easily be adapted to in- or out-of-class exercises.

I've also found that instructors differ on when they like to assign fully developed essays. Some prefer to give assignments at the beginning of each unit so that students have a sense of what they're working toward. Others prefer to coordinate formal essay assignments with the chapter on "Drafting" (that is, after the exploratory stages are initiated). Still others wait until students have worked through each chapter in the unit. To accommodate so many approaches, all "Suggested Writing Projects" are now located in a special section at the end of the book where the variety and levels of writing tasks can be seen in their entirety, and can be assigned at whatever point the instructor feels appropriate.

I have, of course, retained the unique organization of the original edition, an organization based on the essential stages of writing most of us go through when we struggle to place words on the page: first, *exploring* (and that includes exploring language, self, and subject), followed by *identifying an audience, discovering form, drafting, revising,* and *editing.* Each of these stages is repeated and expanded in eight separate units. This pattern of growth is repeated for each phase in the writing process. The text leads students from the personal, imaginative, and concrete to the objective, critical, and abstract: from the senses and emotions to ideas and values. Each stage is repeated at least five times, often as many as twelve, but always at a higher level of difficulty.

I recognize that these stages are never as simple or as orderly as I characterize them in the text. But to present them in all their recursive redundancy seems to create confusion and a threatening ambiguity for our students. Because students need to know how to write, not how to theorize about writing, I have chosen simplicity over complexity. Yet at the same time, the very argument of the text rejects an overly simplistic linear approach to writing. Throughout the book I try to promote the notion that thinking itself is a process, that thoughts occur and shape themselves during the act of writing, and that insights may grow out of any and every phase of the process, including the preparatory stage of looking at and exploring a subject through one's senses, long before one ever puts a word to the page.

Because this process is never identical for any two of us (and perhaps never identical even for the same individual on any two writing projects), it has always seemed important to offer students as many options as possible for discovering their own potential at every level. I have therefore continued to show how professional writing skills—those of the creative writer, journalist, and professional essayist—as well as those skills developed through academic and rhetorical models, should be understood as parts of one unified writing process.

I want to express my appreciation to the many individuals who have given time and energy in helping with this revision. First, to Olivia Bertagnolli whose involvement with the text has been so extensive over the years that I can no longer separate her ideas from mine; her name rightly appears, therefore, on the cover. And second, to the talented staff at Holt, Rinehart and Winston, beginning with Developmental Editor Leslie Taggart, Acquisitions Editor Michael Rosenberg, Production Manager Kathleen Ferguson, and Art and Design Supervisor Serena Barnett.

Special thanks goes to former Humanities Publisher Charlyce Jones Owen, whose vision and talent has inspired the confidence of so many writers.

I am also indebted to the able reviewers who offered valuable insights and suggestions for this edition: Nancy Anderson, Auburn University; Joan G. Brand, Cincinnati Technical College; Roger George, Bellevue Community College; Georgina Hill, Andrews University; Larry Perkins, Jefferson Community College; Alice Sink, High Point College; and Donna Winchell, Clemson University.

Finally, I want to acknowledge my gratitude to Wilson R. Thornley, who taught so many of us that through writing one can discover what it means to be a human being. It is to his spirit, ever alive in his students, that this book continues to be dedicated.

Jeff Rackham

Contents

Exploring

Audience

Drafting and the Discovery of Form

Revising

Editing

PART IV   THE EXTENDED INVESTIGATION   **205**

PART V   WRITING ABOUT IDEAS, ISSUES, AND VALUES   275

Exploring

Exploring

Exploring

Audience and Form

PART VII   CRITIQUING THE ARTS   **395**

Exploring

31 Awareness of the Arts   397

Exploring

32 Literary Significance   412

Audience and Form

33 The Formal Critique   430

Readings

PART VIII · SCHOLARLY RESEARCH   **449**

Exploring

34 The Preliminary Stages of Research   451

Exploring

35 Thoughtful Note Taking   466

Discovering Form

36 Organizing Complex Material   479

Drafting

37 Drafting and Documenting   486

Introduction

The Writing Process

Novelist Robert Crichton likes to tell the story about writing his first novel. He was already in his thirties, an established professional journalist. Writing a novel had been a dream all his life. But the truth was that even when he discovered the perfect story on a trip to Italy, he was afraid of the attempt. He interviewed Italians who could provide him with background material. He took notes. He wrote long letters home. But he was unable to begin the novel. Later, back in New York, he threw away his notes and made more notes from the letters he had written. Yet he was still afraid of starting on the book. He sat at his desk and wrote one word: "If." The next day he wrote, "So now I begin," and could go no further. Finally he tried writing about the weather: "On a cold blustery morning in May . . . ," but it led nowhere.

Crichton admits now that he had become hyperconscious about style and craft. All the rules of writing suddenly seemed foreboding. The moment he wrote a word on the page he began making critical judgments. He wanted what he wrote to be perfect; he wanted it to sound profound and moving. He read Tolstoy to see how a novel ought to read, and it only made him feel intimidated, paralyzed. How could he ever compete with the great writers before him? Each day he struggled with a few sentences and each day he threw away everything he had done. "I couldn't imagine," he says, "who would be listening to me and who would want to read anything I wrote."

Finally, Crichton discovered what all writers must eventually find out: that it matters little whether you're trying to write a book or a college essay, you cannot worry about the finished product before you've even begun. Writing is a process—an action—that requires you to dive in—feet first or head first—it doesn't matter. For Crichton it meant forcing himself through a "Dick and Jane" manuscript of some 125 pages, then revising until it was more than 500 pages long. It was a matter of letting go, becoming immersed in the story he had to tell, letting the writing itself generate ideas, letting the process of exploring images lead him in directions he had not expected.

Learning to write may present you with similar frustrations. You may be one of those for whom writing has always seemed impossible. One reason may be that in the past so many teachers and students approached good writing as a system of rules and forms: they analyzed well-written arguments by George Orwell or profound moral essays by Bertrand Russell; they categorized how great authors organized, shaped, selected, and envisioned their material; and they gave names to the most successful and traditional models—narration, exemplification, exposition, and so on. Yet when students tried to imitate such models they often felt frustrated and helpless. What they wanted to say never seemed to fit conventional rhetorical patterns.

Over the years, I've found a lot of my students feeling discouraged. Compared with the masterpieces of English prose, their essays read like failures, lacking all grace and style. As Robert Crichton learned, he had been looking too long at the rules and forms instead of at the process. The best analysis of a well-written novel (or memo or research paper) cannot reveal the false starts, the thrown-away words and paragraphs, or the agony the author feels each morning staring at the blank page. Nor does it reveal how an author finally discovers what it is he or she wants to say.

This book, then, is about a process. I confess I'll sometimes analyze or explain a rhetorical model, and there will be many discussions of craft, but I hope it will be seen only in a context of helping you find a method for getting ideas onto the page—your method. Because we are individuals, the "process" cannot be identical for each of us, just as there can't be ten rules for playing tennis like Ivan Lendl or sixteen rules for playing the piano like Vladimir Horowitz. But by investigating the methods successful writers go through, we find certain phases seem to recur, enough so that we can identify six general stages most writers move through. The stages are seldom sequential, as I present them here. Writers usually move back and forth between and among phases in a messy, recursive process. However, once the process is understood *as process*, as something essential for all of us to work through and endure, it can free your creative potential.

EXPLORING THE SUBJECT

Perception

All writers need to know about their subject; they also need to learn how to know about it: how to look, how to investigate, how to see relationships. In many ways this first stage in the writing process is the single most important element in achieving meaningful, intelligent prose. Exploration begins with perception, a sensory act. You must see your subject (and sometimes hear it, taste it, touch it, smell it). Ideas do not float in midair. You discover them in the process of looking at specific details, searching out patterns, bringing together seemingly unrelated parts. A business executive makes a special trip to Texas, where she personally observes the market for her product; she listens to opinions from local officials; she surveys the community's needs; she takes notes on facts found in a government report; she studies statistics provided by a university analysis. Only then does she write her report to the company president. A social worker needs funds to develop housing projects for the aged. He searches for supporting evidence in local welfare records; he interviews supporters of the project; he selects two good examples from more than fifty case studies; he makes a visual survey of the neighborhood to gather concrete impressions. Only then does he begin to write his grant proposal. No matter what your goal in writing, the first step is to see the subject clearly.

Yet the mind can be overwhelmed by too many details. Part of the perception process involves learning how to focus intensely on a manageable part of the whole subject and then how to select only the most significant details from that smaller part. Learning how to focus and select requires practice. Most writing assignments, whether in school or in a job, will already have some degree of focus: Write a ten-page analysis of economic relations between Cuba and Haiti; write an essay on character growth in *Huckleberry Finn*. But even these subjects will usually prove too broad. The writer always has the responsibility for narrowing a subject. Otherwise, a jumble of impressions leads to a confused and unfocused paper, like a home movie that jumps from "Our Vacation in the Rockies" to "Esther's Third Birthday." Focusing and selecting must become automatic steps for every writer.

Perception is ultimately the source of your ideas. In working through

facts, details, statistics; in listening to others' opinions; in personal observation, you begin to combine and compare, to differentiate, to see
relationships and patterns. For many, the understanding of a subject,
the ideas and insights, will occur even before a word has been written;
for others, like myself, the act of writing may be the only way to force
the mind to shape and order the material. Obviously, I am using the
term *perception* in a general sense to include a great many acts that go
on in the mind, but the original meaning of the term includes the notion
of "seeing all the way through a subject," of reaching "understanding."
I think then that if we accept the concept in its broadest sense, we can
fairly say that a well-written paper is the result of an intense perceptive
process.

The Writer's Journal

Still, this early, preparatory stage in the writing process raises a difficult
issue. Just how do ideas emerge from observations? The answer clearly
differs for every writing situation. What we do know is that professional
writers—as well as scientists, statesmen, artists, and others who depend
upon their minds for creative ideas—often rely on journal writing as a
primary means not only of recording acts of perception but of stimulating, toying with, and exploring concepts that emerge from perception.
A biologist working on dolphin migration in the Pacific Basin may record
each day's findings, her perception of the data, and then move on to
reflections, hunches, speculations—anything that may eventually lead
her to a deeper understanding of the information she's working with.
Others have used journals to explore memories and emotions, to play,
to invent word games, to draw diagrams of their ideas, or merely to
"warm up," much as a pianist might practice scales before turning to
a piece by Mozart. We have thousands of such journals left by some of
our finest minds: Peter Tchaikovsky, Charles Darwin, Margaret Mead,
Thomas Wolfe, Dag Hammarskjöld. Each kept a notebook of explorations, a sourcebook of half-formed ideas, lists of possibilities, a single
sentence that after days or months or even years of incubation grew into
a fully developed theorem, a novel, a strategy for national defense. And
that is the point. The journal is not an end in itself, but a tool for
preparation and incubation. Few of us think first and then write. We
think *as* we write. In fact, many of us discover what we think only after
we've placed words on the page. Writing in a journal is an act of exploring our perceptions, of tracing vague feelings and half-formed ideas
that observations may stimulate; it is an act of brainstorming ideas that

may go nowhere, of taking risks in order to eventually discover a deeper and more precise understanding of our subject.

IDENTIFYING THE AUDIENCE

Writing is an act of communication with a reader (an audience). Few beginning writers realize how significant the audience is, both in the way they perceive the subject and in the way they write about it.

The audience may well influence the way a writer looks at a subject. If a lawyer writes a brief for a judge, it must be logical and concise; it must be documented with facts and precedents. But, in turn, that means the lawyer must see the subject in the same way. The client may have wrecked a car one warm summer night when waves pounded against the beach and the scent of orange blossoms hung in the air. Those are all good sensory details derived from perception. But they won't influence the judge. A different selection of details is called for. The lawyer needs facts on road conditions: a broken safety barrier and the number of other accidents that have recently occurred on that same curve. The details a writer searches for depend not only on the subject but also on the audience—and on the way the writer hopes to affect that audience.

Writing is often a private act. But the product (the essay, report, critical analysis) is a public performance. As in all social actions, convention and custom influence the parties involved. The shaping of your ideas, the voice you speak in, the level of your vocabulary, the formality of your sentences, even your grammar and punctuation, may be influenced by the type of audience you're trying to reach. You would probably agree that safety instructions to plant employees should be written in short declarative statements that allow for no ambiguity. Regardless of the shop supervisor's poetic spirit or need to express his inner self, that supervisor cannot be allowed to write safety instructions in free verse. Yet an essay written for a Shakespearean scholar assumes a different audience with a different set of expectations. We can speculate that the Shakespearean scholar might quickly become bored with a paper written in short declarative sentences. Why, she asks the student, can't you let a little more of yourself come through? Where is your voice, the flow and rhythm of some kind of personal style? Successful writers anticipate the reader's needs. They recognize that conventions exist not as unbreakable rules but as traditional patterns that have proved successful in easing communication.

Identifying the audience and its needs must occur almost simultaneously with the first phase of the writing process: *exploring the subject.*

Honest writers will not change their ideas to please a particular audience, but they must often be willing to change many other elements—selection of evidence, organization of details, tone and level of vocabulary—all for one reason: to communicate their ideas as effectively as possible.

DISCOVERING FORM

In spite of Wordsworth's famous assertion that poetry is a "spontaneous overflow of emotion," no writing, not even poetry, is ever totally spontaneous. No doubt the best writing often sounds spontaneous, but some sort of organization or form always disciplines content. In prose, most forms, such as the essay or narrative, are open-structured, allowing enormous freedom for exploring and developing a subject. Other than a few obvious requirements like beginnings, middles, and ends, no inflexible patterns exist. You may be suspicious of the whole notion. Organizing, shaping, forming have always been the great stumbling blocks to professional writers as well as students. The reason is easy to identify: Finding form in a subject is a process of ordering chaos. In other words, it's hard work. You may have focused your subject, selected your details, and clearly identified your audience; but if you're like me, you'll still have a head jumbled with subpoints, half-formed ideas, images, and hunches. No outburst of spontaneous writing will magically shape that material into a coherent message. From time to time, exhilarating moments of inspiration do occur, but most attempts to organize require sustained effort.

Placing *discovering form* as the third stage in the process, however, is merely arbitrary. The organization of a paper may be determined by the writer's special perception of the subject or by the limitations and biases of a particular audience. Form may be consciously organized with a roman-numeral outline, or it may evolve gradually from the writing itself. Knowledge and practice of techniques developed by professional writers can often ease your way. For example, professional writers have developed something called the "lead." A lead quickly defines and limits your subject, establishes tone, and suggests a pattern of organization, all in a sentence or two. Other successful writers make line drawings to "design" their work or jot down informal lists of words and phrases. Still others depend on traditional forms, arguing that they can give more attention to internal subject matter if they allow convention to establish external outlines. Each of these different methods will be reviewed later to provide you with a number of options for any writing situation.

DRAFTING

Ray Bradbury once said that "writing must be as immediate as life, or there are no juices, no chance to involve yourself or others in your vitality." I've known many students who approached the act of writing with such dread that the product they produced expressed little of their lives and nothing of their vitality. Many student papers read as if they were written by a faulty computer: awkward sentences, distorted vocabulary, too many words and not enough substance, a stumbling lack of logic. Where are the juices? Where are the human beings that never seem to emerge from these shapings of their native language? And yet other students write with remarkable fluency, with a zest that reveals their own voice and spirit. Some even feel free to let ideas grow out of accidents, to play with words. Surprisingly, the difference does not seem to lie in natural ability as much as in the initial attitude a writer brings to the blank page. Perhaps one of the most serious misunderstandings about the writing process is a failure to envision the first draft and the many drafts that may follow as essential stages requiring separate mental attitudes.

In discussing creativity, psychologist Abraham H. Maslow suggests distinguishing between a primary phase and a secondary phase. During the primary phase, you as a writer must lose your past and future. You must live only in the moment, "immersed, fascinated and absorbed in the present, in the current situation, in the here–now, with the matter-in-hand." While drafting, you must become willing to suspend—at least temporarily—a critical attitude. You must teach yourself to let it flow, to write fast, talking to the page to discover what you know; you must allow digressions to occur. Drafting is the primary phase of creativity, the point where you get down your perceptions, follow your hunches, see the subject intensely in your mind as you write, often ignoring your notes or your outline. Drafting is the stage where you allow yourself to make mistakes, where you don't worry about the rules, the right word, or the conclusion. You just write.

You might think of all this as a process of creating a rough sketch of your ideas, a process of writing an extended note to yourself. You'll have time later to judge what you've written, to revise, to correct. But unless you've explored the subject freely with your own voice, you'll have nothing to improve on.

Like many students, you may feel most free and relaxed when writing in your journal. You keep the journal for yourself. You are your own audience in the journal. You can play, test ideas, scratch out, let your imagination flow—and that is usually the origin of vitality in writing.

REVISING

Once you begin to feel satisfied that you've found what you want to say, a new element enters the picture. Revising is a dual process that includes the continued effort not only to resee the subject and to explore it ever more deeply but also to think about that other audience, the reader, and how you can best communicate your ideas and feelings. Communication begins to become as important as exploration.

I have a friend who claims she never revises. She merely extends the drafting process, beginning again with almost the same attitude she has when she writes her first rough notes, almost without reference to what she has just written. Each draft is composed in the light of what she has learned about her subject in the previous draft. She pushes ahead, trusting her mind to develop ideas further, to clarify logic and order. Each draft is a rediscovery of her subject with renewed excitement and more depth. But each draft also becomes more polished, more directed outward toward her audience. Actually, she does revise, but through a subconscious process.

I envy her. I can't work that way. Once I've created what feels like a semicomplete working copy, I spread out with red pencil, black pen, scissors, and tape. My attitude is more self-critical than during early drafting. I cross out sentences, draw arrows, write new ideas in the margin. I juggle the order by cutting out paragraphs and taping them into new arrangements. From time to time, I stop and retype whole sections. The retyping reveals new flaws. Sometimes I read aloud and let my ear catch the imprecise word, the tangled sentence.

My friend and I approach revising in almost opposite ways. A third method has developed with the widespread use of word processors. Drafting on a microcomputer is surprisingly easy. A fast typist can almost keep up with the mind's release of ideas. And revising is even easier. Studies show that when they work with a word processor, writers are likely to spend more time moving sentences around, changing words, exploring new patterns of organization, and inserting new ideas than when they work with pen and pencil. For many individuals, the word processor has actually made revising an enjoyable act.

Whatever the method, all writers rewrite until the shape of a subject begins to find its wholeness. Some students believe that novels, like *War and Peace*, simply burst forth from the mind of the author, each perfect sentence following another. The experienced writer knows better. Painters, architects, sculptors—and writers—all work from rough sketches that only gradually take on shape and substance.

I heard recently about a business executive who ordered a new advertising campaign. Three days after a team of his best writers submitted the proposed material, he called them into his office. "Is this the best you can do?" he asked. No, they admitted sheepishly. There had been time pressure, other interruptions. They could do better. A week later they submitted the advertising campaign again. Again, three days later, he asked, "Is this the best you can do?" No, they admitted—but with more reluctance and a sense of frustration. No, they could do better. The process was repeated, the material resubmitted. On the third day the executive asked, "Is this the best you can do?" This time the team of writers insisted it was. Yes. This was the best. "Good," the executive replied. "Now I'll read it."

Revising, whether for an advertising campaign or a college-level essay, is obviously one of the most essential stages in the writing process. Some will even say that writing *is* revising.

EDITING

After drafting and revising, much remains to be done. Editing requires a cool, slow, line-by-line examination. For some, this stage may partially overlap the revising phase. For others, it seems most successful as a final and separate act. Often the work is laid aside, the intense involvement in the subject allowed to cool. Later, the writer returns to the paper with a critical eye, acting as his or her own editor.

As an editor you bring to your manuscript the attitude of an old craftsman. You want every word to be precise; you feel every unnecessary word should be eliminated and every verb should be strong. Sentence structures must be grammatically acceptable. You want each sentence to move the idea, the feeling, the rhythm of your voice easily toward the next sentence. Paragraphs must be coherent, focused, and unified. Each paragraph must relate to the preceding and following paragraphs. As an editor you won't hesitate to relocate a paragraph or strike it entirely if it does not contribute. Finally, the order and logic of the whole must seem apparent. The title must be considered as carefully as the conclusion. No detail is forgotten, not even (alas!) punctuation and spelling.

Learning how to edit means learning when to edit. If you begin too soon in the writing process, you may edit out your own personality in favor of safe, anonymous-sounding prose; you may even prevent your ideas from reaching their most developed form. That's why an understanding of writing as a process can be so valuable to your writing.

Editing must constitute the final phase (or at least occur no sooner than the revising phase). Editing must come at the point when what you have to say is important enough that every detail about how you say it seems worth perfecting.

Final editing of your manuscript is your responsibility. Someday you'll need to write a lab report for your team manager or a regional analysis for your county supervisor or a critical evaluation of court procedures for your law firm. No English instructor will be standing by to correct your paper in red ink. And your secretary may not be a good editor. Better to set high standards now and teach yourself how to reach them. Editing will not in itself make for good writing, but good writing is simply not possible without careful editing.

THE FINAL SYNTHESIS

The writing process is not a mechanical formula. At best it should suggest a pattern, not a rigid prescription. As you work on assignments, you'll find many phases in the process merge or overlap. To divide exploring, drafting, organizing, and revising into individual stages is an act of analysis. To draw them all together, as eventually you must, requires an act of synthesis. Just as you learn tennis by studying the forehand, backhand, and serve separately, consciously, you must eventually begin to play the game intuitively. We do not know how intuition works. We cannot teach it in the classroom. Yet this inner thing, this inner sensing for which we have no satisfactory explanation, is as much a part of successful writing as the process outlined here.

Gradually, with hard work and self-discipline, practice in the writing process sets in motion an inner growth. Whether playing tennis, painting a picture, or writing Japanese haiku, grace and beauty do not emerge from simply learning correct skills and techniques; true athletes, like true artisans, must be engaged in a process in which their craft, their art, grows out of some expression of inner self. By working through the writing process, you work through the very process necessary to begin an understanding of yourself; you work with the way the mind perceives, selects, shapes, and envisions the world. Good writing is always an exploration and articulation of intelligence, of the uniqueness of individual human natures. That is why writing is, or should be, a humanistic act. It extends our imaginations and makes us receptive to our intuitions. Writing increases our sensitivity to emotion, clarifies thought, and makes judgment more rigorous. The writing process is the beginning of movement from sight to insight.

PART I

Writing from Experience

Creativity is the encounter of the intensively conscious human being with his world.

ROLLO MAY

Exploring

1

The Writer's Journal

I n high school I remember rewriting a sentence 15 or 20 times. I was determined to be a good writer. My first attempts had to be perfect. After hours of painstaking effort, all I had before me was a single sentence. Writing an entire page seemed impossible. What I had to learn then and what I constantly have to remind myself of now is to trust myself to trust the language.

I began trusting myself when I began keeping a journal. I wrote spontaneously every day for 10 or 15 minutes and the more I wrote, the less threatening the act of writing became. Often I found fragments I wanted to continue working on. As the pages accumulated, I knew I had something to say. In time, I found that a journal becomes a compost of ideas, memories, images, and emotions to be drawn from whenever needed.

At 18, long before he had thought of *War and Peace* or *Anna Karenina*, Leo Tolstoy began to write in a journal that he continued to keep for most of his life. He filled pages with thumbnail descriptions of nature, observations, experiences, proverbs, folklore, strange words, reactions to readings. Tolstoy vowed from the beginning to write truthfully about his thoughts and feelings without fear. He jotted down sketchy notes, simple and clear perceptions of nineteenth-century Russia.

> The night is clear. A cool breeze passes through the tent. . . . Everything in there is dark, except for one bar of light falling across the end of my brother's bed. But just in front of me, in full light, a pistol, sabers, a sword and a pair of underpants are hanging on a partition.
> Silence. A gust of wind. A gnat buzzes past my ear. Close by a soldier coughs and sighs.

Much can be learned from Tolstoy's journals, but the key to writing that he shares, his gift to us, is deceptively simple. Tolstoy tells us to look closely, to tell the truth, and to write always what we feel in our hearts.

Keeping a journal isn't limited to poets or writers of fiction. Historians, scientists, naturalists, explorers, and artists also keep journals. Browse through the journals of Leonardo da Vinci, Käthe Kollwitz, Paul Klee, or Paul Gauguin. Read the notebooks of Woody Guthrie, who wrote over 1,000 songs and never went anywhere without a notebook in his pocket. Glance through any one of a number of naturalists' journals, including Edward Hoagland's, John Burroughs', or John Muir's (over a period of 44 years he compiled 60 journals). Read the journals of anthropologist Margaret Mead, dock worker and philosopher Eric Hoffer, teacher John Holt, or aviator Charles Lindbergh. Study the notebooks of George Washington, John Quincy Adams, or Thomas Jefferson. Lewis and Clark's journals take up an entire library shelf. Winston Churchill based his six-volume history of World War II on his wartime journals. For physicist Jeremy Bernstein, scribbling away in his notebooks was something he did naturally. Although he had never taken a writing class, his journal efforts eventually led to publication in *The New Yorker*.

What we can learn from these authors seems obvious—that writing, like any other activity, requires practice and preparation. Actors practice their lines, football players practice plays, musicians practice scales, and individuals who need to write for any reason, individuals whose lives will be spent working with the mind—scientists, lawyers, inventors, doctors, artists—often keep journals. Journal writing is the mind's way of preparing and practicing.

Despite years of research and investigation, we still know very little about the creative process—how writing begins and how it evolves. What we do know is a gross oversimplification of a complex phenomenon. But from the journals and writings of those who have willingly shared their experiences, we've learned that the creative act almost always occurs in solitude, preceded by two essential phases. The first has been called the preparation phase, that period when we collect and store our experiences and thoughts. The second phase, the incubation period, is the time needed for those experiences and ideas to be stored away, allowed to rest, and germinate. Sometimes hours, weeks, or years later, the writer will suddenly have an idea and put that raw material to use in some more significant work. Henry David Thoreau composed *Walden Pond* from journals written six years earlier while he lived at the pond. Annie Dillard's Pulitzer Prize–winning book *Pilgrim at Tinker Creek* evolved from her journals. William Least Heat Moon's detailed notebook of his trip around America prompted the writing of his best seller, *Blue Highways*.

The value of keeping a journal, then, whether you intend to become a professional writer or just a better writer, seems immeasurable:

- Keeping a journal encourages you to transfer your experiences, observations, reactions, and reflections into written language.
- Keeping a journal encourages fluency and develops confidence.
- The journal allows flexibility and freedom, which encourage you to take risks, to play and experiment with language. Where else is this freedom to explore allowed?
- The journal puts you in touch with yourself and helps you discover your own voice and your own special style.
- The journal becomes a storehouse of ideas and serves as preparation for future writing. It is a place to hold onto fugitive ideas, thoughts, words, images, observations, and reactions.
- The journal is a way to make writing a habit. If you are to write well, you must write often. You must first discover privately who you are as a human being, what you think and feel, and what it is that makes you feel alive.

Write what you can, then, knowing from the beginning that journals are characteristically uneven in quality. Some days you'll write with great ease and you'll feel excited by your attempts; other days the writing will be painfully slow and methodical. Pushing the pen across the paper will be the best you can do. But write every day, no matter how awkward or perfunctory your attempts may be. Accept what comes to you. Trust the language. The act of writing itself leads to thoughts and feelings you never knew existed inside you. It becomes a way of exploring the texture of your life.

Journal Practice

If you've never kept a journal, you may be tempted to begin with something like this:

> Well Steven finally asked me out. B-O-R-I-N-G!! So then I made a list of guys I really like better and really!!! And I'm only a freshman.

But this is diary writing, not the stuff journals are made of. It accomplishes little in terms of generating ideas or probing deeper feelings. It may seem paradoxical to say on the one hand that you are free to write what you want, and on the other to encourage you to avoid superficial diary entries. If you're going to benefit from journal practice, however, you must challenge yourself to think, to reflect, to explore with a sense of commitment.

1. Set aside a time and place where you can practice freewriting every day for ten to fifteen minutes without interruption. Freewriting means to write nonstop on anything without removing your pen from the paper. Write for yourself, not for another reader, otherwise you may feel self-conscious. Write what is important to you. Accept whatever comes to mind. Trust yourself. Keep your pen moving even if you change subjects.

If you can't think of anything to write about, try listing four or five turning points in your life or four or five individuals who influenced you.

Here's how it worked for Peter Winehaus, a 21-year-old tool and die maker, who decided to complete a liberal arts degree. Before he began writing, he took a few minutes to relax and draw a deep breath (in much the same way an athlete may withdraw before a game for a few minutes of inward reflection). Writing spontaneously, without being selective or judgmental, Peter listed the names of several people who were important to him. When he had five names, he trusted his instincts and zeroed in on one name that stood out, "Grandaddy Ruby." Accepting whatever came to mind, without concern for grammar, spelling, or correctness, he wrote:

> Grandaddy Ruby—always working. Bald on top of head with thin gray hair on the side. Wore wire rimmed glasses. Long hard finger nails. Wrinkled skin. Talks to everyone he knows. Baggy pants with suspenders. Thousands of keys lying around. Gets excited watching wrestling. Sometimes smells like grease, other times like sweat. Eats mints. Smokes non-filter cigarettes. Coughs with phlegm in his chest. Stout. Kind of tall. Walks with a slight limp. Looking so lifeless in casket. Cold and hard and pale. Picture of my nephew Clyde in his coat pocket. I couldn't accept him lying there because he loved life and helping people all the time. Took Clyde for strolls in homemade wagon he built. The two of us tearing down houses together. Planting the garden together. Him helping me cut grass during the summer. I was always amazed at his knowledge of everything. Regretting I didn't know all the stuff he knew when he died. Missing him so much. Watching him drink coffee on the front porch. He poured some in his saucer for me. Hearing his rocking chair squeak and crack. Watching him mix shaving cream in a cup.

By allowing himself to leap from one memory to another, Peter has remembered emotions, details, and events that provide him with numerous possibilities for future writing. He could write pages on any one of these memories—cutting grass, tearing down an old house. He might write about how his grandfather built that special wooden wagon or the time they planted the garden together. Or he might write about his grandfather's death and his final realization of how this special human being had influenced his life—all these ideas generated from a few minutes of spontaneous writing.

2. Write freely about anything that has happened to you in the last few days—searching for a new apartment in a strange city, your new roommate, your feelings about leaving home, your fears about writing in a journal. Keep writing. Don't stop until you've filled a complete page.

3. Write about an outrageous prank you've pulled with a friend—the time you rolled old lady Winchell's house with toilet paper; or the time you stuffed a sardine in Frankie Boller's Reeboks; or the time you put Ben Gay in Weasel Cook's jockstrap.

4. Tell a story. Talk to the page about it as if you were telling a story to a friend. The blank page *is* a friend; it will listen to anything you have to say. Retelling a memory provides you with a natural subject and strong feelings to explore. Here's how Tim Conwell began one of his entries.

> I remember catching hog suckers with my father. Every spring the suckers would come up from Osceola Lake and lay their eggs in the soft sand in our creek. The creek wasn't large. Perhaps four to five feet across and two feet deep in the largest hole. We would fashion nets out of old chicken wire which was no use to anyone. Sometimes the wire was so old the suckers were able to escape by swimming through the holes. Sometimes if we were going to keep the fish, a rusty pitch fork was used instead. I could never bring myself to eat hogfish, but an elderly lady who was our neighbor loved them dearly.

Tim now has a number of possibilities for future writings. He could explore a relationship between a boy and his father, set off on an investigation of *Lachnolaimus maximus* (also known as a hogfish), or use the entry as an introduction to a personal essay on the elderly neighbor. He might find himself writing a humorous sketch about a boy realizing and overcoming his fears. Or nothing at all might come of it. As writers, we're free to make choices.

BUT I DON'T HAVE ANYTHING TO WRITE ABOUT

In the beginning you may feel insecure, even frightened. You may believe you don't have anything to write about, that others lead more interesting lives. A common confession, it may be reassuring to know you're not alone. I felt this way when I started my journal, and others have admitted similar doubts. Instead of condemning yourself, or dwelling on your fears, write about those feelings. You'll find they diminish once you start writing. You may even surprise yourself by discovering just how interesting your life is. Reading any of countless journals available through your library may also reaffirm your freedom to explore. A fine example is *Journey Around My Room*, by Louise Bogan, who wrote on the subjects listed below. Merely skimming this list should be enlightening and stimulating.

- Learning to thread a needle
- Living in a hotel as a child, eating rhubarb with salt and raw potatoes
- The women with scarred faces and boils who ate in the hotel dining room
- The fear-filled evening when she and her mother left her father
- Cutting her thumb on a piece of bottle
- Her mother's hands paring apples
- A recurring dream about the Gardner house
- The first book she owned, *Grimm's Fairy Tales*, and the illustrations by Arthur Rackham
- A memory of her mother sitting by the window shelling peas
- Her art teacher, Miss Cooper
- The depression she feels when she returns to her former neighborhood only to discover it has become a slum
- The ever-straining relationship between her parents
- The first house she remembers living in
- The light on leaves in the evening
- Description of a woman sitting beside her on a bus and their conversation
- How it feels to be kissed by a middle-aged man
- The pain she experienced when falling out of love

Exploring

2

The Senses

All human experience begins with sensory perception. We may know some things intuitively, and like most other animals we possess innate drives—to defend a plot of land, to reproduce sexually. But even our awareness of such primal elements in human nature comes from our ability to see and hear. Anthropologists know something about human social development because they have *observed* it in varying cultures. Psychologists know something about the workings of the mind because they have *listened* to thousands of patients. As a child you learned about the world only through your sensory perceptions of it. You learned that rocks taste slick and cold when you suck on them, that dandelions smell pungent, that the touch of your mother's hand feels warm. Our emotions are especially affected by sensory experience. You do not fall in love with an abstraction. You love a specific young man or woman with red or blond hair, with blue or black eyes, with a soft voice and a dimple in the chin—and a name: Lynn, Bob, Garvin, Maria. Most of us even feel differently when we see a sunny sky than when we wake up and see dark rain streaking our window. All intellectual and emotional experience begins with the senses: seeing, hearing, smelling, touching, and tasting.

Your perception of the subject through your senses is also the beginning of almost every writing project. Good writing is essentially good thinking. And good thinking derives from the ability to perceive critically, to discriminate between important details and unimportant details, to be sensitive to subtleties, to recognize relationships. Each of these concepts involves an act of perception. Beginning now to exercise and extend your perceptive ability through the senses—as well as imaginatively and critically—leads to the process of self-education that is the ultimate goal of a university experience.

Professional writers have always known the value of the senses. They know that because we learn about the world through sight and sound, they must use language that communicates as directly as possible to the eye and ear. The more sensory details, the more a reader is likely to become involved, not just intellectually but emotionally and even physically. Advertisers know they can sell dishwashing detergent if they say it smells like lemons; they can sell mouthwash by asserting that because it tastes like medicine, it must be good for us; they can sell automobiles by calling attention to the heavy thunk when the door slams. The appeal to sensory experience actually makes us willing to spend hard-earned money even when we may not need the product.

In 1932, James Agee visited the home of a tenant farmer in Georgia. Agee felt deeply moved by the experience, by the poverty and the shattered lives. He wrote about his first overnight stay with the family. Had he not known the value of sense perception, this is what he might have told us:

> The bedroom was as shabby as the rest of the cabin and very uncomfortable. I lay down on the bed but found it difficult to sleep. It was miserable and the mattress made noises. After a while I discovered bugs. Just lying there was more than I could stand, so I tried to kill as many as I could find.

But Agee knew that if he wanted us to share his experience, he had to provide sensory details. He had to stimulate our sight and touch the way his had been stimulated. Here is what he actually wrote in *Let Us Now Praise Famous Men*:

> [I saw] how the shutters filled their squares of window and were held shut with strings and nails: crevices in the walls, stuffed with hemp, rags, newsprint, and raw cotton: large damp spots and rivulets on the floor, and on the walls, streams and crooked wetness; and a shivering, how chilly and wet the air is in this room. . . .
>
> I sat on the edge of the bed, turned out the lamp, and lay back along the outside of the covers. After a couple of minutes I got up, stripped, and slid in between the sheets. The bedding was saturated and full of chill as the air was, its lightness upon me nervous like a belt

too loosely buckled. The sheets were at the same time coarse and almost slimily or stickily soft: much the same material floursacks are made of. There was a ridgy seam down the middle. I could feel the thinness and lumpiness of the mattress and the weakness of the springs. The mattress was rustling noisy if I turned or contracted my body. The pillow was hard, thin, and noisy, and smelled as of acid and new blood; the pillowcase seemed to crawl at my cheek. I touched it with my lips: it felt a little as if it would thaw like spun candy. There was an odor something like that of old moist stacks of newspaper. . . . I began to feel sharp little piercings and crawlings all along the surface of my body. I was not surprised; I had heard that pine is full of them anyhow . . . it was bugs all right. I felt places growing on me and scratched at them, and they became unmistakable bedbug bites. . . . To lie there naked feeling whole regiments of them tooling at me, knowing I must be imagining two out of three, became more unpleasant than I could stand. I struck a match and a half-dozen broke along my pillow: I caught two, killed them, and smelled their queer rankness. They were full of my blood. I struck another match and spread back the cover; they rambled off by the dozens. I got out of bed, lighted the lamp. . . . I killed maybe a dozen in all; I couldn't find the rest; but I did find fleas, and, along the seams of the pillow and mattress, small gray translucent brittle insects which I suppose were lice. . . .

Half a century has passed, yet Agee still involves us directly in his experience.

sight	shutters held together with string
	crevices in the wall stuffed with rags
	bedbugs bloated with blood running in the matchlight
touch	chill in the air
	wetness on the walls
	slimy sheets
	a ridgy seam
	bedbugs crawling on his body
sound	the rustling mattress
	the striking match
smell	the odor of old moist newspapers
	a pillow that smells like acid and new blood
	the queer rankness of the bedbugs

To use sensory experience as part of your writing, you must first train yourself to perceive more clearly and fully. I know that by the time I reached college, I had become dulled to my senses. I was no longer excited as I had been as a child by the touch of a shiny doorknob or the brand-new taste of chocolate chips melting on my tongue. Nor did I even trust my experience to be important or meaningful to others. Yet writing that omits sensory details leaves out the human element of our world, and, more often than not, the human element makes writing interesting, even vital, to a reader. Using the writer's journal is one way to train and develop your perceptive abilities. With effort and practice, all of us can reinvigorate our senses and make ourselves once more conscious of our aliveness. Only when we begin to see clearly will we begin to write clearly.

Journal Practice

1. Continue freewriting in your journal every day. Write about anything important to you, about anything you value—but always more than a mere account of your daily activities. Recall a memory of your father. Jot down a list of books you want to read. Describe your secret fears. Use all your senses—smell the cafeteria food, the taste of your mouth when you wake up in the morning, the touch of a cold tile floor. Be alive. Write freely. Don't worry about spelling, punctuation, or grammar. Be willing to play. If you can't think of anything to write about, record the immediate sensory reactions you experience as you sit at your desk writing— the sound of your pen, the sensation of its ridges against your index finger, the shadow of your fist as it moves across the paper. Keep writing.

2. Write at least a full page on the sensory qualities of a simple object. Begin by sketching the object in your journal.

Sketching is a technique used by many writers to train and sharpen awareness. Because sketching requires the eye to slow down, it helps you to concentrate, focus on, and discover detail. Leonardo da Vinci sketched the wings of birds, the hand of a man, even light on a piece of fabric. He then described in his journal what he had seen. Henry David Thoreau sketched frost patterns and leaves. Lewis and Clark included sketches of fish as well as other flora and fauna found along their journey to the Northwest. And poet Gerard Manley Hopkins drew cloud formations, stained glass windows, and trees.

Begin with something simple and small—a fruit or vegetable, such as a pickle or carrot, something you're so accustomed to that you take it for granted. Or focus on a small object—a straw hat or a belt buckle. The drawing on page 23 shows how freshman Tucker Sims sketched his old Nike tennis shoe one Sunday afternoon. After spending about thirty minutes drawing, Sims wrote three handwritten pages describing what he had seen. The following is a condensed and edited version.

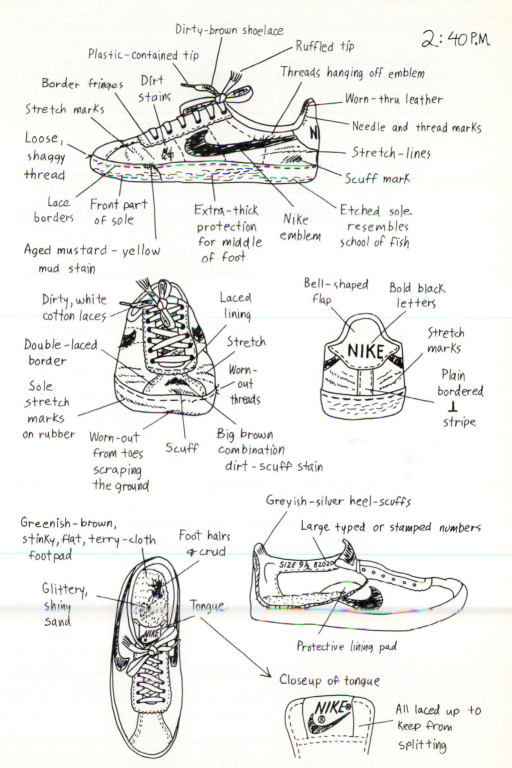

Dirty-brown shoelace

Plastic-contained tip

Ruffled tip

Threads hanging off emblem

Border fringes

Dirt stains

Stretch marks

Worn-thru leather

Needle and thread marks

Loose, shaggy thread

Stretch-lines

Scuff mark

Lace borders

Front part of sole

Extra-thick protection for middle of foot

Nike emblem

Etched sole resembles school of fish

Aged mustard - yellow mud stain

2:40 P.M.

Dirty, white cotton laces

Laced lining

Bell-shaped flap

Bold black letters

Double-laced border

NIKE

Stretch marks

Stretch

Plain bordered 1 stripe

Sole stretch marks on rubber

Worn-out threads

Worn-out from toes scraping the ground

Scuff

Big brown combination dirt-scuff stain

Greyish-silver heel-scuffs

Large typed or stamped numbers

Greenish-brown, stinky, flat, terry-cloth footpad

Foot hairs & crud

SIZE 9½ 82020

Glittery, shiny sand

Tongue

Protective lining pad

Closeup of tongue

NIKE

All laced up to keep from splitting

Nike, Inc. is the owner of the NIKE name and Swoosh Design registered trademarks.

My old Nikes are finally beginning to feel warm and cushy, as if molded to my foot. Stretch lines and scuff marks cover the outside, showing the strain of bending and rubbing against a dozen stadium benches. I can trace the strong thread that lines the border of the leather and rubber sole of the right shoe with my fingertip. The sole itself is etched with numerous niches resembling a school of fish swimming in different directions. The renowned Nike stripe that resembles a black scythe decorates the sides. A few frayed threads have feathered off the emblem. But these are durable shoes. Even the original cotton shoelace has survived although it's now stained brown and one tip is ruffled where the tiny cylinder of plastic has popped off. Fringed borders outline the lace holes. Mud, grass-pucky, and splatters of hot dog mustard stain the sides.

The front of the shoe is lined with a double-stitched border directly ahead of the shoelace, and the sole is worn smooth up front from my toes scraping the ground as I've lifted and lowered my feet and punted imaginary footballs around. The back of the shoe is decorated with a bell-shaped flap at the top of the heel and stitched up like the rest of the shoe. This time the word *Nike* is printed in bold, black letters. A plain border stripe runs perpendicular to the heel of the sole. The inside is soft and mushy, the color of rotted mushrooms, and reeks of sweat and good old toe-jam. I hate wearing socks. The flat terry-cloth footpad has turned a moldy brown and stinks like a sour wash cloth. I remember how cool blue the terry cloth was when I bought them, and the fresh scent of clean cotton and new leather. Now a few curly hairs from my feet sprout beneath the cloth along with crud and a few glittery particles of sand cling to the splayed fibers. This is the way tennis shoes are supposed to be—well chewed.

3. Most of you have known a special place at one time in your lives. It may have been the attic in your grandmother's house or perhaps the clubhouse you built in the woods or even a dark crawl space behind the furnace in an old apartment building—some place you felt was yours. Write a full page about it. Search your memory carefully for smell, sound, touch, and sight images. Select sensory details that would help someone else share your feelings about the place.

Exploring

3

Perception, Language, and Honesty

A long with Shakespeare, Tolstoy, Mark Twain, and other writers who have endured, James Agee knew a simple truth about words: concrete, specific, and particular words stimulate sensory pictures in the mind. They help a reader share your experiences more fully. Concrete words suggest or name something we can see, hear, touch, smell, and taste, such as *trout*, *French bread*, *daffodils*, and *silk*. By contrast, general, abstract terms identify classes, qualities, or ideas—for example, *fish*, *nutrition*, *vegetation*, and *clothing*. The ability to abstract is one of the distinctions that separates our brains from the brains of other animals. Truly to think, we must abstract from sensory experience and reach an understanding of it. Indeed, without higher abstractions like *justice*, *democracy*, *hope*, and *human nature*, our thoughts would be severely limited. But such terms tend to be vague and, when overused, meaningless. More to the point, in writing about personal experience, if you allow yourself the comfort of the easy generalization, you'll find yourself failing to stretch your senses, failing to *look* for the real and immediate level of experience, and, of course, failing to share anything significant with your reader.

Here, for example, is a student's description of his three-year-old cousin:

> Willa has beautiful hair. It smells nice and feels wonderful.

The writer obviously wants us to know how lovely his cousin is. He tries to bring in sight, smell, and touch. But in each case, the choice of words fails to help the reader experience anything. The description is so vague that no one could ever select Willa out of a crowd. *Beautiful, nice,* and *wonderful* are words that express the author's opinion of his subject. They tell us what he thought about his perception, but they don't *share* his perception in a sensory or specific way. The same is true of this effort by student Carol Eisley.

> There was no chance of working well at home. First I dropped my pencil and it made an interesting sound as it struck the floor. I was trying to decide how to describe it when my little brother came in making lots of ugly noises.

The reader has little idea what interesting *sound* the pencil made and cannot even guess at which of the thousands of *ugly noises* the writer's little brother happened to be making. Both *sound* and *noise* are too general; we can think such words, but we can't hear anything specific in them.

Here is the same scene after Carol went back in her memory and attempted to share the actual experience.

> There was no chance of working well at home. First I dropped my pencil. It skittered across the tile floor. I was down on my knees looking for it under the refrigerator when my six-year-old brother skipped in whistling a two-note song he had invented. He watched me, first on one foot, then on the other. He began sucking through the gap in his front teeth. It sounded like garbage water sucked down an open drain. I had my arm under the refrigerator as far as I could reach. All I could find was a broken potato chip sticky with green mold, so old and mossy it seemed to have eyes. The mold smelled like curdled yogurt. My little brother began making a wet plopping sound by sticking his thumb inside one cheek and popping it out.

Concrete, specific words name things or describe sensory details, objects, emotions, and facts in such a way that the reader can actually experience in the imagination the named quality. When a pencil *skitters* across a tile floor or when a little brother *sucks* through his front teeth or makes a *wet pop* by pulling his thumb out of his cheek, readers can hear it in their imagination, just as they can see and smell a *green, moldy potato chip*. Specific names or details call up whole pictures that affect both mind and emotion. By knowing in advance that you must describe details in your experience, you discipline your senses to work more actively. To be specific, you must first look and listen for the specific. Knowing a vocabulary of the senses thus works in two ways: It stimulates you as a writer to search deeply into your experience, and it stimulates the imagination of the reader, helping him or her to share your experience.

Concrete, specific words are not limited to personal writing. Even philosophers have known that the more abstract an idea is, the more difficult it is to communicate. Plato, for example, in writing his famous allegory of the cave, attempts to show that most of us live in darkness and that we are reluctant to face higher truths. Plato describes—in sensory images, not in abstractions—the problem of several prisoners who live their lives in a cave with their backs to the entrance. On the back wall of the cave, the men watch shadows pass back and forth. They insist that shadows are real life. But one prisoner is forced to walk to the cave entrance where he is dazzled by the light. He would almost prefer the shadowy illusions on the wall to the pain of exposure. Yet, Plato argues, after finally accustoming himself to the sun and lake and trees, the prisoner would rather die than return to the misery of the cave. Plato's dialogue deals with the nature of truth and the manner in which people both find and resist it. He constructs his argument on a simple, sensory-based story. The senses provide us with a tangible point from which Plato hopes we can reason to higher levels.

In your writing, you'll need both kinds of words, general and abstract terms as well as concrete, specific terms. You should make yourself aware of the differences and attempt to become rich in both vocabularies. Knowing a language of the senses can increase your powers of perception, just as knowing the words that express ideas helps you to think about ideas.

CREATING IMAGES

The use of concrete, specific words, especially sensory words, creates *images*. An image is a sensory picture in the mind. If I write that *several people came into my shop*, you receive the communication in the abstract. You understand what I mean. I have used proper grammar and good syntax. But you have no particular image in your mind; you don't know whether six Chinese diplomats came into my shop or twenty-two Nebraska farmers. But if I write *the Hells's Angels gang stomped into my shop*, you'll probably have a fairly instant recognition. *Hell's Angels* suggests

motorcycle jackets, chains, greased-back hair, black boots, and perhaps
an undercurrent of tension or fear.

The word *imagination* is built from the word *image*. Our imaginations
are created by sensory experience. A person without an imagination is
a person who neither sees nor helps the reader to see. We might say
then that one of the first principles of good writing is to *show* instead
of *tell*, for showing affects the imagination. Show the reader through
some kind of concrete, sensory-related words, if possible, instead of
merely telling the reader in abstract concepts. General, abstract words
inform the rational side of our minds; specific, concrete words stimulate
the imagination.

Telling is vague.
I hurt my finger.

Showing is specific.
I poked a needle through my finger.

Telling communicates an idea or concept.
Downtown traffic was heavy.

Showing demonstrates an idea or concept.
City buses coughed black smoke; taxis honked at a stalled delivery truck.
Even a policeman on a motorcycle couldn't squeeze through the rumble
of cars.

Many inexperienced writers believe that abstract language sounds
more intellectual. Some writers use abstract generalities in the hope of
impressing the reader with their intelligence. The impression quickly
wears thin. Most of us are soon bored with a continuous dose of abstraction, and often it sounds pretentious. George Orwell once demonstrated this principle by calling attention to how simply and specifically
the following passage from Ecclesiastes is written.

> I returned, and saw under the sun, that the race is not to the swift,
> nor the battle to the strong, neither yet bread to the wise, nor yet
> riches to men of understanding, nor yet favor to men of skin; but
> time and chance happeneth to them all.

Orwell then rewrote the passage entirely in abstractions.

> Objective consideration of contemporary phenomena compels the
> conclusion that success or failure in competitive activities exhibits no
> tendency to be commensurate with innate capacity, but that a con-

siderable element of the unpredictable must inevitably be taken into account.

The passages say approximately the same thing, but the second version speaks only to the mind, whereas the first speaks to our mind, our imagination, and our emotions.

BEING HONEST TO YOUR EXPERIENCE

Nothing should be easier than writing down in simple, concrete terms what you see and hear. Yet not only do your emotions, hopes, and fantasies get in the way, so also do the biases of the world you grew up in—especially when you are writing about personal experience. Ernest Hemingway spoke for most of us when he said that one of the great difficulties for a writer was to discover what "you really felt rather than what you were supposed to feel." Yet honesty of perception seems to be an ideal we constantly slip away from, tempted as we are to produce the familiar response or the trite phrase. We have a seemingly instinctive desire to please by writing down what we think others want to hear instead of what we truly see or think for ourselves.

Here, for example, is what Greg Eaton wrote in his journal when asked to write about the sunrise.

> In that hushed moment before dawn broke and the sky was like black velvet, there was a hovering solitude as all creatures waited for Midnight to disrobe her garments. Suddenly, golden light radiated forth from the trembling clouds. The branches of the trees began to do deep knee bends to get the circulation going again, and all the awaiting animals began a symphony of noise: birdlings warbled in chorus, puppies yapped in counterpoint, insects buzzed in harmony— while the concert master, the breeze himself, tickled the undersides of the leaves in the trees.

Greg wrote down what he thought an English instructor would approve of. He tried to imitate the gleanings of some vaguely remembered poetry, but he did not look or smell or listen for himself, probably because he did not yet have the courage to trust his own perceptions. If, as he thought, writers from earlier centuries had written about the "hovering solitude" before the dawn, then why shouldn't he? Who was he to say that branches don't do deep knee bends or that the breeze is not a concertmaster running around tickling leaves on their bottoms? The journal entry does not express his perceptions because it seemed both safer and easier to describe the dawn in acceptable "literary" terms.

This kind of faking does not necessarily imply a conscious attempt to deceive. Usually, such dishonesty is unintentional. We simply don't know we are not yet seeing for ourselves. We assume that the way we think something has always been done is the way it should be done. We may actually know of no other words to express something because it has always been expressed in the same words. We tend to grow familiar and comfortable with conventional ways of looking at the world. Trying to challenge the norm either leaves us with a dark hole into which our imagination refuses to leap or gives us a headache thinking about it.

But here is what Greg wrote when urged to report the scene again as he honestly perceived it with his own senses.

> I shivered in the dark. My nose started to run. On the other side of Hennly's pasture, about a quarter of a mile away, diesel trucks rumbled along the highway with their lights on. I sat on a mean rock in the dark listening to the trucks.
>
> The last truck by thundered away down the highway. The sound faded away to a mute grumble. For several minutes there was a silent red glow in the distance, and I couldn't hear anything at all because my ears were still filled with the engines and whirring tires. Then the glow faded and my ears went empty. I heard the weeds brushing against my feet. I felt a soft wind come up. Sometimes I could hear water lapping in the creek that wound through the pasture. After a few moments I heard another truck coming, just a whisper at first, mumbling real low like it was pushing the sound ahead of it kind of angry, then louder and louder until it was booming right in front of me, the tires zinging over the pavement, then past me with the engine growing dull and retarded and passing another truck coming from the other direction in a flash of mixed up lights, with the new sound grumbling back toward me.
>
> And somehow it was light. I don't know when or how. I just realized I could see mist hovering over the creek like faint smoke. A few cars appeared on the highway, some without lights, zizzing along like dark beetles.
>
> Just light. Gray at first. On the other side of the highway the woods took shape, black and smoky and wet. While the mist in the pasture faded gradually and the rim of the mountain in the east looked silver.

Little of Greg's second entry deals with the sun coming up at all. In the process of trusting his experience to tell him what was genuine and real, he discovered a sensory world he had previously ignored. Instead of birdlings singing in chorus, Greg had diesel trucks thundering, grumbling, mumbling, whirring, their tires zinging on the pavement. Instead of branches doing deep knee bends, he saw a black and smoky woods.

The light itself appeared so gradually it was almost unnoticed—all this while sitting on a "mean rock" with his nose running. This second attempt convinces the reader. Greg is no longer faking. As an almost inevitable consequence, the writing is more powerful, more memorable. Greg has begun to see honestly, and the reader shares the uniqueness of his experience.

THE VILLAINOUS CLICHÉ

Part of Greg's problem in his first journal entry was his dependence on clichés to do his thinking for him. A cliché is a phrase that has been repeated so often that it no longer communicates anything fresh. A cliché may be false or true, but it is so familiar to our ear that we simply don't think about it. Clichés fool us into thinking that we are saying something meaningful. More than one student writer has found that he or she could pad a whole essay with clichés, although seldom with the wit Peter Carlson uses in this excerpt from *Newsweek*.

> As every school child knows, the cliché has a long and glorious history here in the land of the free. Clichés were here long before I was born and they'll be here long after I'm dead and buried. Clichés traveled from the Old World to the New to follow their manifest destiny. They crossed the Great Plains, forded the rushing rivers and traversed the burning sands of the steaming deserts of this teeming continent until they stretched from sea to shining sea. . . .
>
> And these clichés did not crawl out of the woodwork. Many of our Founding Fathers added their 2 cents to the nation's great storehouse of clichés. Jefferson, Lincoln, and Roosevelt created enough clichés to choke a horse, and Franklin coined more phrases than Carter has pills. Since then, these immortal words of wisdom have become landmarks on the American scene. . . .
>
> Let's face facts: You can fool some of the people some of the time, but you can't change human nature. This is a free country and a man has a right to say what he pleases—even if it's a hackneyed cliché. In this increasingly complex society, where the only constant is change, clichés still occupy a warm spot in our hearts. They are quicker, easier, and more economical than other forms of talk. They also require less energy than thoughtful, carefully constructed sentences. And in this day and age, that's nothing to sneeze at.

Carlson makes appropriate fun of the cliché, but unfortunately there is a serious side to all of this. Because clichés are used so often, they deaden our perceptive powers; they stifle our ability to think for ourselves. Clichés substitute for a genuine attempt to express the uniqueness of our experience.

Here's what one student wrote when asked to describe someone she cared about deeply.

> The first time I met Hodges he came up to the desk in the library
> with determination written all over his face. I could tell he was bur-
> ied deep in thought, perhaps about an assignment that had been
> given in class that morning. I'm sure he didn't know I was in the
> same class with him so I just asked him how I could help, but inside
> I had butterflies in my stomach.

Although the reader gets a certain feel for the situation here, the author makes it difficult for us to trust her perceptions. Did Hodges really have "determination written all over his face"? There must have been some actual physical quality, but neither the author nor the reader has seen it. And what about being "buried deep in thought"? What exactly did Hodges do or say that made the author think so? Is it even possible to be buried in thought and show a face with determination written on it at the same time? The clichés begin to sound like easy substitutions for what really happened in the author's experience. The final statement about "butterflies in my stomach" confirms such a judgment. This is lazy writing in which the author has made no honest effort.

Yet it is not enough to say that a writer must avoid clichés. We must also say how to avoid them. The answer does not lie in turning to a thesaurus for an alternative word or phrase. The fault lies not in language, but in the substitute of old language for new perception. *Only by seeing what is actually there instead of what you think you are supposed to see will your writing become meaningful.* The honesty of the writer demands an honesty to his or her experience—and perhaps the only way to begin is with a series of questions: Is my experience here real, or am I feeling this way because my parents or teacher expect me to? Am I hearing or seeing something in a certain way because the cliché tells me I am supposed to hear and see in that way? Just because something has always been said this way before, are the words true to my experience? Here is a revision of the Hodges paper.

> I was working from nine to midnight behind the checkout desk
> when Hodges came in. He marched straight up to the desk and let a
> book drop on it. I remember how I watched his jaw thrust out and
> pull back. At the time I was so fascinated by him I thought the

thrusting jaw meant that he was a determined young man who demanded his own way, but later I came to realize that he did it whenever he was nervous. He kept his eyes on the lighted computer board behind the desk while his slender fingers twisted the corner of the book. The other girls only giggled and pretended to be busy. I had to cross ten feet of open space to get to the counter. It felt like I had forgotten how to walk. I felt my arms and legs were sponging about in all kinds of directions. When I reached the counter I took hold, hung on, and asked if I could help, all without ever looking at his eyes.

This time, in using her five senses and then in attempting to be exact in describing them, the writer has eliminated clichés. Her experience now seems genuine to us. It may be impossible to eliminate all clichés from your writing. Yet only when you begin to challenge yourself to see and feel what is really there in front of you can you be sure you are at least making an honest effort. Honesty may sometimes be painful, yet it is essential if you are to begin the process of finding truth in your experience of the world about you.

Exercises

1. Consider the type of words each writer below is using. Look closely. Circle the general, abstract terms; underline the concrete or specific terms.

The rain fell periodically on my window. Soundless. Each blurred streak looked gray and warped. I could hear my dog Harper sleeping in the kitchen. He snores when he sleeps and bubbles ooze between his lips. The rain had begun to melt the old rusted snow in the gutters.

Student Journal

The influence of custom is indeed such that to conquer it will require the utmost efforts of fortitude and virtue, nor can I think

any man more worthy of veneration and renown, than those who
have burst the shackles of habitual vice.

Samuel Johnson

Cans. Beer Cans. Glinting on the verges of a million miles of
roadways, lying in scrub, grass, dirt, leaves, sand, mud, but never
hidden. Piels, Rheingold, Ballantine, Schaefer, Schlitz, shining in the
sun or picked by moon or the beams of headlights at night; washed
by rain or flattened by wheels, but never dulled, never buried, never
destroyed.

Marya Mannes

At sunset I sometimes make bread or roast a chicken in a camp oven
on the little islet with twenty eager helpers shrieking, exclaiming,
running to throw rotten eggs in the sea or to fetch firewood for a
dying fire.

Margaret Mead

About three to six gallons of a dyed and perfumed solution of
formaldehyde, glycerin, borax, phenol, alcohol and water is soon
circulating through Mr. Jones, whose mouth has been sewn together
with a needle directed upward between the upper lip and gum and
brought out through the left nostril, with the corners raised slightly
"for a more pleasant expression." If he should be bucktoothed, his

teeth are cleaned with Bon Ami and coated with colorless nail

polish. His eyes, meanwhile, are closed with flesh-tinted eye caps

and eye cement.

Jessica Mitford

My father is a great guy. The whole family looks up to him and

admires him. Ever since I was old enough to walk, I think I wanted

to be just like him and I still find myself imitating him all the time.

Student Journal

2. Revise each abstract "telling" given below. Make it concrete.

a.   She fed us well.
b.   The party was awful.
c.   She dresses funny.
d.   I just love nature and the woods and all that.
e.   Roberto looked terrible after the fight.

Here are three examples:

Original	*Revision*
The door sounded awful.	The door squeaked as I closed it.
The mirror didn't work.	The mirror looked like a car windshield early in the morning after a heavy dew.
We had a pleasant time riding horses.	We took the old gray stallion and a dingy white mare and went exploring gentle rolling hills. The long pasture grass tickled our bare feet. We followed the lazy creek to its source near a jagged clump of rocks where the water was the coldest and clearest I've ever seen. So cold it made your teeth ache. Later we followed the narrow creek for a mile or so until it widened and warmed.

3. Clichéd writing may be caused by laziness, or it may occur because the beginning writer is not yet widely read and not yet aware of phrases and terms others consider hackneyed and worn out.

In which of the following sentences do you detect a cliché? Compare your response to your classmates.

a. Snow blanketed the park.
b. For better or worse, the general died on the battlefield.
c. Movie actors come from all walks of life.
d. In this modern-day society we seldom see students burning the midnight oil.
e. Investing in the stock market when it's down is a tried and true plan.
f. I had a sneaking suspicion that she was guilty.
g. Last but not least, you have to face the fact that writing always requires effort.

Journal Practice

1. Continue freewriting in your journal but challenge yourself to write more than you did the previous try. If you filled a full page on your last attempt, push to fill one-and-a-half pages now. Try recording any first experience—the first time you drove a car; the first time you tried smoking; the first time you saw the ocean. Share the story by using specific concrete words that create images.

2. Write about a single object, something directly in front of you—a battered baseball mitt saved from fifth grade, a shell brought back from the beach one summer. Allow your eyes to trace the outline of the whole object, to wander from left to right, top to bottom. Focus on the minute details, light and shadow. List the details, naming what you see, showing rather than telling. Avoid using a single abstraction or generalization unless it is to discuss the object's significance for you.

Here's how David Knox, a freshman, wrote about his observation of a candle. What images help you share his experience? What can you see? Taste? Touch? Smell? Hear? What sensory details are missing?

> The candle has burned once before tonight. Yellow, cylindrical and four inches wide, streams of molten wax run down the sides of the candle. One side has folded over in the shape of an ear. The flame grows taller as the wax center builds up. A little pool gets deeper before the wax melts on the sides. The wick burns slowly and the blackness creeps down lower and lower. The inside of the candle edge is shaped like the underside of a mushroom, thin ridges between deep valleys. Smooth pollen-like grains make a flat surface

from the mushroom edge to the pool of liquid wax. One edge looks like an apricot all shriveled and curled.

3. Write about an experience you had with someone important to you. Look deeply into your memory for the actual details. Write with feeling for yourself (you are your own audience) but this time write in third person, as if you were watching the experience happen at an earlier time in your life. Use the five senses to help you recall images.

George Powers, a physics major, chose to write about his memory of his grandmother in the hospital just before she died.

The family stood back from the bed as the nurses spread and tucked a blanket over Gran. Skin hung in folds from her thin body. She made a small package wrapped in a yellow hospital blanket. Her eyes stared out of small caves, moving slowly from the face of one person to another. Little brown splotches covered her wrinkled face. One under her left eye, one under her forehead. Many speckled her cheeks.

Her feet poked out from under the covers. Ten toenails grew out at ten different angles, curved and long, like small birds' beaks on small birds' heads. Her feet were almost white and they smelled of old stockings and hospital alcohol. The feet never moved. He thought of her walking through the garden, the feet busy nudging stones away from young corn.

Her arms lay across her stomach. The loose splotched skin on her arms outlined the bones underneath. The IV site on her wrist was black in the center changing to a two inch blue circle. Raw skin surrounded the circle. The arms had shrunk to half their previous size.

Her hands looked worst of all. Thin crooked fingers lay entwined together. Strips of skin peeled away from the ends of her fingers and curled back to expose pink flesh. The tendons on the backs of her hands ran like small tubes under the splotched skin.

"George, is that you?" She could barely whisper now.

"Yeah, it's me." He leaned over and kissed her cheek. A little wisp of white hair tickled his cheek.

4. Reread your journal. Find an entry that could be more concrete, more sensuous, more honest and moving, if you had shared more details. Rewrite it, telling the story through images. Avoid clichés. Find the actual details that make the experience come alive.

Audience

4

The Appropriate Voice

As you've looked at the world about you and sharpened your senses, you've also been redefining yourself. Consciously or unconsciously, you've been exploring concrete relationships between yourself and your immediate environment. In that sense, writing from personal experience may sometimes seem to be a private act. But almost all writing, even a journal, may reach an audience if you choose to share it. Although writing often serves to help us formulate a better understanding of ourselves, it never ceases to function as an act of communication. One of the earliest phases in the writing process, then, perhaps one that occurs as an almost simultaneous act with exploring the subject, is identification of audience. Who are your readers? Why are they reading? What do they expect from you?

THE EVER-CHANGING AUDIENCE

If you were writing an objective research paper for a history professor, you might begin like this:

Our knowledge of Queen Elizabeth's era is limited by the scarcity of unbiased historical data. According to C. P. Sharksey, professor of history at Oxbridge, historical information from the sixteenth century is drawn almost entirely from the men directly involved in making the history and, therefore, must be seen as containing an inherent favoritism toward one party or the other.

But you would not write a letter home in the same manner. Instead, you would probably relax and compose the sentences exactly as they came to you.

> Hi Mom,
>   Working on a history paper for old Donaldson this week. Wants footnotes. The whole works. I've been up until 3 A.M. every night. Got kicked out of the library Thursday night for eating chocolate cake in the computer room.

Professor Donaldson would never accept the informality of your letter; your mother would never accept the rather stiff voice you used for Donaldson. You make such adjustments because you know each reader expects something different from you. All successful writers know they must make repeated shifts in word choice, sentence length, voice, and tone if they are to convince whatever reader they are addressing at the moment. When, for example, advertising copywriters turn out TV scripts for Crispy Pop cereal, they write with a vocabulary and voice that they hope will sway an audience of children; when bank presidents write their annual reports, they write to inform the banks' stockholders; and when students write papers about Freud's Oedipal theory, they usually write to convince a single professor that they understand the subject. Yet writing *for* an audience does not mean that you abandon your ideas or standards; it does not mean "selling out." Rather, it means using common sense. It means learning to be flexible enough to meet your readers where they are, even when the goal may be to lead those readers somewhere else. That requires you to know something about the audience *before* you begin to write.

What, then, should you know about the audience for personal or expressive writing? By its very nature, the writing found in personal letters, journals, and essays is usually addressed to a more intimate group of friends or at least to a sympathetic reader. Such an audience is presumed to be interested in sharing insights drawn from your observations and experiences. Your aim may be nothing more than to entertain, or it may be to inform and persuade your reader about values and personally held truths. Either way, one common element holds all personal writing together: the natural voice. The reader will expect it and may even be offended by overformality.

THE NATURAL VOICE

Listen for a moment with your inner ear to the voice of Virginia Woolf. The year is 1929; the location, a women's college in England.

> Here was my soup. Dinner was being served in the great dining-hall. Far from being spring it was in fact an evening in October. Everybody was assembled in the big dining-room. Dinner was ready. Here was the soup. It was a plain gravy soup. There was nothing to stir the fancy in that. One could have seen through the transparent liquid any pattern that there might have been on the plate itself. But there was no pattern. . . . Next came beef with its attendant greens and potatoes. . . . Prunes and custard followed. . . . Biscuits and cheese came next, and here the water-jug was liberally passed round, for it is the nature of biscuits to be dry, and these were biscuits to the core. That was all. The meal was over. Everybody scraped their chairs back; the swing doors swung violently to and fro; soon the hall was emptied. . . . Conversation for a moment flagged. . . . A good dinner is of great importance to good talk. One cannot think well, love well, sleep well, if one has not dined well. [But] the lamp in the spine does not light on beef and prunes.

Virginia Woolf sees clearly. She senses, names, shares the experience in concrete images. But she also talks to us in a human voice, a warm and familiar voice—almost conversational but a little more rhythmical and controlled, as prose must always be. Look closely and you find simple sentences (*Here was my soup*), simple words (*biscuits, beef,* and *prunes*), mixed only occasionally with a longer, more complex thought. Among other qualities, it is this intimate voice of a real person speaking to our inner ear that makes "A Room of One's Own" such a forceful essay. Yet one misfortune of our educational system is the tendency for all of us to write in the same voice: an objective, impersonal monotone.

Listen to Irwin Parker, in his first term at college, trying to write about a personal experience in high school.

> The most interesting course that was taken by me in high school was taught by Mr. Frank. It was a course in chemistry. Mr. Frank developed student minds by involving them in experiments which were a daily part of the content of the experience that Mr. Frank wanted them to have. One liked the course because of the excitement. One never knew what exciting type of experiment Mr. Frank would come up with next.

After Irwin Parker had read this paper to the class (this is only the first paragraph), he admitted he did not talk that stiffly in real life. It sounded nothing like his voice. In fact, the class decided the essay was rather boring.

One problem was tone. *Tone* is the attitude or feeling the writer takes toward both subject and audience. Parker's tone is distant and rather cold.

> *The most interesting course that was taken by me . . . One liked the course . . . One never knew what exciting . . .*

Any reader would find it difficult to feel "excitement" when the prose is so stiff. The use of the third-person *one* instead of the first-person *I* removes the human element. Other forms of writing—a critical analysis, a laboratory report—demand that the writer take an objective tone toward his or her subject. But the personal essay ought to sound personal.

Irwin tried to rewrite it using a more natural voice. "Begin again," the class told him, "Keep it simple, and try talking to the page."

> I liked Mr. Frank because he was a good chemistry teacher in my high school. He made us think. We were always doing experiments in class, and sometimes we would get so involved that no one would hear the bell. Once, Mrs. Shaw, the principal, had to come in and drive us out because we were all late for our next class.

"Better," the class told Parker after he read the second version. Much more human and more readable. This would probably be an acceptable voice for a personal essay. But it was still not the voice Irwin Parker used outside the classroom walls. Could he tell it to the page as if the page were his friend? Could he tell the page concretely what he saw in his memory and pretend his audience was not an English teacher but a group of his own peers?

> Mr. Frank was a super dude. He wore bow ties so big they held up his chin. A little guy, all squeezed up in an old suit spotted with chemicals and this giant butterfly of a bow tie. We would start experimenting with iron sulfide and hydrochloric acid, and pretty soon the whole room would smell like a rotten egg, and then everybody would be wiping their eyes and gasping and laughing, and old Mr. Frank would be dancing around the room saying, "Wow, it worked. You see what happened? You see what happens when you make hydrogen sulfide?" And that's when old Mrs. Shaw would stumble in gasping and holding a pink handkerchief over her nose. "You've all god to ho to quass." She would turn red and Mr. Frank would act shocked, like how did he know what time it was, and we would all just be laughing so hard you couldn't breathe.

"Good!" said the class. "Now we can hear the genuine voice of Irwin Parker." And notice what has happened in the process of working toward that voice. The first essay is almost totally abstract.

One liked the course because of the excitement.

But in the final paper Parker involves the reader by using concrete, sensory details.

> *. . . pretty soon the whole room would smell like a rotten egg, and then everybody would be wiping their eyes and gasping. . . .*

By finding his natural voice, Parker has been able to let his imagination flow more freely. The tone has become informal, even colloquial; and the reader feels the emotion and excitement of the class.

> *. . . like how did he know what time it was, and we would all just be laughing so hard you couldn't breathe.*

In listening once again to all three versions, the class decided that the first voice probably revealed Parker's nervousness about writing anything. He wrote stiffly, perhaps on the assumption that his audience would expect "dignified," formal writing at college. In the second version, he wrote more directly to a particular English instructor who told him that he could relax and be natural. But in the third version, he wrote for his fellow students, using the same voice he would actually talk in.

The point is clearly that beginning writers should become aware that they have a choice of voices, just as they have a choice of vocabulary, and that the audience as well as the subject helps determine which voice is appropriate for the purpose. Writers who find themselves locked into the same voice in every paper, no matter what the audience or intention, find themselves locked into repetitive dullness. Even the most formal research paper can be made more lively and interesting by the carryover of a genuine voice. What we are talking about here is a matter of degree. The beginning writer must recognize that dull writing lacks any voice at all. It sounds anonymous, as if written by committee. Effective writing, even formal and scientific prose, can still have a voice, a liveliness or felicity or uniqueness that makes the reader say, "This could only come from Irwin Parker or Salinda Rodriquez or Hiawatha Golden."

EXPLORING YOUR VOICE

Finding a natural voice may open doors to your imagination that a wrong voice will permanently block. The right voice relaxes you and frees you to speak your mind. The wrong voice makes you uncomfortable and distracts your attention from the subject to the writing itself.

Listen to Jim Brown, a star football player of the late 1950s and early 1960s.

> I get a little weary of hearing broken homes blamed for 96.3 percent of American youth's difficulties. . . . My guess is that thanks to all the yakking about broken homes, a lot of kids have found a good excuse to get into trouble. The broken home is their crutch in Juvenile Court. I am not dogmatic about this. Looking back on my own boyhood, there were many times when I came perilously close to becoming a no-account.

Compare Brown's voice with that of E. B. White, a novelist and an essayist.

> One summer, along about 1904, my father rented a camp on a lake in Maine and took us all there for the month of August. We all got ringworm from some kittens and had to rub Pond's Extract on our arms and legs night and morning, and my father rolled over in a canoe with all his clothes on; but outside of that the vacation was a success and from then on none of us ever thought there was any place in the world like that lake in Maine.

Both voices sound natural, informal, relaxed. Both put the reader at ease, yet they are not the same voice. Brown uses more colloquial words. The term *colloquial* derives from the Latin for conversation. Hence, colloquial words reflect the vocabulary we use in our most casual speech, for example, *I get a little weary . . . My guess is . . . all the yakking about . . . a lot of kids . . . becoming a no-account.* Of course, no written language is identical with the spoken voice. But good writing almost invariably has the sound of the spoken voice. Brown achieves that sound, the impression that he is speaking to us from the page.

E. B. White achieves the same effect, but his word choice is *informal*, not colloquial. Excluding the more casual or slang vocabulary found in colloquial writing, the informal voice simply uses everyday words and phrases: *We all got ringworm . . . but outside of that . . . and from then on . . . there was any place in the world like. . . .*

The following list contrasts informal and colloquial language with a more formal vocabulary.

Colloquial	*Informal*	*Formal*
yakking	talking	discussing
kids	children	youth
a no-account	a problem child (or delinquent)	a delinquent (or social offender)
my guess is	I would guess	I would estimate

Such a list is arbitrary. Words considered informal by one generation may be considered appropriate formal terms by the next. (For example, contractions like *isn't* and *haven't* were once strongly rejected in a formal paper. Today, even conservative periodicals print essays using contractions.) Still, the contrast reveals that a significant choice is available to a writer—and also confirms that material written in one voice may be changed or translated into another voice.

Jim Brown, for example, must have felt comfortable writing in a colloquial style. His ideas presumably came to him most readily in the voice closest to his speaking voice. But if his audience had been a convention of psychologists instead of the casual reader, Brown might have returned to his material and translated it into formal prose.

> I am disturbed at hearing that broken homes are blamed for 96.3
> percent of American youth's difficulties. . . . I estimate that because
> of excessive discussion about broken homes, many young people
> have found a good excuse to become social offenders.

The point is clear: By writing in your natural voice, you allow your imagination to flow; your attention can be focused where it should be—on the subject. But later you can (and should) return to your first draft and double check the *appropriateness* of the voice you have written in. Once your ideas and experiences are on the page, the voice can be adjusted to match the expectations and needs of your audience.

THE APPROPRIATE VOICE

Every voice has its limitations. A *colloquial* voice may be highly successful for entertaining a sympathetic, casual audience. It is appropriate for humor or light entertainment. But such a voice usually prevents you from discussing more serious material—that is, if you want to be taken seriously. An *informal* voice, however, may be considered a solid bridge between colloquial and formal. It may be either entertaining or serious. E. B. White often shifts easily from pleasant memories into thoughtful reflections on human values. The informal voice is the most flexible of all styles: friendly, relaxed, conversational, yet at the same time more polished and edited than the colloquial. The informal voice is especially appropriate for essays. Unless you are highly skilled, however, the audience for a research paper, critical analysis, or report will probably expect a more *formal* voice. The need for objective data, factual information, and logical analysis requires a tone of high seriousness to convince the reader.

Know your audience, then; know what it expects and needs. But also know yourself. If you write more freely and comfortably in one voice, use it to its best advantage, especially in your journal or on the first draft. Write fast, keeping your subject vividly and imaginatively before your mind's eye. Use the most natural voice. Then be willing to return later and make whatever adjustments are necessary for your ideas and experiences to be communicated effectively to your audience.

Exercises

1. Here are a series of paragraphs, each by a different author and each with a distinctive voice. Consider the audience for each voice, and suggest the type of character behind the voice. Discuss the limitations of each voice—that is, would it be effective for a convention of physicists or for an informal audience reading for pleasure? Are there any voices here you find annoying to your ear? Any you feel you might like to emulate in your writing?

> Among the most comprehensive of the existing synthetic models that do not use human-capital approach is that by Stiglitz, who integrates the distribution of income into its major sources, *viz.*, wages and profits. Stiglitz examines the distribution impact of nonlinear saving functions, heterogeneity of labor skills, material-capital inheritance policies, variable reproduction rates of different income classes, tax policies, and the nature of the stochastic elements in the accumulation process.
>
> Gian Singh Sahota, "Theories of Personal Income Distribution: A Survey," *Journal of Economic Literature*

> Just to paint is great fun. The colours are lovely to look at and delicious to squeeze out. Matching them, however crudely, with what you see is fascinating and absolutely absorbing. Try it if you have not done so—before you die. . . . One begins to see, for instance, that painting a picture is like fighting a battle; and trying to paint a picture is, I suppose, like trying to fight a battle.
>
> Winston Churchill, *Painting as a Pastime*

> Wednesday, Mr. and Mrs. Johnnie Gann went to Kansas City. Sure was a hot day but enjoyed our trip. Couldn't hardly sleep that night. They were gone but they came after we were there for some time. We took the lawn chairs, went out in the back yard to keep cool

until James came. He took us over to Bobby's to get something to
eat. We just got a hot dog when we got to the Bus Station. Bobby
works late, comes home after dark. When James' wife came home
they came to get us. Went over there for supper.

We saw several sight-seeing different places. Was close to an
airplane. Went under several overhead bridges. The Bus Station sure
is a nice large building, has nice seats, two lunch counters.

We saw the Kaw river going down it was full. Steamboats were
sailing.

Mrs. Johnnie Gann, Lily Grove News, Tri-County Weekly,
July 1, 1970

There are, of course, other ways to account for the songs of whales.
They might be simple, down-to-earth statements about navigation, or
sources of krill, or limits of territory. But the proof is not in, and
until it is shown that these long, convoluted, insistent melodies,
repeated by different singers with ornamentations of their own, are
the means of sending through several hundred miles of undersea
such ordinary information as "whale here," I shall believe otherwise. Now and again, in the intervals between songs, the whales
have been seen to breach, leaping clear out of the sea and landing
on their backs, awash in the turbulence of their beating flippers.
Perhaps they are pleased by the way the piece went, or perhaps it
is celebration at hearing one's own song returning after circum-
navigation; whatever, it has the look of jubilation.

Lewis Thomas, Lives of a Cell

a. To what extent does sentence length affect the voice in each
    piece?
b. Does the use of *I, we,* or *you* change the feeling in the voice?
c. Many writers have observed that the use of Anglo-Saxon words
    (simple three- and four-letter terms like *pig, man, live, hand*) cre-
    ates a different reaction in the reader than the use of words of
    Latin origin (*heterogeneous, preterition, lactiferous*). Do you find these
    writers using one or the other with any consistency? Does it
    affect their voice?

2. Here is a student writing about a personal experience. Has he
chosen the right voice? What specific problems, if any, do you detect?

My most embarrassing moment was having the zipper of my pants
split apart during church. Since church services traditionally demand
one's attire to be elaborate, to see a person with his fly open must
be quite striking to the observer and embarrassing to the observed.

The abashment that followed the accident was humorous at the initial thought of the situation. Uncontrollably following was a nervous and very desperate search for the most logical path to use for an exit. The path hopefully would serve the purposes of a stealthy departure from the congregation and to allow unnoticed repairs to take place. Once repairs had taken place to fix the obvious defect, the feeling of complete isolation flooded my brain in order to contribute in dismissing all possibilities of the situation recurring. The end of the service was reached to find my body outside the church in the parking lot hastily waiting the departure home in the most inconspicuous manner possible. Consequently, when the time to dress for church services arrives in the future, a special precaution related to the strength and durability of zippers in pants will be unforgettably performed.

Journal Practice

Experiment with voice. In your journal write three different letters in three different voices. Assume this is your first term at college and you've discovered a serious problem—perhaps you've discovered your roommate selling term papers and one of them is yours, or your tuition payment was not properly recorded, or the manager at your place of employment prevents you from attending one class a week with the toughest professor you have.

a. Write a letter to a good friend in a *colloquial* voice describing the problem. Use concrete, specific details. Be yourself.

b. Write a second letter to someone who might be able to help—a senior dormitory assistant, a school counselor, or the manager at work. Assume you want to demonstrate maturity and tolerance here: Use an informal voice, but be specific and detailed about the problem.

c. Write a third letter to the highest reasonable authority—the college president, the professor himself, the district manager of your company. Use a firm voice and firmly request an immediate solution.

Play

If you've never allowed yourself to play around with words, now's a good time to begin. Many writers, among them Ray Bradbury, Ivan Doig, and Dylan Thomas, have admitted that the willingness to play with language—to accept words spontaneously—is the place where writing begins. Experienced writers know that freedom and play are what imagination loves most. Such play need not have a direct relationship to a specific writing project. As you play with language, you discover its texture, its structure and rhythms. Experimenting with language helps break up predictable patterns of thinking and writing and may even lead to fresh perceptions and original ideas. So have some fun. Write puns, songs, jokes, riddles, poems, slogans, and absurd exaggerations.

1. Fred Chappell, a widely admired contemporary writer, frequently engages his readers' attention by using similes—phrases that show what something is *like* rather than explaining what something *is*. Here are only a few of the many examples of similes that appear in Chappell's novel, *I Am One Of You Forever*.

> darted past like minnows
> his hands dangled out like big price tags
> white as a morning cloud
> flapping his arms like broken wings
> his hands trembled like poplar leaves
> as dark as the dreams of a sleeping bear
> skin as tight on him as a surgeon's glove
> a raspy whisper like a rat stirring a leaf pile
> a dry crackling voice like the sounds of leaves burning

Try your own hand at creating original similes. Be spontaneous; feel free to be absurd. This is just for fun. But avoid clichés. Similes are effective only if they're fresh and help us see something in a new way.

> Her hands trembled like . . .
> Crows darted past like . . .
> A whisper like . . .
> His enthusiasm shone in him like . . .
> His feet clomped about like . . .
> Sunlight floated on the pond like . . .

2. Create a nonsense menu with ridiculous connotations beginning, for example, with cream of esophagus soup, lymphnode pie, and epidermis on rye.

3. List a dozen disgusting images: maggots crawling out of the eye of a dead cat, a one-legged chicken, cold oatmeal floating in the toilet. Choose one image and expand on it. Here's how 21-year-old Sylvia Plath wrote in her college journal about picking her nose.

Do you realize the illicit sensuous delight I get from picking my nose? I always have, ever since I was a child. There are so many subtle variations of sensations. A delicate, pointed-nailed fifth finger can catch under dry scabs and flakes of mucous in the nostril and draw them out to be looked at, crumbled between fingers, and flicked to the floor in minute crusts. Or a heavier, determined fore-finger can reach up and smear down-and-out the soft, resilient, elas-tic greenish-yellow smallish blobs of mucous, roll them round and jellylike between thumb and forefinger, and spread them on the un-der-surface of a desk or chair where they will harden into organic crusts. How many desks and chairs have I thus secretly befouled since childhood?

In spite of this, Sylvia Plath later went on to win a Pulitzer Prize for poetry.

From *The Journals of Sylvia Plath*, Ted Hughes (ed), Dial Press, Doubleday & Company, © 1982.

Drafting

5

Facing the Blank Page

The time arrives. You've been exploring various subjects in your journal; you've practiced several exercises. Perhaps your instructor has already assigned a subject and an audience. (If not, you'll find several recommended topics on p. 534.) One way or another, the preparation stage is drawing to a close. You have to face the inevitable. You have to write a full-fledged paper. Oh, shudder and dread!

You spread out paper, pens, erasers, and dictionaries. You adjust the desk lamp over your typewriter or word processor. Perhaps you drink a Coke or doodle little circles inside of big circles. You punch a cassette into your tape deck, listen for a while to a new British rock group, and remember good times in high school.

But the blank paper remains white and glaring; the cursor light on your word processor blinks on an empty screen. There is no escape. At some point you must face the single most difficult part of the writing process: beginning to write.

HOW THE PROCESS WORKS

One of the great misunderstandings about writing involves the concept of *failure*. We need to get it out of the way at the beginning. For the successful writer, failure is normal to the process. To say such a thing may sound like a paradox, but actually, without failure, most of us would never be able to say what we wanted to at all. In fact, most of us probably would not know what we truly think and feel without first saying what we did *not* think and feel. In the first version of this very paragraph I wrote a dozen sentences that did not express what I wanted to say. Why? Because until I saw the words in front of me, I could not be sure. I "knew" (like an unvoiced urge) that I should say something about failure. But I had never articulated the ideas before. The first two sentences of the paragraph appear here exactly as I wrote them. Success. But the third sentence did not come until I had first *failed* at several false starts. I had to work through some awkward, inaccurate, and actually misleading sentences until I came to the next one that seemed right to me. I wish I could say it wasn't necessary. I wish I could say that with practice each sentence will flow out upon the page. But, in reality, even the best writers know they must work *through* the failures to arrive at success.

In 1926, William Butler Yeats wrote "Sailing to Byzantium," a 31-line poem. The manuscript reveals that Yeats wrote 19 pages of material in pencil, ink, and typescript, each page averaging about 14 crossed-out, reworked, and abandoned lines. No line now in the final poem appears in the manuscript before the tenth page. In other words, Yeats wrote approximately 140 lines before he found even the first few rough images that satisfied him; and he still had another 126 lines to struggle through: a total of some 266 lines to achieve 31 lines of poetry.

Theodore Geisel is author of the famous Dr. Seuss books for children. Simple lines, simple rhymes. Nothing like the complex moral vision of William Butler Yeats.

> The sun did not shine
> It was too wet to play
> So we sat in the house
> All that cold, cold, wet day.

Yet Geisel admits that *The Cat in the Hat*, a book of 61 pages (only 223 words), took ten months to write.

No one, of course, will expect you to spend ten months writing a college paper, but the more words you're willing to explore on any one writing project, the more likely you'll eventually discover what it is you want to say and how you want to say it. What you need to know is what the professional knows: that the first working copy will be only a sketch of the writer's ideas, of the facts and details of perception, and that much of it will be almost inevitably badly written. If you, too, can know in advance that you are never going to show that first awkward draft to any audience, if you can know that the first draft is *your* copy and that its sole purpose is to provide you with a work sheet, a place to sketch out in as much detail as possible your ideas in rough form, and that it is absolutely *normal* for your first draft to seem like a failure, you will probably find yourself less threatened, less fearful of the blank page. What you are about to do is to explore, and every explorer must chop through a lot of tangled underbrush to reach the crest of a hill. You must be willing to take wrong turns, be willing to make mistakes. You cannot know the path in advance, nor can anyone else. So take a chance and start with the first word.

THE HABITS OF WRITING

Certain types of preparation and mental attitudes can make your approach to the first draft, if not easier, at least more productive.

1. Make writing a habit. As long as writing is an occasional thing, it will seem strange, even threatening. If you practice the piano or trumpet or guitar a little every day, it becomes a familiar instrument; you feel comfortable with it. Familiarity in any situation helps you relax. Better to write an hour a day, every day, than to postpone an assignment until the night before and attempt a 12-hour marathon. Work for an hour a day in your journal, on a lab report, on two pages of a 15-page research paper—it really does not matter as long as you're writing every day.

2. Find a regular time and place. Try to write at approximately the same time each day. We are creatures of regularity. Football coaches know how important it is for a team to practice at the same hour, five days a week. The body—and the mind—has its rhythm. Whether you write best in the early morning or at midnight makes little difference so long as you find the tide of your personal rhythm and flow with it every day.

Most successful writers have also discovered they need a special place in which to work. Some prefer absolute silence; others write well immersed in noise. Find what works for you and stick to it. Create your own nest. Surround yourself with books or paintings or bare walls—whatever makes you comfortable. The German writer, Schiller, claimed to work well only when he could smell rotten apples. Most of us aren't that eccentric, but having a special place helps establish a pattern for writing that almost all of us need.

3. Do warm-up writing when necessary. When Kurt Vonnegut was still employed by General Electric Company and not yet famous for his novels of fantasy and science fiction, a story was told about how he would arrive for work each morning, immediately sit down at his type-writer, and pound on it for about ten minutes, describing nothing more than the eggs he ate for breakfast, the rumbling of the subway that morning, and the feel of snow in the air. He called it his warm-up. To use the analogy of an athlete or musician again, trying to perform cold, without preparation, may be possible; but the performance will usually be halting and error prone until the mind or senses are fully tuned in. The best preparation for beginning the first draft may be to write in your journal for ten minutes. A warm-up can never substitute for honest effort on the main writing project. But don't hesitate to play a little at first. Write about anything that comes into your head. If nothing comes, write: *Mary had a little lamb*, then find a new rhyme to go with it, then another. Play. Exercise. But start writing fast. Time yourself and do not stop writing for at least 10 minutes.

4. Write fast. Once you begin work on your real subject, write with as much intensity and speed as possible. Because the mind usually moves faster than the hand, a typewriter or word processor can prove valuable. You might even want to try dictating your ideas into a tape recorder. But work fast.

Most successful writers have found that the more slowly you write the first draft, the more slowly ideas tend to come. The more words you get on the page, the more the words themselves seem to activate the imagination. Words call up words. Images call up images. Slow writing may allow time for you to become overly critical. You may begin con-sciously to challenge the sentence you've just completed. (Is it the best way to phrase what you want to say? Did you spell that word correctly? Should you be varying your sentence structures more?) Once this sort of self-criticism begins, you're no longer writing. You're editing. Writing and editing are different stages in the writing process. During the first draft, fast, intensive writing focuses your mind on the subject. Ideas will grow only out of an encounter with the subject, not out of concern for grammar or spelling. After you've finished a rough working copy, there will be time (and need) to revise, edit, and polish.

FORM AND THE PERSONAL ESSAY

Form refers to the shape of your experience, to the way you organize your material. In personal writing, form is usually subjective. It tends to develop from the natural sequence of events you are writing about (this happened and then this happened) or from subconscious "associations" (one word calls up a second; one image leads to another). I won't tell you not to outline or plan before you write. Many writers find it helpful. But because part of the aim of writing about personal experience is to explore yourself and your voice freely, for the time being you'll probably find that conscious concern for form should follow the first draft, not precede it. Yet two traditional elements of form tend to be associated with most personal essays. Knowing them in advance may help you focus even your rough draft more clearly.

First, although the whole range of human experience is open to you, you cannot successfully write about ten years of life, or even twenty-four hours, in only four or five pages. The personal essay may be organized around a single, unique experience, one that you develop in great detail, helping the reader to see, hear, smell, and touch. Or the personal essay may be organized around two or three smaller experiences that reveal some kind of pattern—a series of ordinary daily situations that are typical or that lead to general insight. Either way, you will need to *select* only the one major incident or the two or three typical incidents and to exclude all the millions of others that compose your life.

Second, the elements of experience you select to write about should show the reader how they led you to some type of growth, insight, or understanding, even if it is a humorous one. You do not necessarily need to explain the meaning of the experience in abstract, general terms (although you can do so), but the meaning must be evident or implied by the end of the essay. After all, why write about it if it has no meaning to you?

Journal Practice

If you've been practicing regularly in your journal, you already have a number of strategies for beginning your first essay—and you may already have the subject for it. Making lists, freewriting, exploring your memory, sharing stories and experiences with the blank page are all ways of getting started.

1. Look back through your journal for exercises you may have written on any personal experience. Select one that seems to have possibilities and make a list of ideas that might extend it into a longer essay. Perhaps you wrote a paragraph about your first meeting with your new roommate. Consider how the topic might be developed further:

> initial encounter in hallway
> luggage with airline tickets pasted on sides
> sweaty palms
> obnoxious parents
> father wearing tennis shorts and talking loud
> mother with sickly smile, left basket of overripe grapefruit
> roommate wouldn't talk for two days
> spent two more days moping about bad cafeteria food
> hated each other
> then found we were both on swim team
> first instinct: competitive, determined to beat each other out
> initial practice session
> water overheated; coach too demanding
> everybody seemed arrogant, everybody for themselves
> roommate only person who talked to me
> stuck together out of necessity
> asked for lockers together
> eye contact said we were both nervous
> cheered for each other in trial heats
> stopped hating, started respecting each other's abilities
> found we could be best friends

Now you've got the potential for a full essay, and it's already beginning to take shape. Sometimes you may find you won't even get to the end of your list before you'll have too many ideas. Instead of listing, you'll find you're already writing. Go ahead. Trust your instincts and trust the act of writing to generate more ideas.

2. If none of your previous entries seem to offer possibilities, or if a new listing doesn't stimulate the imagination this time, try a technique called "webbing." Begin with a key word, *any* word, and follow whatever comes to mind. Allow one word to create associations or memories. Trace them out; draw lines and circles that follow your ideas.

If no ideas come, draw the line and circle first. The very act of showing the mind that it is supposed to fill in the blank often triggers an idea.

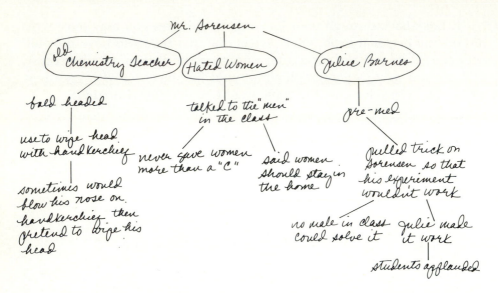

3. If nothing at all seems effective, take a break. Work on some other project or go to a movie. Let the incubation phase do its own thing in your subconscious. Try again later. But don't postpone the assignment until the night before it's due. Keep trying any and all exercises suggested so far, and if nothing works, start writing about anything. Remember, the act of writing itself is almost always more productive than merely worrying about or thinking about what to write.

Revising

6

Precision and Feeling

Interviewer: *How much rewriting do you do?*
Hemingway: *It depends. I rewrote the ending of* Farewell
to Arms *thirty-nine times before I was satisfied.*
Interviewer: *Was there some technical problem there?*
What was it that had stumped you?
Hemingway: *Getting the words right.*

PARIS REVIEW

The real work of writing begins when you determine to make
your prose say exactly what you want it to say. You may find
it effective to create a wholly new second draft, a complete
reworking with the same speed and intensity as in your initial
effort. Or you may find that for you revising is a somewhat slower, more
calculated study. Some inner feeling suggests that the words you've used
do not yet express what you hoped they would; so you rephrase, cross
out, and begin again, testing each new sentence against the old. In either
case, your focus remains primarily on the subject—on ideas and feelings—but you find that your attention edges toward a conscious effort

at finding the right word, the most meaningful sequence of ideas or images, and toward achieving a unified effect.

SEARCHING FOR THE RIGHT MEANING

Many take language for granted. In terms of influencing their lives, they tend to place words somewhere between sunshine and potato chips. But language has a remarkable, almost awesome power over us. Words spoken by someone you love on an autumn afternoon unite the two of you forever. Words written on a letter of application get you accepted to law school. Words spoken on television by a local car dealer campaigning for mayor make you slam a book on the table in anger. The power of language is such that almost two-thirds of the world's governments forbid newspapers to publish freely. Priests in many early cults and religions often were feared because they knew magic words that summoned the gods. Telling stories, fables, and fantasies around the campfire led to complex mythologies that eventually became the cultural fabric of civilization. Indeed, without words, we would have no civilization. Language is inseparable from being human. As a beginning writer, you need at least a rudimentary understanding of some of the ways words affect you and your reader.

Here's how one freshman (who had not yet developed a feeling for words) began an early draft of an essay about his grandfather.

> Royster R. Matting lived an immemorial life. He began as a surveyor in Montana, made and lost a fortune as a miner, once owned a railroad in Virginia, became a judge in Maryland, and raised thirteen children who honored his loins.

Well, maybe, but the writer seems to have encountered two kinds of language problems, both related to accuracy. One is a matter of denotation; the other, a matter of perception.

Denotation is the explicit (or dictionary) meaning of a word. Obviously, using a word with the correct denotation is essential to clear communication. *Immemorial*, for example, means reaching beyond the limits of memory, beyond even recorded history. As admirable a life as Royster R. Matting may have had, it surely wasn't beyond memory's scope. The student has clearly wanted to express the breadth and energy found in his grandfather's life, but the word *memorable* (something worth remembering) probably comes closer and expresses his feelings more exactly. Mark Twain's famous remark still applies: "The difference between the right word and the wrong word is the difference between lightning and a lightning bug." Words are symbols. Unless we use them with generally agreed-upon meanings, confusion and disorder result. In this case, the student has simply chosen the wrong word. Thirty seconds with any dictionary would have revealed the problem.

But dictionaries are not always the solution to achieving accuracy. Accuracy begins in clarity of perception. If you are not seeing your subject clearly, you obviously won't find clear and precise words to communicate it. The freshman who wrote about his grandfather admitted that he felt uncomfortable with the phrase "thirteen children who honored his loins," but it had a biblical ring to it and he hoped it would work. The student accepted the first phrase that sounded good to his ear (something that's fine to do on a first draft), but that uncomfortable feeling should have signaled a need for challenging the phrase in the second draft. Surely, these thirteen children honored more than their father's prodigious sexual abilities. The problem here is not that the student has chosen a wrong word, but that he has not truly identified what it was about his grandfather the children honored. Was it his remarkable career? His achievements? His human compassion? We don't know and neither does the student. At this point a dictionary won't help.

Revising the first draft often means reseeing the subject (from the Latin for "looking again"). This student should have asked himself a series of questions: If I haven't found the precise word, is it because I haven't found the right insight? If I haven't found the right insight, is it because I haven't looked honestly, haven't struggled to find the small details that make up the total? What is it about my subject that I'm not yet seeing?

The answer in this case was not difficult.

> Royster R. Matting lived a memorable life. He began as a surveyor in Montana, made and lost a fortune as a miner, once owned a railroad in Virginia, became a judge in Maryland, and raised thirteen children who always honored the model of courage and discipline he established.

Before submitting a final typed version of his essay, the student reread it and again refined the accuracy by penciling in the term *self-* before "discipline." Now the reader can be convinced. Self-discipline and courage indeed can make for a memorable life. Precise words strike home more forcefully than a page of words that only circle the subject. The "almost right" word is never the right word.

SEARCHING FOR THE RIGHT FEELING

If you were hired to write menus for Top of the Town Restaurant, you might find that correct denotation was only half the problem. Here are two versions of the same menu, each conveying a similar denotative meaning:

> Succulent roast beef served in its own juice with tiny young peas and mashed potatoes . . . $12.50

> Bloody cow's flesh with tiny young *pisum sativum* seed and squashed tubers . . . 75¢

No doubt most of your customers would prefer to pay $12.50 for the first dish, even though the 75-cent meal is identical. Words do more than communicate messages. The *connotation* of a word is the feeling it suggests to us.

Nursing merely names a medical occupation, but the word has about it an aura of feelings: tenderness, care, sacrifice. The nature and intensity of feeling associated with a word may be peculiar to your individual relationship with it. If you appreciate athletics, *jock* might be a term you use with pride, but if you don't like sports, *jock* might be a term you use as an insult. Other words, however, seem to share a general *connotation* throughout a given culture—*snake*, for example.

Sometimes the feelings we have about words become so strong that they actually replace the original denotative meanings. In the Middle Ages, the word *mistress* meant a woman who had control of the house. Possession of numerous keys to pantries, cupboards, and wine cellars symbolized her control. The word was equivalent to the male appellation *master* and projected a similar positive connotation. During Shakespeare's

---

Compare your emotional responses to each of the following words with similar denotations. The positive or negative feeling you experience is the connotation. Words that evoke no feeling are said to be connotatively neutral.

gay	homosexual	fag
female activist	feminist	women's libber
amour	love affair	making it
tumor	malignancy	cancer
rest room	powder room	john

time, *mistress* began to be used metaphorically, as in "mistress of my heart," suggesting the woman who possessed keys to, or control of, her lover's emotions. Apparently the metaphor seemed so right that a *mistress* began to be associated more with love than home. By the seventeenth century, the denotation had actually changed to "an illicit lover" and the connotation had become negative.

Words evoke feelings, but communicating the *exact* feeling is not easy. Several years ago a student of mine, Kiki Nikoni, wanted to write about a painful moment from childhood. Kiki stumbled into what is probably the most common danger among beginning writers—over-writing, telling too much, using words that are too emotional or that suggest an inappropriate connotation. In listening to her first draft, the class argued that her essay sounded melodramatic. Kiki rewrote it several times to make it more genuine, but at the same time she wanted it to be forceful because the real experience had been important to her. Read the original version through before you read the revision.

	Original	*Revision*
1	Where I used to live there was a	In Japan I used to live near a
2	train. I would hear it but I never	train. Each night I would hear its
3	really listened until after my	whistle but I never really listened
4	father died. Once I was alone at	until the night after my father's
5	night by the window.	funeral. I was alone at the
6	Frankenstein-shadows seemed as	window and the shadows seemed
7	deathly cold as I felt inside. Then	thin and cold. Then I heard the
8	I heard the whistle like a	whistle, high and far away, like a
9	moaning screaming animal	child's toy in the dark. The
10	somewhere far outside. The	silence afterward seemed
11	silence roared about me! Then	unsteady, as if something whole
12	the whistle blew again, this time	had been sliced. The whistle
13	closer but still painful and really	blew again, this time closer but
14	lonely. I remember thinking for a	still hollow and lonely. For a
15	moment that it was like I was out	moment I felt some part of me
16	there and my heart was broken	was out there, like my father's
17	and torn out of me and lost, like a	ghost. Then the whistle again,
18	father's ghost crying out! It hurt	but further away, faint and fading.
19	my ears, it hurt my heart until the	After a while I couldn't hear it.
20	tears ran down my cheeks.	There was just moonlight on
21		empty fields.

Both versions reveal problems with connotations, but the first presents serious difficulties. The class objected especially to lines 13 through 20. Kiki's listeners felt she was crying out in abstractions (*painful, lonely, lost, hurt*) and that she was perilously close to clichéd melodrama (*a broken heart, a ghost, tears running down her cheeks*). Kiki had tried to select words and images she thought would convey an honest feeling of pain. The opposite effect resulted. The class doubted the sincerity of her description.

In the second version Kiki tried to resee the scene in her memory. She removed most of the abstractions and substituted concrete images, using words that might *suggest* the feelings of pain and loss (*a hollow whistle, a faint and fading whistle, moonlight on open fields*). She removed the references to her broken heart, replacing it with the generalization: *some part of me*. The class agreed that this was a time when the generalization worked more successfully because it seemed less melodramatic. In the context (and connotation is always affected by context) *some part of me*, by its very abstractness, suggested emptiness and helped promote the appropriate feeling.

Kiki made a number of other changes you might want to consider.

1. Why did she add *Japan* to line 1? How does a specific place suggest feeling? Would the connotation have been different had she lived in Little Rock at the time?
2. Why did she change *after my father died* in line 3 to *after my father's funeral*?
3. Why *shadows seemed thin and cold* instead of *Frankenstein-shadows* in line 6?
4. What was gained or lost in changing *moaning screaming animal* in line 9 to *high and far away, like a child's toy in the dark*? How do the connotations of either one relate to the loss of a father, and which seems most appropriate for the mood Kiki wants to convey?
5. What kind of feelings does *moonlight on empty fields* in line 20 connote for you? Why did Kiki think that it could substitute for the original *tears ran down my cheeks*?

As a young writer you need to develop the confidence that words can be played with. Just because you've written a word on the page, you should not think it's sacred. Indeed, you may not know exactly what you want to say until you've tried to say it in several different ways. By understanding something about how language affects all of us, you learn how to discover and express your ideas with more force.

Exercises

William Faulkner said there are three things a writer needs: paper, tobacco, and whiskey. To that list we need to add a good, large dictionary. It may not do for you what tobacco and whiskey will, but it is an essential tool of any educated person, not just the professional writer.

1. *The Oxford English Dictionary* (usually called the *OED*) traces word histories, providing you with a thorough sense of a word's past and, by implication, its denotative and connotative developments.

Investigate the history of the following terms. In your own words, write up the history as you understand it, giving some of the examples listed in the *OED*.

science	nice
woman	humanities
sophisticated	text

2. Look up the following terms in a dictionary of synonyms. Find three synonyms for each, and in your own words suggest the differences in connotation. For example, *Roget's Thesaurus* lists *dowager* and *relict* among the synonyms for *widowhood*. To me, widowhood suggests loneliness, dark dresses, and silence, whereas *dowager* suggests strength in a woman's old age, a widow with power and authority, and something vaguely Elizabethan. Frankly, I'm surprised to find *relict* there at all. If *relict* is a synonym for *widowhood*, then it suggests a decrepit woman, the leavings of a man's life, a woman without value.

submission	regret
money	marriage
cool	truth
trust	student

3. Identify and discuss the positive, negative, or neutral connotations in each of the following sentences. Which is the key word or phrase that creates the emotional effect? In which sentences can an alternative evoke a different emotional response?

a. The Russians liberated Afghanistan.
b. Grandmama is selling her objet d'art.
c. The President is proposing tax incentives for business.
d. The ingredients on a can of cat food include fish by-products.
e. Juan comes from a Chicano family.

Journal Practice

Select one of your previous exercises—perhaps one on an individual or a place that had special importance to you—and evaluate every sentence in light of what you now know about connotations and denotations.

Does every word contribute to the precise meaning and feeling that you want? Are some words or phrases inappropriate? Rewrite the passage to make it more effective, to make it suggest the emotions you honestly feel. Would the rewritten version make it a stronger piece for you to share with an audience (a reader)?

Editing

7

Cutting
Unnecessary
Words

The distinction between editing and rewriting is somewhat arbitrary. For more experienced writers, editing techniques blend naturally with the process of exploring the subject in second and third drafts. The goal of both stages in the writing process is to improve the effectiveness of writing so that you find means of conveying your subject clearly and convincingly. But many necessary aspects of writing involve the mechanics of effective expression: sentence structure, sentence variety, paragraphing, logical order, accurate documentation. When such qualities are emphasized too early in the learning process, beginning writers tend to be overwhelmed by what they perceive as rules and restrictions. The results can often create stillborn prose and the "I hate to write" attitude. It might be best (even if somewhat oversimplified) to think of rewriting as a phase in which your primary focus remains on developing the subject, and of editing as a phase in which your attention shifts to achieving the most polished and effective form of expression.

THE EDITOR'S JOB

Editing involves selecting, arranging, and correcting a manuscript. Your papers may not be intended for publication, but as most audiences are accustomed to thinking of "good writing" as that which they see published, your writing will usually be judged by similarly high standards. You must become your own editor. You must learn some essential skills of editing. Almost without exception, you'll find their application to every essay, report, or research paper will make the difference between average work and good work.

Editing requires an attitude almost opposite to the one you were urged to adopt in writing the first draft. Instead of spontaneous, fast writing, instead of suspension of all concern for sentence structure and correctness, editing requires a cool, slow, self-critical act. Most writers find that they need to turn away from their writing for a while, distance themselves from it, and later return with a coldly skeptical attitude: Every word, every sentence, must prove its worth. As a student you may not have the ideal amount of time to pause between rewriting and editing, but you can still train yourself to approach your material with an editor's eye.

© 1972 United Feature Syndicate, Inc.

Because the sentence is the shortest complete unit of thought, it seems the best place to begin the practice of editing. The first step in forming a solid, readable sentence is to make it say only what it needs to say and nothing more: That means eliminating unnecessary words. Unfortunately, many students have been taught that short simple sentences should be avoided. Long, complex-compound sentences seem to get all the praise. Some students go out of their way to use as many words as possible in every paper. Editing down to simple, irreducible elements may seem in conflict with everything you've been taught. But a major misconception is at work here. Long sentences in themselves are neither better nor worse than short sentences, but extra words are deathly to all forms of writing. The first goal of sentence editing is to clear away clutter that distracts from meaning. *Every word or phrase that can be cut should be cut.*

Here's a typical early-draft sentence:

Having just finished college myself, I can testify that mental discipline is the greatest asset a college student can have while he's in school.

Fair enough. But not good enough. The simplest editorial act strikes out excess.

Cut: Having just finished college[myself], I can testify that mental discipline is the greatest asset a [college] student can have [while he's in school].

By eliminating six redundant words or phrases, we have a cleaner sentence that directly conveys its message.

Here's another example from a freshman paper.

At an early stage in his career, Pete Rose met a coach who kept urging him to go and analyze his motions while he was up at the plate.

No two editors would necessarily find the same weaknesses in this sentence. Right and wrong answers are seldom clear-cut in editing. But most editors would probably agree that almost half could be eliminated without losing the meaning of the sentence.

Cut: [At an] early [stage] in his career . . .
("Early in his career" says the same thing.)

Cut: . . . Pete Rose met a coach who [kept] urg[ing] him to [go and] analyze . . .
(*Kept urging* adds little to the concept of *urge*, and *go and* simply distracts from the stronger word, *analyze*.)

Cut . . . his motions [while he was up] at the plate.
(As we seldom think of someone being *down* at the plate, *while he was up* contributes nothing to meaning.)

A final edited version might now read like this:

Early in his career, Pete Rose met a coach who urged him to analyze his motions at the plate.

We have eliminated ten words, made the sentence simpler, and, in the process, allowed the meaning to come through more clearly.

Sometimes prepositions are special offenders to wordiness.

The federal government has sponsored several programs *to* assist *in* providing *for* funds *for* the college student.

Prepositions are essential to English grammar, but if you find them popping up like dandelions, do some weeding.

The federal government has sponsored several programs to assist college students.

THE BACKWARD SENTENCE

In early drafts we often tend to write about what something is not rather than what it is. Again, the process seems normal. In trying to figure out what we want to say, we may need to circle and come in from behind. Editing can be the time when we reconsider and consciously reshape the sentence to strengthen its meaning.

> There is no doubt that Ellen looked as though she were not feeling well.
>
> *Cut:* [There is no doubt that] Ellen looked as though she were not feeling well.
>
> (Introductory phrases that use the word *that* can almost always be eliminated.)
>
> as if she were sick
>
> *Tighten:* Ellen looked [as though she were not feeling well].
>
> (It is almost always more effective to say what something is instead of what it isn't. "He was not a weak man" suggests weakness by the very presence of the word; "he was a strong man" suggests strength that is actually there.)
>
> sick
>
> *Tighten again:* Ellen looked [as if she were sick].
>
> (Sometimes a short, blunt sentence is the most forceful of all.)

Here's the sentence before editing . . .

> There is no doubt that Ellen looked as though she were not feeling well.

and after editing . . .

> Ellen looked sick.

The editing process eliminated eleven unnecessary words and reversed the meaning of the sentence from what Ellen was not to what she was. The result is a simple, strong statement that leaves "no doubt"—the point the writer began with.

The word *not* should be a clue. When it shows up in a sentence, challenge the sentence. Obviously, there will be many times when *not* works well; but if you're a good editor, you'll probably find an equal number of times when the direction of the sentence needs reversing or when a single word will substitute for a phrase.

I did *not* remember.   I forgot.

I did *not* believe his statistics.   I distrusted his statistics.

It did *not* seem important.   It seemed unimportant.

WHO, WHICH, AND THAT

Like the word *not*, the words *who, which,* and *that* should be seen as clues. Every time they occur, challenge their necessity. About half the time they serve no function.

Cut: I lived in a room [that was] over the garage.
("I lived in a room over the garage" says the same thing.)

Cut: How could I know that her mother, [who was] short and dumpy, would oppose our marriage?
(Make it sound more like the spoken voice: "How could I know that her short, dumpy mother would oppose our marriage?")

Cut: [I think that] we owe first responsibility to our moral conscience.
("We owe first responsibility to our moral conscience" is stronger and more direct.)

ADJECTIVES

Adjectives modify nouns: a *red* house, a *grouchy* professor. They can be helpful at times. But the beginning writer often overuses them, sometimes attaching a string of adjectives to a single noun or even an adjective to every noun in a mistaken belief that "adjectives are colorful" or that in some way they will make up for weak writing. Successful writers have learned from experience that a strong noun in itself is more colorful than a weak noun propped up with one to six adjectives. Nouns, not adjectives, are the foundation blocks of every sentence. Use of an adjective should cause you to question the noun to which it's attached. Can the adjective be eliminated, either because it's unnecessary or because a stronger noun will supplant it?

Challenge: I ate a [red apple].

Winesap might be a better noun ("I ate a Winesap") because a Winesap is both red and an apple. A concrete noun simplifies the sentence (one less word) while making it more sensuous. *Winesap* does more than suggest red; it suggests a shade of red (wine colored) and a taste (wine plus sap).

Challenge: I studied a [~~small brown~~] insect that I found by an [~~old gray~~] rock.

Why not name the *insect*? A cricket, for example, is both *small and brown* (a two-word saving). And aren't all rocks *old*? In this case, we would know more if the adjective identified some less predictable quality. Was the rock covered with lichen or moss?

> I studied a cricket that I found by a mossy rock.
> > or better yet
> I studied a cricket by a mossy rock.

Challenge: A [~~big, red, growling, thundering, incredible, bell clanging~~] fire engine came down the alley.

A string of adjectives attached to a single noun is called an adjective pileup. In this case, *fire engine* is a strong enough noun, but more than two adjectives in a row should cause the writer to think twice. Here are some steps we might go through to reconsider.

1. *Big* seems weak because of its vagueness. How big is big? In this context, *thundering* probably connotes bigness anyway.
2. *Red* is generally associated with fire engines and, therefore, adds nothing to the image.
3. *Thundering* and *growling* suggest similar sounds but with slightly different connotations. We need to choose between them. As both are stronger than the verb, one or the other might replace the verb.
4. *Incredible* might be valuable, but as it's used here, it seems lost amid the other adjectives.
5. *Bell-clanging* adds another dimension of sound and might be an adjective we want to retain.

Here, then, are several possible revisions.

> A bell-clanging fire engine thundered down the alley.
> A clanging fire engine growled down the alley.
> An incredible, bell-clanging fire engine thundered down the alley.

The context in which a sentence occurs, your purpose, and your ear will have to help you decide. But, in general, two or more adjectives in a row should be seen as a caution signal. Editing is probably called for.

ADVERBS

What the adjective is to the noun, the adverb is to the verb. It helps, but often with only modest success.

Challenge: I [really] felt strange and uptight.

The reader can only respond that *really* feeling is still feeling and hasn't added enough added dimension to justify letting it live in this sentence.

Challenge: Both of us ran [very] fast,.

We can accept *fast* as an adverb (I suppose one could run slowly), but what does *very* add? What is the difference between *very fast* and *fast?* A smidgen at best, and not worth the extra word.

Maybe we can come up with a general principle. Adverbs and adjectives should be used so sparingly that their effectiveness is increased by the rareness of their appearance.

A REMINDER

In each of my examples in this chapter I have edited a sentence out of context. Obviously, in your own papers, word choice and sentence length must be evaluated within the flow and meaning of the whole essay. (See Chapter 22.) But remember that editing occurs at the end of the writing process. Do not worry about it while you are still in the first-draft or revising stages. If you begin to edit too early, you take your mind off the subject matter. Content must precede form. Get the content on the page: then shape and form it afterward.

However, do not think that you can ever skip the editing phase. Content alone is never effective. The way you express yourself is as important as what you have to say. If your ideas are submerged in an ocean of unnecessary words, you'll find your reader unwilling to make the dive for fear of drowning. The best of writers—Hemingway, Fitzgerald, Thomas Wolfe—all had editors. The rest of us must learn to become our own.

Exercises

Although you must eventually learn to edit your own material, it may at first be easier to identify wordiness in someone else's sentences. Try some of the following games before you begin editing your own papers.

1. In each of the following sentences, eliminate every unnecessary word or phrase. Do not change the meaning of the sentence itself. When necessary, replace a cluttered phrase with a single word or with a more concrete and specific word.

a.   Owing to the fact that he was late, he missed seeing the president.

> Because
> *Cut*: [~~Owing to the fact that~~] he was late, he missed seeing the president.

b.   I do not approve of the methods he employs.
c.   His tale is very old and strangely different.
d.   His brother, who is a member of the same firm, was indicted by the grand jury.
e.   This is a subject that has always interested me.
f.   Her sweater has a red glow to it.
g.   The question as to whether he succeeded has not been decided.
h.   The people who stood around outside in the street had a better view than those who stayed inside.
i.   Mike was different from him. His face was quite round, and a pale white color. On his chin he had a beard which was thin and scraggy in some places. He wondered where he was at.

2.   Here is a paragraph from E. L. Doctorow's *Ragtime*, a novel about the 1920s. The main character in this passage is "Mother's Younger Brother." He had no other name. I have rewritten the paragraph as it might have looked in a first-draft version. Edit out every word you feel is unnecessary. Then compare your edited version with Doctorow's, which follows. Don't cheat by looking ahead. Right and wrong answers are seldom available in editing,. Context, purpose, and your inner ear must determine your answers. Test your ear against that of a professional writer.

> The air was very saltylike in your nose. Mother's Younger Brother, in his white linen suit and boater, had rolled his trousers up to almost his knees and taken off his shoes and was walking barefoot in the salt marshes. Sea birds were startled by his approach and flew up into the blue sky. This was the time in our history, which was before most of us were born, when Winslow Homer was doing his painting. A certain type of light was still available along the whole Eastern seaboard. Homer painted the light in his paintings. The light gave the sea a very heavy, dull menace and shone very coldly on the black rocks and rough shoals of the New England coast.

Here is Doctorow's edited version:

> The air was salt. Mother's Younger Brother in his white linen suit and boater rolled his trousers and walked barefoot in the salt marshes. Sea birds started and flew up. This was the time in our history when Winslow Homer was doing his painting. A certain light

was still available along the Eastern seaboard. Homer painted the light. It gave the sea a heavy dull menace and shone coldly on the rocks and shoals of the New England coast.

Journal Practice

1. Edit two of your previous journal entries. Eliminate every unnecessary word. Look especially for clutter words like *of, at, to,* and *the.* Try to eliminate or find single-word substitutes for unnecessary phrases like *the fact that, whether or not,* and *the question of.* Be careful of overusing *who* and *which;* they can be eliminated about half the time.

It is possible to overwork a piece of writing. Sometimes your first instinct is best. If you feel yourself becoming angry or frustrated, stop for a while. Go over it again later when you feel cooler. For many people, the process works better in the back of the mind than on paper. For others, it's always a word-by-word battle, crossing out and starting over. Never think you are alone. Everyone from Thomas Jefferson to William Faulkner has worked in exactly the same way.

2. Edit any one of your previous journal entries by making it at least one-third shorter than the original version. Do not cut anything that is essential to the meaning or feeling, but be brutal; throw away everything that doesn't directly, concretely contribute to the total effect.

Readings

The Writing Process: A Student Example

Fred Cox wanted to major in Sports Medicine. He signed up for my class only because it was required. Fred dreaded "English" and sat in a back row where he could gaze longingly out the window. Early in the semester, I asked the class to use journals for listing any past experience that began negatively and ended positively, and then to write briefly on one item from the list. Here is what Fred wrote:

Chinatown on New Year's Eve
Patty Roger's party
my first wrestling match
learning sign language
taking the SAT exam

I remember the first time I ever wrestled in high school and my dad came and saw me lose. He was the kind who you could tell was angry or something, but he never really talked to me, and when he did it was only to criticize. It was always the silent treatment. We had a real shouting match in the car on the way home, or at least I shouted at him because he wouldn't say anything, and then all he could do was tell me everything I had done wrong, but after we got home he put his arm around me and I've never forgot and I think I never really knew how he felt about me until then.

Later, I asked my students to select one excerpt from their journals and to develop it into a full essay. Everyone brought a draft copy to class for other students to read and react to. Our goal was to help each other by offering comments and questions. Here's the first page of Fred Cox's draft with some of the observations students wrote in the margins.

Lots of generalizations but no details

I remember the first time I ever wrestled and my dad came and watched. It was awful. Even though I had made the team in my fresman year I had to face a guy who had wrestled in the state state tournemnent the year before, and I lost badly. But the hard part was not losing because I had expected to. My dad was the hard part. After the match we drove home and he never said a word. The interior of the car was cold. Almost immediately a thin layer of ice formed on the inside of the windshield. Maybe it was from my hot, sweaty body which only a few

Good concrete details here — we need more

Could we see him?

minutes earlier had been badly beaten. My dad got into the car and you could tell he was angry. I thought to myself, this is what I really hate, the silent treatment. You could never tell what he was thinking, just nothing.

How? Show us instead of telling us

> I wondered whether he was proud of me or
>
> disappointed.

Fred's group suggested that he was *telling* rather than *showing*. He needed to focus on the memory itself, to find concrete, sensory details that would bring it to life for the reader. Fred insisted he had done the best he could. "I just can't write," he complained.

A week later, he brought in a second draft. Even Fred felt he was making progress. The essay seemed richer and more fully developed. My suggestion that he could improve it even more was met with shocked silence. Fred left my office with a sigh. Here's a copy of his first page with some of my comments.

I remember the first time I ever wrestled
and my dad came and watched. It was awful.
Soph? Junior? Be specific → Even though I had made the team in my freshman
year I had to face a guy who had wrestled in the
state tournemnent the year before, and I lost
badly. But the hard part was not losing because
I had expected to. My dad was the hard part.
still seems too general — do we actually need this?

After the match we drove home and he never said
a word. The interior of the (car) was cold. The
Perhaps should begin here (?) Isn't this where the incedent itself begins? →
red leather seat crackled as I slid acorss.
Almost immediately a thin layer of ice formed on
the inside of the windshield. Maybe *I felt hot* it was from
my hot, sweaty body. Only a few minutes earlier
(it) had been badly beaten. It was the first
match my dad had ever attended. I leaned my
body up against the door, slumping in the seat

what kind of car? Is it really "leather"?

simplify!

"slumping" shows that you're tired

> in a tired way. Dad got into the car slamming
> the door. I could see the black <u>outline</u> of my   *〈 right word ?*
> dad's head from the dim light of the gym.
> Without a word, he turned the key in the
> ignition. The engine <u>sputtered</u> as it started.   *〈 good verb*
> I thought to myself, this is what I really hate,
> the silent treatment. My dad never told me how
> he felt, what he was thinking, nothing. I
> wondered whether he was proud of me for making
> the wrestling team my freshman year. Was he
> disappointed in my losing tonight?

Nice images here - you begin to slow down and reader concrete details

Three days later, after struggling through a third revision and some late-night editing, Fred presented another copy. The essay now begins with the actual experience. As readers we participate in the sequence of events and learn about a father-and-son relationship from their own actions and words. Fred's selection of concrete details creates a sense of watching the memory unfold. By the end, we do not need to be told the meaning of the incident. The actions themselves inform us. Best of all, Fred discovered good writing isn't something magical or mysterious. Good writing is the result of a process involving drafting, revising, and editing. His later essays got better and better. And although I can't say Fred ever actually came to like writing, he did discover that with plain hard work, he could be proud of the quality of his effort.

Here's the final version of Fred's first college essay.

The Match

Fred Cox

The interior of our Chevy was cold. The red vinyl seat crackled as I slid across. Almost immediately, a thin layer of ice formed on the inside of the windshield. I felt hot and sweaty. Only a few minutes earlier I had been badly beaten in a wrestling match, the first match my dad had ever attended.

I leaned my body up against the door, slumping in the seat. Dad got into the car slamming the door. I could see the silhouette of my dad's head from the dim light of the gym. Without a word, he turned the key in the ignition. The engine sputtered as it started. I thought to myself, this is what I really hate, the silent treatment. My dad never told me how he felt, what he was thinking, nothing. I wondered whether he was proud of me for making the wrestling team my freshman year. Was he disappointed in my losing to-night?

We started home. The air whistled through the defroster. We passed the high school stadium, crossed the railroad tracks and were halfway through town. He still hadn't spoken. I blurted out, "What did you think, Dad?" He turned his head, glanced at me for a second and then turned his attention back to the road. "Did I do all right?" He only kept driving. The engine strained as we accelerated. I would have felt better if he had said anything, even if it was disheartening, at least I would know where I stood. "Did I do all right?" His hands tightened on the steering wheel.

After a long pause he answered. "He beat you. He was all over you, turning you over on your back, almost pinning you. You have to ask how you did? You were too slow and couldn't get away from him."

Wow! I thought. He's an expert and this was the first match he had ever seen. I didn't think he knew anything about wrestling.

"Are you glad I made the team?" There was a long pause like maybe he really had to think about it.

"You should've played football," he said.

Not this again, I thought. He had really been upset in the fall when I had refused to go out for football. I had tried it in the seventh grade and had not enjoyed playing, but I still enjoyed watching. The main reason I had gone out for wrestling was to try to make him proud of me. But it wasn't working.

"Did you know the guy I wrestled was a senior and went to the state tournament last year?"

No answer.

By this time the interior of the car was unbearably hot. I reached over and turned off the fan. My stomach felt queasy like the hot dog I had eaten earlier was about to come up. I could feel the hair on the back of my neck standing straight out.

My dad was not a cruel man. He had always given me what I needed plus some. Never had he beaten or abused me. He wasn't even overly strict. He let me come and go as I pleased. But he hardly ever talked, and when he did it was to criticize. Nothing I ever did was right. Even if I won the match, he would have said the opponent was a pushover or something.

We were halfway home. In desperation I screamed, "Damn it, say some-thing." He glared at me. His nostrils flared and his jaw tensed. "Don't you ever talk to me in that tone of voice again if you know what's good for you." I pressed closer to the door. I had really made him mad now. Then he started talking about respect and then something about how I had inconvenienced him for the last fifteen years. How your kids never treat you right.

After a short time he seemed to calm down. "I'm sorry," I mumbled, but he didn't answer. By this time my stomach felt all knotted. My body was breaking into a cold sweat, but my face burned.

We were almost home, still riding in silence. "I'm sorry I didn't play football," I said. "I'm just no good at it. You know you're the only reason I went out for wrestling. It was to make you proud of me." Headlights from an oncoming car illuminated his face. He stared straight ahead.

We headed down Lattimore Street to our house, the only one with a porch light still burning. Dad swerved the car into the driveway and switched off the key. I got out slamming the door behind me and stood there in my baggy sweats shivering. I waited while Dad got out, watching as he walked around the front of the car. His breath ballooned in the cold as he walked toward me. I stared at my feet. Then, without saying a word, my dad did something he hadn't done since I was a little kid. He put both arms around me and hugged me hard.

Rita Ann Christiansen wrote the following essay as a second semester freshman. She revised it several times, trying to capture the experience and the feeling with images and concrete details. The essay was almost a page longer in its original version, but in working with other students in class, she edited out unnecessary words and phrases, and sometimes whole paragraphs. "Trying to be honest," she said, "was the hardest part. I kept wanting to make the whole thing sound dramatic." In the end, the class felt she achieved the right balance.

To Catch a Thief

Rita Ann Christiansen

At the age of sixteen, I began shoplifting. Small things like makeup or three-dollar plastic earrings. I did it with a couple of friends from high school. We giggled and smirked and thought the clerks were stupid. It sent a little thrill to the pit of the stomach for a few moments. Then for the rest of the afternoon we strutted around the mall in our tight Levis feeling superior to adults, and enjoying the way guys followed us around. We were pretty hot.

Daniels department store was our favorite: lots of fluorescent lights, chrome and mirrors, busy clerks looking the other way. On the Monday before the Fourth of July, my parents dropped me off to meet my friends, but no one showed up. I wandered about alone, running my fingers over the dresses, trying on belts, watching my face in all the various mirrors, until I came to the fifty dollar silk scarves and the two hundred dollar Gucci purses. I was sixteen years old and I suddenly knew exactly what I was going to do. I was hot, after all, and I knew my friends would be impressed when I told them.

I held up the scarves to my face, the soft pinks, the blues and lavenders. Behind the counter in the brightly lit mirror, I watched the swirl of colors. I watched my own eyes. And I watched the gray-haired clerk turn her back on me and begin talking to another customer. She was complaining about her feet because she'd been standing around all day. Then I carefully folded up the scarf—one that pictured a green parrot on a background of dark blue leaves and fine veins of gold. The scarf folded into a neat little square, no bigger than my wallet in the bottom of my purse.

Every cell in my skin hummed with anticipation. My lungs felt as if I had inhaled the purest air from the top of Mt. Everest. I could feel my blood surging through veins, arteries, capillaries, like hot ice. I could feel it in my face and in my wrists. I strolled through Daniels. I had all the time in the world. I stopped and looked at swim suits. I tried on several pair of shoes. I took the escalator up. I rode it down. All the time my heart was hammering as if I'd just had a date with Tom Cruise.

Then in the lingerie department I saw a woman stuff a satin teddy in her shopping bag. I saw her because she seemed to accidentally knock several teddies to the floor. She bent over and pushed one into a woven bag while she picked up and brushed off the others, returning them to the table. She was in her early twenties, her hair still long and blond, pulled back away from her face. She wore a knee-length sun dress with thin straps and a square bodice. Her arms and shoulders looked tanned, soft, her face lovely and perfectly made up with blue eye shadow. She was stunning. I remember, just for a moment, feeling envious of her.

Then she looked at me. I can still see her eyes. It was like watching my own eyes in the mirror when I stole the silk scarf. Her eyes were as distant and metallic as a clear sky in winter. It was as if she had recognized me. She looked at me and defied me to tell. And I realized she probably wasn't in her early twenties at all. The makeup did not hide the lines around her eyes. It probably wasn't even her own hair; it was probably a wig. Her mouth looked tired, like the skin of an apple that has grown old from the inside. The tan on her shoulders was layered from too many afternoons in the sun, oiled and shiny but tough as cat's hide. Then she looked away, bored and no longer interested. She straightened up the counter of lingerie, picked up her straw bag, and strolled away, stopping here and there to run her hand over a silk nightgown, a pink chemise, fading into the other shoppers.

I wish I could say I learned something on the spot. I wish I could say I turned myself in or became a nun or devoted my life to the poor. Instead, I wandered on through the store, checking my face in every mirror. I was hot stuff. That woman had nothing to do with me. Later, just like I'd planned, I bragged about stealing the scarf to my friends. But when school started the next fall we drifted apart and I didn't see much of them anymore.

I still have the scarf buried deep in a bottom drawer at home. It's not the kind of thing I would ever wear. I came across it when I was packing for college. At first I thought of just throwing it away, but I didn't. I'm not sure why I'm saving it.

David Brendan Hopes has won awards for both poetry and drama. In A Sense of the Morning, *an autobiographical work drawn from his daily journal, Hopes uses concrete images, sensory detail, and a simple, honest voice to evoke the experience of attempting to save an owl that he finds entangled in a coil of wire.*

The Great Horned Owl
David Brendan Hopes

My first great horned appeared years ago, while I played with friends in Goodyear Heights Metropolitan Park in Akron. High in a white oak we spied what we assumed to be a squirrel's nest, and being boys our impulse was to lob sticks at it to provoke some action. It was quite early in spring, and our heavy jackets impeded our throwing arms, but at last I got one high enough to nick the dark shape. The next instant it sprouted wings, and with a sepulchral *Who?* glided from the limb above our astonished heads farther into the deep of the forest. I fell permanently in love.

Years later my relationship with the great horned owl reached a climax that I hope but do not really expect will come again. It was at those green lakes in upstate New York, on a crisp late-autumn day after a spectacular cold snap that had turned the waters of the north to iron. I walked the lake path with my hands jammed into my pockets. The forest stood so utterly bare that every scurrying rodent, every stay-at-home bird shone in blue-white clarity.

Still a way off, I began to scan a brown complication halfway up a tulip poplar tilted over the lake. The mass was out of place on the clean outline of the tree. It reminded me of the "squirrel's nest" of my youth, and I walked faster, hoping for an owl, a tardy migrator, perhaps a ghostly presence from the ultimate north.

A hundred yards off I knew I had an owl, a big one, a great horned, plain as a hillside. I commenced a cautious approach, stepping with a deliberation hard for an impatient man, stopping whenever her head swiveled my way.

Closer.

Used by permission of David Brendan Hopes.

Closer.

Closer than I'd ever stood before. Nearly as close as I'd ever been to a wild thing. I couldn't believe my luck.

There's a point at which the dream of approaching wild things—touching them, tasting acceptance lost since Adam—wavers over into nightmare. We are men; they are beasts. It is our business to stalk, theirs to flee. We are uncomfortable when it turns out otherwise. By those green lakes one summer I stalked a fox in a sunny meadow, hoping to see his den. After letting me stalk a few hundred yards, he turned and looked at me. Assuming it was over anyway, I approached briskly, waiting for him to scurry. He didn't. I took another step. Another. Fox stayed put. No change of expression on the red muzzle, not even the apparent effort to "freeze." He scratched a flea, surveyed the meadow, no more interested in me than in the white moths circling his head. I'd crept close enough to touch him with my boot when the horrific word *rabies* formed in my brain. I backed off, quicker than I had come.

I don't know that the fox was rabid. I know I needed an excuse to get away from an experience more intense than I wanted.

So my emotion was not pure delight when I touched the base of the owl's tulip and she hadn't budged. I gazed up, hand flat over eyes against the sun and the glare of the lake ice, and saw the owl's legs tangled in wire, and the wire tangled in complications of the tree.

I want to say the decision formed instantly, but it didn't. Her branch extended over imperfectly frozen ice, itself over incalculably deep water. Not a tree climber as a boy, I'm no better at it now. The two miles to my car was a long way to go with soaked clothing or broken bones. Still, one knows what one can live with, what one cannot. I began to climb. I remember nothing of the way up until I reached her limb, began to snake out, cooing ludicrously, *Good bird, good bird.*

I keep saying "she" and "her" without knowing whether I can tell male from female owls. She *looked* feminine, at once, vulnerable and haughty, a princess in durance.

As I inched out she leaned back as far as she could from me, until she must have teetered on her tailbone. Her struggling had wrapped the wire tight, so no matter how she pulled, her feet remained immovably involved. The yellow eyes opened incredibly wide in what was inseparably threat and indignation.

The great horned is a very large bird, a hunter, an exquisitely equipped carnivore. Tyrannosaur flows in her blood. I kept flinching from the peck of the skunk-dismembering beak. It never came. She watched as I worked the wire free, blinking, raising her wings to let the loops of it pass under. I removed my gloves to work more freely, working faster against the paralyzing cold. When I touched her body with my naked hand, a thrill went through me like an electric shock. I imagined slipping my fingers under her feathers for a moment to warm them, but never dared.

The wire dived onto the ice—baling wire, I figured, trying to imagine how she'd picked it up. Maybe mousing in a barn. It made a musical note when it hit. The owl cocked her head to the sound but didn't budge. She sat free a beat before she realized. I kept still with imagining a face full of frenzied owl. We stared at each other from the ends of our branch so long I broke concentration, daydreamed of warmth, caught myself slipping. The motion of my grabbing on startled her. She flapped. Her eyes announced that she felt nothing hold her.

Several things happened at once. The owl took to the air, and though the lift-off was absolutely silent, it startled me so that I lost my grip on the limb, plunging as the owl rose. Between us we achieved a mystical balance, mirror images diverging at equal distances from the same tulip branch. She shot straight up, then veered toward the center of the lake.

I, however, did not change directions. Down and backward, with the sky at the same apparent remoteness no matter how far I fell. The tree hadn't seemed so high when I was on it.

If you hit hard enough you actually do see stars. I felt the pain in my bones, savoring it, testing it to see what was broken. It flowed to full tide, then receded. I gave thanks. All that pain meant that the ice had held. I waited for news to shiver down my nerves from the extremities; as the shock laved away, I knew we were whole and unbroken. I rolled the six or seven feet to shore. As I staggered to my feet, the owl beat onward, visible near the far side of the lake, poised to vanish into owl-colored distance. I watched her disappearing-place for a long time, wanting to holler *Who?*, but afraid somebody would hear me, or that nobody would.

Dick Gregory was first known as a stand-up comedian whose political comedy encouraged supporters of the civil rights movement in the 1960s. His two major books, From the Back of the Bus *(1962) and his autobiography,* nigger *(1964), helped draw attention to the pain and injustice of racial prejudice. The following excerpt from his autobiography uses concrete details to help us experience the degradation of growing up poor and black in a segregated world.*

Shame

Dick Gregory

I never learned hate at home, or shame. I had to go to school for that. I was about seven years old when I got my first big lesson. I was in love with a little girl named Helene Tucker, a light-complected little girl with pigtails and nice manners. She was always clean and she was smart in school. I think I went to school then mostly to look at her. I brushed my hair and even got me a little old handkerchief. It was a lady's handkerchief, but I didn't want Helene to see me wipe my nose on my hand. The pipes were frozen again, there was no water in the house, but I washed my socks and shirt every night. I'd get a pot, and go over to Mister Ben's grocery store, and stick my pot down into his soda machine. Scoop out some chopped ice. By evening the ice melted to water for washing. I got sick a lot that winter because the fire would go out at night before the clothes were dry. In the morning I'd put them on, wet or dry, because they were the only clothes I had.

Everybody's got a Helene Tucker, a symbol of everything you want. I loved her for her goodness, her cleanness, her popularity. She'd walk down my street and my brothers and sisters would yell, "Here comes Helene," and I'd rub my tennis sneakers on the back of my pants and wish my hair wasn't so nappy and the white folks' shirt fit me better. I'd run out on the street. If I knew my place and didn't come too close, she'd wink at me and say hello. That was a good feeling. Sometimes I'd follow her all the way home, and shovel the snow off her walk and try to make friends with her Momma and her aunts. I'd drop money on her stoop late at night on my way back from shining shoes in the taverns. And she had a Daddy, and he had a good job. He was a paper hanger.

I guess I would have gotten over Helene by summertime, but something happened in that classroom that made her face hang in front of me for the next twenty-two years. When I played the drums in high school it was for Helene and when I broke track records in college it was for Helene and when I started standing behind microphones and heard applause I wished Helene could hear it, too. It wasn't until I was twenty-nine years old and married and making money that I finally got her out of my system. Helene was sitting in that classroom when I learned to be ashamed of myself.

It was on a Thursday. I was sitting in the back of the room, in a seat with a chalk circle drawn around it. The idiot's seat, the troublemaker's seat.

The teacher thought I was stupid. Couldn't spell, couldn't read, couldn't do arithmetic. Just stupid. Teachers were never interested in finding out that you couldn't concentrate because you were so hungry, because you hadn't had any breakfast. All you could think about was noontime, would it ever come? Maybe you could sneak into the cloakroom and steal a bite of some kid's lunch out of a coat pocket. A bite of something. Paste. You can't really make a meal of paste, or put it on bread for a sandwich, but sometimes I'd scoop a few spoonfuls out of the big paste jar in the back of the room. Pregnant people get strange tastes. I was pregnant with poverty. Pregnant with dirt and pregnant with smells that made people turn away, pregnant with cold and pregnant with shoes that were never bought for me, pregnant with five other people in my bed and no Daddy in the next room, and pregnant with hunger. Paste doesn't taste too bad when you're hungry.

The teacher thought I was a troublemaker. All she saw from the front of the room was a little black boy who squirmed in his idiot's seat and made noises and poked the kids around him. I guess she couldn't see a kid who made noises because he wanted someone to know he was there.

It was on a Thursday, the day before the Negro payday. The eagle always flew on Friday. The teacher was asking each student how much his father would give to the Community Chest. On Friday night, each kid would get the money from his father, and on Monday he would bring it to the school. I decided I was going to buy a Daddy right then. I had money in my pocket from shining shoes and selling papers, and whatever Helene Tucker pledged for her Daddy I was going to top it. And I'd hand the money right in. I wasn't going to wait until Monday to buy me a Daddy.

I was shaking, scared to death. The teacher opened her book and started calling out names alphabetically.

"Helene Tucker?"

"My Daddy said he'd give two dollars and fifty cents."

"That's very nice, Helene. Very, very nice indeed."

That made me feel pretty good. It wouldn't take too much to top that. I had almost three dollars in dimes and quarters in my pocket. I stuck my hand in my pocket and held onto the money, waiting for her to call my name. But the teacher closed her book after she called everybody else in the class.

I stood up and raised my hand.

"What is it now?"

"You forgot me?"

She turned toward the blackboard. "I don't have time to be playing with you, Richard."

"My Daddy said he'd . . ."

"Sit down, Richard, you're disturbing the class."

"My Daddy said he'd give . . . fifteen dollars."

She turned around and looked mad. "We are collecting this money for you and your kind, Richard Gregory. If your Daddy can give fifteen dollars you have no business being on relief."

"I got it right now, I got it right now, my Daddy gave it to me to turn in today, my Daddy said . . ."

"And furthermore," she said, looking right at me, her nostrils getting big and her lips getting thin and her eyes opening wide. "We know you don't have a Daddy."

Helene Tucker turned around, her eyes full of tears. She felt sorry for me. Then I couldn't see her too well because I was crying, too.

"Sit down, Richard."

And I always thought the teacher kind of liked me. She always picked me to wash the blackboard on Friday, after school. That was a big thrill, it made me feel important. If I didn't wash it, come Monday the school might not function right.

"Where are you going, Richard?"

I walked out of school that day, and for a long time I didn't go back very often. There was shame there.

Now there was shame everywhere. It seemed like the whole world had been inside that classroom, everyone had heard what the teacher had said, everyone had turned around and felt sorry for me. There was shame in going to the Worthy Boys Annual Christmas Dinner for you and your kind, because everybody knew what a worthy boy was. Why couldn't they just call it the Boys Annual Dinner, why'd they have to give it a name? There was shame in wearing the brown and orange and white plaid mackinaw the welfare gave to 3,000 boys. Why'd it have to be the same for everybody so when you walked down the street the people could see you were on relief? It was a nice warm mackinaw and it had a hood, and my Momma beat me and called me a little rat when she found out I stuffed it in the bottom of a pail full of garbage way over on Cottage Street. There was shame in running over to Mister Ben's at the end of the day and asking for his rotten peaches, there was shame in asking Mrs. Simmons for a spoonful of sugar, there was shame in running out to meet the relief truck. I hated that truck, full of food for you and your kind. I ran into the house and hid when it came. And then I started to sneak through alleys, to take the long way home so the people going into White's Eat Shop wouldn't see me. Yeah, the whole world heard the teacher that day, we all know you don't have a Daddy.

It lasted for a while, this kind of numbness. I spent a lot of time feeling sorry for myself. And then one day I met this wino in a restaurant. I'd been out hustling all day, shining shoes, selling newspapers, and I had googobs of money in my pocket. Bought me a bowl of chili for fifteen cents, and a cheeseburger for fifteen cents, and a Pepsi for five cents, and a piece of chocolate cake for ten cents. That was a good meal. I was eating when this old wino came in. I love winos because they never hurt anyone but themselves.

The old wino sat down at the counter and ordered twenty-six cents worth of food. He ate it like he really enjoyed it. When the owner, Mister Williams, asked him to pay the check, the old wino didn't lie or go through his pocket like he suddenly found a hole.

He just said: "Don't have no money."

The owner yelled: "Why in hell you come in here and eat my food if you don't have no money? That food cost me money."

Mister Williams jumped over the counter and knocked the wino off his stool and beat him over the head with a pop bottle. Then he stepped back and watched the wino bleed. Then he kicked him. And he kicked him again.

I looked at the wino with blood all over his face and I went over. "Leave him alone, Mister Williams. I'll pay the twenty-six cents."

The wino got up, slowly, pulling himself up to the stool, then up to the counter, holding on for a minute until his legs stopped shaking so bad. He looked at me with pure hate. "Keep your twenty-six cents. You don't have to pay, not now. I just finished paying for it."

He started to walk out, and as he passed me, he reached down and touched my shoulder. "Thanks, sonny, but it's too late now. Why didn't you pay it before?"

I was pretty sick about that. I waited too long to help another man.

PART II

Writing About People and Places

Accuracy of observation is the equivalent of accuracy of thinking.

WALLACE STEVENS

Exploring

8

Description and Narration

To describe is to picture, to create a scene in the reader's imagination.

As I walk along the stony shore of the pond in my shirt sleeves . . . it is cool as well as cloudy and windy, and I see nothing special to attract me. . . . The bullfrogs trump to usher in the night, and the note of the whippoorwill is borne on the rippling wind from over the water. Sympathy with the fluttering alder and poplar leaves almost takes away my breath; yet, like the lake, my serenity is rippled but not ruffled. These waves raised by the evening wind are as remote from storm as the smooth reflecting surface. Though it is now dark, the wind still blows and roars in the wood, the waves still dash, and some creatures lull the rest with their notes.

This is how Thoreau described Walden Pond in a memorable chapter on solitude, and that is how many of us first think of description—as something associated with nature.

But this is also description.

A distractingly pretty girl with dark brown eyes sat at the edge of our group and ignored both the joint making its rounds and the record player belching away just behind her. Between the thumb and middle finger of her left hand she held a pill that was blue on one side and yellow on the other; steadily, with the double-edge razor blade she held in her right hand, she sawed on the seam between the two halves of the pill. Every once in a while she rotated it a few degrees with her left index finger. Her skin was smooth, and the light from the fireplace played tricks with it, all of them charming. The right hand sawed on.

This paragraph, by Bruce Jackson, is taken from a magazine article on drug abuse. The article has nothing to do with rippling wind and whippoorwills, yet the same attention to specific details engages our imagination.

Here, too, is description.

Squirrel monkeys with "gothic" facial markings have a kind of ritual or display which they perform when greeting one another. The males bare their teeth, rattle the bars of their cage, utter a high-pitched squeak, which is possibly terrifying to squirrel monkeys, and lift their legs to exhibit an erect penis. While such behavior would border on impoliteness at many contemporary human social gatherings, it is a fairly elaborate act and serves to maintain dominance hierarchies in squirrel-monkey communities.

Scientist Carl Sagan, writing about the evolution of human intelligence in *The Dragons of Eden*, is a long way from Thoreau, writing about waves on Walden Pond. But both use an identical process of focusing on selected details. All three writers describe the ordinary world about us; yet each has sharpened his perceptions so that the reader's consciousness is heightened, magnified. The commonplace is no longer common when seen by a focused intelligence. We are made to experience the newness of our world.

DESCRIPTIVE FOCUS

How does a beginning writer learn to select the best details from all those thousands of images registering on the senses every moment? Over the years, experienced writers have discovered some general principles that may help.

1. If a detail isn't interesting to you, you probably won't be able to make it interesting to your reader. Don't include it just to fill up the page.
2. Sometimes you may fail to recognize the interest value of a detail because you haven't looked closely enough. If your senses have dulled or your mind has grown lazy from lack of challenge, you

may never see the element in the detail that makes it significant. Look again. Focus your mind like a camera moving in for a close-up.

3. Use all of your senses: listen, taste, touch, smell, look. Make mental or written lists of more details than you can ever use. From thirty visual details, select two or three that will help your reader *see*.

   a. Look especially for light. Without light, other details remain in the dark.
   b. Choose one detail that suggests the predominant character, atmosphere, or impression of the thing observed.
   c. Select one detail that personalizes the subject or that seems to be the unique feature setting it apart from all others.

If I look about my office, for example, I see brick walls, a dull red carpet, shelves of literature books, a Chinese evergreen with yellowed leaves, an ashtray on the desk, a telephone, morning light falling through the window, stacks of unread freshman papers, and so on. What should I choose? Probably the morning light because, in addition to lighting the scene, the word *morning* gives us a type of light, an angle to the light, and a time of day—all of which open the scene to the mind's eye. Then I might select the rows of books or toppling piles of freshman papers; either would suggest the predominant atmosphere. Finally, I might focus on the milk-glass ashtray with red lettering stamped around the rim: COWBOY BAR—PINEDALE, WYO., U.S.A. The ashtray suggests something personal, something that sets me apart from other college instructors. (Do I spend my summers herding cattle in Wyoming? Could I have stolen it one wild and drunken night?)

4. Select the small detail most representative of the larger whole. Flyspecks on a water glass in a restaurant may be the only detail needed to suggest an unsanitary restaurant. A comb poking from the pocket of a teenage boy may suggest his pride or vanity. A hesitant pause before answering a question may give a clue to a congressman's use of slush money.

5. Look for details that reveal contradictions, conflict, or contrast, either in the subject itself or in what you anticipate the audience expects from the subject. A white picture is heightened by contrasting it with a dark matting. A man's strength may be emphasized by the tenderness with which he holds his six-month-old daughter. The character of a 60-year-old woman may be revealed when she jogs in the Boston Marathon.

Obviously, every subject may call for special treatment, yet these guidelines can suggest a starting point for observation. Here's part of an essay in which freshman Gary Svoboda described an occurrence on a beach in North Carolina—before he had trained himself to select.

> Later on that night I went out to the beach and met several people who were hauling in a fishing net. One was named Jim and there was a woman whose name I didn't catch. I asked if I could help, just for the fun of it, and I worked with them for about an hour pulling fish and all kinds of sea life out of the net. They gave me a couple of fish for my help. We worked hard and I was tired by the end.

Gary has described, but he has failed to evaluate the effectiveness of his details. Both randomness and abstraction show that he hasn't yet disciplined his perceptions. A woman whose name he didn't catch creates no picture in our mind; neither does feeling tired after an hour's work of pulling "sea life" from a fishing net. Nothing here engages our imagination. After hearing a peer editing group react indifferently to the essay, Gary complained that in his hometown this was just an ordinary event. How could he do more than write an ordinary description? As an experiment, we asked him to name 20 details from the experience. Here are only a few that Gary listed on the blackboard.

Gary's details	Peer response
a man named Jim	The detail lacks significance.
fish tossed in piles	What kind of fish?
croakers, sand sharks	Good, the names create images. What did they do with the sand sharks? Do croakers croak?
The fish got tangled in the net.	Fair. Keep going.
Skates made a clapping noise trying to escape.	What are skates? How do they clap? Why didn't you tell us this before?

The interest shown by his peer editing group in certain types of details helped Gary rewrite.

> Later on I went out on the beach and walked along the sand in the moonlight. There was a small crowd gathered around some fishermen hauling in a net. I watched for a while and then asked if I could help. The rope felt like a steel cable cutting into my hands. When the net came out of the waves it sounded like someone clapping, like applause. At first I thought it was the bystanders, and then I realized it was the skates caught in the net and clapping their

winglike bodies, trying desperately to escape. I put on a pair of
gloves borrowed from one of the fishermen and knelt in the wet
sand and helped them untangle the fish from the net. There were
croakers and sea trout, sand sharks, and horseshoe crabs. The fish
were tossed in a heaping pile on the sand. We heaved the skates and
crabs back into the surf. We let the two-foot-long sand sharks die on
the beach. They were still there the next morning. They had their
mouths open and I felt like their eyes were staring at me.

Although the writing here needs editing, Gary's second version contains
details that involve the reader in the experience. Gary has omitted dull
points (surely a man "named Jim" did not stir interest even in Gary),
and he has replaced them with sensory details (moonlit beach, a cutting
rope), with details that contrast to the reader's expectations (skates that
clap their bodies in an effort to escape), and with small details that
suggest a larger significance (their mouths gape open; eyes seem to stare
at him).

A unique style, correct grammar, a large vocabulary—all are wasted
unless you also develop a disciplined mind eager to encounter the realities of an ordinary world—the "fabulous realities" as Thoreau calls
them. To describe with precision, you must see with precision.

NARRATIVE FOCUS

In the process of reseeing details in his subject, Gary Svoboda also discovered a natural, chronological ordering for presenting his experience.
His description moves clearly from a nighttime setting to early the next
morning; the rope is pulled; the net hauled onto the beach; the fish
removed—all in the sequence in which they obviously occurred.

Few students experience any difficulty with narrative. Chronological
sequence seems to come naturally to us: this happened; then this happened; then this happened. But good narrative—the ordering of events—
requires a mental discipline similar to that required by description: To
order or arrange, you must select. Some aspects of an event must be
omitted in favor of other aspects. Time must be shortened here, dwelt
on in more detail there.

Not all narrative is chronological, of course. Sometimes a writer
begins with the present, moves to the past, then to the distant past and
back to the present. This is the beginning of form: selection and ordering
for the sake of emphasis, clarity, interest. All professional writers, writers
of fiction as well as of nonfiction, know that the ordering of events affects

the reader's ability to follow a story or essay logically, as well as the pace or speed with which the essay seems to flow.

Here is an example of superb ordering and pacing from *Black Elk Speaks* as recorded by John G. Neihardt. Black Elk describes the butchering at Wounded Knee.

> I had no gun, and when we were charging, I just held the sacred bow out in front of me with my right hand. The bullets did not hit us at all. . . .
>
> The soldiers had run eastward over the hills where there were some more soldiers, and they were off their horses and lying down. . . .
>
> We followed down along the dry gulch, and what we saw was terrible. Dead and wounded women and children and little babies were scattered all along there where they had been trying to run away. The soldiers had followed along the gulch, as they ran, and murdered them in there. Sometimes they were in heaps because they had huddled together, and some were scattered all along. Sometimes bunches of them had been killed and torn to pieces where the wagon guns hit them. I saw a little baby trying to suck its mother, but she was bloody and dead. . . .
>
> When we drove the soldiers back, they dug themselves in, and we were not enough people to drive them out of there. In the evening they marched off up Wounded Knee Creek, and then we saw all that they had done there. . . .
>
> Many were shot down right there. The women and children ran into the gulch and up west, dropping all the time, for the soldiers shot them as they ran. There were only about a hundred warriors and there were nearly five hundred soldiers. . . .
>
> It was a good winter day when all this happened. The sun was shining. But after the soldiers marched away from their dirty work, a heavy snow began to fall. The wind came up in the night. There was a big blizzard, and it grew very cold. The snow drifted deep in the crooked gulch, and it was one long grave of butchered women and children and babies, who had never done any harm and were only trying to run away.

Notice how the flow of this narrative is maintained by the first sentence in each paragraph.

> I had no gun, and when we were charging . . .
> The soldiers had run eastward over the hills . . .
> We followed . . .
> When we drove the soldiers back . . .
> Many were shot down right there . . .
> It was a good winter day when all this happened . . .

Of course, the power of Black Elk's story depends equally upon the descriptive details. Narration almost always works hand in hand with description. Practice in describing and narrating is practice in perceiving and shaping experience. Teaching yourself how to *select* and *order* is the first major step in disciplining the senses and in moving eventually toward logic and critical judgment.

Journal Practice

1. Write about the worst place you ever spent a night—inside a tent that leaked; curled behind the steering wheel of a pickup truck; the Dreamland Motel where cockroaches and a lumpy mattress kept you awake; on the kitchen floor at Aunt Mildred's with 20 other relatives. Share the event in narrative or story form with focused selection of sensory details. (Sometimes the best way to discover the best details is through freewriting. Let the images flow. Then look back over your work, select the most striking images, and rewrite with more focus and order.)

2. Description should have a direction or purpose. A random listing of details has little interest even for the writer. The purpose may be nothing more than creation of mood or feeling. Here is Joan Didion's opening paragraph from a short story. By focusing her perceptions on selected details, she creates an atmosphere that suggests the quality of life along a particular stretch of highway in California. Her purpose is to make you see and feel that quality.

> Imagine Banyan Street first, because Banyan is where it happened.
> The way to Banyan is to drive west from San Bernadino out Foothill
> Boulevard, Route 66: past the Santa Fe switching yards, the Forty
> Winks Motel. Past the motel that is 19 stucco tepees: SLEEP IN A
> WIGWAM—GET MORE FOR YOUR WAMPUM. Past Fontana Drag
> City and the Fontana Church of the Nazarene and the Pit Stop A Go-
> go; past Kaiser Steel through Cucamonga, out to the Kapu Kai Res-
> taurant-Bar and Coffee Shop, at the corner of Route 66 and Carne-
> lian Avenue. Up Carnelian Avenue from Kapu Kai, which means
> "Forbidden Seas," the subdivision flags whip in the harsh winds.
> HALF-ACRE RANCHES! SNACK BARS! TRAVERTINE ENTRIES! $95
> DOWN. It is the trail of an intention gone haywire, the flotsam of
> the new California. But after a while the signs thin out on Carnelian
> Avenue, and the houses are no longer the bright pastels of the
> Springtime Home owners but the faded bungalows of the people
> who grow a few grapes and keep a few chickens out here, and then
> the hill gets steeper and the road climbs and even the bungalows are

few, and here—desolate, roughly surfaced, lined with eucalyptus and lemon groves—is Banyan Street.

Write a paragraph describing a street that leads to your home or school. Focus your perceptions in such a way that you select only details that suggest what it would be like to live there. Do not *tell* through abstractions; *show* in carefully selected concrete images.

3. A change of scene may stimulate perceptions and awaken awareness. If you shop exclusively at large supermarkets, this week shop at a small Chinese grocery store; instead of eating at a fast-food restaurant, eat at a local Greek or Vietnamese restaurant. Make a spontaneous list of your observations before you leave the site; then, back at your desk, re-create a sense of place through a descriptive narrative focusing on selected details.

4. Describe and narrate the most important two or three scenes from some significant event in your childhood—perhaps the moment when your brother came home from the hospital, or the day your mother sat you down in the kitchen to tell you of your parents' divorce. Select carefully both descriptive details and the *chronological ordering* of events. Try to help the reader see and feel the flow of your experience. Write as if the whole of it were occurring in a story.

Now rewrite the experience with a different narrative pattern. Begin at the end of the event, then flash back to the beginning. Narrate up to the same point you described in the first sentence of your version.

What is the difference in effect? Is one version stronger than the other? More effective?

Copying

Copying is an old technique first practiced by medieval monks but continued in our own time by writers as diverse as Tennessee Williams and Malcolm X. Benjamin Franklin copied paragraphs from writers he admired, then paraphrased the passage, and later wrote a paragraph or so in the same style exploring his own ideas. Ralph Ellison has acknowledged he taught himself to write by copying Dostoevsky. Like sketching, the act of copying requires you to slow down and to pay attention to details you might otherwise miss. You learn to see how others have used language to re-create experience. One writer's style—the lengths and rhythms of sentences, his choice of words, his gift for the unexpected—may encourage you to take more risks with your own writing. More important, it may gradually help you discover more and better choices for expressing just what it is you need to say.

Turn back to Dick Gregory's essay, "Shame," and copy the paragraph on page 85 beginning "Now there was shame. . . ." Pay particular attention to Gregory's use of specific nouns and concrete details. What discoveries can you make? What word does Gregory repeat and what is its effect? Following Ben Franklin's method, can you use a similar style to describe in your journal the last time you experienced shame or embarrassment or humiliation?

Exploring

9

Character

At one time I lived in a small village on the side of a mountain in South America. The village priest, Padre Bolanos, was also the mayor. A thin, almost gaunt man who wore a faded black cassock and drove a jeep, the padre seemed to be everywhere—organizing a festival, laying a water pipe from a spring to the village, building an electrical generator to light the church, petitioning for government funds to construct a small bridge, initiating a soccer game in the rain in which he ran wildly through the mud, his black cassock flaying the wind, his boots kicking the splattered ball high into the air. Everyone loved Padre Bolanos.

As I was one of the few outsiders ever to stay in the village, the padre invited me to live in his home behind the church. I had hardly settled in when I discovered that a young woman and her small son also lived with the padre. The very mention of the young woman to others in the village caused raised eyebrows and knowing smiles. "The padre is only human," one man told me. I quickly found a room with another family. For six months I felt contempt for the priest. That the villagers loved him made him only more hypocritical in my eyes. I avoided him, spoke coolly to him. And then once, in an emergency of sorts, I found I had to ask him to drive me to the nearest large town where I could find a doctor. Padre Bolanos acted without hesitation. Within minutes he had the jeep bouncing down the mountainside. On the way, he told me a story.

He told how a priest had once visited the capital city of his country and walked late at night through the poorest *barrio*. As he walked among the broken streets, the priest heard muffled cries from an alley and found there a young girl who had just given birth among the rags and ashes. The girl was fourteen. She had been a prostitute since she was eleven. The priest had taken the girl home with him where for several years now she served as housekeeper. He knew many people felt horrified that a priest should have an ex-prostitute for a housekeeper; others, more cynical perhaps, felt certain the priest kept the girl as his mistress. In a few weeks she would be eighteen and leaving for the capital city again. She did not like living in a rural village. The priest would continue to raise the little boy, at least for a while, until the girl found a job. The priest's only regret was that the girl was still not a Christian. She did not believe in God.

I sat quietly, ashamed. How could I have misjudged him so badly? As we pulled up to the doctor's office, Padre Bolanos turned to me. "You know," he said, "for a long time I thought you were a sullen young man, perhaps even a little arrogant. But I apologize to you for my mistake. I see now that you are only shy." I had climbed out of the jeep. "Character," he said, "is a difficult thing. Too often I don't know what to look for, or I judge too quickly." He smiled at me and added in English, "I must learn to look most closely."

After two years in South America I returned home. I wanted to write about the economic consequences of a village market on sociological development—big words, big ideas. Most college writing deals with ideas and issues. But I found I could not separate my ideas from the people I had known. Ideas and issues do not exist in a vacuum. People with complex characters create ideas, cause events, stir up issues, invent machines, change the course of history, and indulge in little acts of human kindness. Describing people requires that we learn to look "most closely" and is perhaps the best training we can have for the development of writing skills. Good writing begins with perception of the subject. Teaching yourself to perceive people in all their complexities is a major step toward teaching yourself to perceive the complexity of the world people have created—and perhaps toward making us all a little more human.

PERCEPTION OF CHARACTER

What exactly is "character"? What do we mean when we say (in the abstract) that "Gomez is a real character"? Or "Loretta has a super personality"? Even though you may not plan to write novels, novelists are one of the better sources to learn from, for a major tradition in the novel for 200 years has been the creation of character.

Here is David Copperfield describing (concretely) his stepfather's sister, whom he has never met and who has just arrived by stagecoach.

> It was Miss Murdstone who was arrived, and a gloomy-looking lady she was; dark, like her brother, whom she greatly resembled in face and voice; and with very heavy eyebrows, nearly meeting over her large nose, as if, being disabled by the wrongs of her sex from wearing whiskers, she had carried them to that account. She brought with her two uncompromising hard black boxes, with her initials on the lids in hard brass nails. When she paid the coachman she took her money out of a hard steel purse, and she kept the purse in a very jail of a bag which hung upon her arm by a heavy chain, and shut up like a bite. I had never, at that time, seen such a metallic lady altogether as Miss Murdstone was.
> . . . Then she looked at me, and said:
> "Is that your boy, sister-in-law?"
> My mother acknowledged me.
> "Generally speaking," said Miss Murdstone, "I don't like boys."

Charles Dickens is famous for his ability to create a sense of character within a short space, sometimes by exaggeration, but more often by seeing with an accurate eye the precise details that contribute to making a person unique. If we look closely at this description of Miss Murdstone, we find—either through direct concrete description or by implication—almost all of the major qualities that create in our minds an image of character.

PHYSICAL DESCRIPTION

As always, we begin with *seeing*. The way people look, the way they dress, the physical qualities of their person—all suggest something about character. Miss Murdstone is dark with heavy eyebrows that almost meet over her large nose (suggesting a perpetual scowl); she carries a hard steel purse in a jail of a bag with a heavy chain. Now, although it might be possible that Miss Murdstone is actually delicate, kind, happy, and charming, her physical appearance suggests the opposite. And although we have always heard we should not judge a book by its cover, we do. We tend to judge people, rightly or wrongly, by their physical appearance.

We can begin to distinguish between fact and inference. A *fact* is a direct observation of the senses that can be verified by someone else making the same observation. "John has a black eye." An *inference* is a conclusion about something that you cannot observe directly but that facts suggest to you. "John has probably been in a fight."

The facts of physical appearance lead us to inferences about character. If we see a teenage girl with purple lipstick, orange hair combed straight up, a safety pin stuck through one ear, and the name MARVIN tattooed on her bare shoulder, the facts, which all can be verified, lead to inferences about her character, inferences that may or may not be correct. Physical appearance, then, is our first contact with character. But we need more details of another nature to confirm our impressions.

ACTIONS

Actions can overcome the impressions made by outward physical appearance, or they can confirm our impressions. In the paragraph by Dickens, Miss Murdstone is seen performing only two significant acts: paying the coachman for her ride and speaking to David Copperfield's mother. We see her in more action later in the novel; but even at this stage, in our introduction to her, we begin to sense a quality of her personality by the way she takes her money from a steel purse (that shuts with a bite) and by the bluntness—could one say rudeness?—of her speech. Dickens tells us nothing in the abstract. He never says, "Miss Murdstone was greedy and cruel." But the *fact* of her actions causes us to *infer* that she is.

Look at the actions of people around you. Perhaps you have a grandfather who locks himself in a fruit cellar when your grandmother gets angry. Perhaps you have a college roommate who sticks wads of used chewing gum on the bottom of a desk. You've probably encountered the college instructor who is never in his or her office during posted office hours. You make inferences about all their characters. Neither physical appearance nor actions by themselves give a complete picture of character, but together they build impressions.

SPEECH

What we say and how we say it reveal an almost infinite number of qualities. Miss Murdstone's blunt dislike of children could not be made more stunning than by her single line, "Generally speaking, I don't like boys." Physical details and physical actions can suggest inner qualities, but speech has the potential of directly revealing values, ideas, rigor of intellect, attitudes, beliefs—even educational and cultural background. There is a striking difference between the character who says, "I ain't gonna put up with no more crap!" and another who says, "Your suppositions about me are highly distressing, and I refuse to tolerate further insinuations."

Yet speech, too, must be weighed against other perceptions. When you've just caught a man at midnight leaving your room with your TV set, and he says, "Gee, I guess I must be sleepwalking again," you may find yourself skeptical about the *fact* of his statement.

SELF-CREATED ENVIRONMENT

The type of environment we surround ourselves with, the physical nature of the rooms we live in, the condition of our homes, the cars we drive—all contribute to perception of character. For example, Miss Murdstone apparently surrounds herself with metallic hardness. She carries her belongings in *hard* black boxes on which she has her initials pounded in *hard* brass nails. She even carries her money in a *hard* steel purse hung on her arm by a metal chain. Dickens would have created a different character in our minds had he described her as carrying a silk umbrella, a purse made of see-through wicker with wild straw flowers on top, and a trunk painted with fragile blue forget-me-nots.

BACKGROUND

Background may or may not be important in creating a sense of character. We know nothing about Miss Murdstone's background when we first meet her, and we probably don't need to. At other times, background can be the single most vital quality in explaining why someone acts as he or she does—for example, an actress may have had a "stage mother" who drove her relentlessly to become famous, or the president of a giant corporation may have learned his dedication as a boy by getting up at 4 A.M. to milk cows on his father's Missouri farm. But writers must be cautious about background details. If you tell us, "Mr. Harper was born on July 9, 1932. He lived in a small town until he was six, then he moved to a large city where he attended elementary school . . . ," you will bore all of us to death. Background details must be striking and essential to understanding current qualities of character, or they must be avoided altogether. Dickens, like other successful writers, uses background material with careful selectivity.

OTHERS' REACTIONS

Finally, the way other people react to character helps to establish the validity of a writer's observations. Any writer may be biased in judgment. As we've already seen, it's possible to select only details with negative connotations or only those with positive connotations to sway the reader's impression. A second and third opinion can help us as readers to believe that the writer is reporting fairly and honestly. In the scene of Miss Murdstone's arrival, we have no reactions from other characters, but later in the novel we find that people tiptoe around Miss Murdstone, no one dares speak loudly to her, and others obey shamefacedly when she commands. Their reactions to her confirm our original impression of her character.

Although one could probably name several more aspects of life that shape our attitudes toward character, the following six attributes—balanced off against each other—seem to be the most frequently observed and used by successful writers.

> Physical appearance
> Actions
> Speech
> Self-created environment
> Background
> Others' reactions

As Dickens shows, a writer need not present all six qualities to evoke a sense of character. Some writers have achieved solid, believable characters by using only dialogue or by using only action and speech without physical description. You must train yourself to look for the most interesting and important qualities in your subject, the unique elements of human nature that separate the person you're writing about from all others.

HOW DESCRIBING CHARACTER RELATES TO OTHER FORMS OF WRITING

Of course, you're not going to write novels or short stories—at least not most of you. So why learn how to describe character?

First, any training in how to select factual details that lead to logical inferences is simply good training for every paper or report you'll ever write in college or in your career. But the suggestions for selecting those details that I've listed in this chapter are also crucial: It is one thing to say, "Learn how to select good factual details"; it is another to question, "How?" The strategy of looking for *physical details, actions, speech, environment, background*, and *others' reactions* provides you with a focus for selection that goes beyond "character." For example, with only slight modification, you might use the same criteria of selection for a history paper on the battle of Marathon:

1. What physical details were significant? What type of armament, protective shields, and supplies affected the outcome?
2. What actions were significant? Why did the Athenians form a battle line that was thin in the middle and heavy on the flanks?
3. What speech was significant? Who convinced the Greeks to meet the Persians on the plain of Marathon instead of awaiting battle at Athens?
4. What elements in the environment were significant? How did the shape of the hills and the narrow passes affect the outcome?
5. What elements of background are important? Why were the Plataeans willing to aid the Athenians? Where did the Athenian generals learn their tactics?
6. How have other historians reacted to the battle? To what good fortune does Herodotus attribute the victory?

In other words, the six attributes a novelist looks for in "character" can be used as six strategies any writer can look for in developing almost any subject. In later chapters, I'll develop this approach more fully.

But it must also be said that perception of character—and the ability to share that perception in writing—goes beyond a mere set of techniques. The need to extend our awareness, to sense and feel the qualities of another person's life, is one of the great steps out of self-centered adolescence and into adulthood. Only by training ourselves to sympathize (and ultimately to empathize) with other people in their fears, their ideals, their frustrations, and their convictions—only in developing the ability to project ourselves into others—can we begin to know and better evaluate our lives by contrast. As Padre Bolanos said, we "must learn to look most closely."

Journal Practice

1. Try some thumbnail sketches—one- or two-line descriptions of people you observe. Try to reveal something about character by focusing on physical details, speech, or actions. Here are a few examples.

He wore shorts and a white shirt and he was smoking a European
cigarette out of a flat silver box.

Student Journal, Sharon Grant

The Arab nurse who nails down the coffin has a cyst on her nose and
wears a permanent bandage.

Notebooks of Albert Camus

She had a face like a collapsed lung.

Notebooks of Raymond Chandler

A horrid priest came to the back door of the mansion yesterday, raw,
bright red face looked to have gone under a carrot scraper. Black
coat, white neckband. . . . He chewed gum of some sort,
harrumphed, rubbed some coins together.

Sylvia Plath's Journal

2. Write at least two full pages about an experience you had with
someone important to you. Look deeply into your memory for actual
details; don't depend upon clichés to express what you saw and felt.
Focus on your memory. Show actions, physical details, speech, and any
other details that re-create the character. Here is how Eva Figes described
a child's perception of her grandmother and artist grandfather, Claude
Monet, in her novel *Light*.

Grandmama leaned forward and put her white plump hand on her
arms, so she could smell the funny odour that always seemed to
come from her.

"Is there something you want, child?" she asked kindly, but Lily
just shook her head, pressing her lips together. It always seemed to
come out of her clothes, thought Lily, sitting rigid, watching the
brown flecks on the back of her grandmother's hand, and half the
smell was sweet, like flowers, like the bottle which stood on her
dressing table, but under it was something not so nice, something
sharp and acrid, a mixture of skin and powder and sweat, and
through it all something even more powerful, the pungent odour of
mothballs. Her clothes smelt of years of folding, putting away, as
though the fresh air could not get at them, however much she
walked about.

Everything was different about old people, she thought, their
shape under the clothes they wear, their colour, everything. Those
little brown flecks on the skin, for instance, and something flaccid,
soft and loose about grandmama's cheek when she was expected to

kiss her. Soft and dry, not unpleasant: just different. But grandpapa, who also had brown flecks on the back of his hands, his skin was anything but soft, firm and bristling with beard, and from his clothes came an odour of tobacco, which she liked. Strong earth smells which came from out of doors, and sometimes tiny particles of colour caught round his fingernails, which she thought fun. As though he had come away with bits of river, field or sky clinging to him, after making such things. Like she and Jimmy after using plasticine. Everything about grandpapa, she thought, staring at his bearded head on the far side of the water jug, everything about grandpa was on the surface, outside where you could see and hear and touch it, but grandmama was concealed in her black dress, in the folds of her gown and what she might wear underneath. It was buried in her face, too, in the slack mouth and soft white cheeks, and the pale eyes that said nothing. Only now and then one got a whiff of it, her secret, in the faint odour coming from her clothes.

3. You are your own character. Have some fun with it. Look into a mirror and study your face—forehead, eyes, nose, mouth, teeth, cheek, pores, flaws. Close your eyes and explore with your fingertips the textures of your skin, the ridges and hollows of your bone structure. When you've finished, create your own caricature. Exaggerate your imperfections—maybe you have a nose shaped like a turnip or eyebrows like two confused woolly worms. Let yourself go. Accept the images that come to mind.

4. Reveal the character of someone you don't know through their actions. Actions may be as small as gestures made by the hands or as large as decisions made in the face of a great crisis. Here is how historian and essayist Paul Horgan recorded in his journal a scene observed in passing on the street.

The man paralyzed from the waist down being wheeled on a winter afternoon in a small neat compact chromium wheelchair to his Rolls Royce limousine parked at the curb in 54th street. On his lap is balanced an attaché case. There is a young woman waiting at the car—a nurse?—in a winter overcoat. The man wheeling him turns him to the open front door of the car. The nurse takes away the left armrest of the chair and attempts to remove the attaché case. He slaps her away from it. With his right hand and arm he arranges his inert legs to a slanting position for moving. She sets a smooth board from the car's front seat to the raised footrest of the wheelchair. He turns himself to sit on the board. He then hunches and grubs himself along into the car. His movements are like those of a seal out of water. Finally he is in, the board removed, the chair is folded and stowed in the rear of the car, the attendants get into the car, she driving, and all the doors are shut. During the maneuver the slim, shiny, black attaché case has remained on his lap and as they drive away, he clutches it to his breast.

5. Interview your roommate or a friend. If possible, keep the interview going informally on-and-off for several days. Watch for gestures, actions, physical details, speech patterns, and so on. Look for anecdotes or elements from your subject's past that might be meaningful. Look for conflicts or contradictions and gently probe their origin or significance.

Most important of all, find a central "idea" your subject believes in and make that the focus of your paper. Let us *see* and *hear* your subject, but also let us *understand* his or her character as revealed through ideas or beliefs.

Select only the most significant details to write about. Be concrete. Randi Devine, a sophomore business major, handled the exercise like this:

> "Personally, I think the bomb is OK. And it makes me mad to see all these know-it-all liberals protesting something they really don't know anything about."
>
> Ferrell Freeman leaned forward and stuffed another bite of hot dog in his mouth. He gripped the hot dog so hard mustard oozed out the other end.
>
> I met Ferrell last year in an economics class where he kept arguing with the professor about supply-side economics. He had a way of overwhelming you with facts and confidence. Even the professor seemed wary of him.
>
> For the last two days I had hung around asking him questions about himself. We had just witnessed some two hundred students at a nuclear freeze rally, and Ferrell was growling and grumbling. "If we hadn't used the bomb to end World War II," he said, "thousands and thousands of Americans would have died." His round blue eyes became rounder as a new idea came to him. "These jerks wouldn't even have been born if their fathers hadn't been saved by the bomb."
>
> He finished his hot dog, chewing vigorously and talking at the same time. "Don't they know conventional warfare can kill you just as dead? It's sort of like as if people in 1914 protesting mustard gas but not saying a word about machine guns." A slight grin crossed his face. He was pleased with his own argument.
>
> His father had been a colonel in the marines and was now a chief executive at Bellcraft Corporation. Ferrell planned to start his own electronics company. He stood up and brushed the crumbs from his Izod polo shirt. He laid one hand on my shoulder as if he were my father.

"Forget these jerks," he said. "The bomb is here to stay. And, believe me, it's for your own good."

Copying

Sometimes it may be helpful to copy two or three paragraphs by different writers to see how they perceive and reveal a character in writing. Copy any of the following passages to see what you can discover about writing from these writers: Eva Figes' description of her grandmama, pages 105–106; Charles Dickens' paragraph on Miss Murdstone, page 100; or Paul Horgan's observation of the man confined to his wheelchair, pages 106–107.

After copying the passage slowly, use it as a model and write your own passage about a person still alive in your memory.

Play

1. Create a ridiculous two-line rhyme:

Can't think, born dumb; inspiration won't come;
Bad ink, bum pen, best wishes, Amen.

2. Think of any stranger you have observed working even briefly: the high school janitor, the executive in the striped suit at a bank, a barkeep in the local bar, the attendant in the women's restroom at the Indiana State Fair. Imagine you are that person, enter the mind of that person, share his or her thoughts, feelings, actions, reactions, and voice. Become that person. Write about your life and work as if you were writing an imaginary autobiography.

3. Create an absurd recipe using concrete, specific ingredients with detailed instructions.

> ### *Elephant Stew*
> 1 elephant (medium size)
> Optional: 2 rabbits
> Salt and pepper, to taste
> Brown gravy (lots)

Cut elephant into small bite-size pieces. This will take about 2 months. Reserve trunk to store pieces in. Add enough brown gravy to cover. Cook over kerosene fire about 4 weeks at about 465. This will serve about 3,800 people. If more are expected, 2 rabbits may be added. But do this only if necessary, as most people do not like to find hare in their stew.

Anonymous Recipe from *Mountain Elegance*

Drafting and Discovery of Form

10

The Scene

That night Demirgian lay in his combat clothes—his steel helmet, the damp fabric of his shirt and trousers, his canvas boots—and Demirgian had a wet black rifle on the soil beside him as with intricate fingers he made himself a glass of grape juice. Slower than a caterpillar chews on a maple leaf his fingers tore a small paper packet of Kool-Aid and quieter than a dandelion loses its fluff his hand shook the light purple powder into his Army canteen. The cold stars above, the cool earth below him kept their complete silence as Demirgian tilted his rubber canteen to its left—right—left—right with the slow periodicity of a pendulum. One long minute of this and Demirgian took a quiet sip. And ah! Demirgian had come alive! He's in the grape-juice generation! He buried the torn paper packet quietly in six inches of Vietnam's soil.

This paragraph is not taken from a short story or a novel, although it seems to have all the qualities we expect in fiction. Actually, it was written by John Sack, a professional writer describing in an article for *Esquire* a true character involved in the Vietnam War. Sack writes nonfiction, but like many successful writers, he incorporates the techniques of fiction into his work to make it more interesting. In almost any type of personal writing and in many other kinds of writing, the various elements of perception, language, and form that have been covered in the first nine chapters of this book (especially in description and narration) can be drawn together into a fiction technique labeled *scene*. Understanding the components of scene can give you both an effective device for beginning an essay and a structural unit for shaping your first draft.

ELEMENTS OF SCENE

A highly respected teacher of writing, Wilson R. Thornley, identified six major elements in the prose scene.

Light. The stage in a theater cannot be seen without light, nor can your reader see a prose scene in his or her imagination without some mention or implication of light.

Time. Light often suggests time: a "November dawn," for example, gives time of year, time of day, and type of light. We do not need time as given in detective novels (it was 6:42 P.M. when the murder occurred) but we do need a general range of time like morning, evening, noon, or whatever.

Place. We all live in a real world, in a real setting, and we cannot imagine people functioning in a vacuum. A sentence or two can suggest the gates of a castle, a Victorian living room, the path in a dark forest.

Character. Common sense tells us that character is the focal point of any scene. Light, time, and place are all background to the character who walks, talks, acts, and reveals for us the vital qualities of his or her life.

Purpose. Nothing can be more dull than a scene that doesn't go anywhere. No scene in a play or in your writing should exist without some clear intention. Purpose can lie in demonstrating some aspect of character, in setting the mood for what is to follow, or in presenting a problem or conflict that will need to be solved.

Five senses. The theater can successfully suggest only sight and sound to the audience. Prose can involve as many of the five senses as possible or necessary to absorb the reader physically or emotionally in the scene.

If we go back for a moment to John Sack's opening paragraph about a soldier in Vietnam, we will find all of these qualities: The first sentence establishes time (night, stars out); we know immediately that a character (obviously a soldier wearing combat clothes and a steel helmet) is lying on the ground, a detail that indicates both his position and our first indication of place—which turns out to be Vietnam soil; the larger setting of the article will follow. In addition to sight, sensory details include touch (a wet rifle, cold earth) and sound (quieter than dandelion fluff). Sack's purpose here is not as immediately clear. We do gain some insight into the soldier's personal, human qualities as we see him mixing Kool-Aid grape juice in his canteen. Actually, it is not until the next paragraph (which I have not quoted) that the author makes his point: While a soldier is on ambush patrol, nothing ever happens. The scene becomes clear. The soldier is doing what soldiers have always done—lie in the mud, wait, and find some way to pass the time.

Scene is a literary device, but it is so only because we all live every day in a scene, as you are doing at this moment. Knowing the elements of scene gives you a method for observing and recording. Description and narration should not consist of random details. Selection should be made from those qualities most likely to convey to the reader's imagination the actual and most vivid elements of life itself. Thus scene: *light, time, place, character, purpose,* and *sensory experience.* Scene provides you with the first major step in creating form; a scene *is* form.

ORGANIZING WITHIN THE SCENE

The elements of scene can be organized into whatever pattern is most effective. There are no rules, but there are some conventional organizations that you should be familiar with and that might help you in your writing.

General to Specific

Because a reader needs orientation, it often helps to begin with the larger frame and focus in step-by-step toward the more significant detail. Here is how one 17-year-old student began an essay.

> On Saturday morning I crossed the hollow to Leo Auffman's house and sat on the back porch where the sunlight pooled and dropped into the narrow slats between the wooden steps. I watched the round speckled sparrows with purple ridged beaks squatting along the chicken wire fence that stretched behind Leo's woodshed. The sparrows chattered and scratched the sides of their beaks back and forth against the wire.

I whistled just to be whistling. I didn't feel seventeen years old sitting there in a white blouse and Levis the color of blueberry stains on cheesecloth. I didn't even feel eight, or ten, or twelve, but just as old as the ripening blueberries that grow blue-misted in summer.

July brought yellow days, warm wind, and blueberries. Blueberries as big as the end of your thumb; blueberries so bloated with thick, purple juice that the tight skins burst when the sun touched them; and the ebony meat slipped from the tarnished sacks leaving the wrinkled skins to hang from the stems like bits of purple rag. The blueberries didn't ripen all at once, but just a few at a time, some still clinging to the stems as hard as green peas. The plumper berries pushed a few of the smaller ones away from the sun, squeezing the blueness from their skins. They turned yellow and shriveled against the stem leaving the others waiting to be picked.

The student writer begins with the larger frame. She leads us across a "hollow" to Leo Auffman's house, then to his back porch. We scan the general area, observing a few sparrows, a chicken-wire fence, a woodshed (although within that general frame the writer still points out specific selected details such as the sparrows' purple-ridged beaks). The second paragraph again begins with the general—this time a general feeling, an emotion caused apparently by being young and alive and free in summer sun. But in that general emotion, a single image is evoked ("blueberry stains on cheesecloth"). The image seems to trigger a focusing of memory, and the third paragraph moves quickly from July to yellow days and warm wind (the general) to blueberries and all their particulars (the specific). The third paragraph focuses on a single ordinary element of life with such accuracy and precision of observation that every element of our imagination is stimulated.

This pattern of movement is often used at the beginning of essays. The same pattern, usually called the *panoramic scene*, can be seen in a number of TV shows and movies: we begin with the overview, a large city with tall buildings. The camera zooms in toward a single building, then focuses on a single window in the building; we move inside, where we find Don Johnson in a pink sports jacket. Movement from the general to the specific orients the audience, leading its attention toward the detailed point the writer wants to make.

The panoramic technique can be especially helpful for the writer during the first draft because the mind, too, needs orienting, needs to follow a process of focusing. By allowing yourself to begin with the general, you help the words flow. It is usually easier to write about large elements than about small ones (easier to begin with "It was a July morning" or "All over Brooklyn the rain was falling") and then to lead into the finer details.

Specific to General

The alternative is obvious. John Sack's scene about Demirgian begins with the soldier lying in the mud. Not until the end do we find out he is in Vietnam. We move from the focused detail to the larger frame. Here is Billy Whitmore, a sophomore, following such a technique in an essay about his coach.

> His hand reached out and slapped my helmet. An explosion like a dull boom thundered inside my head. His shoulder clipped my shoulder and the pads made a vicious smack! I felt myself spinning for a moment off balance, the sun flashing past my eyes, blue sky, then the cold plastic grass coming up at my nose. I was reaching out to catch myself when something hit me from behind like three heavy mattresses falling on me at once, smashing me down. Then someone's knee drove itself into my kidneys and the pain arched across my back. My ribs poked into my lungs. For a moment everything was just still, only the sounds of several people panting. Huffing. Then the weight lifted off me and I heard the coach yelling, "Jesus H. Christ, Whitmore, where's your head? You were out of position! Get yourself up before I kick your ass all the way to Rolf Hall!"
>
> It was the third day of practice. Coach Harley was standing over me, and between his legs I could see the afternoon sun dripping down over the empty bleachers. The dull thundering in my ears had not gone away. His voice sounded as if he were shouting at me through a cloud. I got to my knees and in spite of the pain burning in my back I pulled myself up. The other guys trying out for the team had drifted back over to the scrimmage line and were looking away from me, pretending not to notice. It was the third major mistake I had made that day and something in Coach Harley's face told me it would be my last.

Although the reader can quickly tell that the author is writing about football (the helmet and the shoulder pads appear in the first three sentences), we know nothing of the larger situation until the second paragraph. Only gradually do we perceive the more general setting (a sinking sun, empty bleachers, other football players, the coach). And not until the final sentence of the second paragraph do we get a suggestion of purpose or direction.

Beginning with selected details plunges the reader immediately into your writing. The audience is caught up in an event or a description without knowing exactly why and must keep reading to find out. Therein lies the risk. The reader will stay with you only so long—perhaps a few paragraphs or a page—before you must provide some general orientation. But either organizing technique—general to specific or specific to general—provides you with a relatively easy and sequential pattern to follow for getting the first few paragraphs of an essay flowing.

DRAFTING SCENES

As the first draft often presents the most difficult obstacle to overcome in writing, an understanding of scene and its components can provide you with an immediate place to begin writing: Create a scene in which you show us your subject; write a series of scenes showing different aspects of your subject. In early drafts, the scenes need not be logically connected. You can always return later and fill in the relationships, add commentary or personal reflection, and draw conclusions. A scene or a series of scenes can be the organizing unit of a complete essay: It can serve as a sensory and dramatic introduction to an essay or it can provide an effective and often moving conclusion. The readings collected at the end of this unit provide several examples.

The function of a scene is not to tell but to dramatize. A scene helps you select and order your details by focusing your attention on light, time, place, character, and purpose. It provides a manageable shape for organizing details, either from specific to general or general to specific. Ford Madox Ford, an early twentieth-century writer, said you must always write as if your subject were acting out its life before you on a stage. If you see nothing in your mind's eye, you can be sure your reader won't see anything either. Especially in writing about character or in writing any form of description and narration, keeping the elements of scene in the back of your mind while keeping a picture of the thing you're describing in the front of your mind can help make words flow onto the page.

Exercises

Analyze the following scene by John Knowles, from his novel *A Separate Peace*. Identify each of the elements of scene. Has he left any out?

> No one else happened to be in the pool. Around us gleamed white tile and glass brick; the green, artificial-looking water rocked gently in its shining basin, releasing vague chemical smells and a sense of many pipes and filters; even Finny's voice, trapped in this closed, high-ceilinged room, lost its special resonance and blurred into a

general well of noise gathered up toward the ceiling. He said blur-
ringly, "I have a feeling I can swim faster than A. Hopkins Parker."

We found a stop watch in the office. He mounted a starting box,
leaned forward from the waist as he had seen racing swimmers do
but never had occasion to do himself—I noticed a preparatory loose-
ness coming into his shoulders and arms, a controlled ease about his
stance which was unexpected in anyone trying to break a record. I
said, "On your mark—Go!" There was a complex moment when his
body uncoiled and shot forward with sudden metallic tension. He
planed up the pool, his shoulders dominating the water while his
legs and feet rode so low that I couldn't distinguish them; a wake
rippled hurriedly by him and then at the end of the pool his position
broke, he relaxed, dived, an instant's confusion and then his suddenly and metallically tense body shot back toward the other end of
the pool. Another turn and up the pool again—I noticed no particular slackening of his pace—another turn, down the pool again, his
hand touched the end, and he looked up at me with a composed,
interested expression. "Well, how did I do?" I looked at the watch;
he had broken A. Hopkins Parker's record by .7 second.

_____ light   _____ sight
_____ time   _____ touch
_____ place   _____ sound
_____ character   _____ taste
_____ purpose   _____ smell

Journal Practice

1. Glance through the pages of your journal and select any entry you
could now shape more powerfully by writing it as a complete scene.
Begin by listing all the elements of scene that should have been in the
passage—light, character details, time, place, and so on. Then select the
most effective elements and revise the old entry.

2. Observe and create an indoor scene. Melinda Wilson, a freshman,
began by concentrating on the elements of scene as she woke up one
morning.

"Cincinnati is playing Oakland tonight. The game is to be televised
at 8:00 P.M. . . . ."

Groaning I rolled over and turned down the volume on my radio
to a low whisper. My eyes watered as I yawned and my back arched
in a stretch. I opened my eyes and looked at the clock. All I could
see was a red glow. I pulled my hands from under my pillow and
rubbed my eyes. With one fingernail I scraped the hard crumbly

mucus from the corners. My eyes stretched wide and I blinked the water away. The red glow had become numbers: 7:34. The door was open and the light from the kitchen illuminated the bedroom. I could see the remnants from my midnight snack on the floor near the foot of the bed. A bowl of milk with a few Cheerios still floating in it and half a box of Fig Newtons. I pulled my pillow against my chest and wrapped my arms around it. The sheet felt warm and smooth against my legs. I wet my lips with my tongue and grimaced as I realized I didn't brush my teeth last night. I pushed my feet from under the covers and over the side of the bed. Still hugging my pillow, I pushed myself upright. Everything went black as the blood rushed to my head. I pushed my face into my pillow and waited for the fuzziness to go away. The hard wood floor felt cool under my feet.

3. Practice writing a *panoramic scene*. Look out of your window. Describe the general location; record the light (try to imply "time" through the light); then focus in, step by step, on a simple but important or characteristic detail selected from the whole. Here is how freshman Mark Bostic attempted it.

General overview	It was another gloomy Monday, and the light was beginning to fade for the day. The clouds in the sky grew darker and darker. Then the rain began, lightly at first,
Focusing in *Smaller focus*	barely touching the leaves of the trees outside my house. I saw my neighbor in his driveway with his car hood up. Then the rain began to fall harder. I saw it bouncing furiously against the top of his car. He slammed down the
Specific focus	hood with a disgusted look on his face. As he ran around the side of his car he tripped over his tool box. "Damn," he yelled, "who in the hell set this here?" He raced into the house to get out of the rain.

4. Write a scene involving two characters. Do not fictionalize. Observe and listen to two secretaries as they go about their work or two janitors leaning on their brooms in the hall or two professors having a cup of coffee. Catch the actual dialogue, the gestures. Look especially for opposition. Select details about each character that reveal their personalities. Focus on actions and speech. Include all other elements of scene necessary to orient the reader: light, time, purpose, place, and the five senses. Writing about two characters is at least twice as difficult as writing about one. Ease the way by organizing either from the general to the specific or the reverse. Do not merely list details at random.

5. Now write an imaginative scene involving the same two characters in the same place in the midst of an imaginary conflict, one you have invented. Pretend it is the day after the original scene, and let the

characters debate or argue according to the characteristics revealed in the first scene; allow them to act out their inner qualities.

Copying

Copy any one of the following scenes (or if you're feeling ambitious, copy two for contrast) to study how the elements of scene are put to use in each:

    a. The scene from Tolstoy's journal, p. 14;

    b. The scene from Hopes' essay, p. 81, beginning with "So my emotion" and extending through the following six paragraphs;

    c. The scene from student Melinda Wilson in exercise 2, pp. 115–116.

Revising and Editing

11

Using Strong Verbs

As a student I remember *style* always seemed one of those vague things others "had" and I was supposed to "get." But no one could tell me how. For a long time I thought that style meant being flowery or dramatic or writing like William Faulkner. Only gradually did I come to discover that it meant, among other things, using your most natural voice. Indeed, some professional writers insist that style *is* voice, the revelation of your spirit, your biases, your vitality as it speaks to us from the page. In an earlier chapter I emphasized that you could probably discover your natural voice while writing spontaneously during the first draft. Another surprising way of finding that voice, of developing strength and vigor in your style, is through the conscious search for strong verbs during the revising or editing phase of the writing process.

WEAK AND STRONG VERBS

You may think of verbs (if you think of them at all) as grammatical elements in a sentence, as words that connect subjects with objects. Verbs do much more. Successful writers have found verbs the most important element in creating lively prose.

We can divide verbs into two general categories:

1. Strong verbs create a sense of direct, specific action, and because they are often concrete words, they tend to create an image in the reader's mind (*slump, crackle, shove, roar*).
2. Weak verbs use some form of the construction "to be" (*is, was, were, am, are, has been,* and so on), or they use what is generally called a "passive voice" (*The line was hit by the fullback,* instead of *The fullback hit the line*). Sometimes weak verbs are merely those vague little words like *get, do, make, come,* and *go* that fail to give statements a forceful impact because they are so innocuous.

Most of us tend to rely on weak verbs, especially in the early stages of writing. Yet an overdependency on weak verbs leads to dreary, styleless prose. Because only a dozen "to be" forms exist in the language, their repetition in sentence after sentence becomes predictable and monotonous. Just as you should train yourself to avoid clichés and generalities in your writing, you should train yourself to eliminate all weak verbs. Why?

Strong verbs create the image of an action:
jump, smile, whistle, swivel, dive, pivot, float

Strong verbs focus an idea:
narrate, condemn, expose, recount, argue, define, explore, criticize

Strong verbs tighten and strengthen a sentence.
(Good writers never use seventeen words when eleven will do.)
It was brought to my attention by Dr. Lewis that I had failed to define my terms.
(17 words)
Dr. Lewis told me I had failed to define my terms. (11 words)

The best writers know that strong, active verbs create a sense of imaginative, original prose. Notice how Annie Dillard uses verbs to evoke strength and emotional force in this simple passage describing a moth flying into a candle.

I *looked* up when a shadow *crossed* my page; at any rate, I *saw* it all. A golden female moth, a biggish one with a two-inch wing-span, *flapped* into the fire, *dropped* her abdomen into the wet wax, *stuck, flamed, frazzled* and *fried* in a second. Her moving wings *ignited* like tissue paper, enlarging the circle of light in the clearing and creating out of the darkness the sudden blue sleeves of my sweater, the green leaves of jewelweed by my side, the ragged red trunk of a pine. At

once the light *contracted* again and the moth's wings *vanished* in a
fine, foul smoke. At the same time her six legs *clawed, curled, blackened,* and *ceased,* disappearing utterly. . . . And her antennae *crisped*
and *burned* away and her heaving mouth parts *crackled* like pistol fire.

Writers make choices. As they work to revise and edit their writing,
they search for the strongest nouns, the most accurate verbs. Contrast,
for example, the almost infinite number of strong verbs available for the
single sentence, *A snake is under the porch.*

A snake *coiled* under the porch.
A snake *rattled* under the porch.
A snake *hissed* under the porch.
A snake *died* under the porch.

The list might go on for pages. Strong verbs offer you an almost
unlimited number of choices. And strong verbs make writing more precise, more sensory. *A snake is under the porch* locates the snake but nothing
more. It doesn't show us anything for the imagination to grab hold of.
Coiled, slithered, rattled, hissed, and *died* convey concrete details about the
snake. The specific choice you make gives your writing a voice that
distinguishes it from the choice someone else makes, even for the same
sentence on the same subject.

Professional writers, like journalists, must be especially conscious of
verbs. Stories have to move; action must keep the reader interested. Few
reporters could get away with a story that relied on weak verbs. Notice
how the writer of this *Newsweek* article used strong verbs to make the
event more concrete, more specific, more active, and more interesting.

She *strolled* into a New Orleans motel, calmly *demanded* money in the
cash register and *warned* the clerk: "I'm going to spill your guts."
When the disbelieving clerk *resisted,* the teenage holdup girl *stepped*
behind the reservations counter and *slashed* the clerk in the belly
with a 3-inch knife.
While he *lay* bleeding on the floor, several motel guests *walked*
in. The girl *made* change for one of them from the stolen money,
handed a room key to the second and *checked* out the third.

Even the newspaper-headline writer knows that verbs sell a story by
capturing the reader's interest:

PRESIDENT WRESTLES WITH DEFICIT
STRANGLER STRIKES AGAIN
PROFITS SOAR ON WALL STREET
YANKEES CRUSH RED SOX

The value of adding strong verbs to your writing cannot be over-emphasized. More active verbs make sentences more concrete and sensory, they eliminate extra words, they emphasize the most important facts in the sentence, they make details more precise, they make all forms of writing sound vigorous, and they offer you the opportunity to express your own voice, to make your writing stand out.

EDITING FOR STRONG VERBS

For the beginning writer, finding strong verbs is usually an editorial act. After several years of practice, such verbs may come to you as early as the first-draft stage: The weak passive voice may seem almost unnatural. But too much conscious effort at the first-draft stage may cause inhibitions as much as excessive concentration on proper punctuation. Unless you already write using active verbs, it would be better to work with them during the revising or editing phase of the process.

As in other forms of editing, there are few clear rights and wrongs. Some sentences may work successfully with a passive verb, and every effort to change it to an active verb will only distort or strain the flow. *Never force a strong verb into the sentence merely for its own sake*, but do test every sentence you have written.

1. In many cases, the strong verb is already in the sentence. Find the word that seems to carry any action at all and rebuild the sentence around it.

Original
The truck was overloaded by the workmen with watermelons.

Find the action.
overloaded

Rebuild the sentence around the action.
Workmen overloaded the truck with watermelons.

Original
His work shirt had dark rings where it had been stained with sweat.

Find the action.
stained

Rebuild the sentence around the action.
Dark rings of sweat stained his work shirt.

Note that in both of these examples, editing for the strong verb also eliminates several unnecessary words. In each case, the active sentence reads more smoothly, simply, and effectively.

2. Avoid especially the "to be" verb form at the beginning of sentences. Such constructions as There are, There is, It is, *and* It was *can often be eliminated.*

Original
There are two basic types of verbs you may have studied in high school. [*a sentence taken from my first draft of this chapter*]

Find the action.
studied

Rebuild the sentence around the action.
You may have studied two basic types of verbs in high school.

Original
It was her decision to become a banker.

Find the action.
decision

Rebuild the sentence around the action.
She decided to become a banker.

Changing verbs may also change the meaning, of course. "It was her decision" may suggest that a question existed regarding *who* made the decision. "She decided" loses such an implication. You must make editorial changes within the context of your whole essay. If the passive construction is actually more accurate, then use it. But if a strong verb can be substituted without distorting the accuracy or if it actually increases the accuracy, then by all means make the change.

Original
The elderly are thought by some people to be a burden on society because wages are not earned by most of them.

Find the action.
thought . . . earned

Rebuild the sentence around the action.

Some people think the elderly burden society because they earn no wages.

3. Finally, certain active verbs in themselves remain dull and empty because they lack concrete imagery. Got, have, come, go, *and* made *serve better than a passive form, but not much better. Usually, a more precise action can improve the sentence.*

Original

I got in late at night.

Revision (that is, reseeing in more precise or sensory terms)

I tiptoed in late at night.
I slipped in late at night.
I stomped in late at night.
I thundered in late at night.
I crept in late at night.

Most readers consider Shakespeare the finest writer in English because of the combined breadth and depth of his perception into human nature, but also because of the superiority of his craftsmanship. Critics long ago identified his use of strong verbs as a major element in that craftsmanship. One scholar estimates that Shakespeare uses approximately four active verbs for every passive verb. In the following passage from *King Lear*, Shakespeare uses no passives at all.

> LEAR: *Blow*, winds, and *crack* your cheeks! *rage! blow!*
> You cataracts and hurricanes, *spout*
> Till you have *drench'd* our steeples, *drown'd* the cocks!
> You sulphurous and thought-executing fires,
> Vaunt couriers to oak-cleaving thunderbolts,
> *Singe* my white head! And thou, all-shaking thunder,
> *Smite* flat the thick rotundity o' the world!
> *Crack* nature's moulds, all germens *spill* at once,
> That make ingrateful man!

It would be misleading to state that style or voice is nothing more than the use of strong verbs. Style is ultimately the reflection in language of your total personality. But the conscious search for vigorous, forceful verbs can be a major step in learning to control language so that it speaks for you and through you. The verb may be the key element in making your writing sound fresh as well as energetic and exact.

Exercises

1. In the following paragraph from *Ragtime*, E.L. Doctorow narrates Houdini's first flight in a biplane with boxed wings. Almost all verbs have been left out. First read the paragraph to grasp what's happening, then fill in every blank with a strong, vigorous verb. Don't try to guess what verbs Doctorow might have used; try to come up with your own. Compare your choices with the choices of others in your class. If you're like most people, you'll find that you overlap with someone else on no more than five or six out of the sixteen blanks. Selection of the strong verb almost automatically helps you find your own voice.

Houdini _____ into the pilot's seat, _____ his cap backwards

and _____ it down tight. He _____ the wheel. His eyes _____

in concentration, he _____ his jaw firmly and he _____ his head

and _____ to the mechanic, who spun the wood propeller. The engine _____. It was an Enfield 80-horsepower job, supposedly better

than the one the Wrights themselves were using. Hardly daring to

breathe, Houdini _____ the engine, _____ it, _____ it again.

Finally he _____ up his thumb. The mechanic _____ under the

wings and _____ the wheel chocks. The craft slowly _____ forward.

2. Although not all of the following sentences use passive verbs, all contain at least one weak verb. Rewrite each sentence to make it as strong and vigorous as possible. In the process, eliminate other unnecessary words.

a.   Several important statistics were found in the document by the search committee.
b.   The torn drapery was repaired by the stage crew.
c.   For many years the country was under the totalitarian rule of a dictator. The dictator was self-appointed.
d.   The Dimley brothers were thought by many of us to have grown up on a farm.

e. It is very important for speakers to have the gift of being able to give their speeches emotional force.

f. Mrs. Roosevelt's feelings for him are shown by her staying with him when he was ill with polio.

g. A satisfactory decision was made by the students regarding the use of the campus union.

h. All men possess certain doctrines of natural rights that have been instituted by God.

3. Editing verbs in context is more difficult. Try to improve the following paragraph by changing at least 50 percent of the weak verbs into strong verbs. In the process, you'll find yourself eliminating many unnecessary words throughout the paragraph.

> In the 1930s scientists were beginning to be suspicious of cigarettes as a cause of illness and death. One reason was an increase in lung cancer. Around 3,000 people were listed each year as dying from lung cancer. Today there is an increase to 18,000 annually. Also, many smokers have got emphysema, a disease that is destructive of the wall of the air sacs of the lungs. All other related diseases, such as cirrhosis of the liver, pneumonia, bronchiectasis, and even stomach ulcers, are contributing factors to an even higher death rate. If all related diseases are combined, there is a 57 percent increase in the death rate among smokers over nonsmokers.

4. Read two of your earlier journal exercises. Circle every weak verb. Rewrite both exercises, substituting strong verbs in every possible case (but don't make the sentence sound unnatural to your ear). Try to eliminate each case in which two or more passives appear in a single sentence or in which two or more sentences in a row use weak verbs. If Shakespeare used an average of four active verbs for every passive, set yourself a goal of using at least one active for every passive. If you fall below the 50–50 ratio, you're probably not seeing the potential for vigor and action in your own material.

Readings

Charles S. Rathbone was a returning adult student taking night classes to complete his bachelor's degree in management when he wrote the following sketch of his grandfather. Rathbone uses narration and description, as well as several focused scenes with sense details, dialogue, and action to express the fullness of his memories.

Grandpa Was a Big Man

Charles S. Rathbone

Grandpa's big hairy hand gripped my two wrists and I felt helpless. He had just locked the door of his little country store and stepped down the wobbly steps. I started poking and grabbing at him as usual when I wanted to scuffle.

I pulled and tugged, wrestled and jumped about on the hard packed dirt of the store yard trying to break his hold. In a few minutes I began to tire. I had no chance of getting loose. I was ten and I thought pretty strong, but all I had to show for my efforts were the heel marks and furrows my feet made in the store yard that Grandma kept swept as clean as her front porch.

Grandpa Harley was a big man, six feet three inches tall and two hundred and fifty pounds. He filled a door frame, and even the horses he occasionally shod seemed smaller when he stood next to them. The boys on Fines Creek liked to scuff with him and test his considerable strength. He was in his sixties, but he could hold all their hands with one of his.

Grandpa was the patriarch of the Methodist Church we went to every Sunday. I could not imagine sitting in that little church and seeing anyone else but Grandpa standing up at the pulpit conducting the Sunday School and hymns. For this occasion each week he substituted his overalls for his old beige suit which looked good on him. Perhaps it was the contrast between it and his overalls. He stood erect before the congregation and even leaned back slightly to balance the tilting pull of his stomach. He wore his coarse, grey hair permanently parted down the center of his head. Tight stiff waves rose up from the part, then faded toward each side of his head. He wore his hair clipped short on the sides making his big ears look even bigger, especially the lobes. The wrinkles on his weathered face swelled in and out as he sang.

Any time a member or close friend of the church died, Grandpa rang the church bell the next day at noon, one ring for each year lived. "It's a tribute to the deceased," he once told me, "and the family knows we share their loss."

I remember walking the half mile or so with him to the church to ring the bell for an eighty-nine-year-old man who had died the day before. I jumped along and played as we walked up the gravel road, and occasionally picked up a rock and sailed it into the creek, but Grandpa walked in a quiet steady stride. He felt even the walk to and from the church was a solemn ritual.

Grandpa unlocked the church door and we walked in. Several days with the door and windows closed had left the air hot and stale. The quiet left by the absence of worshipers caused our every movement to echo off the walls.

I opened the little belfry door and Grandpa, hat in hand, stooped through. He took hold of the plow rope hanging from the bell, and in a quiet somber manner he began pulling. As I stood next to him, I could hear the rope scuff against the ceiling hole. The clapper struck the bell interrupting the calmness of that summer afternoon. I imagined everyone within earshot silently contemplating the loss of Mr. Tom Kirkpatrick.

After about forty rings, beads of sweat covered Grandpa's brow. Some trickled down his cheeks. Sweat covered the bib of his overalls below the pocket where he carried the gold colored watch with a steam locomotive engraved on the back.

"Son," he said between breaths, "do you think you can help me for a while?"

I felt grown up. "Sure," I said.

"Now, before I stop you take hold of the rope and follow it up and down a few times so you can keep ringing at the same pace." I took the rope loosely in my hands; I could smell his sweaty body as his arms came up and down above my head. "Are you ready?" he said.

"I think so."

Slowly he turned the rope loose and backed away still counting the rings and keeping time with his hand. He leaned against the wall, and with his other hand, fanned his face with his old felt hat. I concentrated on every pull, being careful not to swing the bell over the top and cause two or three rings out of time. After a few minutes, the cords of the rope cut into my hands. My arms grew weak. My earlier enthusiasm and feeling of being grown up disappeared. To ease my aching arms, I pulled with my whole body, bending my knees at the bottom of each stroke. The bell no longer seemed to communicate a compassionate message but rather the deadening clang of heavy metal at the end of each exasperating tug. Grandpa knew I couldn't last much longer. He took the rope from my hand and I leaned back against the wall sweating and panting.

After eighty-nine rings, he put his hand on my shoulder and we walked out of the church. The bright sun and cool air felt good as the blood returned to my arms. As I walked down the road, perhaps a little slower than before, the bell continued to ring in my ears with the same cadence.

Grandpa and one or two men in the congregation dug all the graves in the church cemetery, sometimes taking three days in the winter if the ground was frozen deep, or if they hit rock. I often walked to the cemetery with him carrying the spade or shovel. It always amazed me how different the grave looked compared to other holes he dug on the farm. Perfectly shaped from top to bottom, the walls never varied more than a half inch. The spade marks on the sides were smooth and never gouged. Grandpa said the care taken in digging a grave, like ringing the church bell or taking off your hat as a funeral procession passed by, showed respect for the dead.

Grandpa talked once about the number of stray cats that had taken up out at the barn and how something had to be done. A day or two later I heard a shot out at the barn and ran to see what happened. I saw Grandpa coming out of the barn into the sunlight. He walked slowly, his head down, his face hidden by his hat. He carried his rifle loosely by his side as if he wanted to drop it. When he met me, he raised his head slightly. "What's wrong, Grandpa?" I asked as I looked up into his face. The wrinkles on his brow stood out.

"I shot the black and yellow spotted cat," he said.

The next day he discovered five kittens under a pile of boards in back of the barn. He knew the mama was the cat he had killed. Afterwards he carried milk to the kittens every day for two months.

When Grandpa died several years later some of the lining had to be removed from the casket to make room for him. On Sunday after Thanksgiving, his body was brought to Mom and Dad's home before the funeral. Family and friends passed in and out of the house offering condolences. The weather was particularly distressing that day. A cold wind blew and the naked maple trees swayed back and forth as their last leaves fell to the ground. Dark, thick clouds raced across the sky. The grass, the ragweed, and the plantain had withered and turned brown.

The day of the funeral, Jeff and Jim, his two other grandsons, two funeral home attendants, and Dad and I carried the big casket out of the hearse. As we struggled through the door and across the porch one of the attendants looked at me and said, "There lies much of a man." The brass handle felt heavy in my hand, but not as heavy as the weight I felt inside.

Jeff Roberts was a freshman on a soccer scholarship when he wrote the following. "This was the hardest thing I've ever written," he said afterwards. "I was trying extra hard to use similes and active verbs."

The Triumph of Mr. Edgars

Jeff Roberts

None of us liked Mr. Edgars. He lived in a house built up on cinderblock stilts near the railroad. He had been a brakeman on the railroad until the night he fell from a boxcar and lost both his legs. I don't know why that made us dislike him, but I think it was because he seemed like a freak, something horrible who clumped about in his hollow house on hollow legs. On the way home from school, Larry and Rick and I would cross the tracks. Sometimes Mr. Edgars would peer out at us from behind his smoke smudged windows. His hair stuck up wildly about his head. We knew he couldn't chase us so we would chant and dance about on the railroad tracks, pretending we were daring a train to run over us. I don't think any trains had used those tracks in years. Sometimes Larry would lie down on the tracks and cry, Oh my legs! Oh I've lost both my legs! Then we would run in all directions howling with laughter. On nights after leaving our Boy Scout meetings, we would crawl under the house itself, wearing our brown uniforms and our merit badges, then each of us would take a rock or a bottle and pound on the floor over our heads, screaming Earthquake! Earthquake! Run for your lives!

When my mother found out, she dragged me in deep fear and shame to Mr. Edgars' house to apologize. He met us at a tattered screen door using two canes to balance on. I avoided looking at him as I came in but I could smell him, sort of like a mixture of sour milk and old cheese. Inside the house was dark, like a tunnel inside a mountain where the light seeps in from a distant opening. We sat on an old stuffed sofa that sank and sank and sank when we sat on it. Our knees were level with our chests. Mr. Edgars lowered himself into a straight-backed chair. The thing I remember most was that when his artificial knees bent, I could hear the whoosh of escaping air, the kind of sound that comes when you open a can of vacuum-packed coffee. Next to him was a monstrous old television set that must have come from the 1950s. Old *TV Guides* littered the floor. In one dark corner I could see a cat curled up asleep in the middle of a toppled pile of old newspapers. What light there was filtered through a curtained window behind him so that his hair seemed to float about his head. If it hadn't been for his breathing, I wouldn't have even known he was alive. Mr. Edgars never wavered. He sat straight and still, waiting for whatever it was we had come for.

So my mother said I had something to say and then she waited too, and I tried to say I was sorry but I could feel all the blood draining out of my face in shame and what I said came out mumbled. She told me to speak up, so I said it again, but it still wasn't much above a whisper. I felt dirty and humiliated. Then we all waited in silence, as if we were listening for a far away train that never came. Finally Mr. Edgars used both his canes to push himself up and his knees whooshed again. My mother decided it was our signal to leave. We crawled up out of the sunken sofa and walked ahead of him to the door.

As we started out, he said, "Who did you say you were?"

My mother told him again, and we stepped out onto the rickety wooden porch in the sunlight. From the porch I could see the railroad tracks running off like two rusty blades until they curved into a woods.

"And what was it you wanted?" Mr. Edgars asked. "I never give to charity." His voice sounded faint and rusty. You could tell he wasn't used to talking much.

My mother held my hand hard and told me to tell him again. So I said it real loud this time. "I'm sorry Mr. Edgars for being mean to you."

He let the screen door close and the two of us were outside trying to see him through the dark mesh screen. Inside in the cold darkness he was leaning forward on both canes and peering out.

"I'd like to help," he said. "You can count me in."

My mother squeezed my hand until I though it would break and after a moment she forced a smile and nodded. Walking back up the gravel path, my mother kept her eyes fixed straight ahead. Then we heard him shout something behind us.

Mr. Edgars had come out on the porch. He was wearing old railroad overalls and his long hair flew about in the sunlight like white bats' wings. "Tell them I'm all for it," he shouted. "You tell them, I'll be there."

And he raised one cane over his head, jabbing it at the sky, as if in triumph and joy.

Maya Angelou might be called a "Renaissance woman." Beginning as a singer and dancer, she has starred in off-Broadway productions, acted in movies, written plays, published numerous volumes of poetry, produced a PBS-TV series on Africa, and served as coordinator for the Southern Christian Leadership Conference. Her autobiography, I Know Why the Caged Bird Sings, *from which the following excerpt is taken, received national acclaim. Two other volumes of autobiography have followed, as have numerous awards. Yet as the following piece illustrates, her life began in the poorest of circumstances. It took a special person to show her the way out.*

Sister Flowers

Maya Angelou

For nearly a year, I sopped around the house, the Store, the school and the church, like an old biscuit, dirty and inedible. Then I met, or rather got to know, the lady who threw me my first life line.

Mrs. Bertha Flowers was the aristocrat of Black Stamps. She had the grace of control to appear warm in the coldest weather, and on the Arkansas summer days it seemed she had a private breeze which swirled around, cooling her. She was thin without the taut look of wiry people, and her printed voile dresses and flowered hats were as right for her as denim overalls for a farmer. She was our side's answer to the richest white woman in town.

Her skin was a rich black that would have peeled like a plum if snagged, but then no one would have thought of getting close enough to Mrs. Flowers to ruffle her dress, let alone snag her skin. She didn't encourage familiarity. She wore gloves too.

I don't think I ever saw Mrs. Flowers laugh, but she smiled often. A slow widening of her thin black lips to show even, small white teeth, then the slow effortless closing. When she chose to smile on me, I always wanted to thank her. The action was so graceful and inclusively benign.

She was one of the few gentlewomen I have ever known, and has remained throughout my life the measure of what a human being can be.

Momma had a strange relationship with her. Most often when she passed on the road in front of the Store, she spoke to Momma in that soft yet carrying voice, "Good day, Mrs. Henderson." Momma responded with "How you, Sister Flowers?"

Mrs. Flowers didn't belong to our church, nor was she Momma's familiar. Why on earth did she insist on calling her Sister Flowers? Shame made me want to hide my face. Mrs. Flowers deserved better than to be called Sister. Then, Momma left out the verb. Why not ask, "How *are* you, *Mrs. Flowers?*" With the unbalanced passion of the young, I hated her for showing her ignorance to Mrs. Flowers. It didn't occur to me for many years that they were as alike as sisters, separated only by formal education.

Although I was upset, neither of the women was in the least shaken by what I thought an unceremonious greeting. Mrs. Flowers would continue her easy gait up the hill to her little bungalow, and Momma kept on shelling peas or doing whatever had brought her to the front porch.

Occasionally, though, Mrs. Flowers would drift off the road and down to the Store and Momma would say to me, "Sister, you go on and play." As she left I would hear the beginning of an intimate conversation. Momma persistently using the wrong verb, or none at all.

"Brother and Sister Wilcox is sho'ly the meanest—" "Is," Momma? "Is"? Oh, please, not "is," Momma, for two or more. But they talked, and from the side of the building where I waited for the ground to open up and swallow me, I heard the soft-voiced Mrs. Flowers and the textured voice of my grandmother merging and melting. They were interrupted from time to time by giggles that must have come from Mrs. Flowers (Momma never giggled in her life). Then she was gone.

She appealed to me because she was like people I had never met personally. Like women in English novels who walked the moors (whatever they were) with their loyal dogs racing at a respectful distance. Like the women who sat in front of roaring fireplaces, drinking tea incessantly from silver trays full of scones and crumpets. Women who walked over the "heath" and read morocco-bound books and had two last names divided by a hyphen. It would be safe to say that she made me proud to be Negro, just by being herself.

She acted just as refined as whitefolks in the movies and books and she was more beautiful, for none of them could have come near that warm color without looking gray by comparison.

I was fortunate that I never saw her in the company of po-whitefolks. For since they tend to think of their whiteness as an evenizer, I'm certain that I would have had to hear her spoken to commonly as Bertha, and my image of her would have been shattered like the unmendable Humpty-Dumpty.

One summer afternoon, sweet-milk fresh in my memory, she stopped at the Store to buy provisions. Another Negro woman of her health and age would have been expected to carry the paper sacks home in one hand, but Momma said, "Sister Flowers, I'll send Bailey up to your house with these things."

She smiled that slow dragging smile, "Thank you, Mrs. Henderson. I'd prefer Marguerite, though." My name was beautiful when she said it. "I've been meaning to talk to her, anyway." They gave each other age-group looks.

Momma said, "Well, that's all right then. Sister, go and change your dress. You going to Sister Flowers's."

The chifforobe was a maze. What on earth did one put on to go to Mrs. Flowers' house? I knew I shouldn't put on a Sunday dress. It might be sacrilegious. Certainly not a house dress, since I was already wearing a fresh one. I chose a school dress, naturally. It was formal without suggesting that going to Mrs. Flowers' house was equivalent to attending church.

I trusted myself back into the Store.

"Now, don't you look nice." I had chosen the right thing, for once. . . .

There was a little path beside the rocky road, and Mrs. Flowers walked in front swinging her arms and picking her way over the stones.

She said, without turning her head, to me, "I hear you're doing very good school work, Marguerite, but that it's all written. The teachers report that they have trouble getting you to talk in class." We passed the triangular farm on our left and the path widened to allow us to walk together. I hung back in the separate unasked and unanswerable questions.

"Come and walk along with me, Marguerite." I couldn't have refused even if I wanted to. She pronounced my name so nicely. Or more correctly, she spoke each word with such clarity that I was certain a foreigner who didn't understand English could have understood her.

"Now no one is going to make you talk—possibly no one can. But bear in mind, language is man's way of communicating with his fellow man and it is language alone which separates him from the lower animals." That was a totally new idea to me, and I would need time to think about it.

"Your grandmother says you read a lot. Every chance you get. That's good, but not good enough. Words mean more than what is set down on paper. It takes the human voice to infuse them with the shades of deeper meaning."

I memorized the part about the human voice infusing words. It seemed so valid and poetic.

She said she was going to give me some books and that I not only must read them, I must read them aloud. She suggested that I try to make a sentence sound in as many different ways as possible.

"I'll accept no excuse if you return a book to me that has been badly handled." My imagination boggled at the punishment I would deserve if in fact I did abuse a book of Mrs. Flowers's. Death would be too kind and brief.

The odors in the house surprised me. Somehow I had never connected Mrs. Flowers with food or eating or any other common experience of common people. There must have been an outhouse, too, but my mind never recorded it.

The sweet scent of vanilla had met us as she opened the door.

"I made tea cookies this morning. You see, I had planned to invite you for cookies and lemonade so we could have this little chat. The lemonade is in the icebox."

It followed that Mrs. Flowers would have ice on an ordinary day, when most families in our town bought ice late on Saturdays only a few times during the summer to be used in the wooden ice-cream freezers.

She took the bags from me and disappeared through the kitchen door. I looked around the room that I had never in my wildest fantasies imagined I would see. Browned photographs leered or threatened from the walls and the white, freshly done curtains pushed against themselves and against the wind. I wanted to gobble up the room entire and take it to Bailey, who would help me analyze and enjoy it.

"Have a seat, Marguerite. Over there by the table." She carried a platter covered with a tea towel. Although she warned that she hadn't tried her hand at baking sweets for some time, I was certain that like everything else about her the cookies would be perfect.

They were flat round wafers, slightly browned on the edges and butter-yellow in the center. With the cold lemonade they were sufficient for childhood's lifelong diet. Remembering my manners, I took nice little lady-like bites off the edges. She said she had made them expressly for me and that she had a few in the kitchen that I could take home to my brother. So I jammed one whole cake in my mouth and the rough crumbs scratched the insides of my jaws, and if I hadn't had to swallow, it would have been a dream come true.

As I ate she began the first of what we later called "my lessons in living." She said that I must always be intolerant of ignorance but understanding of illiteracy. That some people, unable to go to school, were more educated and even more intelligent than college professors. She encouraged me to listen carefully to what country people called mother wit. That in those homely sayings was couched the collective wisdom of generations.

When I finished the cookies she brushed off the table and brought a thick, small book from the bookcase. I had read *A Tale of Two Cities* and found it up to my standards as a romantic novel. She opened the first page and I heard poetry for the first time in my life.

"It was the best of times and the worst of times . . ." Her voice slid and curved down through and over the words. She was nearly singing. I wanted to look at the pages. Were they the same that I had read? Or were there notes, music, lined on the pages, as in a hymn book? Her sounds began cascading gently. I knew from listening to a thousand preachers that she was nearing the end of her reading, and I hadn't really heard, heard to understand, a single word.

"How do you like that?"

It occurred to me that she expected a response. The sweet vanilla flavor was still on my tongue and her reading was a wonder in my ears. I had to speak.

I said, "Yes, Ma'am." It was the least I could do, but it was the most also.

"There's one more thing. Take this book of poems and memorize one for me. Next time you pay me a visit, I want you to recite."

I have tried often to search behind the sophistication of years for the enchantment I so easily found in those gifts. The essence escapes but its aura remains. To be allowed, no, invited, into the private lives of strangers, and to share their joys and fears, was a chance to exchange the Southern bitter wormwood for a cup of mead with Beowulf or a hot cup of tea and milk with Oliver Twist. When I said aloud, "It is a far, far better thing that I do, than I have ever done . . ." tears of love filled my eyes at my selflessness.

On that first day, I ran down the hill and into the road (few cars ever came along it) and had the good sense to stop running before I reached the Store.

I was liked, and what a difference it made. I was respected not as Mrs. Henderson's grandchild or Bailey's sister but for just being Marguerite Johnson.

Childhood's logic never asks to be proved (all conclusions are absolute). I didn't question why Mrs. Flowers had singled me out for attention, nor did it occur to me that Momma might have asked her to give me a little talking to. All I cared about was that she had made tea cookies for *me* and read to *me* from her favorite book. It was enough to prove that she liked me.

Pete Hamill served as an award-winning correspondent during the Vietnam war. His writings include several collections of essays and more than a dozen screenplays. His most recent work has appeared in such periodicals as The New York Times Magazine *and* Esquire. *In the following essay, he focuses on a single house in Brooklyn where he grew up. By using almost all the qualities of "scene" (sights, smells, sounds, light, purpose, and so on), plus specific names and concrete details, he reveals not only the character of the place, but the quality of his experience and memories there.*

Home

Pete Hamill

The house was at 378 Seventh Avenue. There was a small butcher shop to the left and Teddy's Sandwich Shop to the right, and when I went in, I saw that the mailbox was still broken and the hall smelled of backed-up sewers and wet garbage. There were, of course, no locks on the doors, and I stood for a while in the yellow light of the thirty-watt bulb, and shifted the sea bag to the other shoulder. Two baby carriages were parked beside the stairs, and in the blackness at the back of the hall, I caught a glimpse of battered garbage cans. A small shudder went through me; the back of that hall had always been a fearful place when I was small, a place where I always felt vulnerable: to sudden attacks from the open door leading to the cellar, to rats feasting on the wet garbage, to unnamed things, specters, icy hands, the vengeance of God. Once, I'd had to go to the cellar late at night. To the right, inside the cellar door, there was a light switch, covered with a ceramic knob. I reached for the knob and it was gone, and there was a raw wire there instead and the shock knocked me over backwards, into the garbage cans, my heart spinning and racing away, and then rushing back again. I thought of that night trip, the strangeness later when I realized for the first time what it must feel like to die, and I started up the stairs.

It was a hall as familiar as anything I've ever known before or since. First floor right, Mae McAvoy; on the left, Poppa Clark; second floor right, Anne Sharkey and Mae Irwin; left, Carrie Woods. Carrie was a tiny sparrow of a woman who kept dogs and drank whiskey, and the dogs started a ferocious attack on the locked door, trying to get at me—alarmed, I suppose, by a smell they had not sensed for many weeks. All the apartments had the feeling of tossing bodies within, and I remembered fragments of other nights: the scream when a husband punched out a wife, and how he left and never came back; the glasses breaking at some forgotten party and the blood in the hall later; how they all hated one of the women because she was a wine drinker and therefore a snob; the great large silent man in one of those apartments, who played each Christmas with a vast Lionel electric train set, while forcing his only daughter to play at an untuned upright piano, who rooted for the Giants in that neighborhood of Dodger fans, and who had a strange tortured set of eyes. At each landing there were sealed metal doors where the dumbwaiter once had been, a pit that dropped away, like some bottomless well, to a boarded-over access door in the cellar, and which I thought, when I was eight, was the way to Hell itself, or at the very least, to the secret cave where Shazam granted Billy Batson the magic powers. There were two more baby carriages at the top of the second floor, the floor where my father had so often stopped on his way home, emptied of songs, dry and hoarse, unable to make that one final flight of stairs to bed. Billy Batson. Billy Hamill. Shazam.

There were traces of dinner smells in the hall, as if you could chew the air itself. It was almost three.

The door to our apartment was not locked. I dropped the sea bag, pushed the door open easily, and stepped into the dark kitchen, groping for the light cord in the center of the room. I bumped into a chair, then the table, and then found the light cord. A transformer hummed for a few sec-

onds and then the round fluorescent ceiling light blinked on. The room was
as I had remembered it: a white-topped gas range against the far wall where
the old coal stove had once stood, a tall white cabinet to the left, and then
the sink, high, one side shallow and the other deep, next to the window that
never opened. A Servel refrigerator with a broken handle was next to the
bathroom door. A closet loomed behind me next to the front door, with a
curtain covering the disorder within, and there was a table in the center of
the room, linoleum on the floor, and a clothesline running the length of the
room because there was no backyard, and in winter the clothes froze on the
line on the roof. There was a picture of Franklin Roosevelt on one wall, a
map of Ireland from the *Daily News* on another, and beside it I saw some of
the drawings I had sent from boot camp. Some of them were cartoons, drawings of soldiers and pilots I had copied from Milton Caniff; the others were
something new, drawings of sailors' faces, done in ink washes, the first
drawings I had made that didn't look like comic-strip figures. Roaches scur-
ried across the table, panicked by the harshness of the sudden blue-tinged
light. I could hear movement at the other end of the railroad flat, the smell
of heavy breathing and milk, and then my mother was coming through the
rooms.

"Oh Peter," she said. "You're home."

And she hugged me.

PART III

Objective Reporting

Someone once said, "There is no such thing as a true generalization, including this one," but we can come pretty close to a true generalization when we say that every writer must first be a reporter.

JOHN DE WITT MC KEE

Exploring

12

Emotions, Opinions, and Inference

For thousands of years, no one understood how typhus was spread. Some thought by touch; others, by air; still others speculated that typhus dropped from moon rays. Not until Charles Nicolle saw the relationship of several previously ignored facts did he discover the true carrier. Nicolle was a medical doctor in Tunis when a typhoid epidemic struck in 1909. Nicolle noticed that patients already inside his hospital did not catch the disease from newly arrived victims. Nor did the nurses and doctors catch it. One day, in the act of stepping over a typhus victim who had collapsed on the hospital steps, Nicolle realized that something must be actually stopping the spread of typhus at the hospital doors. He traced procedures back to the admission process and found that new typhus victims were bathed and their clothing burned. The carrier obviously had to be something the patients carried on the outside of their bodies. Nicolle determined that it could be nothing but a flea.

> The fact that I had ignored this point, that all those who had been observing typhus from the beginnings of history . . . had failed to notice

the incontrovertible and immediately fruitful solution of the method of transmission, had suddenly been revealed to me. I feel somewhat embarrassed about putting myself into the picture. If I do so, nevertheless, it is because I believe what happened to me is a very edifying and clear example. . . . I developed my observations with less timidity.

He developed his observations with less timidity. Perception of specific factual details that others had never bothered to investigate literally led to insight.

Heraclitus told us more than 2500 years ago:

Men who wish to know about the world must learn it in its particular details.

Only by observing the details of a subject—and then only after observing them with imaginative concentration—does sight lead to fresh understanding or, more importantly, to discovery of new and previously unseen relationships. But there are many different ways of "observing." Charles Nicolle suspended his emotional reactions, ignored all previous opinions, and tried to see the facts—and their relationships—with an objective eye. The key word is *objective*.

In the first two units of this book I have urged you to pursue sensory details to intensify awareness of yourself in relation to the world around you. The pursuit of objective detail requires the same type of concentrated effort and uses the same sense receptors: sight, hearing, taste, touch, and smell. But a search for factual detail requires a shift from emotional experience to reasoned experience, from an extension of emotional awareness to an extension of intellectual awareness.

OBJECTIVITY VERSUS EMOTION

Objectivity requires the observation of phenomena uninfluenced by feelings. For most of us, subjective feeling comes first. We have to train ourselves, consciously, to suspend feeling and to see only the fact itself.

Subjective observation	*Objective observation*
That's a beautiful sunset.	The sunset has streaks of yellow and lavender in it.
This fried chicken tastes terrible.	This fried chicken has a burned metallic taste.
Burt Reynolds is in this movie, so it must be good.	Burt Reynolds is in this movie.

If all life were this simple, the distinction between objective and subjective observation would also be simple. Unfortunately, emotion may be subtle and may influence observation without our knowledge.

Abortion is murder.
(Here an implied judgment based on some deep inner belief—on some inner feeling about what is good and what is evil—may cause the observation to *seem* like an objective fact to the observer, but the term *murder* has such negative connotations that we should be immediately alert to a subjective intrusion.)

Abortion is the removal of a fetus from a woman's womb.
(Here a simple description retains objectivity because no judgment about good or evil and no hidden emotion apparently influence the observation. The connotations are neutral.)

Industry has poisoned our air and water.
(This observer may believe he or she has stated an objective fact, but again the connotations suggest a negative emotion underlying the observation.)

Industry has often disposed of its waste material and by-products through the air and water.
(Without the word *poisoned*, the observation seems more readily acceptable as objective fact—no negative feelings intrude. The modifier *often* also qualifies the statement.)

The various emotional influences in our lives and how they affect observation and judgment can be a complex subject. The problem will be explored more fully in the later chapter on critical thinking in Part VI. In the meantime, two common forms of *subjective* influences need to be understood now.

INFERENCE

While walking across campus this morning, I noticed a student who wore shoes but no socks. Such a sight might have disgusted me, and I might have inferred that the student was lazy or dirty, or I might have felt sorry for him and inferred that he was poor, or I might have laughed and inferred that he was following the latest fad. A *fact* is a quality that can be verified by a second observer. A second person could easily have verified that the student I saw wore no socks. But an *inference* is a conclusion drawn from the fact. Inferences may be logical and true. Or, as my examples here show, an inference may be influenced by emotion; my disgust, my pity, my laughter, could each lead me to interpret the objective fact differently. *An inference is not a fact.* A second observer cannot verify which, if any, of my conclusions might be true. The first step in removing emotional elements from my observations is to suspend judgment, to withhold inference, until I am in possession of more facts.

As a beginning writer, you may observe facts accurately; but because of this confusion between fact and inference, you may report the inference (the judgment) as if it were the fact. Here is what one student wrote when sent out to interview a local official.

> The warden was unhappy when the noon whistle drowned out his conversation.

The student insisted this was a fact. Yet the term *unhappy* is an inference drawn from concrete details that the student observed with his senses but that he has not reported to the reader. Perhaps the warden stopped talking in midsentence and held his breath until his face turned red, or perhaps he chewed on his lower lip and pounded the table with his pistol butt until the whistle stopped blowing. Any or all of these concrete details may have led the student to infer that the warden was "unhappy." The student's judgment may have been accurate. But the facts, the concrete details, should have been presented to us so that in our role as readers, we could also function as the second observer.

Here is another student, reporting on how college women feel about changing their last names after marriage.

> I surveyed one hundred and eleven women in Howard Hall. Forty-seven indicated that they desired to retain the use of their own names after marriage. Thirty-one desired to use a hyphenated version of their maiden name with that of their future husband, such as Smith-Jones or Harrison-Williams. The remaining thirty-three women had obviously not had their consciousness raised since they desired to exchange their names for their husbands'.

The first three sentences can be accepted as fact. A survey has been taken, and a specific number of answers has been collected. A second observer could verify the information. But to infer that the first two groups of women have a higher degree of consciousness is unwarranted. No information has been given as to why any of the women offered the answers they did. Individuals in the third group might have varying reasons for adopting their husbands' names—religious, legal, or traditional. Some of them might even have last names they dislike, such as Jane Zarlostowhimp.

OPINION

Although somewhat different from an inference, an *opinion* raises a similar problem. In an older, legal sense, an opinion represents a judgment based on available data and logical argument, as in "The judge delivered the court's opinion on the Harris case." But more current and popular use of the term reduces opinion to personal taste. "Henrique loves jazz." "Ann Marie thinks ankle-length skirts are ugly." Such opinions cannot be substantiated by another observer because they deal not so much with the thing observed as with personal feelings. In the most extreme use of the term, an opinion may not be drawn from any objective evidence at all, as in "I feel sure life exists in many galaxies besides our own" or "People are by nature loving and good." Although such opinions may be held with confidence, they're based on speculation or intuition, not on verifiable, objective facts. Yet because opinions, like inferences, are expressed as conclusions—as judgments—they often sound more forceful and convincing than facts.

> People who want gun control are un-American.
> Acid rain is a hoax created by environmentalists.

Such bold, declarative statements are simplistic and easy to grasp. An opinion stated or held with conviction uses language itself to obscure our perceptions, to make us think no more seeking of fact is necessary because we supposedly already possess the truth.

If you are to train yourself in objectifying perception, you must be aware of the difference between a fact observed, an inference drawn from it, and an opinion expressed about it.

Objective fact	*Inference or opinion*
Toadstools are growing in the forest today.	It must have rained last night.
	I think toadstools are pretty.
	The soil there is probably rich in humus.
Rembrandt once painted a picture only three inches by five inches.	Small paintings sell for much less.
	He was too poor to afford a large canvas.
	Rembrandt was the world's greatest painter.

The stock market fell 14 points in April.	The stock market is for gambling fools. Investors are afraid of inflation. Now's the time to buy stock.

OBJECTIVITY AND ABSTRACTION

Finally, I've found that some students confuse being objective with being abstract. These qualities are not related. Objectivity is an attitude of the mind. It is a way of approaching a subject. The subject itself may be concrete (a scientist looks objectively at a very tangible frog; a medical doctor looks objectively at the specific colorations and flesh tone of his or her patient), or the subject may be general and abstract (a philosopher attempts to study the question of justice by withholding all personal bias; a sociologist studies the relationship between poverty and behavior by quantifying the data). To be objective does not require you to be abstract *or* concrete. It requires you to perceive the subject—whatever it is—with as little intrusion of your emotion as possible.

Obviously, as human beings, we can never be totally objective, nor would we want to be. But training ourselves to observe and report with an objective attitude provides excellent mental schooling; it sharpens powers of observation; it clarifies the separation between self and non-self, strengthening the ability to think and argue with finer distinctions; and it improves linguistic awareness, helping us to recognize how language itself may influence observation and judgment. A sound objective attitude continues to require all our sensory and perceptive powers.

Exercises

1. In the following conversation, identify which observations are influenced by emotion and which might be considered factual—that is, which could be verified by a second observer.

> Bob: That drunk almost hit me.
> Mary: What drunk?
> Bob: The one in that weaving car. He drove right up over the curb and I had to leap out of the way.
> Mary: What did he look like?
> Bob: A big ugly guy. He was aiming at me. You could see in his eyes he wanted to kill someone.

Mary: The car had a license from Montana.
Bob: It was some cowboy who's never been in the city before.
Mary: Are you all right now? Your face looks pale.
Bob: I'm OK. I just don't like drunken cowboys.
Mary: I read in the paper that there are still 15,000 people who make their living as cowboys.
Bob: Boy! Are you gullible! Not everything in the paper is fact, you know.

2. Here is a statement containing both opinions and inferences. Rewrite it so that the same information is conveyed as objectively as possible.

Grade-point averages are higher today than twenty years ago, but the fact is that kids aren't smarter; teachers are just easier. Twenty years ago, a *C* was considered a good grade in college. The average grade was 2.2 on a 4-point scale. Today anybody who goes to class can get a *B*. The average grade across the country is 3.2. Over 86 percent of the Harvard class of 1982 were graduated with honors, which proves how low the standards have fallen. One report from the U.S. Office of Education stated that teachers blamed grade inflation on the Vietnam War. A lot of cowards who didn't want to fight for their country hid out in college and as long as they got good grades, they were draft-deferred. But once the teachers started giving grades for reasons other than performance, there was no more objective standard to judge by, so everyone had to get *A*'s.

3. Your instructor will select a particular incident or topic currently in the news. Your job is to find at least three news reports on it in your local newspaper or in news magazines such as *Time, Newsweek,* and *U.S. News & World Report.* How objective is each report? Underline all signs of emotion, opinion, or inference. Are opinions attributed to a source or presented *as if* they were objective? Consider whether even verifiable facts are slanted; that is, are they preselected or heightened in such a way as to affect the reader in a calculated way? After carefully considering your findings, bring your material to class for discussion.

4. Study the painting by George Tooker on page 146. Based on the specific details portrayed in the painting, draw a reasonable inference about what is happening. Now write a brief paragraph that begins with your inference and is then supported by a description of the painting that can be verified by a second observer. Compare your paragraph with those written by others in your class. Were your inferences the same? Can more than one inference be supported by the same data?

William Hogarth, *Hudibras Catechized*, engraving.

Journal Practice

1. Choose any early entry that you have written subjectively—one that you have deep personal feelings about—and write about it again objectively. Give no opinions; avoid all emotionally charged words. Present only facts that could be verified by a second observer.

2. Take your journal to a student meeting, a classroom lecture, or the cafeteria. Pretend you are a journalist and describe a single incident. Avoid inserting your opinions, but try to select the most interesting facts. From the facts you have observed and presented, draw what seems to be a reasonable inference. (Learning to draw an inference that can be supported by facts is the first step in writing a sound conclusion to any essay.)

Play

Even though your classroom discussion and assignments may begin to shift toward more objective writing, your journal remains a place for you to continue freewriting, playing, and copying. The connection may not at first seem apparent, just as a football player may not at first see the value of running through old tires on a playing field. But the continued exercise of your imagination always relates to any kind of writing you may be engaged in.

Here are a few suggestions you might try.

1. Scribble out a list of puns. For starters, begin with hairstyling establishments: *From Hair to Eternity, United Hairlines,* or *Curl Up and Dye.* Or how about a hot-dog joint called *Mustard's Last Stand,* or a pet grooming shop called *Groomingdales?* Try creating your own puns on some of the following:

the local mall
your school cafeteria
a fraternity or sorority house
your local radio or TV station
the chem lab

2. Make a list of ridiculous song titles.

The Hills Are Alive with the Smell of Doobage
Baby, You're My French Fry
Get Down Little Guadalupe
Toast-lusters

3. With your mental eye, focus on the images listed below. Allow the images to lead you, dictate where you will go in your writing. Accept anything that comes to you. Reject nothing. Create your own story, including the elements of scene, powerful verbs, and forceful specifics.

the broken mirror
the enchanted forest
the spring
the childless couple

Exploring

13

Interviews and the 4 *C*'s of Observation

Until a few years ago I thought my job complete once I had advised students to pursue facts objectively, once I'd established the proper "attitude." What more could I do? That the writer also needed to select only the most important facts about a subject was self-evident. How the writer was to separate the significant from the insignificant seemed more mysterious—something I could explain only by the words *intuition* or *experience*. Then I had the opportunity of spending several days with a reporter for a large city newspaper. I hurried after him through the corridors of a state-government office as he pursued a story on alleged payoffs to several low-ranking bureaucrats. I stood to one side while he researched dusty files and ledgers. I watched in amazement as he flirted with secretaries, all the while drawing out fragments of information. I waited outside closed doors while he interviewed officials. As it turned out, no evidence for payoffs could be found. For my friend the story was a dead end, but for me it had been a revelation.

THE 4 *C'S* OF OBSERVATION

A reporter knows a great deal about how to seek and find facts that could benefit any writer in any career. Reporters know, for example, that whatever story they write has to be interesting because it has to sell papers, and to make it interesting they need to search out facts that affect the largest number of readers. They know that details with the most impact tend to be found by training the mind to look for certain aspects of a subject that I've grouped under four headings: *change, contrast, consequence,* and *characterization.* Although my friend would wince to hear his methods so labeled, I've come to call them the 4 *C's* of observation. They are guidelines only. Any subject may suggest its own unique approach, and audience requirements may place restrictions on any writer. But the 4 *C's* provide an effective *starting point* for developing an eye for factual observation.

Change

Events, ideas, values and social customs can all be studied according to how they are changing (or sometimes failing to change). Here is how sophomore Larry Kinde approached the subject of childbirth.

> At the center of the delivery room was a soft, padded chair, something like a dentist's chair, only angled more, so that a woman in it would have been half-reclining, half-standing. Toward the bottom of the chair were stirrup-like contraptions for the woman's legs to rest in. The room was painted a soft blue and there was even a speaker on the wall for music. Where was the white sterility of the old-fashioned delivery room? Where was the flat table with leather straps that held the woman down? Where the bright overhead lights?

We could study childbirth delivery rooms for many qualities other than change. But in this case change was the key element for entry into the subject. It provided the focus for selecting important facts about new developments, and even though Kinde's report is objective, there is nothing dull about it. The focus on change stimulates interest in the subject.

Contrast

People clash and so do ideas. Republicans battle Democrats; psychotherapists disagree with behaviorists; environmentalists fight industrialists. Forces in opposition provide a natural focal point around which a writer can approach a subject.

> . . . a basic contention developed from the whole philosophy behind
> prisons. Those who guard and manage the prison tend to believe that
> its function is to punish the prisoners. Those who counsel and serve
> as probation officers tend to believe that a prison should reform the
> prisoners. Both sides were able to provide me with statistics and facts
> supporting their position.

This student writer has stepped into the middle of controversy. Almost
every issue or event stimulates an opposing view. Contrast, conflict, contradiction, and opposition are not only eternally interesting to readers,
they also provide natural ways of selecting, shaping, and organizing
factual information. Looking for contrast in every subject should become
habitual as you develop a reporter's eye.

Consequence

Interesting facts are useful. Significant facts are vital. To find the significance in a subject, a writer must look for facts that have the most
impact, the most consequence, on people directly involved. Here is how
a student reporter for a college newspaper zeroed in on the consequences
of an action.

> The faculty voted Wednesday to change from a "course system"
> meeting four days a week for an hour per day, to a "credit-hour sys-
> tem," meeting on Monday, Wednesday, and Friday for an hour a
> day. The majority of the faculty argued that the credit-hour system
> was used by most colleges and that we were out of step.
>
> However, it could also be considered that while faculty members
> would teach a lighter load under the credit-hour system, students
> would need to take five courses per semester instead of four in order
> to graduate in the same number of years.

On the surface, a change in the organization of credits and class
hours is being carried out to increase conformity with other colleges.
Those are the facts. But the significance is revealed only by questioning
the consequences of those facts: Students will need to carry more courses
per semester; instructors will teach fewer hours. Actions, ideas, events—
all produce consequences. To describe the action, idea, or event objectively is important. By asking whom the consequences affect, the writer
begins to focus his or her attention on what is most significant.

Characterization

In an earlier chapter I described a number of ways for selecting details
that would characterize a person. Because ideas, values, and issues seldom exist or have interest for us apart from the human beings whose

lives are affected by them, knowing how to bring people—character—into almost any essay or report can increase the impact it has on the audience. But "characterization" has a larger potential: The same techniques that bring people alive on the page of a novel can be applied as guidelines for selecting details from other types of subjects. If you wanted to report on a business operation in the Bahamas, for example, or on current developments in nuclear reactors, you could look for the same categories you sought out in characterizing your grandfather: *physical details, actions, background, speech, environment*, and *others' reactions*. To characterize is to give a full, rounded view of a subject. Here is how Kathleen Mills characterized the physical education facilities at her high school.

Physical details	The gymnasium was drafty and cold. The old wooden floor had splinters in it and the windows at either end were broken out and boarded over. Lockers had no locks; the
Others's reactions	showers had only cold water. The basketball team from North High refused to dress in our locker rooms. They dressed on their bus and their coach was quoted as saying,
Speech	"It was nothing personal." The students at Jefferson were
Actions	part of the problem. They had torn out the toilets two
A self-created environment	years before after losing a game. They ripped locker doors off the hinges. Three times during the four years I
Actions	attended, the local PTA tried to raise funds for restoring
Background	and painting but the neighborhood had deteriorated since the 1950s. Some apartments were empty and boarded up. A large percentage of the population was on welfare. The tax base no longer supported the school, we were told, and
Action	the remaining residents would not support the PTA. Finally, in my senior year, ten seniors took to the school board a petition signed by over two hundred students.
Lack of action	They demanded better facilities. The school board promised to look into the situation but nothing was ever done.

Using the 4 *C*'s of observation offers no guarantee you'll find the most important factual details in every subject, but if you encounter a subject you don't know how to write about or if you don't know how to begin a report, ask yourself:

1. Is there an element of *change*? Is it the most interesting or important point in the subject?
2. Does any element of the subject involve *contrast, conflict, contradiction*, or *opposition*? Could the best details be organized around one of those categories?
3. What quality about the subject has led to significant *consequences*? To whom or to what aspect of the subject are the consequences important? Whose lives are affected?

4. How could this subject be *characterized*? Which of the elements of characterization seem most consequential? (Physical description? Action? Background? Speech?) Is a full, rounded view of the subject what the reader needs or expects?

OBTAINING FACTS FROM OTHERS

Relying solely on personal experience suggests obvious inadequacies: We cannot be in all places at once; we cannot always separate our emotions from the facts observed; we cannot be experts in all subjects. Others' views are necessary to formulating an objective and balanced understanding of a subject. In careers outside the academic world, writing often depends on interviewing as a major source of information. Historians talk to those who were there; biographers talk to those who remember; technical writers talk to engineers; medical writers talk to researchers. Even within the university, a student of political science, social work, anthropology, psychology, or sociology will recognize that significant amounts of data, almost all in many cases, are derived from surveys or interviews. An interview often provides information unobtainable from any other source, and it offers the writer a natural way to introduce human interest—and a human voice—into an otherwise objective report.

Preparation

Almost everyone agrees, the more you already know about a subject, the better you can question someone else on it. The first step in interviewing begins with research into whatever subject you're investigating—the university parking problem, the success or failure of the antischoolbook committee in your locality, the farm crisis—it really doesn't matter. You need background details. If it's a campus controversy, begin with back issues of the student newspaper. If it's a local or national topic, search through city newspapers or national news magazines. Know as much as possible before you begin the interview, not to show off, but to seem reasonably well-informed and intelligent—and to make your questions more substantive.

The second step is to ensure a positive reception for the interview. Don't just "drop by." Make an appointment. Tell the person you want to interview what your subject is, why you want the interview, why you think he or she can be indispensable in helping you, and how much time you will need (fifteen minutes to half an hour is usually enough). All this is only courtesy. It makes you seem levelheaded and professional.

Third, before you go, create a list of five to ten questions. Be prepared, of course, to follow up new points or unexpected answers that arise during the conversation. Your prepared questions are only a guide, not something to stick to religiously.

Fourth, don't take a tape recorder. A number of wonderful interviews have been accomplished with tapes, such as Studs Terkel's *Working*, but difficulties abound. Microphones inhibit many individuals. Batteries fail. Tapes run out. More important, you may depend on the machine rather than on your intellect and imagination. Better to carry an old-fashioned note pad and jot down answers as you go. If necessary, don't hesitate to say, "Wait a second while I write that down." Don't be embarrassed to take notes. That's why you're there.

Questioning

The value of the information acquired in an interview is determined in part by the type of question you ask. Avoid the question that requires only a yes-or-no answer.

> Do you believe we ought to have a better campus police force?

Such questions might be valid for a survey, but you want more depth from a personal interview. Always formulate a number of questions in advance based on what you already know and on what you need to know.

> Thirteen rapes were reported on the State University campus last year. What kind of problem do we face here?

> Recently a number of letters to the editor in the campus paper have complained about theft in the dormitories. Do you think the problem is "out of control," as one letter writer suggested?

The phrasing of each question is vital. If you reveal bias or seem to be attacking the person you are interviewing, you may bring the interview to an abrupt end.

> Campus security is obviously inadequate. What are you going to do about it?

The shape of such a question, the emotional tone, inhibits a free exchange of information. Take time in advance to compose wording that makes each question seem open-minded, fair, and objective.

What measures are being taken to improve campus security, or do you feel current procedures are working effectively?

Follow up answers by asking for supporting facts or concrete examples.

Can you give me statistics on that?

Exactly how many cases of theft were reported to your office last year?

Are records available to show whether crime on campus has increased or decreased?

Listening

Most professionals insist that learning how to listen is the most vital element in an interview. A good interview must flow like a good conversation. If you merely read off that prepared list of questions or if you fail to follow up on answers, you might as well conduct the interview by mail. Here is the wrong way to go about it:

Question:	Do you feel America has an evenhanded policy in the Middle East?
Answer:	We've had one of the most biased and misguided policies that could have been devised.
Question:	How important is Saudi Arabian oil?

The second question ignores the answer. The person interviewed can only assume you haven't listened or that you're not genuinely interested. Future answers will become more perfunctory. You'll probably find it more helpful to repeat the central point of an answer (this helps you remember it while making clear to the person interviewed that you're listening) and then to ask for further clarification or explanation.

Follow-up question:	You say "biased and misguided." Could we look at each of these points separately? In what way has American policy been biased? In whose favor? And why?

Now you've engaged in a dialogue. Perceiving that you're alert and interested, the person interviewed will freely expand on his or her ideas.

A dialogue, however, does not mean you should take sides. Even if you personally disagree or find flaw in what you're hearing, avoid a direct argument.

But you're contradicting yourself now. You don't have a single fact to prove your point.

Instead, phrase your follow-up in such a way that you press hard for the answer but seem to be attributing your aggressiveness or disagreement to what others might say when they read your report.

> I wonder if others would see this as a contradiction to a point you made earlier?
>
> Could you give me any evidence to support that point?

Listen intently. Follow up. Train your ear to select important facts from others' observations in the same way you train your eye to observe minute details from personal experience.

Taking Notes

Although I said earlier that you should feel perfectly comfortable taking notes during the interview, it can sometimes prove best to avoid writing notes until *after* the interview. Except for a few direct quotations where actual wording is important, plan to write the rest from memory. After all, most of any interview will be summarized, and what you really want is the essence of someone's view on your subject, not the whole of it. During the interview select only a few important or colorful quotations to record. Then immediately afterward—in the hall, in the park across the street, on the bus going home—write out the whole interview. Use the techniques practiced in earlier assignments: Describe the place of the interview, the light, smells, sounds. Show the character, the physical details, speech patterns, actions. Put all of it into a scene. Leave yourself out of it for the most part. Focus instead on the opinions, ideas, and attitudes of the person interviewed. Blend in the specific quotations you wrote during the interview. Summarize the rest in your own words. Be fair and honest. Present the person's position objectively and accurately.

Now you have *complete* notes, even if scrawled roughly in pencil. From them you will probably select only a small portion to use in your final essay, but the full record is down on paper, far more thoroughly than a tape recorder could have captured it. Even better, in the act of writing down a complete record of the interview, your mind will select, organize, and evaluate all that you saw and heard. The act of writing stimulates the act of evaluating.

Evaluating

Just as you cannot always separate your own emotions from external facts, neither can others. You must assume that many answers you hear will reflect some degree of self-interest or bias. It will always be your job, both during and after an interview, to distinguish facts from opinions or inferences. You must ask yourself, Does this answer show a hidden emotional element? What are the consequences of such an answer? Am I hearing an opinion or a verifiable fact?

Opinions may form a part of any objective report so long as they are attributed to your source ("Dr. Harrison believes. . . ." "Captain Miller thinks. . . .") and do not derive from your own bias. For some subjects, opinions may be as important as the facts themselves. But any interview that tends to be opinionated should be balanced with an interview providing another side of the issue. You have no control over others' opinions, but you must demonstrate your own objectivity by presenting a balanced and fair report that includes equal representation of every point of view.

Learning how to obtain information from others extends your range of observation. Combined with the 4-*C*'s approach, it provides you with a tool for moving outside the limitations of personal feelings and personal experience—as you must if you are to begin to explore and write about the world you live in.

Exercises

1. Discuss how *change, contrast, consequence,* or *characterization* might be a way of finding the best factual details about the following. Which of the 4-*C*'s methods or which combination might be useful in investigating each topic?

tuition increases
the grading system at your
  college
drinking or drugs on campus
off-campus housing conditions
censorship policy for the student
  newspaper
parking regulations

professional college athletes
bookstore profits
budget-cutting effects
class attendance regulations
coed dormitories
campus security
cafeteria food

2. With others in your class, make a list of people you might ask for information about three or four of the above topics.

Journal Practice

In addition to your daily freewriting, challenge yourself to move outside your immediate self. Begin writing about broader issues.

1. Make a list of concerns you have now about problems on your campus—something you'd like to know more about. Perhaps you're annoyed by bookstore prices, by the limited availability of campus computers, or maybe a community issue has you worried. List your concerns in question form. Questioning often triggers more questions, more possibilities.

2. Select one issue from your list and begin writing about it spontaneously, voicing your concerns and your questions. What do you know about your subject? What do you need to find out about?

3. The first step in finding out is to ask someone who should be in a position to know. Think of anyone you might talk to who could provide more information.

Before you talk to the person, create an interview web in your journal to provide a quick visual reminder of what you need to know.

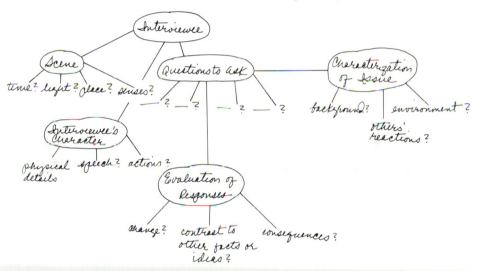

Take your journal to the interview with you but don't fill it in until you've finished. Jot down material you want to quote and brief words and phrases that will jostle your memory later. Once you're back at your desk, and within an hour or so after the interview, fill in the web with specifics. Then write a rough draft of the interview in your journal, trying to fill three full pages.

Audience

14

Context, Purpose, and Voice

Unlike personal writing, for which you could expect a sympathetic audience, perhaps even a friendly audience that wants to share your feelings and experience, no such simple generalization can be made for informative writing. Too many variables exist. In certain situations, the audience for informative writing may want straightforward, no-nonsense facts. In other situations, your audience may appreciate a more informal voice, even a personal voice, while still reading for objective information. Everything depends on four interacting elements: the subject, the audience's needs, the context (or situation), and your own purpose.

Most of the time these four factors are defined for you in advance. In college your instructor assigns an essay on the French Revolution (*subject*); your paper will be evaluated to determine how well you know the subject, and it will count as part of your final grade (*context*); your instructor alone will read it (*audience*); and in the process of investigating the subject, you determine which particular aspect you wish to explore and what you want to say about it (*purpose*). In the career world, a similar situation will usually influence your writing projects. Your supervisor will assign you to write a report on whether your company is meeting environmental regulations (*subject*); the report will be used by company officials to prepare for an upcoming federal inspection (*context*); your supervisor, the company vice-president, and several government agents will read it (*audience*); and although the report must be accurate, it must also present the company's efforts in a positive light (*purpose*).

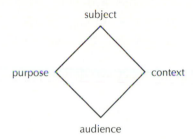

Once you make the leap from personal writing into more objective forms of writing, the demands on you increase rapidly. Yet this relationship of subject-audience-context-purpose does not necessarily make the act of writing as difficult as it may sound. In many cases, knowing the four points of influence actually simplifies your job by clearly defining what you need to write about and how you must approach it. All four points in combination also determine the voice and tone you will use. Because that voice can be significantly different from the voice you use in personal writing, we need to look at some of the options open to you.

OBJECTIVE REPORTING: THE FORMAL VOICE

The most objective writing is usually found in scientific work where the voice must be formal and the tone objective. No element of your personality or inner feelings should be apparent. In scientific reporting, your audience will desire facts alone. Here is a report on Martian landing sites from *Scientific Results of the Viking Project.*

> Both sites are dominated by a variety of rocks among fine-grained material, and both have the brownish to orange color of the surface and the sky. Beyond this superficial similarity the sites are quite different in their appearance. The Chryse site topography is undulating and has a great range of rock size and type from rocks a few centimeters across to one nearby large rock almost 2 m across and others

in the distance much larger. . . . No evidence of life has been found
in the pictures at either site.

The tone here is factual and unemotional. The avoidance of either positive or negative connotations modulates the voice and creates a neutral effect. Even the last sentence shows no trace of personal emotion (although it may have stirred a feeling of regret in the scientists). Instead, we receive only a straightforward statement of observable fact—in this case, concrete, sensory details observed in a photograph.

The use of the pronoun *one* in place of *I* or *we* is sometimes associated with formal writing. The *one* creates a distance between writer and reader and may sometimes be necessary. But note that the NASA scientists who reported on the Viking Project avoided its use altogether. The use of *one* too often creates awkward sentences where the pronoun tends to pile up in clusters that sound contrived. Here is how a university scholar misuses it in a book on poetry.

When one begins writing poetry one tends to use language that convinces one that it is truly poetry that is being written. One uses a special voice . . .

Try reading such sentences aloud, and you find that the excessive repetition of *one* begins to feel like marbles in the mouth.

The use of *one* can be necessary at times, but it works best when it does not call attention to itself. Here is an objective report on Alaskan snow in which the *one* blends easily and unobtrusively.

There are different kinds of snow. New-fallen snow yields almost silently underfoot. Midwinter snow is dry, and squeaks and crunches as one walks through it, while spring snow is tired and crackles as the crust resists, then breaks. Wind-driven snow is riffled like lace or like the whitecaps of the sea, and it sparkles with flashes of blue, yellow, orange, and green.

Tom Walker, writing in a book entitled *We Live in the Alaskan Bush*, has so skillfully blended the objective *one* into this passage that a reader might miss it entirely—which is what should happen.

OBJECTIVE REPORTING: THE INFORMAL VOICE

In many situations, when context and audience are appropriate, the informal voice may be used quite successfully with objective writing. Naturally, the author must still avoid intrusion of personal feelings or emotions, but the notion that all objective writing must be dull is mistaken. The following is a report on the sloth bear from the *Audubon Society Book of Wild Animals.*

> Termites are a staple of the sloth bear (*Melurus ursinus*) of the Indian subcontinent and Sri Lanka, and to get at the insects this dim-sighted creature has evolved a snout that approximates a vacuum cleaner. The lips of the sloth bear are hairless and flexible and can be protruded like a tube a considerable distance from the mouth. The bear can close its nostrils whenever it wishes. After digging open a termite mound, the bear literally huffs and puffs to uncover and ingest its prey. Puckering its lips into a tube, with its nostrils shut to keep out dust, it blows away the loose dirt to expose the termites, then sucks them in, a process facilitated by a gap in its teeth resulting from the absence of two upper incisors.

Although the reporting here is objective—each fact can be verified by a second observer—the tone is lighter and more casual. The active verbs (more than ten in five sentences) and the humorous imagery (a snout like a vacuum cleaner, huffing and puffing, sucking termites between a gap in the teeth) make the writing lively and interesting. Yet no personal emotion, opinion, or bias appears. The Audubon Society has produced a book for informative reading but one meant to entertain at the same time. Context and purpose justify the informal voice.

OBJECTIVE REPORTING: THE FIRST PERSON

Writers for more popular magazines often use the first person while still reporting objective information. The admission that a human being is behind the observation tends, naturally, to create a more personal and informal tone. At one time, such reporting was avoided. Writers went to great length to objectify or disguise their presence, sometimes using such awkward phrases as "This reporter saw . . ." or "The writer has noticed that . . ." Today the trend is toward an honest admission that *I,* the writer, exists as a person but that he or she also has the ability to report objectively. After all, the use of *one* or the neutral, objective tone in the scientific voice is only a subterfuge. A writer still exists. He or she is a human being, and because the writer has consciously selected some details to present while omitting others, we know that the writer's personal imagination is actively involved. Total objectivity is impossible.

   Here, then, is how Jane Winslow Eliot reports for *The Atlantic* on winemaking in Spain in the 1930s.

By the light of one candle I saw three men inside the vat. Their coats were off, their trousers rolled above the knees. They hung onto knotted ropes which were looped over the rafters, and, barefoot, they rhythmically stomped the slippery grapes. Sweating, faces distorted by candlelight, they shouted back and forth as friends came to watch. Fumes began to rise, and their footing became less sure, their laughter louder. A new basket of grapes was tipped into the vat. Twirling around and around, one man lost his grip. With a splash he fell into the richly reeking mash.

The concrete details make the scene rich and sensuous, perhaps even evoking emotion in the reader. Yet the writer herself injects no undue inferences or opinions. Eliot presents a verifiable report, but she uses a personal voice that candidly admits, "I was there, and I'm reporting what I saw." In a different context, of course, and for a different purpose and audience, this voice might be highly inappropriate. You must determine the subject-audience-context-purpose *before* you begin to write; otherwise, you will find yourself working in a vacuum and merely guessing or hoping that the way you treat your material will be successful.

Exercises

1. Read each of the following selections. (a) Identify the level of formality or informality. (b) Describe a *context, purpose,* and *audience* for which each passage might be appropriate. (c) Describe a *context, purpose,* and *audience* for which the voice and tone would be highly inappropriate or less effective.

(1) Some hermit crabs have developed a relationship with a group of anemones that benefits both creatures. Relations like these are called symbiotic relations. Once it has found a shell, the hermit crab finds a special kind of anemone that has tentacles which sting and irritate fish and other potential enemies. In some cases the anemone climbs on the hermit crab's shell and plants itself there. In other cases there seems to be some complex communication based on touch between the hermit crab and the anemone. They tap and touch each other, and the anemone then releases its grip on the rock it clings to and plants itself on the hermit crab's shell.

Judith and Herbert Kohl, *The View from the Oak*

(2) The top of a maple leaf is dark green with green-yellow lines running through it. These lines are fairly straight and seem to

branch off into smaller and smaller lines, which give the surface of the leaf a scale-like appearance. The leaf is thin, about the thickness of two sheets of paper. It is about four inches wide, measuring from tip to tip, and about four inches long. At the bottom of the leaf there is a thin, pliable tube which seems to connect with the largest of the green-yellow lines.

Student Report

(3) The eel is a fish which believes in long journeys. It is spawned in the Sargasso Sea in the western Atlantic, and from there will travel back to its fresh water haunts in this country or in Europe to feed and grow up in the rivers and streams frequented by its parents. The young eel or elver is still only 2 or 3 inches longer after its immense journey, and is transparent and yellowish. . . . As with cats, there is more than one way to skin a fresh eel. We prefer the following. Slip a noose around the eel's head and hang the other end of the cord on a hook, high on the wall. Cut the eel skin about 3 inches below the head all around, so as not to penetrate the gall bladder which lies close to the head. Peel the skin back, pulling down hard—if necessary with a pair of pliers—until the whole skin comes off like a glove.

Rombauer and Becker, The Joy of Cooking

(4) Committing the mind to one approach for a long period of time with no evident prospect of success is a mistake. Of course, the length of time one should devote to any one approach cannot be stated in advance. It depends on the difficulty of the problem. But if one does not seem to be making any progress the thing to do is to try to break from that pattern of thought, though it is very hard to give up once one starts to think along that line. What one should do is probably forget the whole thing and come back to it sometime later when that mental groove has disappeared.

Morris Kline, The Creative Experience

2. Rewrite the following passage to make it more informal. Use the personal *I* instead of *one.* Try to find strong verbs to replace weak ones.

A decline in energy is observed as the team continues its workout. The gymnasts who are on the rings show fatigue early. One notices that the faces begin to turn red and the veins bulge in the throat. If one looks closely, one also sees a slight quivering in the biceps as the exercises continue. Even after the rings have been released and the student is back on the mat, the shoulder and back muscles often can be observed to twitch involuntarily.

Journal Practice

1. Copy three different voices. Try the scientific voice of the Viking Project (pp. 159–160), a more informal voice in the passage on the sloth bear (p. 161), and the personal voice used to describe winemaking (p. 162).

2. Here is how the Brothers Grimm wrote about "Little Red Riding Hood."

> "But Grandmother," she said, "what big eyes you have!"
> "The better to see you with, my child," was the reply.

And here is humorist and journalist Russell Baker telling the same tale in the voice of exaggerated objectivity.

> "Grandmother," she said, "your ocular implements are of an extraordinary order of magnitude."
>
> "The purpose of this enlarged viewing capability," said the wolf, "is to enable your image to register a more precise impression upon my sight systems."

Retell a folk or fairy tale in a different voice. Use a hyped-up streetwise voice or the formal voice of an official government notice.

Drafting and the Discovery of Form

15

The 5 *W* Lead and the Inverted Pyramid

For most writers, not just beginning writers but all of us, finding the right order for the right content becomes a major stumbling block to success. To avoid the struggle and to save time, news reporters sometimes use a formula for organizing factual information. This formula gives them a ready form in which to shape their material. You should know it as well, because it is the simplest and easiest of all forms to learn and because it provides a natural starting point for objective reporting. It teaches you how to discipline facts, and it can be used for many other types of informative writing.

THE 5 *W* LEAD

As you develop your writing skills and become involved in complex interpretation and analysis of a subject, you will need to practice the art of creating an effective *thesis statement* (Chapter 26), but straight reporting of objective facts requires a simpler, although equally effective, type of introduction. Professional writers call it the *5 W Lead*. A lead informs the reader of the five most important facts about the subject: *who, what, where, when,* and *why*. The facts may be organized in any sequence, according to which elements are most important.

The 5 *W* lead began as a journalistic device, and an experienced reporter can usually handle all five elements in the first sentence alone.

> *who*   *where*   *when*
> Sen. Howard M. Metzenbaum, D-Ohio, said in Washington Saturday
>   *what*
> he will introduce a major piece of legislation next week,
>   *why*
> designed to upgrade parks, playgrounds, and other recreational areas in American cities.

> *where*   *when*   *who*   *what*
> In Baltimore last week Peter L. McCrystal, 15, broke the world's
>   *why*
> chewing gum record just to win a ten-cent bet.

The 5 *W* lead groups and organizes information that might otherwise have appeared randomly throughout a news story. By shaping the material in this way, the reader receives all major facts immediately. Everything that follows the lead will support or elaborate on the major facts. But just as you probably don't plan to become a novelist who writes about character, you probably don't plan to become a journalist. How, then, does the 5 *W* lead apply to the type of writing you may be doing?

Here is how one student began a report for a sociology class.

> *who*   *where*   *what*
> A white, Anglo-Saxon Protestant in America is socially mobile because
>   *why*
> achievement rather than background is the determining factor. For
> *who*   *what*
> blacks and Jews, social mobility is restricted regardless of achieve-
>   *why*
> ment since color and religion are influencing factors.

By selecting all the important facts and organizing them according to the 5 *W*'s, the student has pulled together a surprisingly clear statement about her subject. The reader knows immediately what to expect in succeeding paragraphs—development or elaboration of details that support the statement and perhaps, depending on the type of report, an explanation of why such different patterns of social mobility exist.

Here is another example of the 5 *W* lead used for a business report in a class on macroeconomic theory.

>   *when*   *who*
> During his first administration, Ronald Reagan initiated
>   *what*   *why*
> supply-side economics, in part to end deficit spending, but by 1986,
>   *when*   *what*
> the mid-point of his second term in office, deficit spending exceeded
> $200 million per year.

This student has begun an informative essay by shaping his opening sentence around the most important facts. The reader is now prepared for succeeding paragraphs to provide evidence that supports the 5 *W* claim.

Even students of the humanities have found the 5 *W* lead effective. Here is how one sophomore began a report for a literature class.

>   *where*   *when*   *who*   *what*
> In *The Bell Jar*, first published in 1963, Sylvia Plath recounts the
> events of a young girl's twentieth year, her attempted suicide, and
> her struggle to avoid madness.

The 5 *W* lead is an all-around serviceable introduction for almost any kind of informative writing. It communicates the facts clearly and concisely. And because starting a first draft is often the point at which writers have the most difficulty, the 5 *W* lead offers a simple strategy for organizing information and getting the first sentence or first paragraph on the page.

Equally important, the lead can immediately suggest an organization for the rest of your report.

THE INVERTED PYRAMID

Let's return one more time to how all this was developed by journalists. Because of the constriction of space in a newspaper and because hurried readers often do not read to the end of a news story, the 5 *W* lead became a technique for presenting vital information as quickly as possible. But the nature of journalism also imposed another constriction on the reporter and predetermined the organization of remaining material. Until the final moments before a newspaper goes to press, neither the reporter nor the editor may know how much space is available for any one story. The writer must be prepared, then, for the editor literally to take scissors to a report (or more likely, to press the delete button on his word processor) so that it will fill the appropriate column. This means that all important supporting details must be presented early, followed by interesting details, and finally mere details. The editor can easily delete "mere" details without any great loss. The editor can even cut the story in half and remove the "interesting" details, still without damaging the important supporting information that follows the lead. The reporter has thus learned to envision the organization of his or her story in the form of an upside-down pyramid.

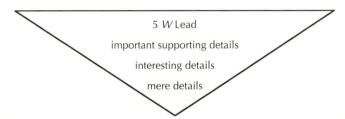

5 *W* Lead

important supporting details

interesting details

mere details

The technique is also used in laboratory and engineering reports as well as in formal business reports. A busy executive, for example, does not necessarily have time to read through twenty pages of details. The executive wants and needs to know important information immediately, at the beginning of the report. He or she does not want to be kept in suspense as to what it all means. But the inverted pyramid design also creates a problem because, by its nature, it fails to come to a conclusion. Other than in the field of journalism, few situations exist in which you will ever be allowed to drift off with "mere" details. On the assumption that you have engaged your intelligence with the subject at all, you will want to do more—and your reader will expect more. If nothing else, you must at least summarize your findings. Better, you must draw a reasonable inference from the facts you have gathered and come to a concluding generalization. Even the business executive will expect a final paragraph that at least restates or reinforces the 5 *W* lead. Here, then, is how we might modify the inverted pyramid so that it can serve you as a visual pattern for organizing objective essays in college and in other career situations.

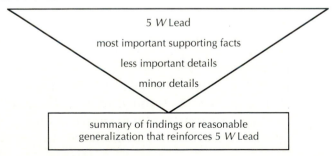

5 *W* Lead

most important supporting facts

less important details

minor details

summary of findings or reasonable
generalization that reinforces 5 *W* Lead

Freshmen Michelle Newburg and Ted Larkin used such a form to organize a report assigned as part of a group project on pornography for a class in religion and contemporary values. Here are excerpts from that report that illustrate the pattern.

5 W lead	According to Ralph Hendleman, the manager of the World Cinema, customers for his X-rated movies are generally upper-class businessmen from the exclusive suburb of Marlborough Heights, where the theater is located. . . .
Most important supporting facts	We spent a total of six hours observing the type of customer entering and leaving the theater on two separate afternoons. During that time we counted sixty-one men and four women entering the theater, all well dressed, some carrying briefcases. Only seven seemed to be younger than twenty-five. The majority seemed to be in their forties and fifties. Forty-seven arrived alone in automobiles that were parked to the side of the theater. Of the forty-seven cars, nine were Cadillacs; nine were Buicks, Oldsmobiles, or Toronados; seven were foreign sports cars, including one red Porsche driven by a woman. . . .
Interesting details (background)	Until 1981 the theater showed traditional Hollywood films but lost money, according to Hendleman. Since the introduction of X-rated films, the theater has shown a profit each year. . . .
Least important details	The theater is located next door to a shoe store and an exclusive jewelry shop. . . .
Concluding generalization	Since we did not interview any of the customers, we cannot speculate on the psychology that motivates attendance at this particular X-rated theater. But from our observations we believe that the customers seemed to be financially well off, primarily male, and probably of the upper managerial level. Other theaters might attract a different type of customer. We believe, however, that it is reasonable to conclude that the World Cinema shows pornographic films because there is a willing-to-pay audience among the supposedly better educated and socially higher classes in our society.

This most-important-to-least-important method of organizing is not the only pattern that can evolve from the 5 *W* lead. Any one element or combination of elements from the lead may form the focus of your organization. The lead for the student's paper on social mobility (page 166), for example, might suggest that the *why* is the key question a reader would be interested in. The writer could supply supporting factual evidence to defend the lead, then move quickly into an interview with a sociologist on why such a social pattern exists. The lead might equally suggest that the report will be organized around the contrast between the two groups being discussed (in several later chapters I will develop the contrast design more fully). In turn, the lead for the student business report (page 167) implies that the *what* and *who* will be pursued: What went wrong and who was responsible for a huge deficit? In other words, the value of the 5 *W* lead lies in its potential for serving you and the reader with a concise, clear statement of your findings in the first sentence or paragraph and then in *suggesting* a possible organization to follow. The very act of looking for the 5 *W* lead in your material actually forces you to begin a process of discovering your purpose, selecting the most important facts, and organizing them concisely.

AND THEN THERE'S *HOW*

I've left out a final but important element. To the 5 *W*'s, reporters often add an *H*—for *how* an event happens, *how* an engine works, *how* the civil rights act was created, *how* the stock market reacts to interest rates. Obviously a factual report for business, science, medicine, engineering, history—even advertising or a creative art—may be more concerned with *how* than almost any other approach to the subject. Yet because the how of something is often complex and detailed, it is seldom used as a lead. Instead, the lead may consist of some element of the 5 *W*'s plus the *H*.

> *what*   *who*
> Industrial alcohol is produced by the Gehrneight Corporation for use in
>   *how*
> antifreeze and industrial solvents. Through a process of fermentation,
> glucose and fructose (usually derived from cane-sugar or beet-sugar
> molasses), alcohol, and carbon dioxide are created by a catalytic
> action of enzymes. The molasses is first distilled with water. . . .

And so on. The remainder of the report takes its own organic shape, that is, it follows the natural step-by-step process of *how* industrial alcohol is made. Chronological order, spatial order, and logical sequence, rather than a predetermined form, usually determine the organization of the report. Yet note that even when objectively describing *how* something works, or *how* it is created, or *how* it is accomplished, *what* happens, *when* and *where*, by *whom*, and *why* will often remain key elements.

The strategy of searching out 5 *W*'s and one *H* can therefore be one of the most valuable techniques you can train the mind to use. A word of caution, however: Your writing will quickly become dull if you use such formulas in everything. Be selective. When the subject-context-audience-purpose calls for a simple but factual presentation, the strategy will serve you well. Other audiences, other contexts, may be responsive only to fresher, more creative designs. Eugene O'Neill once said that "a man's work is in danger of deteriorating when he thinks he has found the best formula for doing it."

Exercises

1. Identify the 5 *W*'s in the following leads.

   A spokesman for the firefighter's union said Wednesday that negotiations with city hall have been broken off until the mayor is willing to be more flexible.

   Marketing conditions have remained unstable during the last six months because of inflationary pressures. The Federal Reserve Bank in Washington has increased prime interest rates three times. Investment conditions could not be worse.

   The English Advisory Board believes that current requirements in the English department are arbitrary and inflexible. A review of requirements at other colleges shows that students elsewhere have more opportunity to make selections from clusters of related-area courses.

   Professor Mike Kepple, chairperson of the chemistry department at Milligan College, has been elected chairperson of the National Honors Colloquium, to be held on the University of Southern California campus next fall.

2. Write three different 5 *W* leads based on the same set of facts.

   a. John Smith is director of public relations at Simkon Foundry.
   b. The foundry has decided to donate $5,000,000 to the United Appeal.
   c. United Appeal will divide the money among the Boy Scouts, the Children's Hospital, and Mothers for Peace.
   d. Bentley V. Cunningham is chairman of the board that made the decision.
   e. The stockholders voted last April on the issue.
   f. The vote passed by only 52 percent.
   g. Smith made the announcement public on Tuesday, August 7.
   h. Cunningham hopes the gift will create goodwill for the foundry.
   i. Simkon Foundry has been located in the city for twenty years.

j. Claire Wilson, representative of a minority group of stockholders, spoke out against what she called a "giveaway" of stockholder profits.

k. Cunningham personally delivered the check into the hands of Bennett Goodman, president of the United Appeal.

Revising

16

Reshaping, Rearranging, Integrating

I can't understand how anyone can write without rewriting everything over and over again.

LEO TOLSTOY

The most serious error the beginning writer can commit is to write only a single draft and assume the writing process is complete. You might at first believe that objective reporting would require less rewriting than a personal essay. After all, you're dealing with facts, not struggling to express inner feelings. Although the problems seem different, the demands on you are similar: to find precise words, to discover the best arrangement of parts, to blend or join each part so that the whole of it reads clearly. If we consider the various needs for informative reporting, the complexities become more apparent.

1. Objective observation of factual detail.
2. A focus on elements of change or contrast (if significant).

3. A focus on major consequences.
4. Characterization of the subject as a whole (including actions, physical description, background, and so on).
5. Understanding of the subject-audience-context-purpose.
6. A lead that clearly presents all major facts in a sentence or two.
7. An organization that flows naturally out of the lead and serves the subject-audience-context purpose.

To do all of this well in a first draft would be impossible for most of us. Even when we feel we have a subject well in hand, some elements of a paper always seem to get muddled. Here are four paragraphs of a rough draft by freshman Melvin Chase. In the first paragraph the 5 *W* lead shows he has found his purpose and made a clear statement that ought to lead him into an easy-flowing organization. With only minor editing the second paragraph can probably stand as it is, for it does provide specific support for the lead. But the next two paragraphs present serious problems.

5 W lead

A new organization in Cleveland, the Committee Against Cancer, is working to ban all cigarette advertising. The CAC claims that dangerous products should be forbidden public promotion. A pamphlet distributed last Wednesday on the Western Reserve campus claimed that an average reader of newspapers and magazines is exposed to 3,000 advertisements for cigarettes each year. But not only is the CAC claim suspect, the organization's efforts may be unconstitutional.

Specific factual details

First, to test their claim, I surveyed newspapers and magazines subscribed to by my own family. In the October issue of *McCall's*, I counted five cigarette advertisements. There were nine in the same month's issue of *Playboy* and three in the Wednesday, October 3, edition of the *Cleveland Plain Dealer*. The Sunday, October 7, edition of the paper contained one full-page color advertisement for True and four other half- or quarter-page ads for other brands.

Evaluates facts

If my family is typical, it might read as many as 100 advertisements for cigarettes each month in such publications—a total of approximately 1,200 per year and far below the CAC claim.

Source not identified fully—who is Brooks?

Connection with first paragraph is unclear— doesn't speak directly to the issue

When I interviewed Benjamin Brooks, he said, ''The evidence is tenuous. Our own research is ongoing and not yet conclusive either way, but we've found that moderate smoking does no more damage to your health than moderate drinking of wine at mealtimes or moderate eating of candy or almost anything else taken in moderation. I'm just not convinced that because rats get cancer when forced to smoke a hundred cigarettes a day

Quotation becomes too long, rambling

that people who are smoking only maybe twenty a day are going to get cancer. There are dozens, hundreds of kinds of cancer, you know. Well, I can't understand why people want to ban advertising tobacco as if it caused all those kinds.

Finally relates to advertising

No one wants to ban alcohol or beer or candy advertisements and they could cause cancer too for all we know. It's our legal and constitutional right to advertise like any other product. Even if you ban all cigarette advertising it won't stop people from smoking. After they banned it on TV our sales actually went up."

Good, but his authority should come earlier

I asked him about his qualifications to speak on the subject and he told me that he had worked as a district representative for the R.J. Reynolds Tobacco Company for ten years.

Characterization details are adequate but seem tacked on

He is a large, robust man with blond hair that is going bald. He smoked a cigarette while I interviewed him in his office. He spoke very forcefully.

Chase was aware of the problems encountered in his report as it moved along, but he felt unsure about how to solve them. For him, as for most of us—especially when working with facts and opinions collected from others—revising is often a process of selecting only the best statements for quotation, summarizing other parts, and integrating the two. We must sharpen the focus of our essays while being careful not to distort the meaning of the information provided by the source.

SUMMARIZING

To summarize is to restate concisely in your own words the essence of a larger work or idea. A person you interview or material you read may provide more information than you need or material not directly relevant to your paper. The long quotation in Melvin Chase's report is an example. Much of it could be selectively omitted; most of it can be summarized in a sentence or two.

Professional writers know that good quotations make writing seem lively. But lengthy quotations or too many quotations can become as tedious as none at all. The reader expects a balance between summary and direct quotation. In general, approximately 80 percent of material taken from other sources (through interviews or reading) should be summarized in your own words. You should summarize only the information or ideas that directly relate to your subject, while being careful not to distort, oversimplify, or in any other way change the meaning of the original. Only the most important element should actually be quoted.

Here is how Melvin Chase summarized a portion of Brooks's statement. Note that although unrelated details have been omitted, the essence of Brooks's ideas has not been changed, only condensed.

Original	*Summary*
The evidence is tenuous. Our own research is ongoing and not yet conclusive either way, but we've found that moderate smoking does no more damage to your health than moderate drinking of wine at mealtimes or moderate eating of candy or almost anything else taken in moderation.	Cancer research by the cigarette companies is inconclusive. The companies believe that moderate smoking is no more harmful than moderate drinking.
I'm just not convinced that because rats get cancer when forced to smoke a hundred cigarettes a day that people who are smoking only maybe twenty a day are going to get cancer. Well, I can't understand why people want to ban advertising tobacco as if it caused all those kinds. No one wants to ban alcohol or beer or candy advertisements and they could cause cancer too for all we know.	The result of laboratory experiments on rats may not apply to people. Brooks doesn't understand why tobacco should be selected for an advertising ban when products like beer and candy are not.

The summary has shortened the original by half. By restating only the main points, the reader's attention is focused more clearly on ideas that contribute directly to the subject.

QUOTING

To quote another person means to use the *exact* words you've heard or read. Although you have a great deal of flexibility in how you integrate those words into your text, you will seldom be forgiven even the smallest inaccuracy. A word omitted or a phrase inverted can change the total meaning of an idea. If you cannot be sure of the exact words, place the idea in your own terms and give credit to your source. Do not use quotation marks unless you can be precise.

The most important element of Benjamin Brooks's statement came at the end. Melvin Chase decided that here Brooks's exact words should be retained.

> "It's our legal and constitutional right to advertise like any other product. Even if you ban all cigarette advertising, it won't stop people from smoking. After they banned it on TV our sales actually went up."

Only three of Brooks's nine sentences will now be used as direct quotation.

INTEGRATING

Finally comes the task of blending all the parts.

Because the purpose of Chase's report is to discuss cigarette advertisements, the beginning of the third paragraph needs to show a related emphasis. Brooks' statement on advertising originally appeared at the end of the interview and seemed lost in all the discussion about cancer, candy, and alcohol. Moving it to the beginning of the third paragraph will more clearly focus the report on the main subject. Many students aren't aware that they have the right to alter a sequence of information from the way it appeared in an original source. *So long as no change in meaning or emphasis is created*, however, you have every obligation to your reader to reorganize and shape your material so that it seems clear and unified.

Here is how Chase joined related concepts.

Original end of second paragraph	. . . If my family is typical, it might read as many as 100 advertisements for cigarettes each month in such publications—a total of approximately 1,200 per year and far below the CAC claim.
New third paragraph	To hear the cigarette companies' side of the issue, I interviewed Benjamin Brooks, who said, "It's our legal and constitutional right to advertise like any other product."

Now the reader moves smoothly between paragraphs, and the connection between related ideas is clearer.

The next step is to identify Brooks's authority to speak on the subject. In general, a speaker needs to be described or identified *before* his or her ideas are given. Chase rewrote the opening of the third paragraph one more time.

Authority inserted	To hear the cigarette companies' side of the issue, I interviewed Benjamin Brooks, district representative for R.J. Reynolds Tobacco Company. Mr. Brooks said, "It's our legal and constitutional right to advertise like any other product."

Depending on the audience, context, and purpose, details describing character may have no place in a formal report. But for a more informal report, or one in which you want to add an element of human interest, such details should be integrated as if you were creating a scene. We need to see actions and description at the same time that we *hear* Brooks speak. Here, then, is how Melvin Chase pulled everything together in the third and fourth paragraphs, omitting unnecessary elements, summarizing related points, and integrating character details and authority into the quoted passages.

> To hear the cigarette companies' side of the issue, I interviewed Benjamin Brooks, district representative for the R.J. Reynolds Tobacco Company. Mr. Brooks, a robust, balding man, spoke forcefully about the "legal and constitutional right to advertise like any other product." He leaned forward in his chair to emphasize his point. "Even if you ban all cigarette advertising," he said, "it won't stop people from smoking. After they banned it on TV our sales actually went up."
>
> Mr. Brooks stressed that cancer research by cigarette companies is inconclusive. The companies believe that moderate smoking is no more harmful than moderate drinking. Brooks himself feels that tobacco products are unfairly selected for an advertising ban when advertisements for other potentially dangerous products such as alcohol and candy are ignored.

The function of drafting is to explore ideas, to get facts on the page. One function of revision is to reshape, rearrange, integrate, and develop these facts and ideas. As Donald Murray has said, "Rewriting is like rubbing a dirty window with a cloth. The more you rub, the clearer the vision on the other side becomes." The normal process for almost all of us is to move from awkward, stumbling prose toward a gradually emerging clarity.

Exercises

1. Summarize in class the following passage in no more than two sentences. A summary should be written in your own words and should constitute the essence of the original without distorting the central idea. Compare your summaries with others in class.

> The mentally healthy freshman comes with a basic sense of industry. Industry is the positive identification with those who know things and know how to do things, with workmanship and task mastery; it

is the capacity to learn how to be, with skill, what one is in the process of becoming; it is the sure knowledge of personal competence. . . . This sense of industry is severely tested. Not necessarily because the academic tasks are too difficult or onerous, but because of the unimaginable number of distractions, temptations, annoyances, and interruptions that ensnare and drag one down to exhaustion. The student is surrounded by seducers, exploiters, entrepreneurs, manipulators, and many hedonists, and a few nihilists.

Hal Crowley, *Forum for Honors*

2. Summarize Denise Levertov's poem on pages 441–442. In your own words, capture the feeling and tone of the poem as well as the reflective pattern of ideas.

3. Assume that you are writing a report on the community relations—or lack of relations—between your college and the surrounding neighborhoods. You obtain an interview with the local mayor or borough representative. From the following exchange, select the most important statement for quotation, decide which material is irrelevant to your study, and summarize the remainder in no more than a couple of sentences.

Interviewer: Do you feel Learning University has achieved satisfactory community relations?

Mayor: We're very proud to have Learning University as a part of our great community.

Interviewer: Some people have suggested that the university locks itself away in an ivory tower and ignores the concerns of the surrounding neighborhoods.

Mayor: Well, you know, I am an alumnus of old Learning U. and it was a fine school. Class of 1955. We had a winning football season for the first time in a decade. Do you play a sport?

Interviewer: No, sir. But I wonder if you might elaborate on how the community looks at the university. Are there specific problems that 10,000 students create? How do the merchants feel? Or the police force?

Mayor: Well, there are always problems, you know. I suppose that we are concerned about the off-campus parking. A lot of residents complain about cars blocking their driveways, that type of thing.

Interviewer: What about the tax base? The university pays no taxes as I understand.

Mayor: That's a particularly sore point with me. Everybody's taxes in
                this community are higher because of the university. There are
                four streets, fifteen light poles, a dozen sidewalks that all cut
                through the university, but the city has to maintain them.
                That means some little old lady on social security has to pay
                property taxes to repave streets for freshmen to ride their bicy-
                cles on. And then there's the cost of fire and police protection.
                Yet the university doesn't pay one cent for all the services we
                provide!

   4. It is sometimes easier to identify faults in others' papers than to
see them in your own. Here is a portion of a first draft. Rewrite it by
rearranging whatever is necessary, omitting irrelevant detail, summarizing, and integrating related parts. The focus of the paper should be
on the lack of social life at this student's college.

> I did a survey of Milligan Hall and found that only 40 percent of
> the students remained on campus last weekend. One student, who
> shall remain nameless because he doesn't want to be identified, told
> me: "I just hate it around here. For kicks I go down and do my
> laundry or maybe watch the squirrels bury nuts in the south quad-
> rangle. I mean, I think the school ought to bring in more movies or
> speakers. We were supposed to have a dance in February but only
> fifteen people showed up. Thirteen were girls." As I talked to this
> student, he told me that he came from a small farm in Iowa and
> that his father owned over one hundred milk cows. He is a freshman
> planning to major in economics.
>
> Another comment I got came from a junior. She told me, "I
> think everyone complains because they don't have enough imagina-
> tion to think of something on their own. I've never been bored a
> minute here. The school has a choral group, a theater club, a dance
> ensemble, a chess tournament, you name it, but everyone wants to
> be entertained instead of getting involved in something and enter-
> taining themselves. Do you see what I mean?" Her name is Barbara
> Walker, and she is a chemistry major from Detroit. She also plays
> flute in the university symphony and paints for a hobby. The day I
> interviewed her, she wore patched Levis and an old paint-spotted
> sweatshirt.

Editing

17

Creating a Professional-Looking Manuscript

She was the first one to complete her course evaluation, and she flipped it defiantly on the table in front of me.

I think you where unfare. every paper I wrote you just bers cut up for commas; and spellings. Grammer. You nver paid attention to my ideas not once so you don't worsb where a hipocrit because you kep't saying the content was the most important think. But when came to my papers it was picky picky like all the other english teacher.

I sometimes wonder how she might have felt had she bought a new Pontiac and found the heater connected with the air-conditioner, the left rear-door handle broken, and both windshield wipers missing. Would she have considered such problems "picky"? Or would she have felt General Motors had been irresponsible?

In your papers the ideas you express do constitute the most important element, but, as in judging automobiles, the overall product, not just engine size, determines quality. The problem seems to arise when, in our role as writers, the ideas we discover seem stimulating and the pleasures of learning overshadow hours of painful reading and note taking in the library. We think our readers should feel equally excited, equally pleased. In the burst of energy it takes to pull together a major paper, such details as spelling and punctuation seem trivial. I used to think so as a student. But the role of the reader is obviously different. The reader has no way of approaching a paper for anything other than what he or she reads on the page. If the reader must study every sentence twice because punctuation is confused or omitted or must pause to decipher words because spelling is erratic, attention is unavoidably diverted from meaning to mechanics. Worse, the reader becomes annoyed and irritated. Like the owner of a carelessly built car with a hidden rattle, the reader of a carelessly constructed paper may well overlook strong points and become obsessed with distracting errors.

The solution is time-consuming but simple. By summoning up a final effort, by proofreading your manuscript for every detail, details that are *your* responsibility, you ensure that the reader will focus on the more important element—your ideas. This final but mandatory phase in editing contains several basic components. You will probably find it necessary to edit for *grammar, usage, spelling,* and *punctuation* before you type your final draft. Attention to *manuscript form* and *proofreading* will then become the last steps you take in the writing process.

The following constitutes an outline of only the most basic elements you should be familiar with. It can never substitute for a full review of grammar and mechanics found in any major handbook.

GRAMMAR

Elementary grammar must be mastered because grammar affects meaning. It may seem annoying when an instructor tells you that your pronouns fail to have a clear reference, but it simply means that in some way you have not communicated successfully. Surely you wouldn't say, "John bought herself a car." You knew from the first words you formed as a child that *he*'s were different kinds of people from *she*'s. Attention to grammar then is little more than attention to the arrangement of words and phrases for the purpose of making them express what you intended to express all along.

Subject-Verb Agreement

Singular subjects take singular verbs; plural subjects take plural verbs.

> John *loves* Jill and Mary.
> Jill and Mary *love* John.

Most of us already know the rule, but most of us also make mistakes from time to time. A problem can arise from confusion about the subject itself. Here are some clarifications:

1. *Collective nouns take singular verbs:*
   The committee *is* being formed.
   The government team *is* in trouble.
   Politics *is* a noble profession.

2. *Compound subjects connected by* and *take plural verbs:*
   Dotty, Betty, Gloria, and Jane *are* feminists.
   The registrar and I *are* having a disagreement.

3. *Compound subjects connected by* either . . . or, neither . . . nor, *or* not only . . . but also *take a verb that agrees with the nearest part of the subject:*
   Neither your mother nor my friends *believe* that you will fail.
   Neither my friends nor your mother *believes* that you will fail.

4. *A subject composed of a complete clause usually takes a singular verb:*
   Whether it rains before breakfast *is* of no concern.

5. *Some words that refer to a plural subject actually take a singular verb* (either, neither, everyone, everybody, anybody, *and* nobody):
   Everyone *loves* a parade.
   Nobody that I know *wants* to see the film again.

Pronouns and Antecedents

Pronouns also should agree in person, number, and gender with the term to which they refer.

1. *A third-person antecedent takes a third-person pronoun:*
   The *girls* rode bicycles to school; *they* all got wet.

2. *A singular antecedent takes a singular pronoun:*
   Roger ran his boat aground where *he* had first sighted the marker.

3. *A masculine antecedent takes a masculine pronoun:*
   Mark Twain was born at an early age; *he* said so himself.

And so on. Few people have problems with pronoun agreement unless the pronouns are separated by too many intervening words or clauses, in which case the solution is usually to repeat the antecedent instead of using a pronoun.

But many of us have problems with *unclear antecedents*. We write too quickly, knowing full well in our minds what we are referring to when we use *it* or *they* or *those*. But the reader, without benefit of insight into our minds, may feel confused unless an antecedent is clearly indicated:

> Steven told his roommate that *his* cat died.

Whose cat? Steven's? Or his roommate's?

> He searched the parking lot but *it* couldn't be found.

The parking lot couldn't be found?

> Botesius destroyed cities, plundered and pillaged the farms, raped helpless women, and then committed himself to the church. *This* was the cause of his downfall.

Which of all those actions does *this* refer to?

As the writer, you know what you mean. But editing is the point in the process where you must read as if you were the reader. Will your reader understand? Not unless each pronoun refers to a specific antecedent.

Misplaced Modifiers

A clause or phrase must modify the word that its position in a sentence suggests it's supposed to modify. When it doesn't, the result can be puzzling:

> Walking along the sidewalk, the falling safe almost struck me.
> Being bright orange, I loved the sunset.
> I wanted a roommate to share expenses with my own moral values.

In the first sentence, the safe seems to have been walking along the sidewalk before it mysteriously fell on the writer. In the second sentence, the writer has turned orange. In the third, the writer apparently has expensive moral values. And yet we know that no such nonsense was intended. The solution is to be more specific . . .

> *As I* walked along the sidewalk, the falling safe almost struck me.

or to rearrange the sentence structure . . .

> I loved the bright orange sunset.

or to pull related phrases more closely together . . .

> I wanted a roommate with my own moral values to share expenses.

Tense Consistency

In general, the reader will more clearly follow an argument if verb tenses are consistent. When you begin in the past tense, make every effort to stay with it unless you have a logical reason for shifting to the present tense. If you begin in the present tense, try to remain in the present. Naturally, occasions arise when shifts in tense are necessary. It is the accidental shifts that cause confusion.

> If my own small experience *is* any guide, the main difficulty in approaching the problem of juvenile delinquency *was* that there *was* very little evidence about it. It *is* unknown, for instance, what the actual effects of prison sentences *were* on the delinquent. Statistics *will be* few and not generally reliable. The narcotics problem alone *was* an almost closed mystery.

By this point the reader's mind is reeling. Past, present, future—just where are we? In the above example, the writer begins in the present and seems to be referring to a current situation. The complete paragraph, then, should probably take the present tense.

> If my own small experience *is* any guide, the main difficulty in approaching the problem of juvenile delinquency *is* that there *is* very little evidence about it. It *is* unknown, for instance, what the actual effects of prison sentences *are* on the delinquent. Statistics *are* few and not generally reliable. The narcotics problem alone *is* an almost closed mystery.

Here are a few general principles regarding verb-tense consistency.

1. If possible, use the same tense throughout an entire paragraph.
2. If possible, use the same tense throughout an entire essay. (Obviously there may be occasions when you are describing a movement from one time period to another in which a shift in tense is necessary.)
3. When a shift in verb tense is essential, signal the reader by moving to a new paragraph or by using a strong transition.
4. Use the present tense in statements that express general philosophical concepts, religious principles, or timeless truths.

Person Consistency

For the same reason that you would hold to a consistent verb tense, logic requires that you hold to a specific use of *person* (first person *I, we,* or *us;* second person *you;* third person *he, she, it,* or *one*).

> If we are unable to function during periods of relatively normal stress, *a person* may revert to actions and thoughts that *you* used in childhood. *He* may withdraw into himself, he may cry, and sometimes *you* can actually see him begin to have a temper tantrum.

Shifts of person distract the reader and disrupt the unity. In general, the same person should be used throughout a paragraph and, if possible, throughout an essay. Many instructors will object especially to using the second person *you* because, as in the above example, the reader may not have seen or felt the qualities being attributed to him or her. Other instructors may object equally to using the first person *I* because it often misleads an inexperienced writer into discussing himself or herself more than the subject. The third person is probably the safest of all forms, especially in formal writing.

> *One* who is unable to function during periods of relatively normal stress may revert to actions and thoughts that *he* or *she* used in childhood. *The person* may withdraw into himself or herself, may cry, and sometimes may actually have a temper tantrum.

Sentence Fragments

Although we frequently use sentence fragments in informal conversation, they may create problems in writing. Encountering a sentence fragment is like reaching the bottom of a staircase and stepping off again as if expecting another step. The sudden jolt makes us realize that something anticipated is missing. When a writer begins a sentence with a capital letter, we anticipate a complete thought. The fragment itself may make perfect sense within the context, but the jolt to our expectations disrupts the flow of the reading.

Sentence fragment	*Revision*
We all hurried back to the hotel for our bags. *Thereby missing the parade.*	We all hurried back to the hotel for our bags, thereby missing the parade.
	or
	We missed the parade because we all hurried back to the hotel for our bags.

I had to make a decision before the end of the term. *To become an economics major or a used-car salesman.*	I had to make a decision before the end of the term: to become an economics major or a used-car salesman.
	or
	Before the end of the term I had to decide whether to become an economics major or a used-car salesman.
The idea is an old one. *Imitating the writing of others to improve your own.*	The idea is an old one: Imitate the writing of others to improve your own.
	or
	Imitating the writing of others to improve your own is an old idea.

Most fragments are grammatically or logically connected with sentences that precede or follow, so most can be eliminated either by joining the fragment to the related sentence with proper punctuation or by incorporating the fragment into the sentence.

However, sentence fragments may be effective even in formal prose if used sparingly and with a sense of control.

> Should we allow ourselves to be dominated by foreign oil interests? *Absolutely not.*
> She began to write poetry for one reason. *To save her life.*
> *Of course!* The answer seemed so simple after all.

USAGE

By custom and long tradition some forms of words and phrases have been accepted as correct or socially acceptable in formal writing. Errors may be considered signs of ignorance. One could argue over whether it should be so, but nonetheless it is so. Here is a very brief list of some common problems young writers often face in *usage*.

Contractions

Contractions like *hasn't, can't, you're,* and *didn't* were once strictly forbidden in formal expository prose. In recent years, books, popular magazines, and most prestigious scholarly journals have shifted toward acceptance. In general, however, contractions are acceptable and effective for personal essays and other types of informal prose, but too casual for a serious formal paper on an idea or value or for a scholarly research paper.

Double Negatives

The old admonishment that two negatives equal a positive is true in mathematics, but for communicating, a double negative succeeds well: *I don't have no pencil* leaves little doubt in the reader's mind about whether you have a pencil. The problem is that a double negative is socially unacceptable. Here are some of the worst offenders.

> *can't hardly* tolerate [for: one can *hardly* tolerate]
> *can't help* but understand [for: *can't help* understanding]
> *did not have scarcely* any [for: *had scarcely* any]

PARAGRAPHING

Every paragraph usually has a focus to which all other ideas in the paragraph relate. It may have a *topic sentence* (a main sentence that expresses the primary idea, often located at the beginning or end). Contemporary writers have somewhat abandoned rigid adherence to using a single controlling sentence. The paragraph today may be glued together by tone or attitude, related images, connecting thoughts, lists, or concepts. Whether you use a single focusing sentence or some other "implied" relationship, the mandatory requirement remains: There must be *unity* and *coherence*. All sentences, all ideas, all elements of tone or image appearing in the same paragraph, must relate in a clear, unified, logical manner.

> ### Weak paragraph
>
> Most men probably don't believe that smoking Marlboros makes them more masculine. They didn't even have this much advertising until after World War II according to *Advertising Age*. What is it exactly that the advertiser is trying to do? The latest advertisement for the Corvette pictures three girls in bikinis playing volleyball on the beach with the car parked behind them. You have to look through the girls to see the car. Vance Packard wrote a book on *The Hidden Persuaders* in advertising that tries to make us afraid of our body odors or makes us have a false hope that our lives will be better if we buy a new toaster oven.

This paragraph lacks coherence and unity. All sentences relate to advertising but they don't relate to each other. The paragraph does not yet have a focusing idea around which to develop supporting ideas.

Strong paragraph

Advertising seems to have two goals—first, to seduce us into looking at or reading the advertisement, and then to convince us in some way that our lives will be better if we only buy. The latest advertisement for the Corvette pictures three girls in bikinis playing volleyball on a beach with the car parked behind them. The girls obviously function only as a means of attracting our attention to the ad. The words on the page then deal with gear ratios, engine horsepower, and electronic ignition. Not sex. Yet sexual elements now seem inescapably associated in some mysterious way with the car. In a similar fashion, a recent advertisement for Marlboro shows a cool green mountain setting with a masculine cowboy on his horse. The object is obviously not to sell real estate or horses, but to attract your attention. The words on the page talk about low nicotine and tar. Yet again, the image of cool masculinity seems as important as the facts. In both cases, and in almost all other examples one might search out, the pattern is the same: Attract the reader's attention, then promote something which seems factual but which also conveys a feeling that the product will enhance your image, if not your life.

Here we have a clear focusing sentence followed by supporting facts and interpretation. The ideas are all related to the topic sentence at the beginning, and the reader finishes the paragraph with a sense of unity and logical coherence.

PUNCTUATION

The goal of punctuation is simply to provide symbols that tell your reader how you want your sentence to be read. The "rules" are actually customs we all agree on, in the same way we agree to drive on the right-hand side of the road. When you break custom, you may feel daring, but you take an undeniable risk.

Commas

1. Use commas to separate clauses, especially in long sentences:

We worked for several hours debating the proposition, a motion to repeal the rights of homosexuals, but it became clear we would never agree.

*In a short sentence, you may omit the comma if the rhythm seems more
effective without it:*
We debated the proposition but we could not agree.

2. *Use commas to separate items in a series:*
His laughter was obnoxious, offensive, and hysterical.
*The final comma may be omitted, although it's best to read the sentence
aloud and determine whether the omission will lead to confusion.*

3. *Use commas to set off long introductory phrases or clauses:*
With the worst of her ordeal yet to come, Barbara decided to
forgo her lunch.

In addition to other errors, he committed a crime against
nature.

4. *Do not use commas to connect two independent clauses (this is often
termed a "comma splice"):*
We watched the boat come in, the people on the dock laughed
at us.
Complete thoughts should obviously be separated by a period.

5. *Do use a comma to connect independent clauses already joined by a con-
junction such as* for, so, but, and, nor, *and* yet:
Professor Harris was unprepared for the question, and his
students were unprepared for the answer.

I knew that she was attracted to me, but I could not find the
courage to ask her out.

Semicolons

1. *Use a semicolon to separate two independent clauses that show a close
relationship (an independent clause is one that can stand alone as a separate
sentence; the semicolon draws such clauses together to emphasize the
relationship):*
All of us supported the political activity; all of us did not
support Mr. Arnold.

2. *Use a semicolon to separate independent clauses that are connected with
a conjunctive adverb* (however, consequently, therefore, moreover, *and*
then) *or by a modifier* (in fact, in the first place, on the other hand,
for example):
His argument was based on emotion; *however*, it could have
been based on appeal to reason.

The antique clock turned out to be the most valuable item in her collection; *in fact,* we were offered over $5,000 for it.

3. *Use a semicolon in a series where other internal punctuation is also used:*
We found several items for sale: sombreros, for only $2; ruanas, for about $15; and estrebos, a type of brass stirrup, for about $100.

Colons

Use a colon to set off the introductory portion of a sentence from items in a series or from a directly related statement or clause:
He developed 3 theories: the theories of magnitude, of discrepancy, and of middle-ends.

Note that the clause preceding the colon must always form a complete sentence.
I had something important to say to him: "You have changed my life, but not my mind."

QUOTATIONS, ELLIPSIS, AND BRACKETS

1. *Use quotation marks for speech or for material taken directly, word for word, from a printed source:*
According to the *Times* report, "A toehold of the antidemocratic left at Berkeley has become an established beachhead in both universities and the larger society."

2. *When you wish to* omit *a word or phrase from a quotation, use an ellipsis (three dots with spaces between them):*
According to the *Times* report, "A toehold of the antidemocratic left . . . has become an established beachhead in . . . universities. . . ."

Note that when the omission occurs at the end of the sentence, four dots—a period plus three spaced dots—are added.

3. *When you wish to add a word or phrase to a quotation to clarify some aspect of it, use brackets, not parentheses. Because many typewriters do not have bracket keys, you may have to draw them in with dark ink:*
Mark Twain once said, "I believe that the impact of a single book for good or harm is shown in the effects wrought by it [*Don Quixote*] and by *Ivanhoe.*"

If this quotation were used without the editorial insertion in brackets, the reader would not know what it referred to.

PUNCTUATION INSIDE QUOTATIONS

1. Periods and commas always go inside quotation marks:

The Surgeon General reports that "smoking causes lung cancer, heart disease, emphysema, and may complicate pregnancy."

Since the *American Journal of Psychiatry* first observed that there "is no evidence for neurosis in guinea pigs," we have turned to other mental health problems.

2. Colons, exclamation marks, and question marks are located inside the quotation when they form an original part of the quotation:

J.D. O'Hara raises a serious issue: "Do we feel that the nation's oil companies alone can solve the problem?"

But colons, exclamation marks, and question marks are located outside *the quotation when they represent* your *punctuation rather than the author's.*

Did Richard Nixon really say, "Your President is not a crook"?

She made herself quite clear by stating, "I believe in the right to censor schoolbooks for children"!

Note that, in such cases, the author's original terminal punctuation is omitted. Your punctuation marks the end of the sentence.

TITLES

1. Use quotation marks for titles of short works:

Magazine articles:	"A New Look at China"
Short stories:	"Young Goodman Brown"
Poems:	"To His Coy Mistress"
Chapters:	"The Social Effects of the New Deal"
Song titles:	"Does Your Chewing Gum Lose Its Flavor on the Bedpost Every Night?"

2. Use underlining for titles of major works or works that enclose shorter works:

Magazine titles:	Harper's
Books:	Twenty Ways to Better Health
Plays:	Death of a Salesman
Record albums:	Beethoven's Pop Hits
Government documents:	The Congressional Record
TV and film titles:	Gone with the Wind

In printed material, *italics* serve the same function as underlining.

3. Never use both quotation marks and underlining in the same title unless the title contains a title of another work:

Dr. Harris's first essay, "A Study of Walt Whitman's Leaves of Grass," received an enthusiastic response.

4. Do not underline or place quotation marks around the title of your own paper. However, your title may include the title of another work:

Moral Turpitude in Shakespeare's Macbeth

A reminder: All writers need two basic tools—a dictionary and a good handbook. When in doubt, don't guess, look it up.

MANUSCRIPT FORM

Preparing a manuscript to look professional is not difficult. The method shown starting on the next page is not the only way, of course. Many businesses, professions, and professors require that you follow a particular style sheet. But the form described on pages 194–195 is recommended by the Modern Language Association and is fully outlined in the *MLA Handbook for Writers of Research Papers, Second Edition.*

PROOFREADING

The term *proof,* when used by publishers, refers to a trial sheet of printed material that is checked against the original manuscript and on which corrections are made. To *proofread,* then, is to look for any kind of mistake that may have been made in transferring your essay from the last rough draft onto a typed page. This is not the place to make your original inspection for *errors of grammar, usage, spelling,* and *punctuation.* Those items should have been corrected in various drafts. But obviously spelling

1

Rosa Rightly

Prof. Vern Dogood

Owen Hall 331

22 Mar 1988

How to Prepare Your Manuscript

The first page of your paper should look like this. Manuscripts should be typewritten on one side of the paper only. Always double-space and use margins of about one inch at top and bottom as well as on each side. If you are writing on a word processor, follow the same guidelines and be sure to print on a high-quality printer.

Number the first page one-half inch from the top of the page in the right-hand corner. Your name should appear in the upper left-hand corner, along with your instructor's. It's also wise to include the instructor's campus address or box number. If your paper becomes misplaced or lost, it can be forwarded. And most instructors will want you to give the date or the assignment number.

Double-space and center your title. Capitalize the first word, the last word, and all principal words. Then quadruple-space and begin your paper. Each paragraph should be indented five spaces.

Rightly 2

The second and all succeeding pages of a
professional-looking manuscript should look like
this. Some instructors will not want you to
number the first page, but all other pages
should be numbered in the upper right-hand
corner along with your last name. Attach all
pages together with a paper clip. If you submit
loose papers and pages become lost, you must
assume responsibility.

No matter how good a typist you are, you
must always proofread the final copy. Use dark
ink and make corrections clearly. Few
instructors will expect you to be a perfect
typist, and few will object to a few, clear
corrections.

Finally, don't conclude by signing your
name or adding a "P.S." to explain why the paper
is late. After you've typed the conclusion,
simply stop.

or punctuation errors may have crept in again during typing. Even worse,
words and phrases may have been accidentally omitted. No matter what
the error, it remains your responsibility to make a final check, line by
line, and to correct the smallest mistake, especially if you have someone
else type your paper for you.

How do you proofread effectively?

1. Read what you've actually written, not what you think you've written. This may require a minimum of several hours or several days to pass so that the paper can "cool" and you can develop some objectivity about it.
2. Read aloud. The ear will catch missing words or phrases. Sometimes the ear will detect incorrect punctuation because rhythms will seem awkward.
3. Check for spelling errors by skimming from right to left or bottom to top. That way the mind can focus on words alone without becoming absorbed in the context.

Does it all seem petty? Surely no more so than our expectation that a doctor will not leave a pair of scissors inside a patient after surgery, that a plumber will not leave a pipe disconnected, or that a lawyer will not omit your name from your rich uncle's last will and testament. Mistakes always occur. All of us are guilty. But for an instructor to demand high standards is no more than your employer will someday demand and no more than you expect from others.

Exercises

Here are two student paragraphs that need some careful proofreading.

1. The newest adition of George Wilsons' new book: "The Whiplash Industry" accuses Congress, which is mostly composed of laywers, of having a self-serving interest in preventing laws that further auto safety. Like requiring head restraints that are high enough to prevent the head from snaping backwards. "Today's head restraints . . . he said, "are only token restrains that often cause more harm than good". He is attacking lawyers for there greed.

2. There is very little real evidence for the existance of UFOs. Professor of astronomy, Richard Carleton observed "There is over a billion stars in are own Galaxy and its only one of a hundred billion Galaxys yet we have no evidance of life anywhere besides on earth. Dr. Carleton admitts that with the possiblity of as many as 640,000,000 planets in the Universe life in some form is a mathmatical probability, still there seem's little likelyhood of one of them sending out extra terrestrial space ships to harass us.

Readings

Deborah Earl, a freshman planning to major in Art Education, wrote the following report on the AIDS controversy at her university. Deborah first determined that four key individuals were involved and she sought interviews from each. But Deborah also sought out back issues of her student newspaper and used statistics reported in a current issue. The result is a brief but rounded report in which she strives for objectivity and then evaluates her findings.

AIDS vs. Morality vs. Reality

Deborah Earl

Several weeks ago, University President, Kyle Duffy, announced that he would allow the Student Health Service to place condom machines at three locations on campus this spring.

"This was not an easy decision," he told me last Wednesday in his office. "We've had a study commission looking at the controversy for over a year." Dr. Duffy, a former economics professor and advisor to two governors, found the issue on his desk when he assumed office two years ago. A lean, athletic man with salt-and-pepper grey hair, Duffy leaned back in his chair and looked out over the campus through a rain-smudged window. He summarized the situation for me as he found it then. Some students were demanding condom machines in the residence halls, he told me. The Health Service was frightened about AIDS and supported the students. But the campus pastor was threatening to organize local churches in a campaign to stop what he considered an encouragement to immorality. "I had several local businessmen in my office the first day telling me that the reputation of the university was at stake." Everybody, the President claimed, disagreed with everybody.

A search through the back issues of the student newspaper two years ago confirms President Duffy's position. The lead editorial for September 7, 1988 is titled: "How Many Students Will Die from AIDS?" The editorial writer quotes a *New York Times* story on the possibility of 10,000 students in America catching AIDS in the next decade, and then calls for the new president to install condom machines immediately on every floor of every residence hall. But the next issue of the paper, September 14th, contains six letters to the editor protesting the editorial. One student claims that "God uses AIDS to punish homosexuals and liberals." Another claims that enrollment at the university will decline because parents will not want their children to attend a school that promotes sex. And the campus pastor, Walter R. Unruh, writes that the "consequences of immorality cannot be solved by encouraging more immorality."

I sought out Dr. Unruh in his office in the basement of the chapel. Unruh is an ordained minister who is hired by the university to conduct non-denominational services and provide pastoral counseling to students. He wore a dark suit and drank coffee throughout the interview. "Let's face it," he said. "The President has made a political decision, not a moral one. He is reacting to political pressure from the board and the governor, but he's not thinking about the spiritual health of our students." Dr. Unruh said that he might not be able to continue at the university, even though he has served here for ten years. He has asked the advice of his bishop. Whether he will organize a public campaign against the condom machines hasn't been decided. "I don't want to bring even more bad publicity to the university, but I do have an obligation to a higher power," he said.

Connie Sleuder, Student Government President, is unhappy with both President Duffy and with Pastor Unruh. Sleuder was elected last spring on a campaign theme of "Students's Shouldn't Have to Die for Sex." A senior biology major, Sleuder has had conversations with both men several times. She believes that both have "their own agenda." Neither is thinking about AIDS. The President, she told me, has let two years go by while his commission studied the problem. "How many lives might be lost because of the delay?" she asks. And what was there to study? We know what causes AIDS. We know what prevents it. She claims the President just did not want to make a decision, so instead he asked others to make it for him and then he can blame the commission if there is a public outcry.

On the other hand, Pastor Unruh wants to be elected a bishop in his church. He needs to show that he has acted righteously, regardless of the consequences to the students. Sleuder claims that Unruh, a member of the commission, used delaying tactics to prevent it from even meeting for six months. After it finally became apparent that the commission was going to recommend condom machines for campus, he worked to get the number of machines reduced, and the locations difficult for students to find.

According to Margerie Miller, a nurse at the Student Health Service, only five condom machines, instead of the originally proposed twenty, will be installed. One will be located in the Health Service. One each in the men's and women's rest rooms in the basement of Horace Library, and one each in the rest rooms of the Student Union. Miller agrees that the locations mean that most students will need to go out of their way to purchase condoms on campus. For many, the Revco Drug Store on Leigh Street, directly across from the women's residence halls, will probably still be the most convenient source.

The consequence is that no one seems to be satisfied, and students who are sexually active will probably not seek out the campus condom machines for protection. Miller points to a final discouraging fact. National statistics show that most college students don't use condoms on a regular basis anyway, even when they are easily available. A recent poll by the U.S. Student News Service showed that 74% of college males claim to be sexually active, but only one fourth had used a condom in the last month.

The result is that all the arguing and shouting may have been mostly over symbolic issues rather than substance. The university's public image, religious morality, and even student politics, were central to the controversy. But the real issue of how to educate students as to the genuine danger of AIDS, and to convince them that each one of them is truly mortal—that issue has never been addressed.

Rebecca Morris was a second term freshman when she wrote the following short report. Hearing that the dining service had adopted dramatically new policies since the previous year, she let three of the 4 C's (change, conflict, and consequence) guide her investigation.

Student Power

Rebecca Morris

Last year six students, led by Terri Shaw, decided they'd had enough of nuked hot dogs, corned beef hash, chipped beef on toast, rubbery Swiss steak smothered with tomato sauce, and macaroni and hamburger. Clark Dining Hall, they claimed, was serving the same kinds of meals it had served half-a-century ago to returning GI's after World War II. The six students first complained by writing a mimeographed letter to other students in the residence halls. "We know students have probably always complaned [sic] about cafeteria food, but the world has changed and the management of Clark has not." Where, they asked, were the options for people who didn't want to eat meat at every meal? They wanted to know why they couldn't have fresh fruit? Why couldn't the dining service install a yogurt machine? Why did everything have to be heavily salted? Did vegetables have to be over-cooked? Why not fresh vegetables instead of canned peas? They concluded their letter with a plea: "If you agree with us, then let the food service management know. After all, we're the ones who pay for this 'glop' and we're the ones who have to eat it."

Terri Shaw, who is now a senior theatre major, says she had no idea that their letter would have such an impact. "We were just really sick of having to spend fifteen dollars a week to buy our own groceries when our parents had already paid for us to eat at the dining hall." Terri is twenty-two and starred this winter in the university production of *A Mid-Summer Night's Dream*. But she's best known on campus as the girl who gets up at five every morning to run five miles before breakfast. "I come from a health-conscious

Used by permission of Rebecca Morris.

family," she admits. "We ate yogurt and bananas for breakfast, not greasy eggs and bacon. My father was always playing golf or tennis, and my older brother was a long distance biker. I think it was just trying to keep up with them that made me health conscious."

Margaret Williams is the new food service manager. She remembers what happened next. She still has a copy of Terri Shaw's letter under a glass top on her desk. "Students do always complain. That's just part of the business. We don't prepare food like Mom does. But this time everyone was caught off guard by the size of the rebellion."

Mrs. Williams had been assistant manager of the college food service for only a week when Shaw's letter came out. She had previously worked for two other college cafeterias, first at Kent State and then at Virginia Tech. She has an Associate Degree in food preparation from a community college in Ohio.

For the next three weeks Terri Shaw and other students picketed the dining hall with signs and posters. Many of the faculty also complained, including Dorsey Leighton, the coach of the women's basketball team who joined the picket line. Then several students called for a boycott of weekend meals. On the first weekend only about fifty students stayed away, but on the second weekend several hundred students sat outside the entrance and sang songs and chanted.

"We had to throw away thousands of dollars worth of food," Mrs. Williams said. "And I think maybe a hundred other students blocked the hall in front of the Dean of Students' office." After that, the dean met with the former manager, Harry Bosworth, asking why the food service couldn't try some of the student suggestions. "But Harry resisted," Mrs. Williams said. "He had directed the food service for twenty years and he didn't want to change." Bosworth finally announced to an *Eagle* reporter that "if the health nuts are going to take over the world, I would rather retire and go fishing." Which he did.

Mrs. Williams then took over and met with both students and faculty for about six weeks to work out a new menu. Students now have choices, she pointed out during a tour of the kitchen. Every meal offers a traditional meat dish, a vegetarian dish, and simple snack food such as bagles and cream cheese, peanut butter sandwiches on whole wheat bread, or fresh fruit. Each offering has a "nutrition sign" which lists total calories, sodium count, cholesterol, and carbohydrates. Along with low-calorie dressings, the new salad bar offers bowls of raw vegetables such as chopped cauliflower, broccoli, and sliced carrots on ice. Yogurt is available at every meal from a shiny new machine. And for dessert, sugar-free brownies or some other low-calorie offering is prepared.

"I couldn't be happier," Terri Shaw says. "We haven't taken anything away from students who want to eat traditional Americana stuff like meat, potatoes and gravy. But everybody now has a choice." Shaw will graduate in two months, but she thinks students should be aware that they have more influence than they think. "They've been silent for so many years they don't know their own power."

For this study, first published in U.S. News & World Report *in 1987, David Whitman, a professional journalist, relies heavily on the 4 C's of observation. His opening paragraph uses all of the 5 W's, then contrasts their surface appearance with behind-the-scenes reality. As you read further, consider how Whitman continues to use* change, contrast, *and* consequences, *both to probe his subject and to organize the essay.*

Trouble for America's "Model" Minority

David Whitman

When 12-year-old Hue Cao shyly read her prize-winning essay at last year's nationally televised Statue of Liberty centennial celebration, she seemed the very model of a thriving Indochinese boat person. Only six years before, Hue, her mother, four brothers and two sisters fled Vietnam in a fishing boat, and now she was the center of national attention, having bested 2,000 other children in a highly competitive essay contest. "This nation has given my family a brand-new life," Hue recited proudly as tens of millions of equally proud Americans looked on.

Unfortunately, however, what they saw on their TV screens was something of a sham. Far from flourishing in the U.S., the Cao family turned out to be on welfare, unable even to accept the contest prize—a new automobile—because it would have meant surrendering their public-assistance benefits. "The girl's mother was in tears," recalls Reg Schwenke of the Aloha Liberty Foundation, sponsor of the essay contest. "She was both anxious and ashamed."

The problems of Hue Cao and her family illustrate a major but long-hidden difference in social backgrounds between the two groups that make up the more than 800,000 Indochinese who sought refuge in the U.S. in the past 11 years. The first wave of 130,000 refugees—those who arrived in the immediate aftermath of the fall of Saigon in 1975—was largely an elite group. They were officials of the deposed South Vietnamese government, employees of the American military, dependents of U.S. servicemen and upper-echelon staffers of multinational corporations. Given their experience and contacts, these refugees made a relatively easy transition to life in the U.S. and created a near mythic image of the Indochinese as brilliant students, flourishing entrepreneurs and altogether successful symbols of the American dream. After only four years in the U.S., the first wave of Indochinese refugees earned 18 percent more than the average American.

The story, however, is far different for the second wave, the 640,000 who arrived in the U.S. following Vietnam's invasion of Cambodia in 1978. For many of them, life in America has been far less satisfying and considerably more precarious. In contrast to those who preceded them, the second wave of refugees had little education and few skills to bolster them in their new homes. Instead of sophisticated city dwellers, they were mostly rural people—farmers, fishers, small merchants and mountain tribespeople—many unable to speak English and illiterate in their own language. Half came from Laos and Cambodia, nations considerably poorer and socially less developed than Vietnam. And unlike the earlier refugees, those in the second wave often suffered brutal physical and psychological traumas before arriving in the United States. Many had been imprisoned in Vietnamese re-education camps, nearly starved and tortured in Pol Pot's Cambodia, or raped, beaten and robbed by the Thai pirates who preyed on the boat people in the Gulf of Thailand.

"This was the largest nonwhite, non-Western, non–English-speaking group of people ever to enter the country at one time," says Peter Rose, a Smith College professor who has written widely on the refugees." The public assumed they succeeded just because the first wave did." Adds Ruben Rumbaut, director of the Indochinese Health and Adaptation Research Project at San Diego State University: "The Southeast Asian success stories play well in Peoria. Those of the losers don't."

Even when compared with depressed minorities in the U.S., "second wave" Indochinese fare poorly. A staggering 64 percent of the Indochinese households headed by refugees who arrived after 1980 are on public assistance—three times the rate of American blacks and four times that of Hispanics. And among refugee groups as a whole, the newly arrived Indochinese are by far the most dependent upon the dole.

"In our old country, whatever we had was made or brought in by our hands," *says Chong Sao Yang, 62, a former farmer and soldier who moved to San Diego from* *Laos. Yang and three family members have been on welfare for seven years. "We are* *not born on earth to have somebody give us food. Here, I'm sure we're going to starve,* *because since our arrival there is no penny I can get that is money I earn from work.* *I've been trying very hard to learn English, and at the same time look for a job. But* *no matter what kind of job—even a job to clean people's toilets—still people don't trust* *you or offer you such work. I'm not even worth as much as a dog's stool. Talking* *about this, I want to die right here so I won't see my future."*

Many in the newer wave of refugees grew up in Laos and Cambodia without electricity, running water, clocks or stoves—much less banks, savings accounts and credit cards. And Hmong tribesmen like Yang from the highlands of Laos feel even more isolated because of their illiteracy and traditional beliefs in witchcraft and shamans. "What we have here are 16th-century people suddenly thrust into 20th-century life," says Ernest Velasquez of the welfare department in Fresno, Calif., home for an estimated 18,000 Hmong. . . .

Nao Chai Her was the respected head of a Hmong village of more than 500 people in Laos. Here, he is on welfare and shares a cramped three-bedroom apartment with 20 relatives. "We are just like the baby birds," says Nao, 61, "who stay in the nest opening their mouths, waiting only for the mother bird to bring the worms. When the government doesn't send the cash on time, we even fear we'll starve. I used to be a real man like any other man, but not any longer. The work I used to do, I can't do here. I feel like a thing which drops in the fire but won't burn and drops in the river but won't flow."

Many Indochinese experience similar sieges of depression but manage to carefully disguise the condition behind a mask of hard work and traditional courtesy. In one standardized psychological test given in San Diego, 45 percent of the adult refugees showed distress symptoms serious enough to require clinical treatment, four times the proportion among the population at large. Cambodian women, many left husbandless by Pol Pot's genocide, are especially troubled. Lay Plok, 34, of Arlington, Va., lost her husband in 1977 when they fled the famine in Cambodia. "I'm down," she says quietly, "and yet I don't know what would make life feel better."

Like U.S. veterans with painful memories of Vietnam, some Indochinese refugees suffer repeated nightmares and evidence a variety of stress-related disorders. Indeed, emotional trauma among the new arrivals is so extensive and little understood that Dr. Richard Mollica and social worker James Lavelle of St. Elizabeth's Hospital set up the Indochinese Psychiatry Clinic in 1981 in Boston just to assist refugees. One woman treated at the clinic wandered from city to city in the U.S., fearful that her Communist jailers were out to recapture her. She told clinic doctors a harrowing but not atypical story of having been repeatedly raped, tortured and given mind-altering drugs while imprisoned.

For all their problems, however, the newer refugees don't fully fit the underclass stereotype. Most cherish hard work and stress the value of family and education. Divorce and out-of-wedlock pregnancy are still taboo. Drug and alcohol abuse is minimal. Studies of the refugee children, including those with illiterate Hmong parents, indicate they do quite well in school. And even where most of the family gets public-assistance payments, at least one member has a paying job, sometimes off the books. "The refugees make exemplary use of the welfare system," argues Nathan Caplan of the University of Michigan, an expert on the second wave of refugees. "They tend to have large families, so they pool resources to finance education and training. And they rely on welfare less as time goes by."

In the end, however, whatever their cultural liabilities, the refugees' greatest asset may be simply that they are survivors. Puthnear Mom, 22, also of Arlington, lost her husband while crossing the Cambodian border to Thailand. She can't read or write, and has been unemployed for two years. "I'm unhappy to receive welfare," she says through a translator, "but life is better now than in Cambodia or the refugee camp. I can learn anything here I want. Freedom does matter."

PART IV

The Extended Investigation

We assume all too readily that observation comes by nature, that we are born "naturally observant." But the truth is that most of us are born lazy, and observation beyond the necessities of life has been too great for voluntary exertion. The result is that we live in a world of which we know little more than a dog or a cat; we are familiar with a few things from long association; we have a nodding acquaintance with a number of other things; but as far as our scientific observation of them goes, we can scarcely be said to be even curious.

A. E. ORAGE

Exploring

18

Seeing Beyond the Surface

Imagination is more important than knowledge. For knowledge is limited, whereas imagination embraces the entire world.

ALBERT EINSTEIN

Cathy and David Mitchell were still in their twenties when they graduated with master's degrees in journalism from Stanford. After drifting for a number of years through low-paying jobs from Florida to Iowa, they took a desperate chance and purchased a small weekly newspaper in northern California. With new enthusiasm, they worked 14-hour days gathering and writing stories about local school board meetings and local ranchers, all the while living in a single back room of the newspaper office and sleeping on a sofa bed.

Meanwhile, a few miles away, one of the country's largest drug rehabilitation centers attracted national attention after purchasing $60,000 worth of guns and 3.8 million rounds of ammunition. Normally the Mitchells left state and national news to the San Francisco dailies, but something told Cathy Mitchell that this story should be pursued. After all, it was practically in their backyard. David began the investigation and almost immediately turned up a number of seemingly incredible facts.

What had begun several years earlier as a highly successful and respectable center for aiding drug addicts now seemed to have become an alternative lifestyle community with its own schools, medical clinics, lawyers, and even its own internal police force. The organization had expanded by opening centers in half a dozen states and several foreign countries. But the Mitchells began to uncover a more significant story involving accusations of child abuse, beatings, totalitarian mind-control, and a surprising accumulation of wealth from tax-exempt business dealings. Yet even after a grand jury investigation, local officials refused to look into the allegations. Even more frustrating for the Mitchells, other newspapers dropped the story or seemed afraid to investigate, especially after the rehabilitation center's 48-member legal staff threatened multimillion-dollar lawsuits. The Mitchells had only courage and their belief in the truth to keep them going.

For the next year, the two young newspaper owners pursued the case alone. They checked out thousands of clues, talked to officials in county and state government, researched financial records, and made hundreds of phone calls. No information was printed unless it could be verified by a second source. At several points the investigation seemed to die. The Mitchells were accused of being obsessed. Some readers suggested they stick to local weddings and birth announcements. Yet the pile of seemingly incredible facts kept growing. Children attending the special school operated by the center were reported to be running away at the rate of thirty every month. Former members of the center, and even passing motorists, were often beaten by "goon squads" with shaved heads and blue overalls. Several individuals claimed to have been kidnapped and held against their will. No one seemed to listen. It all seemed too strange to be true—until a Los Angeles lawyer who had sued the rehabilitation center on behalf of a client was almost murdered: Two of the organization's members had dropped a rattlesnake in his mailbox.

Truth is difficult to define, difficult to prove. At best we can work toward probable truth. We can have the curiosity, the skepticism, the open mind—all needed to pursue the facts beyond a mere surface accounting—but, ultimately, success seems to rely on our ability to evaluate and interpret the facts, on our persistent desire to find an order, a pattern, a meaning that the facts reveal. Cathy and David Mitchell were not solely responsible for exposing the drug rehabilitation center. But their tenacity and courage in the face of such overwhelming odds won them the Pulitzer Prize for Meritorious Public Service—only the fourth time in the history of the award that it had been given to a weekly newspaper.

A serious inquiry into a subject goes beyond mere reporting, beyond observing the facts or listening to facts or gathering facts. *To investigate means to pursue detail in such a way that you begin to perceive a pattern or association that suggests a reasonable meaning, a probable truth.* Although there are as many ways of organizing an inquiry as there are subjects to investigate, three general phases can be identified in the inquiry process: narrowing your focus to a single, manageable portion of the subject; pursuing and selecting facts or informed opinion that seems most significant; and interpreting results.

NARROWING THE FOCUS

Your eye functions as the lens of your imagination. You have the ability to see the whole of something or to focus on minute detail. Successful writers have found that the most effective and significant work usually has a narrow focus on one or two specific areas of a larger subject. The Mitchells did not write about "drug abuse in America." They focused on a single drug rehabilitation center in their neighborhood. They tirelessly investigated each small activity, incident, and event. Although the results of their work eventually produced enough information to fill a book, their focus never shifted.

Many, if not all, topics you'll be assigned in college will be too large to handle successfully. Train yourself to break down the topic into its various components, then to focus on only one or two specific segments. Here's an example of how you might begin.

Assignment: *Investigate dormitories at Slippery Sands State College.* As a topic, "dormitories" is too broad. It covers hundreds of categories composed of various components and specific details. If you try to write on dormitories, you'll end up producing either vague generalizations or a very large book.

First, break down the subject into its major categories.

dormitories {
physical buildings
student facilities
residents
social life
traditions
rules
living conditions
administration
cost
maintenance
student counselors
}

Next, select one category and break it down into its various components.

social life
{
movies
organized floor activities
charity drives
entertainment council
beer blasts
dances
fall picnic
regulations
participation
pool tables
expenses
}

Now you've got enough material for only a small handbook. If you want to write an essay or report, better break it down one more time. Focus on *one* specific area. Begin asking questions, specific questions that can produce facts from which you can reasonably expect to draw conclusions.

Here's a more complex example.

Assignment: *Investigate an ethnic custom.* First, break down the subject into its major categories.

ethnic custom
{
types of food
funeral ceremonies
initiation rites
hand gestures
marriage ceremonies
dress
greetings
sibling relationships
}

Next, select one category and break it down into its various components.

marriage ceremony
{
dress
bride's family
traditional music
invitations
groom's family
religious ritual
food
blessings
traditional gifts
announcements
}

Finally, concentrate on one or two areas and investigate the specific facts.

groom's family
bride's family

{ What is expected of the bride's parents?
What is expected of the groom's parents?
Why? Where do the expectations come from?
Why does the bride's father "give away" his daughter?
Why doesn't the groom's father "give away" his son?
Are the families expected to meet? To exchange symbolic gifts?
Who offers the first toast at the reception? Why?
Are the families aware of the reason behind the customs? If not, why do they follow the customs?
What is the function of custom and ceremony in this situation? }

The answers to these questions will require much research. You'll probably need to investigate written sources, perhaps a book on history, anthropology, or sociology. For some questions you may find no concrete facts at all. You may need to rely on inference and informed opinion. But with enough persistence and enough determination, a probable truth can still be found.

Here is a general topic for you to practice on. Narrow the focus by breaking it down, first into its general categories, then into major components, then into one specific area of concern around which you can formulate some initial questions for inquiry.

topic: funeral customs   categories

_____

_____

_____

_____

choose one category   major components:

_____

_____

_____

_____

choose one component   specific questions:

_____

_____

_____

_____

PURSUING AND SELECTING DETAILS

Almost half of the previous chapters in this text have dealt with the pursuit or selection of specific detail. Each method and technique discussed earlier may apply at some point during an investigation of any subject. It would probably be best to keep them all in the back of your mind, selecting from them as the subject itself seems to call them forth.

Look for the 5 W's Think of the 5 *W*'s as more than a technique used in writing a lead. *Who, What, Where, When,* and *Why* are questions that apply to every subject as a whole.

Look for change. Change may be the key element. Why is change occurring or not occurring? Whom does the change affect? When will it occur? How will it be brought about?

Look for contrast. Contrast, conflict, contradiction, or opposition may lead to the center of an issue. Why is there a conflict? What does it grow out of? Who is involved? Where and when did it begin?

Look for consequences. How does one fact influence another? What facts have the most serious impact? Who is affected? When will the impact take place? What will be the result?

Look for characterization. Major actions, speech or written documents, background, others' reactions or opinions, and physical description or environment (when appropriate) all contribute to the total pattern of almost any issue or event.

Look for the elements of scene. The concrete, sensory elements of a scene are the elements of life. Subjects for investigation exist in a real world, in a place and setting, in a time frame, and with people who have purpose or motivation. An objective search for truth does not mean we abandon the concrete world for the sake of abstractions. See your subject in its real setting, in its world context, both for yourself and for your reader's fullest understanding.

Look for the people behind the subject. Whether through observation, interviews, or library research, keep your eyes open to the human element, both to make your writing more interesting and to retain a human perspective on the issue.

THE ROLE OF FEELING

To all these previous techniques, we should add a few points about mental and emotional attitudes during an inquiry. We've already seen that to reach even a probable truth, we need an objective approach. It seems self-evident that personal bias or an emotional attitude will only lead a person to prove what he or she already believes. Yet we face a paradox here. The best writing and probably the more important discoveries derive from intense involvement, from deep personal feelings about a subject. I began this book with two units on personal writing because my experience with students has led me to believe that the human voice speaking out of honest personal observation rings truest in the ear of the reader. Unless we are able to *feel* a subject as well as perceive it objectively, we have not truly explored it in all its fullness.

You must approach a subject with an open mind, but also with a sense of caring. That is what it means to be sensitive. Pierre Curie, a French scientist and the husband of Marie Curie, entered into a ten-year investigation of piezoelectric crystals because of their beauty. Beauty involves aesthetic appreciation. In other words, it was an emotion that motivated and sustained objective research. In Curie's case, the emotion and the objective facts complemented each other and enriched the inquiry process. On other occasions, you'll find that objective facts oppose inner feelings. You can never ignore the facts or slight them or distort them because of that. The facts must always be fairly and accurately presented, no matter how painful it may be. Emotion and objectivity may oppose or complement each other. Either way, your research and your writing will be enhanced by an intense commitment that effectively balances the two qualities.

THE ROLE OF IMAGINATION

I also feel I should say something about imagination because no successful inquiry functions without it. A scientist, for example, trained in analysis and logical procedure, may suddenly follow an illogical hunch, a leap of the imagination toward an unexpected breakthrough. The years of objective empirical study may at first seem unrelated, yet it is exactly this previous preparation that helps him or her use intuition productively. You have been training your eyes and ears to perceive specific details and facts, and it may have begun to seem like an end in itself. But it has only been preparation for a more important goal. Possession of the facts is never a substitute for understanding their meanings.

Here is what one student wrote when asked to investigate the campus cafeteria. He began with description.

> Students enter through the south door. They stand in line and have their identification cards checked. They gather up knives, forks, spoons, napkins, and trays from a stand. Then they push their trays along an aluminum rack in front of steaming kinds of food. Each student can select one item from meat, two items from the vegetables, one salad, one dessert, bread, butter, and a choice of five or six drinks. Students then separate and choose tables, usually with their friends, where . . .

No need to go on. This is objective reporting with a vengeance. Everything the writer says is verifiable by a second observer. He has successfully prevented emotional influences from affecting his observations. But nothing he says has been seen as significant. He reports objective facts without concern for their value or meaning. The real problem is that the author has made no commitment to the subject. He has not engaged his imagination. It is easy to misunderstand the nature of objectivity and to believe that your mind must act like a machine, like a camera that records but does not evaluate.

Yet here is what Tina Hawthorne wrote for the same assignment. She, too, began with description.

> The young woman sat down at the lunch table with two books under her arm. Her tray contained only a small salad of cottage cheese on wilted lettuce, and a slightly brown orange. She placed one book flat to the side of her tray. She opened the other—a nursing text on cancer—propping it against the first so that it was raised slightly. The edge of the tray held open the pages. She pushed her heavy rimmed glasses against her nose with her thumb, glanced around the line of students still shuffling past the milk machines, and then began to peel her orange and read at the same time.
>
> She used her fingernails to dig at the orange while her eyes studied the chapter on "Multiple Primary Tumors." As she read, the juice ran between her fingers and she slurped each finger slowly, never taking her eyes from the text. Again she thumbed her glasses up her nose, then began to break the orange into segments, popping each one open with small white teeth. A fine spray of juice squirted out over her tray. She leaned into the tray pushing out her chin so the juice wouldn't dribble into her lap. Eyes fixed on the book, she fed each orange slice automatically into her mouth.
>
> She reached out and turned the page with the tips of her wet thumb and forefinger. The subheading read "Malignant Melanoma." She licked her lips and fingers, skimming fast. Feeling about with one blind hand, she found her fork and speared the cottage cheese.

Like the first author, Tina Hawthorne observes facts. Yet Tina's work is not only more interesting, it also strikes me as more meaningful. Tina does not merely report objective details, she also begins to write toward an idea. We begin to sense something about the nature of education, about the excitement of learning when involvement becomes intense and absorbing. The incongruities of the scene heighten our awareness. Tina looked at selected facts (the rest of the cafeteria is ignored), and through her eye we begin to explore the world.

John Ciardi, a poet and essayist, once wrote: "The fact is that anything significantly looked at is significant. And that is significant which teaches us something about our own life-capabilities. The function of detail when ordered by a human imagination is to illustrate the universe." I know of no finer way to make the point. The eye of the scientist and the eye of the poet are not that different. Both perceive the world with imaginative discipline; both select details and weigh them for their value and significance; both reject those that are mere gloss while retaining those that illuminate larger wholes. Facts are lifeless and boring only when perceived by an unengaged mind that does not imaginatively relate them to the world we live in.

EVALUATING AND INTERPRETING

To *evaluate* is to judge the worth of something. Each fact you obtain during an investigation must be evaluated for its worth. So must the source of each fact, for the source may affect the value of the fact in several different ways. To *interpret*, on the other hand, means to clarify or to explain the significance of something. When you evaluate, you ask whether a fact is any good. When you interpret, you ask what the fact means or what it suggests about the subject as a whole.

Evaluating Sources

Before you can evaluate the worth of a fact, you need to consider its source. For example, Cathy and David Mitchell received dozens of tips from local ranchers, clerks in county offices, and deputy sheriffs who suspected a coverup by higher officials. As sources of information, each of these individuals proved valuable, but each had only a limited point of view. None was an authority on drug rehabilitation and few if any had actually been inside the rehabilitation center. Fortunately for the Mitchells, Richard Ofshe, a professor of sociology at Berkeley, had been studying utopian communities for years and at one time had spent several months visiting and interviewing the members of the rehabilitation center. He not only possessed inside knowledge of its operations but he was also an authority on the subject of communes—and he wanted to help.

Yet an authority does not need to possess a fancy title or a degree. A housewife may be an authority on the need for women's liberation, a baker may be an authority on the nutrients in bread, and so on. Authority may derive from experience or from scholarly study. Each source must be tested against the subject. And, in fact, the title of "expert" or even a national reputation does not necessarily give a source inherent value. Motivation behind the release of information may make it suspect. Someone with a grudge or someone acting out of self-interest may provide biased or incomplete information. You must weigh each of your sources with as much care as you weigh your own personal observation. Be skeptical. Human nature is always involved. Withhold judgment until more facts or evidence can be obtained. No matter who or what your source, attempt to verify all data from a second source.

Evaluating Evidence

Once the evidence has been gathered, it must be evaluated on its own terms. Is it fact, inference, or opinion? If the evidence seems factual, can it be verified? How or by whom? If the evidence is an inference, can you trust the source that made the inference? Is the inference confirmed by more than one source? Do other facts support the inference so that one could reasonably consider it a *probable* truth? Finally, if your information derives from opinion, is it informed opinion—that is, does it come from someone likely to be informed on a subject, or does it come from a random person on the street?

You must decide whether each fact is typical of the whole or special to a particular situation or context. Either may be valuable, but exceptions can always exist and may prove little more than that exceptions exist. You need information that forms an association, that seems consistent or typical, for what is typical may suggest a pattern. In the Watergate burglary, five of the original burglars were Cuban exiles. A number of people suspected that various Cuban exile groups were behind the whole plot. Because the ringleader was a former CIA employee, others suspected the CIA of direct involvement. Yet when pieced together with other evidence, these facts turned out to be exceptions. As other data accumulated, the *pattern* of the evidence suggested the burglary was directed by someone inside the White House. The nationality of the people committing the actual break-in seemed to play no significant role in that pattern. Obviously, in some cases an exception to the whole may become the focal point of your research, but you'll usually find the pattern or relationship of facts, rather than the exception, leads to the most reasonable conclusion.

Interpreting the Results

One of the most human qualities is the desire to know, the desire for certainty. As a result, we sometimes begin to interpret or judge before we have finished an investigation. In our impatience to find the truth, we may jump to hasty conclusions before all data are available. We then find ourselves forced to distort the remaining evidence to support interpretation, or else we must back up and endure the tedious process of reevaluating and interpreting anew. But writers, artists, scientists—everyone engaged in trying to make sense of the world—report that chaos is a natural phase in the creative process and that we must move through chaos before we can discover order. In other words, we must learn to accept temporary uncertainty and confusion as normal. Few investigations move in logical, step-by-step fashion. Facts, data, quotations, and opinions pile up without seeming relationship or significance. The mind seems boggled. Hours or days of struggling with the material may follow. But the intuitive or subconscious elements in our mind eventually become our ally. Psychological studies have shown that alternating periods of intense work with relaxation encourages a breakthrough. A pattern forms. A relationship is discovered.

The original meaning of the Greek and Hebrew words meaning "to know" included the concept of sexual relations: to know was to join together, to unite opposites. If we wish to know the significance of something, we must join the parts; we must discover how seemingly opposite or disparate facts relate. Interpretation, then, is a process of reasonable inference applied to an accumulation of data. A hasty inference may cause a distorted or false interpretation. A carefully considered inference, based on all possible evidence, usually leads to a verifiable interpretation.

The human mind finds its truths in qualities that shape themselves into patterns or associations that have order and form. It is your job as a writer to discover the pattern and show it to the reader.

Exercises

1. The ability to discern relationships is a major element of evaluation and interpretation. Study the three advertisements on pages 220–222. What common features do you find? Are there qualities that suggest a

pattern? Make a list of the typical qualities. What reasonable inferences might you make about the nature of advertising? How could you verify your inferences?

2. Here are three sources providing information on a student's application to join a college honors program. Evaluate each of the sources. Evaluate the information provided by each source. Look for patterns or relationships. Interpret the evidence by drawing a reasonable inference about the student's qualifications for honors work.

Excerpts from Student Application Forms

a. Describe the most important book you've read this year.

The best book I've read this year was *The World According to Garp*. Usually I read biographies.

b. What are your goals and ambitions?

I plan to open my own successful law office and go into politics. I'd like to be a congressman or senator someday.

c. Describe an accomplishment of which you are particularly proud.

Last spring my father had a stroke while running our family's business—a dry cleaners. My brother and I kept the store open and profitable for two months by ourselves until my father recovered.

d. Why do you want to participate in an honors program?

I am applying for honors because it would be a personal accomplishment. It also might help me get into law school.

Excerpts from Letters of Reference

I have known Randolph for several years. I once treated him for hyperactivity when he was younger. Throughout the years he has matured and turned out to be a fine young man. I understand from his mother that he has applied for your honors program, and I feel he would be a welcome addition.

John L. Morando, M.D.

It is a pleasure for me to recommend Randolph as a candidate for your honors program. As his guidance counselor I have known him for three years. I also taught him in a class on interpretative dance, for which he received an *A* plus. He is an excellent student whose chief areas of interest are history, psychology, and political science. We would be very proud here at Easter High School for Randolph to be selected for such a fine program.

Kathleen Spangler, Counselor

Excerpts from High School Transcript

National Test Scores: SAT Verbal 601/SAT Math 545

Grades in Senior Year: English . . . A
Algebra II . . . C
History . . . A
Physical Education . . . B
Psychology . . . A
Social Studies . . . A
French II . . . A

Activities: Debating Club, Young Men's Republican Club, Chess Club, President of Senior Class, Honors Society.

Awards: Junior Chamber of Commerce Award for Business Competition—Youth Class, Wisconsin High School Chess Tournament Honorable Mention, Junior Achievement Award, Honorable Mention in the "I Speak for Democracy" Competition, delegate to the Midwest United Nations Conference.

3. Here are several broad topics. Choose one and narrow it to a single component. Design a series of questions that would help you find specific facts and informed opinions about it.

public school attendance
church attendance
local art galleries
grading practices
SAT exams
cheerleading
law schools
core requirements

Sothys Skin and Body Care Products. Sothys, USA Inc.

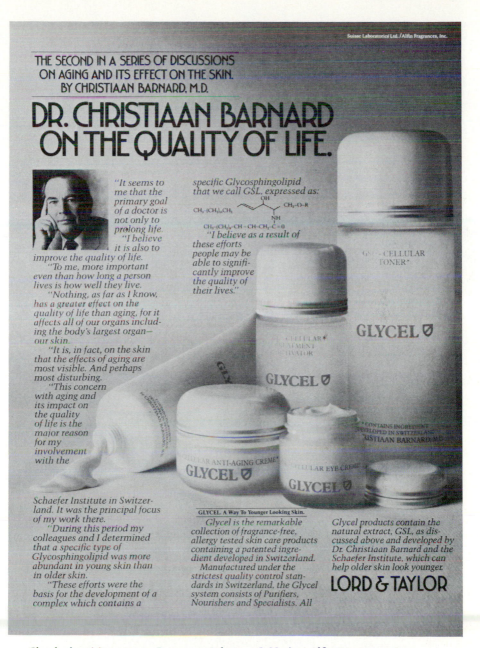

Glycel advertising agency: Drossman, Lehmann & Marino. Alfin Fragrances, Inc.

Lancôme advertising agency: Intermarco Advertising, Inc. Photo: Bill King.

Journal Practice

By this time, opening up your journal every day should seem a natural part of your routine. If you're serious about it, you may be one of those fortunate individuals for whom journal writing becomes a lifelong activity that enriches feelings, memories, thoughts, and imagination. You should continue to use it for freewriting, for spontaneous entries on anything that moves you. But journals should also be used for more objective work. As you begin to narrow a subject for upcoming essays and assignments, use the journal for keeping track of your mental notes, questions, and late-night insights. Explore your hunches about a subject, take risks by pursuing an idea that might lead nowhere but that might open up new interpretations. In other words, journal writing is just as important for exploring your intellectual life as it is for your emotional life.

Exploring

19

Primary and Secondary Sources

A s John DeWitt McKee once wrote, "No writer who is any good writes solely from the contemplation of his navel. He must *know*, either through personal experience or through research." We're now ready to put together the full process by which a writer sets out to explore a subject and, one hopes, to learn something about it. We might describe a full investigation as a triangular process involving, first, your own personal observation; second, the extension of observation by using others' eyes and experience as reported directly to you in an interview or as recorded in an original document; and third, the research of secondary sources, the use of knowledge and insight accumulated throughout history by other authors.

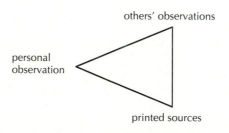

others' observations

personal
observation

printed sources

PRIMARY MATERIAL

A primary source provides information to you in some direct way—through a personal interview, telephone conversation, letter, diary, journal, ledger, memo, manuscript, or book that presents a firsthand account. Even personal experience might be considered a primary source if it directly involves your subject of investigation. If, for example, you were reporting on racial prejudice in the public schools and you had personally experienced or been involved in a racial incident, your observations would constitute a primary source. So would interviews with others directly involved or with those who might be informed on the subject: a school superintendent, a psychologist or sociologist at a nearby university, a police report written about the incident, or an extract from a diary kept by a teacher.

SECONDARY MATERIAL

A secondary source provides secondhand information or analysis and interpretation of original documents. Secondary sources may constitute the largest body of material available to you on many subjects. Your personal ability to observe is limited, as is the number of interviews or primary sources you usually have access to; but the number of books, newspapers, magazines, films, records, government reports, pamphlets, and so on, is almost unlimited. A racial incident in your city's public schools may be investigated almost exclusively through primary sources, but for a fuller understanding of racism and of how the incident in your school forms part of a larger pattern, you would need to turn to secondary sources.

Students often feel that investigation of secondary material is somehow taxing, more duty than pleasure—all those hours in the library, all that note taking. But every subject is interesting when pursued imaginatively, critically, and skeptically. If you bring a dull mind to the work, it will indeed seem dull. If you involve yourself with some sort of personal commitment, even the evolution of the aardvark can become fascinating. What is always necessary is a focused question—the question that grows out of the narrowing of your subject: Does this fact relate to others? Does it conflict with others? How is it significant? Whom does it affect? Does it constitute part of a larger pattern? Is it true? Can the truth be known?

IN-TEXT DOCUMENTATION OF SOURCES

Because the source of any information you obtain affects the value of the information, a writer must always provide complete and accurate documentation. In formal papers you'll want to provide identification of sources within the text and in a separate listing of "works cited" at the end. In a report or critical essay, however, identification of sources within the text is usually enough.

Both primary and secondary sources need to be documented. Some instructors may provide you with a preferred method; some businesses and institutions may provide a "style sheet" that lists a prescribed form. Without such guidance, you can rely on any number of methods for integrating the documentation into your material so long as it provides, in general, *who, what, where,* and sometimes *when.*

Primary Sources

Who

The first time information from a source is used, give the full name of the source. In addition, give the source's full title or a description of his or her authority to speak on the subject.

What

If a manuscript, original document, or book is used, give the full title (or a description if it doesn't have a title). If the source is an individual, give his or her location.

Where

Should the reader wish to verify the information. (If the source is a published book, you would not, of course, want to say that it is located in the library. Instead, provide the same in-text documentation described below under *Secondary Sources.*)

    what   *who*   *where*
A letter from Roger T. Jerome, California state assemblyman and a

   authority
self-professed expert on aardvarks, claims that aardvarks have become an uncontrolled problem near the campus area.

   who   *where*
Bud Walker, University of Missouri freshman, claims he had never heard of aardvarks until he became mixed up with a bad crowd.

         authority
Today, however, Walker raises aardvarks in his basement.

Secondary Sources

For secondary sources (or published primary sources), the same general information is necessary, although *when* the information was published must be added.

> *who*
> Ex-President Richard Nixon declared, "There were no aardvarks in
>
> *where*   *when*
> my administration" (*Time*, Sept. 2, 1974).

> *who*   *authority*   *where*
> Dr. Harold Bley, professor of zoology, Arizona State University,
>
> *when*   *what*
> asserts in his classic 1931 study on aardvarks, *Cognitive Configurations of Snout Development,* that aardvarks will inherit the earth (231).

Direct quotations, paraphrases, and summaries all need to be attributed to a fully documented source.

Statistics, facts, ideas, inferences, and opinions should all be attributed to a fully documented source.

The reader needs to know specifically *who* your source is, *what* information you obtained from that source, *what* authority the source had to speak on the subject, *where* the subject can now be found (if primary material) or *where* and *when* the information was printed.

You should recognize that this demand for accurate documentation exists not only so that material can be verified by a second observer but also because the stronger the source of information, the stronger the facts will seem to your reader, and the more thorough your investigation will appear.

(For other examples, and for an explanation of the "Works Cited" format, should your instructor wish you to use it, see pp. 493–495.)

THE FULL INVESTIGATION

Many college students spend almost all their research time in a library. The professional writer recognizes that the variety of primary and secondary sources—and their location—is so extensive that actual library research is only one small area of the imaginative investigation. Depending on the subject, here's a partial list of sources that might be considered for an inquiry.

memos	college catalogues
court proceedings	business firms' libraries
accountant's ledger journals	U.S. government libraries or depositories
surveys	office files
medical libraries	museum and art-gallery libraries
state or city historical societies	diaries
private libraries	police reports and logs
newspaper files	magazines
letters	record-album covers

Not all of these sources would be available to a college student, of course, but the writer who makes the extra effort—to interview, to write a congressman, to check a telephone log, to dig through some dusty archives—that is, the writer who is alive to the richness of his or her subject, knows that all ideas are related to the world we live in.

Here is how sophomore Mary Jo Loufman investigated the profits earned by a student-run book exchange. Mary Jo interviewed two student employees, an accountant, and the finance officer at the university. She studied the regulations published by the student senate several years earlier, the quarterly statement provided by the accountant (with permission of the president of student government), and the minutes of the student committee that supervised the exchange at the time. Her final report was six pages long. Here are the first four paragraphs.

5 W lead	During the last three years the Student Book Exchange has accumulated more than $1,200 in excess profits because the SBX Committee has lacked authority to deal with the
Inference	money. Apparently when the Student Book Exchange was founded in 1978, no one considered that a profit might be
Verifiable fact	earned. Today, the $1,200 sits in a savings account of the First National Bank drawing 5.5 percent interest.
Primary source	Carl Green, an outside accountant hired by the SBX
Authority	Committee three years ago when he was a student working on his master's in business administration, states that there was no real bookkeeping procedure when he began.
Quotation	"Even though there had always been a 10 percent handling charge on every exchange, no one seemed to have any permanent records on how that money was
Summary	handled." Green claims to have found a shoe box of receipts for various expenses, but no ledgers or accounts.
More authority	Green now runs his own accounting business but has continued to work once or twice a month at the SBX

Secondary source

office—an enlarged closet in the basement of the Student Union. It was Green's introduction of accounting practices that revealed that SBX could and did earn a profit. That was three years ago. But the *Student Book Exchange, Governing Rules and Procedures,* a four-page dittoed pamphlet written and signed by members of the 1977–1978 student government committee that formed SBX, contains only one line dealing with how that 10 percent handling charge is to be spent: "Money accrued from the handling charge

Sources compared

will be used to pay for all overhead expenses and student salaries." Green claims that is exactly what is now done. But SBX still has approximately $400 a year left over.

Summary of findings

The student government committee that oversees the SBX is aware of the problem. The published minutes for September 9, 1986, and for October 22, 1986, both reveal that concern was expressed. On both occasions a motion was considered to bring the issue to the full senate for a recommendation. No action was taken. However, the same concern was shown in minutes from March 3, 1984, and

Lack of action

September 13, 1985. No action was taken at those times, either.

Mary Jo Loufman eventually gathered enough facts to demonstrate that a pattern of inaction and lack of leadership had allowed the profit to accumulate. Nor did she fail to evaluate the consequences in human terms. The two part-time student employees of the SBX might have earned an extra $200 each if the money had been paid in salaries. Mary Jo sifted through pages of unrelated material to discover the evidence she needed. She read three years' worth of published committee minutes and studied financial accounts, even though she knew little of accounting. When she combined the findings with other sources, she discovered a pattern—a lack of action and a feeling by each person involved that it was someone else's concern.

An inquiry into probable truth requires responsibility, initiative, and determination. By combining personal observation, primary sources, and secondary sources, you will have all the tools you need to investigate almost any subject.

Exercises

1. Once you've narrowed the focus of your investigation, you will need to consider the types of sources you might seek out. Here's an example of how you could begin.

TOPIC: Grade Inflation at St. Mary's College

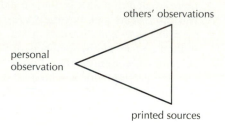

others' observations

personal
observation

printed sources

Personal observation	*Others' observations*	*Printed sources*
classroom experience	several instructors	computer printouts of
attitude of those you	dean of college	grades
interview	registrar	current grade averages
	alumni	from dean
	several students	statistics from registrar
		Time, Newsweek, Chronicle
		of Higher Education
		(for comparison with
		national patterns)

Not every source will be available to you. Some sources won't provide you with information. You probably need a list twice as long as you actually plan to use just to allow for those sources that won't work out.

2. Discuss the following topics. Make a list of the various types of sources you might consider for a full investigation: minority coaches in athletics, the monetary value of a B.A. or B.S. degree, foreign-language requirements at your school, reductions in grants and scholarship support by the federal government.

3. Here are four documented sources taken from student papers. Consider which are complete and informative and which have omitted essential elements needed for verification.

    a. Samuel B. Goldman, commission chairman, indicated in a speech to the accounting class on Friday that Minneapolis business conditions were unstable.

    b. As part of my study, I wrote to North Carolina's Republican Congressman, Bill Hendon. In a letter from his Washington office, dated January 3, 1989, he claimed to support the college-tuition tax credit for the following reasons: . . .

    c. Bilingual programs were begun nationwide in all cities with more than a 5 percent Chicano population, according to a *Time* magazine interview with Dr. Kenneth Kriester, Title VII Coordinator for the U.S. Department of Health, Education and Welfare (*Time*, September 23, 1988).

d. CBS News reported that the divorce rate had risen again in 1990, but so had the marriage rate.

4. In a sentence or two, provide all necessary documentation and the main facts for each of the following notes:

a. "I believe the Charismatic Christian movement is just reaching its peak," *Religion Today*, Reverend Charles Mathaies, Jr., page 21, June 1981, Church of the Good Pastor, Baltimore.

b. Telephone conversation with Marilyn Chase, mayoral candidate, councilwoman from 6th district, October 28th, indicating that unemployment in the inner city areas is now 13 percent.

c. p. 369, *The Origins of Evolutionary Theory*, P. Samuel Wyndcotyl, "Darwin was not the first to propose the concept of evolution," professor of biology, chairperson of the biology department at the University of Toronto, has published six books on evolution since 1955, copyright 1972.

d. "We are approaching an ecological disaster," Boston, Mass., John Pittston, Staley Lecture series, Thursday, March 5, 1987, Boston University, editor of the *Ecological Drift*, a collection of essays, spokesman for the Sierra Club.

Drafting

20

Imaginative Leads

It was a pleasant summer day—warm with just a hint that it would grow hot and humid later on. Doctors moved quietly among a score of patients at the Jewish Chronic Disease Hospital in Brooklyn, giving them injections under the skin of one thigh. It was just a test of their immunity, the patients had been told. There was no real danger, though they "might feel a little discomfort and perhaps see a lump for a while." But there was one thing the patients weren't told: that the injections contained live cancer cells.

William Barry Furlong wrote the above paragraph as an introduction to an article in *Good Housekeeping*. Furlong might have written, "The subject of my report is about doctors who are experimenting with cancer on live human beings." He might have, but he didn't. Few professional writers begin an informative article or essay or even a business report with such a dull statement of purpose. As a writer you want to tell your reader the subject of your paper. But why be boring when you can be interesting?

You've already studied the 5 W lead in Chapter 15. Knowing other types of more imaginative leads can give you a surprising range of alternatives for effective introductions. Imaginative leads may be anything from a sentence to a page or more (depending on the length of the total writing project). Their intent is to involve the reader directly in some concrete element of the subject while also directly or indirectly presenting the underlying idea. The imaginative lead attempts to catch the reader's interest through the use of a quotation, a question, a dramatized conflict, suspense, humor, or shock—and then to lead clearly and logically into the subject itself. The lead should set the tone, provide the underlying idea of your paper, and even suggest to the reader the organization of the essay that follows. A lot for a few sentences to accomplish, but perhaps it explains why professional writers put so much emphasis on the value of the lead. Donald M. Murray, essayist, novelist, journalist, Pulitzer Prize winner, and teacher, says that many writers spend 85 percent of their effort on the lead—not just to catch the reader's attention, but because of its focusing and organizing potential (Chapter 21 will go into more depth on how the lead suggests an organization).

THE PROVOCATIVE LEAD

A bold, provocative statement may be the easiest way to grab your reader's attention.

> The women's liberation movement was a spectacular failure. Instead of freeing women to find the best qualities in themselves, it condemned them to adopt the very worst qualities found in men.

Here a student writer has used a strong, declarative first sentence. It is actually a conclusion based on his investigation. The author does not present the facts, only the meaning he has interpreted from them. The result, standing by itself as the first sentence, can seem striking, challenging, even opinionated. But the reader is captured into reading on to see if the author can indeed support such boldness with concrete factual evidence or logical argument.

A provocative lead may come from the situation itself rather than from a judgment about the situation as above. Here's the best example and probably the most famous lead of all time.

> In the beginning God created Heaven and earth.

Hard to stop reading at this point. The audience is almost trapped into continuing to see how God did it.

THE CONTRAST OR CONFLICT LEAD

Aldous Huxley was a master of the contrast lead.

> The most distressing thing that can happen to a prophet is to be proved wrong; the next most distressing thing is to be proved right.

> In the twenty-five years that have elapsed since *Brave New World* was
> written, I have undergone both these experiences. Events have
> proved me distressingly wrong; and events have proved me distress-
> ingly right.

The paradox of this lead is so intriguing that the reader's interest is
immediately captured. At the same time, Huxley clearly implies his topic
(events confirmed or denied since the writing of his novel) as well as
the probable design of the essay (half on events that proved to be right,
half on events that proved wrong).

For some reason human beings have an eternal interest in conflict:
cops and robbers, cowboys and Indians, girls and boys. Find a conflict
or a clearly defined contrast, especially an unexpected one, and you'll
probably have a natural lead paragraph.

> The process of cloning may be one of the most beneficial discoveries
> ever made by humankind.
>
> But cloning may also lead to loss of individual rights and free-
> dom, political dictatorship, and a more frightening world than even
> George Orwell imagined in *1984*.

This student writer has emphasized conflicting opinions by using two
one-sentence paragraphs. Many teachers dislike the one-sentence paragraph and rightly so when it is used to make a random statement
without further development, evidence, or support. In general, one-sentence paragraphs should be avoided except when a strong emphasis is
desired—and that makes the lead an almost perfect place because a strong
emphasis may be just what you need to catch the reader's attention.

THE QUESTION LEAD

The question lead can fail miserably if it seems to be a substitute for a
more thoughtful or imaginative introduction. Try to avoid the rhetorical
or dead-end question: *Can human beings live without love? What is the meaning of life? Should disease be wiped out?* A truly thoughtful question, however,
can stimulate interest if it raises the reader's curiosity or seems to suggest
an impact on the reader's values, beliefs, or whatever. Here is a student
lead that raises legitimate issues.

> In 1974 the American Psychiatric Association voted to remove homo-
> sexuality from its category of mental illness. The ruling came after
> extensive gay lobbying. The new official definition uses the term
> "sexual orientation disturbances." But the action of the APA raises
> serious questions about psychiatry as a so-called science. Can the dif-

ference between illness and social deviation be determined by a vote instead of by empirically gathered evidence? If medical doctors decided to vote that a ruptured appendix is not an illness, would we accept the decision? And if psychiatrists have no more sound method for determining mental illness than by voting on it, how can we accept their testimony in, say, a trial for murder in which the accused has pleaded innocent by reason of insanity? Can psychiatry really be called a science if we know that, through lobbying and organized pressure, psychologists can so easily redefine the nature of abnormality?

In an age dominated by psychology, such questions have direct impact on us all. The question lead also sets up a natural organization for your paper: You have to answer your own question.

THE CUMULATIVE-INTEREST LEAD

Seven dead of wounds. A twenty-one-year-old woman paralyzed from the neck down. Four widows. Twelve children left without fathers. Over $158,000 in medical and funeral expenses. Two hundred and six robberies. These were the statistics for one city—Los Angeles—during a single month without gun-control legislation.

The cumulative-interest lead attempts to overwhelm the reader with a ''pileup'' of facts, sometimes without attaching the facts to any specific subject until several sentences into the essay. Dramatic lists or statistics seem to stimulate interest automatically.

The above lead comes from a student report. Even though it does not directly state the subject of the report, the tone and focus—even the conclusion—are implied. The author has presented a series of objective facts, yet each fact has been carefully selected for its impact. And the final sentence suggests the remainder of the paper will deal in more detail with gun-control legislation. If, for some reason, the paper actually focused on robberies committed with guns, then the lead would be a failure because the last sentence implies a larger issue.

Here is a cumulative-interest lead from an essay in *Smithsonian*.

For years now the stuff has been insidiously creeping into the nooks and crannies of our lives, firmly but unobtrusively shouldering aside the traditional materials of which our world is made. Cars are constructed of it, and boats and even airplanes, to say nothing of computer housings and camera bodies and fishing rods and watch cases and suitcases and cookware and roller skates and toothpaste tubes.

It has replaced the glass in our spectacles, the paper in our grocery bags, the wood in our tennis rackets, the cotton in our clothing and, in an especially pernicious peanut-shaped form used for packing material, it has exploded from a million cardboard appliance cartons to lodge under our couches and drive us to intemperate language.

It can be brittle or brutishly strong, dirt cheap or astonishingly expensive, fragile or virtually indestructible. It can go anyplace from outer space to the depths of the sea, and once there it will do just about any job it is called upon to do. For decades, as a society we have denigrated it even as we have consumed more and more of it. If in our fanciful moments many of us imagine ourselves in a world free of it, in *fact* most of us would sorely miss its extraordinary versatility and usefulness. By now the stuff has—literally—found its way into our hearts.

The stuff is, of course, plastic.

Like all leads, this one establishes a tone and a sense of direction. Although the lead begins with negatives, the clear suggestion is that a positive essay on plastic will follow.

THE DESCRIPTIVE LEAD

The descriptive lead might also be called the literary lead because it takes as its model the concept of the scene (see Chapter 10). Human beings have a natural interest in hearing stories. A scene, in effect, presents a story in miniature and is, therefore, one of the most popular and most effective means of concretely involving the reader.

For more than half an hour thirty-eight respectable, law-abiding citizens in Queens watched a killer stalk and stab a woman in three separate attacks in Kew Gardens. Twice the sound of their voices and the sudden glow of their bedroom lights interrupted him and frightened him off. Each time he returned, sought her out, and stabbed again. Not one person telephoned the police during the assault; one witness called after the woman was dead.

The horror of this news story is intensified by *The New York Times* writer who takes us step-by-step through the event. We hear the voices, we see lights in bedroom windows, and perhaps in our imagination we see the killer's shadow stalking the young woman. Not until the final word of the paragraph do we learn the result. The emphasis we placed on sense perception in earlier chapters can be used with dramatic effectiveness in a descriptive lead. Here is student Laura Stone's opening paragraph for a sociology report on aging. She began by visiting a nursing home.

> The old woman sat with her hunched back to me. Her wheelchair faced the window that looked out on a Sunoco gas station. Greasy barrels and stacks of used rubber tires and cardboard boxes of worn-out auto parts lined the back of the station. The light coming through the window seemed greasy and faded. The old woman's hair was curled in ringlets and the light shone through giving her a halo effect. From the next room a TV voice announced that The World Turns. I made a halfhearted attempt at saying hello but the old woman did not move an inch. Over her bed hung a crucifix with a plastic rose taped to it. On a nightstand there were several bottles of green pills, pink false teeth soaking in a glass of water, and several worn copies of *Reader's Digest*. I tried again. "Hello!" This time louder. "Hello!" Still the woman sat unmoving. The tile floors were polished, the white walls were newly painted. The bed was made. It was not a bad place. But the hunched old woman sat staring out through the window at the rear of a gas station, at the worn-out tires and generators and dead batteries.

Actually, the various types of leads are limited only by your own imagination. Furlong's lead, used at the beginning of this chapter, describing doctors injecting cancer cells into live patients, is a combination of the literary lead and the surprising statement. You could easily combine a question lead with a contrast lead or a literary lead with conflict, and so on.

It should be emphasized that a lead is not necessary. You can write an adequate informative investigation or essay without one or by using a factual 5 *W* lead. Most students and beginning writers never use leads. Yet a lead establishes a feeling of professionalism from the first sentence; it catches our imagination and makes us think, "Now here's a writer who seems to have something to say." Leads can do for you what almost no other writing technique can: capture the audience, set mood or tone, suggest the focus and organization of your essay, and psychologically prepare the reader to be more receptive to your ideas—all at the same time.

FINDING THE LEAD

Few professional writers wait until they have gathered all details on a subject before writing the lead. They train themselves to search out leads at the same time they are investigating the subject. Leads, therefore, directly relate to the exploration phase as well as to form and the first draft. If you come across a good quotation, an element of conflict, a dramatic change, a sensuous scene, or some startling fact, test it immediately in your mind: would this make a good lead? If you can come up with a lead *before* you ever sit down to write, you will have solved one of those inhibitions to writing: facing the blank page. There won't be a blank page. Instead, you'll already have a sentence or a paragraph in mind. Leads thus are vital to the writer as well as the reader. Knowing in advance that you've got the first sentence or first paragraph helps release tension, helps to release the flow of ideas so that writing gets off to a good start.

Never trust yourself, however, to accept the first lead that comes along. Keep looking. A better one may turn up as you further explore your subject. Always try to write out several leads before you settle on the best. Try them on friends. Read several leads aloud to a roommate. Find out which one the listener would be most responsive to, which would make him or her want to hear more. Some professional writers admit that they spend as much time on the lead as on all the rest of their essay.

On the other hand, if you haven't been able to identify a good lead during the investigation of the subject, go ahead and begin your first draft. You may find that in writing the paper a lead will appear in the middle of it or even in the last sentence. Many a writer has discovered that his or her conclusion made a better lead than it did a final paragraph. Don't be afraid to move sentences and paragraphs around. Remember that drafting is only a process of discovery, and what you may discover is that a scene or fact or detail you hadn't recognized as striking makes a natural introduction around which the rest of your ideas logically group themselves. In other words, let the lead work for you. Try to find it while studying the subject, but if you can't, don't panic. Let it find you during the writing process itself.

Exercises

1. Read each of the following leads. Discuss the technique the writer seems to be using. What type of tone or mood, if any, is established? From the brief sentence or paragraph provided, what probable design or organization of the material would you expect to follow? What specific quality in each lead makes it interesting or makes you want to read on?

All happy families resemble one another, but each unhappy family is unhappy in its own way.

> Leo Tolstoy, *Anna Karenina*

George Kastrides said it was like "being in the eye of a tornado with a high wind blowing." The passengers aboard TWA Flight 840 from Rome to Athens last week heard a loud bang. Then there was a flash of light. Oxygen masks dropped. A woman screamed. Several Arabs began chanting "*Al hamdu lil lah*" ("God be praised"). In the sudden swirl of wind and dust and flying particles, pilot Richard Peterson did not realize that four people, all Americans, had been blown out of the gaping hole in the Boeing 727. But Janet Chaffee looked behind her and saw sky where seat 10F had been. And on the ground, construction worker Alberto Ospina was still strapped into seat 10F when it hit the earth in a terrible tangle of blood and metal.

> *Newsweek*

Some hold that sports are childish, at best adolescent. "When one becomes a man, one ought to put aside the things of childhood." But what if participation in sports is the mark of a civilized person? What if it deepens and mellows the soul?

> Michael Novak, "The Metaphysics of Sport"

In the past few decades, man has become capable of controlling almost every aspect of life through modern equipment and increased knowledge and insight into and about the human body. But these medical and technical advances are having a dual effect. True, in many instances, they are prolonging life. But in many other cases, they are, more accurately, prolonging death.

> Student Research Paper

Once upon a time and a very good time it was there was a moocow coming down along the road and this moocow that was coming down along the road met a nicens little boy named baby tuckoo. . . .

His father told him that story: his father looked at him through a glass: he had a hairy face.

He was baby tuckoo. The moocow came down the road where Betty Byrne lived: she sold lemon platt. . . .

When you wet the bed first it is warm then it gets cold. His mother put on the oilsheet. That had the queer smell.

> James Joyce, *A Portrait of the Artist as a Young Man*

When in the Course of human Events, it becomes necessary for one
People to dissolve the Political Bands which have connected them
with another, and to assume among the Powers of the Earth, the
separate and equal Station to which the Laws of Nature and of
Nature's God entitled them, a decent Respect to the Opinions of
Mankind requires that they should declare the causes which impel
them to the Separation.

Thomas Jefferson, Declaration of Independence

2. Create three different types of leads based on the following collection of material. Assume that this material represents the core of
observations and research you have made on your subject. Which elements would be most interesting to begin with? Which elements might
suggest a way of organizing the rest of the material?

   a. Marietta Bowker has lived in Bay's End, Maine, for her whole
      life, some ninety-three years.
   b. She raises strawberries, cabbage, corn, and tomatoes.
   c. She now walks with a cane.
   d. When she was sixteen, she married Harold Bowker and gave birth
      to thirteen children in the next fifteen years.
   e. "I drink a nip of whiskey every day, and sometimes I smoke a
      cigar," she says, laughing.
   f. She wears a red dress with white lilies on it.
   g. The ocean breezes blow through the open window of her house.
   h. Her six books of poetry have never sold more than fifty copies
      apiece.
   i. There are geraniums on her windowsill.
   j. She has outlived her husband and seven of her children, but she
      has thirty-two grandchildren and nine great-grandchildren.
   k. She last went to the movies in 1932.
   l. She walks five miles a day.
   m. She doesn't know why she has lived so long.
   n. "I just regret I didn't write more poetry," she says.

3. Return to one of your earlier assignments and write at least three
different leads for it. For example, if you wrote an objective report for
Part III, try to come up with three new ways of beginning the same
paper. Write a descriptive lead, a contrast lead, and a bold statement.

4. Audience and intention make a difference in how you begin anything you write. Choose a previous assignment or exercise, and write
new leads addressed to several different audiences. For example, if you
wrote a character sketch for Part II, use the same material to create

three new leads: one for an essay to be published in a psychological journal; another for an essay to be distributed anonymously to your peers in a sociology class; a third for an essay to be included in a new anthology entitled *Interesting Americans*, intended for sale to a general audience.

Journal Practice

Here are some suggestions for this week's freewriting.

1. Write about a time you bought something you desperately wanted but later regretted. Describe the object, sharing details that made it so enticing to you. Include your feelings about it before you bought it and after. What made you regret the purchase, and why? How did your feelings and attitude change?

2. Write about a haunting agony: a sister who was accidentally killed; the day you were fired from your first job; being kicked off the soccer team your senior year; the time you discovered your younger brother was doing drugs. Focus sharply on a single specific scene and include characters and dialogue.

Copying

Practice copying leads (which may vary from one sentence to full paragraphs). Copy at least three different kinds of leads from this chapter. Watch for particularly striking leads while reading newspapers or magazines and be sure to copy them into your notebook.

Discovering Form

21

Visual Forms

Aldous Huxley has stated that the writer must have the urge "first of all, to order the facts one observes and to give meaning to life." To discover the pattern formed by a series of facts is to find order and meaning. Your audience shares that need with you. It cannot see meaning in your work without form or pattern. Random facts are like those disconnected dots on the page of a child's coloring book. Only when the dots are connected and only when they are connected in recognizable shapes is meaning communicated. Without order, without form or design or plan, we have only chaos, and chaos is not meaningful.

The most simple example proves the point. Try mixing up the sequence for a butterscotch brownies recipe:

Bake for 20 minutes.

Stir into the butter mixture.

Sprinkle flour on the dates and figs.

Cut into bars and serve.

Sift ½ cup of flour.

Pour the batter into a greased pan.

Chop the dates and figs.

Grease pan.

Melt ½ cup of butter in a saucepan.

Cool the ingredients.

Preheat oven to 350°.

Beat in one egg.

Without the proper arrangement, nothing makes sense.

And just as there is no one recipe that serves all types of cooking, you should not expect any one pattern or method of organization to serve all types of writing. In a personal essay, the arrangement of the parts usually grows organically out of the experience you've had with the subject. In more objective writing, form may sometimes grow out of the complex subject-audience-context-purpose or it may be based on an imitation of a traditional design. In a formal research paper, organization is usually constructed around a conventional thesis design. The frustrating part about "ordering the facts" is that for every set of facts there always seems to be a different order.

HOW THE LEAD SUGGESTS FORM

In many cases the organization of a paper can be discovered in the process of searching out the best lead. We've already noted how the 5 W lead suggested a natural sequence for an objective report. As the 5 W structure provides all major information in the first few sentences, it follows logically that less and less important information must trail behind. The visual design illustrates the form.

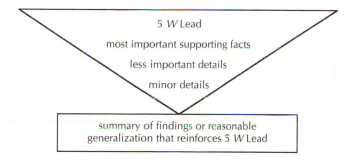

5 W Lead

most important supporting facts

less important details

minor details

summary of findings or reasonable
generalization that reinforces 5 W Lead

Note, however, that the lead does not *create* form. Rather, in the process of searching for a lead, you find that you must sift through all the information you have gathered; you must question the value, meaning, and worth of it; and you must consider your audience, purpose, and context. Each of these factors affects your choice of a lead. But these are the same factors that influence overall organization. In the process of looking for a lead, the mind wrestles with the shape of the subject itself. Just as the 4 C method of investigation gives you a strategy for finding potential meaning in a subject, so the lead gives you a strategy— a method—for finding an effective form. A lead is never something patched onto the beginning of an essay merely to make the introduction interesting. A lead is integral to the whole body of material you are working with.

Because we are visually oriented creatures, professional writers have developed several specific diagrams to help themselves envision forms that often grow out of the imaginative leads discussed in the previous chapter. Remember, however, that these patterns of organization are only suggestions, not rules.

THE PROVOCATIVE LEAD DESIGN

Because the provocative lead is usually a bold generalization of some sort—and usually judgmental—the nature of the lead demands that it be supported with objective evidence. Once the facts and data have been given, the strength of the lead is then reinforced by repeating it as the conclusion, usually with different wording.

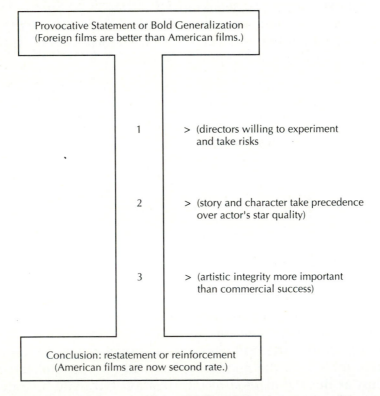

The sequence of facts in the middle of the paper may be organized either from most important to least important or the reverse. Good arguments have been presented for both methods. By starting with your weakest facts and building to your strongest, you raise the intensity of your paper as you progress and hope to sweep the reader along with you. On the other hand, by beginning with your strongest points, you hope to demonstrate immediately the truth of your bold generalizations by providing overwhelming evidence. In the above example, I've organized from "least to most." To me, artistic integrity is the final and most important critical judgment. Either organization method may be effective. But do have a method: Don't jump randomly from strong point to weak point. Begin forcefully, present your facts in a planned sequence, and end forcefully.

THE CONTRAST DESIGN

A lead that calls attention to some type of opposition implies to the reader that you will deal equally and fairly with both sides of the conflict. For example, if you investigated the latest increase in tuition, you would find many students opposed; but you would also find explanations in support of it, perhaps from administrators. On a larger scale, an investigation of welfare costs might turn up many who would justify a large federal budget and others who would oppose it. The easiest way of organizing such information is to group all facts supporting one position in the first half of your report and all facts supporting the other position in the second half. This organization has the benefit of simplicity for both you and the reader.

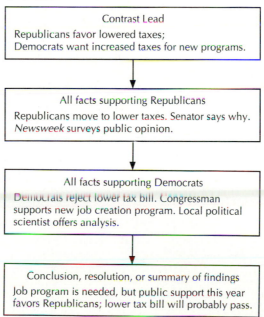

But it is not the only way to contrast material. A second method reveals the conflict more directly by alternating facts supporting one position with facts supporting the other (this is usually done by giving a paragraph or a page to each in alternating sequence). Most of us like a good debate. A back-and-forth exchange creates the tension and interest of two good debaters.

A word of caution, however. The alternating method of organization is more difficult for both reader and writer. Unless clear transitions are used at each changeover, the reader can easily become lost. Gather a good supply of transitions before you begin: *however, by contrast, in opposition to that view, but, on the other hand,* and so on.

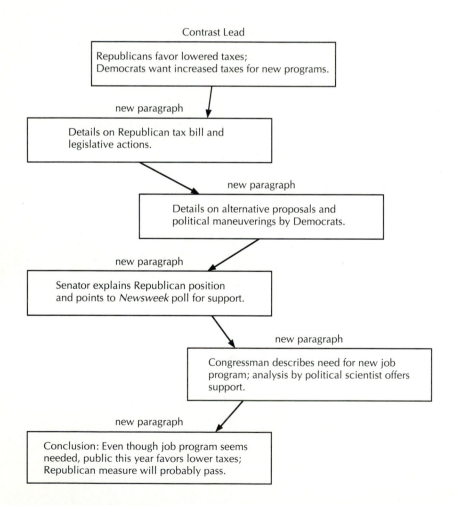

Contrast Lead

Republicans favor lowered taxes;
Democrats want increased taxes for new programs.

new paragraph

Details on Republican tax bill and
legislative actions.

new paragraph

Details on alternative proposals and
political maneuverings by Democrats.

new paragraph

Senator explains Republican position
and points to *Newsweek* poll for support.

new paragraph

Congressman describes need for new job
program; analysis by political scientist offers
support.

new paragraph

Conclusion: Even though job program seems
needed, public this year favors lower taxes;
Republican measure will probably pass.

THE LITERARY DESIGN

Both the *cumulative-interest lead* and the *descriptive lead* suggest the possibility of moving from the specific details with which each begins toward a more general or abstract understanding of the details. The conclusion, as in a work of literature, remains in suspense until the final page. This type of organization is the opposite of the inverted pyramid.

The literary-lead design has several major advantages for the objective investigation or personal essay written in a humanities or social science course. The nature of the lead captures the reader's interest immediately; the ever-increasing importance of the details maintains interest and builds step-by-step toward what you hope will be seen as an inevitable conclusion. The form suggests a logical mind at work and tends to lead the reader toward accepting the concluding generalization. As in reading a mystery novel, the reader continues to the end in order to discover the fullest realization of facts you've perceived.

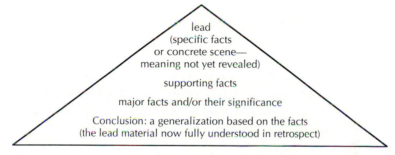

lead
(specific facts
or concrete scene—
meaning not yet revealed)

supporting facts

major facts and/or their significance

Conclusion: a generalization based on the facts
(the lead material now fully understood in retrospect)

If we now consider the *lead* in retrospect, we see that its role in writing can be central both for reader and writer. For the reader, a lead creates interest and captures attention. It suggests tone, mood, and direction. For the writer, it provides an excellent method of getting started on the first draft. And it suggests a design or organization for the report as a whole.

Finding order in your subject need not be quite as overwhelming if, in the process of selecting the best lead, you also discover an organizational pattern for all that follows. Perhaps that's why professional writers willingly spend so much time on leads. They know that once the lead is set, the remainder of the paper will flow more easily.

Ultimately, of course, form grows out of content, not out of a predetermined diagram. Visual designs are not a substitute for engaging your mind with the subject. They offer only outlines that may help you "see" the content and discover its potential.

Exercises

1. Three groups of facts are collected below. Study the relationship within each group, and determine which of the visual designs discussed in this chapter might be best for organizing the facts. Draw the design on a full sheet of paper, and test your proposal by filling in the appropriate spaces.

  a.   Trucking should not be regulated, according to Congressman Smith.

Government statistics show higher costs owing to regulation.

Trucking owners want regulations to continue.

Some costs are double because of regulations.

Economic analysts in Washington say that industry fears competition if regulations are removed.

Regulations allow small companies to survive, according to the secretary of commerce.

  b.   The price of gold has gone down.

Oil nations want more dollars for oil.

Unemployment is increasing.

The President announces, ''I will support the dollar.''

A local economist fears a depression.

The danger to our economy was never greater.

  c.   The board of regents is concerned about a balanced budget.

Six men have gathered in the board-of-regents room; afternoon light filters in; coffee cups clank; discussion is heated; voices rise.

Board members agree to reinvest the funds in a South African gold mine.

Outside the windows two hundred students with signs march in a circle.

The return on the investment is enough to pay for five faculty salaries.

The students are concerned about moral values.

Students are protesting having university funds invested in a foreign country.

A student leader says the funds support racism and dictatorship.

An investigation of the financial statement reveals that ten percent of the funds are invested in foreign countries.

2. Study the readings included at the end of this unit. What relationship between the lead and overall design can you identify?

3. Draw a visual outline of the last paper you wrote for this or any

other class. It does not need to look like any of the designs discussed in this chapter, but it ought to reveal the organization—or lack of organization—in your essay.

Journal Practice

Play

1. Messed around in your journal lately? Written any songs? Told any jokes? Invented the world's lousiest poem? Why not try inventing your own titles for books you'll never write? Be outrageous.

Here are a few examples to get you started: *Radical Chic and Mau-Mauing the Flak Catchers, The Oranging of America, Why Smaller Refrigerators Can Preserve the Human Race, Let's Stop Exalting Jerks, Four and Twenty Golden Umbrellas, Fast-Fish and Loose Fish, The Yogurt of Vasirin Kefirovsky, The Kandy-Kolored Tangerine-Flake Streamline Baby.*

2. List a dozen haunting images: a mottled sea turtle surfacing in the moonlight beneath a pier; letters blowing across a field; the skeletons of two bighorn sheep locked together; Pauline's pet pig caught and frozen in the electric fence. Select one image and expand on it in your journal.

Revising and Editing

22

Rhythm, Variety, and Emphasis

H ave you ever "listened" to your writing? Here's a paragraph from a student who hasn't.

Professor Shirley Baxton is in the English department. The interview was held in her office. She told me that she believed writing should be required in the whole university. She didn't believe it should be just required for English. She has a reputation for having high standards. She says writing is an expression of the inner self. She says it should be part of the experience we have in every class.

These are perfectly correct sentences, but not the sentences of real life. This student has not listened with his inner ear, and the result is Dick-and-Jane monotony. People don't talk this way. And even though good writing is not identical to speech, it should sound like speech. Good writing should reflect all the variety and points of emphasis found in the best conversation; it should express the rhythms of the human voice.

RHYTHM

Rhythm means flow. Effective writing has a flow to it that suggests the sound patterns of living speech. And yet rhythm involves more than sound; it is inseparable from clarity, coherence, unity, order, and all the other elements of style as they work together within a specific context. Prose with little meaning is almost always accompanied by weak rhythms, and, in turn, weak and awkward rhythms signal that meaning may not yet be clearly expressed. Many of our best writers insist that one must develop an ear for the silent rhythm of the printed page. The best method for doing so, and the one least likely to be attempted by most students, is to listen to good prose as it's read aloud. The ear is more sensitive to rhythm than the eye.

Read aloud the following passage from Abraham Lincoln's First Inaugural Address. Listen to the voice you hear.

> I am loath to close. We are not enemies, but friends. We must not be
> enemies. Though passion may have strained it must not break our
> bonds of affection. The mystic chords of memory, stretching from
> every battlefield and patriot grave, to every heart and hearthstone,
> all over this broad land, will yet swell the chorus of the Union, when
> again touched, as surely they will be, by the better angels of our
> nature.

Lincoln begins with a short sentence, followed by another short sentence lengthened only slightly by a second clause. He returns to the short pattern and then moves on to what might be considered a sentence of medium length. The final sentence begins a long sweeping roll where clause after clause delays the most important words, like a symphony building toward a final musical statement. Read it aloud and the passage sings. But did you? I've taken surveys of my students and found that when I give this exercise, two-thirds continue to read silently. Yet rhythm, which is so essential to effective prose, cannot be learned in silence. If you would learn to play the drum, you must bang on it and listen to the sounds; if you would learn to write well, you must read aloud both good prose by professional writers and your own prose. And you must listen to the rhythms. If, out of laziness or shyness or whatever, you choose not to read aloud, you ignore one of the primary techniques our best authors have found successful. Quite simply, the student who reads aloud will have an advantage over the one who doesn't.

Let's return to the Lincoln passage and see what can be learned. Perhaps most important, we discover that rhythm is not a part of any one sentence. Rhythm is always found in context. That is why neither

I nor anyone else can establish a "correct" or "model" sentence for you to imitate. There are none. A sentence is not a static or rigid absolute. A perfectly good sentence in one context will fail miserably in another. The *subject-audience-context-purpose* and your own voice must all be considered—consciously at this stage, where you may feel unsure of yourself, intuitively at a later stage, when practice and experience can be supported by the ear of your imagination. Lincoln's prose reflects his personality, his voice. We know that to be true because, in this particular instance, we have not only the four drafts that Lincoln worked on but also a first draft written by William H. Seward, who was to become Lincoln's secretary of state. Here are Seward's words.

> I close. We are not, we must not be, aliens or enemies, but fellow countrymen and brethren. Although passion has strained our bonds of affection too hardly, they must not, I am sure they will not, be broken. The mystic chords which proceeding from so many battlefields and so many patriot graves, pass through all the hearts and hearths in this broad continent of ours, will yet again harmonize in their ancient music when breathed upon by the guardian angel of the nation.

Seward's proposal has its own rhythm, but Lincoln improved on it. Compare Seward's blunt and unsatisfactory first sentence with Lincoln's still brief but more melodious version. In turn, compare the simplicity of Lincoln's second sentence with Seward's choppy (and somewhat clichéd) second sentence. Read both versions aloud. What other changes in the next three sentences improve the flow? Can you determine how changes in rhythm parallel the clarification (and simplification) of meaning?

If we represent Lincoln's sentences with graph lines, we might diagram the paragraph so:

Sentence 1: _____.
Sentence 2: _____, _____.
Sentence 3: _____.
Sentence 4: _____.
Sentence 5: _____, _____, _____, _____,
            _____, _____, _____,
            _____.

Obviously, variety of sentence structure and length are key elements. In art, music, dance, and language, rhythm is always achieved by theme and variation, by establishing a pattern and then varying the pattern.

EDITING FOR VARIETY IN SENTENCE PATTERNS

Sentences can be simple, compound, complex, or even compound-complex. If you're unsure of the differences, you might want to look into a handbook on grammar. Yet knowing definitions for sentence structure is not as important as knowing that every sentence ought to organize a thought into a clear, coherent pattern that flows well within the larger context of your essay. Two editing steps discussed in earlier chapters (omitting needless words and using strong verbs) should help you begin. Return to the student example on page 250. If we graph-lined that paragraph, it would look something like this:

Sentence 1: _____ .
Sentence 2: _____ .
Sentence 3: _____ .
Sentence 4: _____ .
Sentence 5: _____ .
Sentence 6: _____ .
Sentence 7: _____ ____ .

The variation here is slight at best. Each sentence makes a simple statement with a subject-verb-object sequence; each is approximately the same length as its neighbor. The monotony is deadening. But through careful editing, we can combine some of those Dick-and-Jane constructions into sentences of varying lengths and rhythms.

Circle unnecessary or repetitive words. Find the action and rebuild around it:

action

Professor Shirley Baxton (is)(in)(the) English department. (The) interview (was) held in her office.

Result:

I interviewed English Professor Shirley Baxton in her office.

Two sentences reduced to one saves six words and eliminates choppiness.

Again, circle unnecessary or repetitive words. Find the action and rebuild around it:

action

She (told)(me)(that)(she) believed writing should be required in the whole university. She (didn't)(believe)(it) should be just required for English.

Result:

She believes writing should be required throughout the university curriculum, not just in English classes.

Even though I've added new words for clarity, we still save eight words and improve the flow.

Circle unnecessary or repetitive words. Find the action and rebuild around it:

action

(She)(has)(a) reputation for having high standards. (She) says writing is an expression of the inner self. (She)(says)(it) should be part of the experience we have in every class.

Result:

Baxton, who has a reputation for high standards, says writing is an expression of the inner self and should therefore be a part of every classroom experience.

In the process of performing this type of editorial act, we not only clarify meaning, but also enhance it by creating a more natural rhythm. Yet when I read these new sentences aloud as a complete paragraph, the second sentence still jars my ear. It seems out of place. Because I'm at a loss on how to change the sentence further, my "ear" suggests that the second sentence might exchange places with the third. A fortunate discovery. When this is done, the logic itself proves more convincing.

I interviewed English Professor Shirley Baxton in her office. Baxton, who has a reputation for high standards, says writing is an expression of the inner self and should therefore be a part of every classroom experience. She believes writing should be required throughout the university curriculum, not just in English classes.

Now I think we have a more precise statement supported by a rhythm that, without calling attention to itself, suggests a natural, if somewhat formal, speech pattern. *The first step in editing for variety in sentences, then, is not deliberately to make sentences longer or shorter, but to make them better.* Almost inevitably, the rhythms will begin to flow.

Here is the process.

1. Circle unnecessary and repetitive words.
2. Locate the action.
3. Combine or rebuild around the verb.
4. Read aloud.

THE PARALLEL SENTENCE

Effective writing needs more than just a mixture of long and short sentences, however. Rhythm does not exist for its own sake but to heighten clarity and emphasize important or related elements. For that reason, you must develop a familiarity with the concept of *parallelism*—a method of shaping sentences so that a series of related ideas is expressed in a related grammatical structure. What that grammatical structure might be does not matter—a series of similar verb forms, a series of similar prepositional phrases, a series of nouns—so long as each follows a parallel pattern on the page.

Let's begin with a single idea.

Roger's dad promised to buy him a new bicycle.

But what if Roger's dad made two promises, and the two promises were related?

Roger's dad promised to buy him a new bicycle *and* that he would let him ride it before Christmas.

Now we have two related ideas, but the sentence structure does not show that relationship. The promised idea before the *and* is expressed differently from the promised idea after the *and*. Here's how we could make each clause show the relationship.

Roger's dad promised to buy him a new bicycle and to let him ride it before Christmas. ⟶ ⟶

In this case, infinitives have been made parallel (*to buy, to let*). The result forms a closer psychological relationship in the mind of the reader. The ideas seem to cohere more closely.

We can create the same parallelism with other grammatical structures.

The company wants a new taxi driver who knows the city and who has a good safety record. (*adjectives clauses are parallel*)
Chinita believes in God, motherhood, and country. (*nouns are parallel*).

Parallelism is not merely a grammatical device made fetish by English teachers. Parallel structure is one of the oldest techniques in our language, existing long before English grammar itself was ever set down in rule books. We can trace its importance in English to the influence of the Bible, where parallelism was a basic element of Hebrew poetry.

Blessed are the meek, for they shall inherit the earth;

> Blessed are those who thirst for righteousness, for they shall be satisfied.

The effectiveness of parallel structure can be most clearly emphasized if we take such a well-known passage and rewrite it out of parallel.

> Blessed are the meek, for they shall inherit the earth;
> And we should also bless those who thirst for righteousness so satisfaction can be obtained by them as well.

What we discover is that a failure to provide parallel structure not only makes relationships between ideas less clear but also weakens the forcefulness of writing in general.

Poets and statesmen have long used parallel structure for the sense of dignity and strength it creates in the ear of the reader.

> Let the word go forth from this time and place, to friend and foe alike, that the torch has been passed to a new generation of Americans, born in this century, tempered by war, disciplined by a hard and bitter peace, proud of our ancient heritage, and unwilling to witness or permit the slow undoing of those human rights to which this nation has always been committed, and to which we are committed today at home and around the world.
>   Let every nation know, whether it wishes us well or ill, that we shall pay any price, bear any burden, meet any hardship, support any friend, oppose any foe to assure the survival and the success of liberty.
>
>   John F. Kennedy, Inaugural Address

In every case, the rhythm emphasizes and clarifies a relationship. The result is a coherence that can seldom be more effectively achieved.

THE BALANCED SENTENCE

A *balanced sentence* is related to parallelism, but the emphasis is achieved through the equal "weight" of each clause, not necessarily through grammatical structure.

Both parallel and balanced structures tend to be found more often in formal prose than in informal writing, but even the most casual essay may reach a point where the relationship of ideas needs to be stressed clearly, and an otherwise informal style can often increase its impact on the reader by using carefully selected balanced sentences. Such symmetry not only is appealing to the ear, but it also suggests an almost irrefutable logic and can be especially effective in clarifying contrasts or in ending an essay with dramatic finality.

I come to bury Caesar, not to praise him.

Shakespeare

We have won our battle against necessity, but we don't know what to do with victory.

Sam Keen

The difference between tragedy and comedy is the difference between experience and intuition.

Christopher Fry

Do writers create balanced sentences or parallel structure on a first draft? No doubt, some do. After becoming familiar with the technique, you might do so, as well. But the place to teach yourself such forms is in the revising or editing phase. Any series of related ideas can be expressed in similar grammatical form, whereas contrasting ideas can be expressed in a balanced style. Do not be afraid to rearrange the parts of a sentence or to combine several sentences to achieve the desired emphasis.

THE PERIODIC SENTENCE

Emphasis can be achieved in other ways. The most amateurish way is to add an exclamation mark! Or worse, to underline important words just to make sure your reader gets the point!!!! Both exclamation marks and underlining have a place, but they quickly grow tiring, and in the long run they are merely external punctuation. A truly good sentence should achieve its emphasis from within. By arranging word order to fall at exactly the right point in a sentence, you can control the reader's reaction. When a sentence delays the most important words for last through the use of several interior clauses, we call it a *periodic sentence*. The trick is to postpone the important words, as Lincoln did in the final sentence of his First Inaugural Address, to delay and create suspense, to build the reader's anticipation, and then to fulfill it with a bang.

Simple sentence:
Beverly decided to run for president.

Periodic sentence:
Beverly, who had so often thought of herself only as a housewife, a servant of others, and a woman of no special talents, decided to run for president.

The order should follow the natural intensity of the details. Build from the least important to the most important, and the rhythms as well as the suspense will create a sense of controlled tension.

The dictator exploited his country's resources, stole from the common people, executed those who opposed him, and trampled over their corpses.

Sentences have movable parts and you should feel free to experiment with their arrangement. Move the parts about. Combine and recombine. Read each of your experiments aloud and test it with your ear.

We have a responsibility to look further into how we were drawn into war. A nation like ours has a high moral tradition. Perhaps what we find will teach us a lesson about the future.

Try an experiment. Combine and rearrange the parts:
To learn what lessons it will teach us about the future, we have a responsibility, as a nation with high moral traditions, to know how we became drawn into war.

Experiment again. Recombine the parts:
A nation like ours, with its high moral tradition, has a responsibility to discover how we were drawn into war and to learn what lessons it will teach us about the future.

By attempting several versions and by reading each aloud, you will quickly detect the difference in emphasis and rhythm. Of course, if you turned every sentence into a periodic sentence or a balanced sentence, you would not have theme and variation. Lincoln used three relatively short, simple sentences and one medium-length sentence before building to a crescendo in a final periodic sentence. The short rhythms made the long rhythms more effective. A blunt sentence can often be the best way to emphasis, especially at the beginning or end of an essay. Short sentences have force. They make a point. Use them. But use them with recognition that they must be rhythmically varied with other types of sentences for the total effect to seem natural to our human patterns of speech.

EMPHASIS THROUGH WORD ORDER

The components of even a simple sentence may be arranged to affect emphasis. Your purpose determines what is placed at the beginning of each sentence.

Purpose: to emphasize Eisenhower's leadership
Dwight D. Eisenhower directed the Normandy invasion from a small base in England.

Purpose: to describe the invasion
The Normandy invasion was directed by Dwight D. Eisenhower from a small base in England.

Purpose: to recount England's role in the invasion
It was from a small base in England that Dwight D. Eisenhower directed the Normandy invasion.

But the traditional point for emphasis in the sentence (as well as in the paragraph) is at the end.

Weak emphasis:
The concept of "giving until it hurts" derives from an irrational guilt, in my opinion.

Strong emphasis:
In my opinion, the concept of "giving until it hurts" derives from irrational guilt.

By arranging your words so that they build toward the most forceful term or phrase, you lead the reader toward the most important idea. Your purpose is more effectively achieved.

Weak emphasis	*Strong emphasis*
Our neighborhoods are still unsafe and dirty, Councilman Moody told me.	Councilman Moody told me our neighborhoods are still dirty and unsafe.
My father remained a widower for twenty years. The women he met always lost out, and Dad lost out, too, because he compared them with my mother.	For twenty years my father remained a widower. Because he compared the women he met with my mother, the women always lost, but Dad lost, too.

In some ways, all of this is only common sense. The order of words affects the meaning. Writers and speakers knew that long before textbooks were dreamed of. And, no doubt, you already knew it and make use of it in your everyday speech, especially when trying to be forceful or "make a point." Rhythm, variation, and emphasis are natural to speech. You must make them equally natural to your prose. During the editing phase, read aloud, *listen* to what you have written, and be willing to combine, rearrange, or rewrite until each sentence sounds strong and natural, as if spoken in your own voice.

Exercises

1. Identify the method by which each of these sentences achieves its effectiveness.

>   a. There is an appointed time for everything, and
>   a time for every affair under the heavens.
>   A time to be born, and a time to die;
>   a time to plant, and a time to uproot the plant.
>
> Ecclesiastes

>   b. In proportion as men delight in battles, bullfighting, and combats of gladiators, will they punish by hanging, burning, and the rack.
>
> Herbert Spencer

>   c. The best writing, both prose and poetry, as Shakespeare preeminently shows, makes use, with condensation and selection, of playful, impassioned, imaginative talk.
>
> Sidney Cox

>   d. Consider what had happened to me: I had thought myself lost, had touched the very bottom of despair; and then, when the spirit of renunciation had filled me, I had known peace.
>
> Antoine de Saint Exupéry

2. Rewrite the following passages to achieve a more natural rhythm. First, circle unnecessary and repetitive words. Second, find the action. Third, combine sentences or rebuild sentences around the verb.

>   a. The *College Chimes* is the campus newspaper. I interviewed Tony Rosenblatt, who is the editor of the *Chimes*. The interview was conducted in the *Chimes* office located in the basement of the student union. Tony Rosenblatt is a senior majoring in English.

Tony was dressed in faded jeans and a wrinkled shirt that said, "Country Time Lemonade" on the front.

b. Brown's family was not a particularly religious one at all. His grandmother made him attend a religious revival that was taught by a man with particularly narrow views about the Bible and religious areas. He was a traveling evangelist. The man's name was LeRoy Jedson. His sermon was filled with hell fire and brimstone and threats of what would happen to sinners.

3. Make each of the following sentences parallel. First identify areas that need to be related. Then choose a pattern of expression and rewrite each idea to fit the pattern.

a. The ballerina is light, very agile, and moves with grace.

Identify related ideas:
light
very agile
moves with grace

Choose one pattern:
light ← *possible choice*
very agile
moves with grace

Express each idea in the same pattern:
light
agile
graceful

Rewrite the sentence in parallel form:
The ballerina is light, agile, and graceful.

b. Henry advised him forget time and to forge ahead for victory.
c. All work and not playing makes life dull.
d. Julio promised to bring a copy of the play and that he would not be late.
e. A few generations ago children learned early in life to obey their parents without question, to consider all adults their superiors until told differently, and they had much better table manners.
f. It was a time not for words but action.
g. The French, Italians, the Spanish, and Portuguese all speak a form of language that derives from the Romans.
h. A perfect croissant is tender, flaky, and, of course, good tasting.
i. My objections are, first, the injustice of the measure; second, that it is unconstitutional; and third, an inhumaneness.

j. Each room in the dorm is complete with little closet space, no air conditioning, bedroom and living room combined in one room, no appliances, and the sharing of bathroom facilities with forty other students.

k. We shall not always expect to find them supporting our view; but their freedom is something they have to put their support behind.

4. Edit your last writing assignment for rhythm, variation, and emphasis. Do not make changes merely to make changes. Read each passage aloud. Rewrite only those sentences that need to be improved so that the whole of it sounds natural to your ear.

Journal Practice

Copying

As you've already learned, because it slows down the eye, copying is one of the best ways to learn about composing. At the same time, it helps develop style. Many rhythms and varieties of sentence structure that seem new to you become assimilated through copying and will resurface at some future time in your own writing.

1. Copy Abraham Lincoln's paragraph on page 251 or John F. Kennedy's on page 256. Turn back to David Hopes' essay and copy the final paragraph on page 82, or to the paragraph of Jane Winslow Eliot on page 162.

2. Over the period of a week, copy each of the following passages, one per day, before you do your own freewriting. You'll find the rhythms become infectious.

> For everything there is a season, and a time for every purpose under heaven: a time to be born, and a time to die; a time to plant, and a time to pluck up that which is planted; a time to kill, and a time to heal; a time to break down, and a time to build up; a time to weep, and a time to laugh; a time to mourn, and a time to dance; a time to cast away stones, and a time to gather stones together. . . .
>
> The Bible, King James Version

> Persons attempting to find a motive in this narrative will be prosecuted; persons attempting to find a moral in it will be banished; persons attempting to find a plot will be shot.
>
> Mark Twain

She was very old and small and she walked slowly in the dark pine shadows, moving a little from side to side in her steps, with the balanced heaviness and lightness of a pendulum in a grandfather clock.

Eudora Welty

It was the best of times, it was the worst of times, it was the age of wisdom, it was the age of foolishness, it was the epoch of belief, it was the epoch of incredulity, it was the season of Light, it was the season of Darkness, it was the spring of hope, it was the winter of despair, we had everything before us, we had nothing before us, we were all going direct to Heaven, we were all going direct the other way—in short, the period was so far like the present period, that some of its noisiest authorities insisted on its being received, for good or for evil, in the superlative degree of comparison only.

Charles Dickens

When I awoke in the morning she was already at her machine, or in the great morning crowd of housewives at the grocery getting fresh rolls for breakfast. When I returned from school she was at her machine, or conferring over *McCall's* with some neighborhood woman who had come in pointing hopefully to an illustration. . . . When my father came home from work she had somehow mysteriously interrupted herself to make supper for us, and the dishes cleared and washed, was back at the machine. When I went to bed at night, often she was still there, pounding away at the treadle. . . .

Alfred Kazin

Readings

Holly Paterno was a freshman majoring in French and Spanish when she investigated one of the principal controversies in her future profession. After beginning with an imaginative lead, Holly blends primary and secondary sources. Notice how her conclusion is strengthened by using various rhythmic devices including parallel structure.

Do You Speak American?
Sí Señor!

Holly Paterno

Let's say you move to Portugal because you want more opportunity for you and your family. Prices are low, the chance to make a fortune is great. Along with your wife and children, you take your grandmother, three cousins, and an aging uncle. When you arrive you join other Americans living in a small colony. Later, even more Americans follow. But the children have trouble in school. It seems that school teachers conduct classes in Portuguese. So you and the other Americans go on a public campaign to require schools to teach all subjects in English as well as Portuguese. That way your children won't fall behind. What surprises you is that the Portuguese get angry. They claim that if you choose to live in Portugal, raise your children there, earn your income there, you ought also to learn their customs and language. Are the Portuguese right? Or are they prejudiced against Americans and merely trying to deny your children an equal opportunity to compete?

All this would be hypothetical and silly if it weren't happening here and now in America.

In 1968, to assist students of immigrants who couldn't speak English, the United States government approved of funding bilingual education—instruction given in a child's native language while he or she also learns English. According to Woodrow Wilson University's Associate Professor of Spanish, Peter Valdez, the attempt had a noble aim: to prevent foreign-speaking children from being denied an equal opportunity because of language difficulties. *U.S. News* reports in its March 31, 1986 issue that many of the bilingual programs have been successful. In such places as Spring Valley Elementary School in San Francisco's Chinatown, three-fourths of the school's 580 pupils speak little or no English. They come from homes where not only is English not spoken, literacy itself often does not exist. "Such disparity between home life and school demands this type of instruction," says

Reprinted by permission of the author.

[Principal Lonnie] Chin. "It is incumbent on schools to bridge that gap, and that is the real purpose of bilingual education" (20). Test scores often support the claim. In Houston and Michigan, national scores in such subjects as math and science show that students (both native Americans and immigrants) who participate in multi-lingual programs have test scores at least equal to those in regular programs, and often better (21). In other words, there seems to be no particular evidence that the program has been educationally unsound.

But Professor Valdez is now concerned that the effort has been taken over by members of his own discipline (foreign language teachers) and by ethnic politicians for self-serving ends. "We now have several thousand teachers employed in bilingual programs, and several thousand government administrators, all who want the program to grow even bigger," Valdez says. "It means more job security. And we have street-corner councilmen who want to stay in office by arousing racial and ethnic emotions over the issue because it means more votes and more local power." Valdez claims that any opposition to the aims of these groups has been labeled as racist. And there is evidence on both counts. The same issue of *U.S. News* indicates that by 1986 the government was spending $139 million on only 210,000 students involved in bilingual classrooms (20). The list of languages taught has spread from only a handful to hundreds. Describing "The Case Against Bilingual Education," Tom Bethell, writing in *Harper's* (February 1979), offers a partial list of the languages the U.S. government now provides. The list includes Central Yup'ik, Aleut, Gwich'in, Athabascan, Tagalog, Pima, Plaute, Ilocano, Punjabi, Keresian, Tewa, Chamorro, Trukese, Paluna, Ulithian, Yapese, and many others (32).

Not only does such evidence suggest the concept has grown topsy-turvy, Bethell claims that the original intention has become lost in the process. Students apparently are not being moved through the programs—from native speaking to English speaking and out—but being retained in the native speaking portions of the program by teachers and administrators who claim it is necessary for "maintenance" of the native language and customs. According to Bethell, a government report showed that 85% of the students are kept in bilingual programs after they are capable of learning English (32), and that fewer than one-third of the students now in the programs are there because they have not yet acquired sufficient English (34).

Yet this in itself might cause little controversy. Professor Valdez indicates that the real problem is that because of Cuban refugees and legal and illegal aliens from Mexico, the Spanish language dominates 80% of the bilingual programs. The number of Latin-speaking immigrants in the South and Southwest is now so large that Valdez believes they no longer feel they have a need to blend into the dominant culture. That is, they no longer need to learn English as part of the traditional melting pot, because their numbers are so large that in those areas Spanish *is* the dominant culture. *Newsweek* (June 30, 1986) provides evidence as support. It reports how in Miami, Florida, commercial signs, as well as radio and TV broadcasts, are often entirely in Spanish. Two women in Florida recently sued and won because they were actually turned down for jobs because they could not speak Spanish (24).

The consequence seems to be a creation of racial, ethnic, and cultural divisiveness. Backlash proposals to make English the official language are causing emotional and political tensions in numerous states, most recently in California. According to an editorial in *The Atlanta Constitution* (Oct. 4, 1986), proponents such as California Senator S.I. Hayakawa fear that bilingual culture will create a divided nation where Hispanic politicians will keep Spanish-speaking people in ghettos for a power base. Opponents such as Los Angeles Mayor Tom Bradley charge that trying to make English compulsory is "evil," "unjust," and "prejudiced" (4).

An objective look at other countries shows that language conflicts repeatedly cause this kind of political and cultural divisiveness. In Belgium, a long-standing conflict between those who speak Dutch and those who speak French has so divided the people into warring camps that a "language border" was actually drawn across the country in 1963. And in Canada, the province of Quebec has repeatedly raised the issue of secession as a separate French-speaking nation. Quebec currently requires French as its "official" language even though it is surrounded by an English-speaking culture.

The fact would seem to be that bilingual education in itself is not bad. The study of multiple languages has repeatedly proven to be a valuable educational exercise that increases intellectual acumen while creating broader understanding of differing cultures. The danger seems to arise when any group begins to think that multiple languages can exist side by side as part of a single culture. America may be a multi-racial, multi-ethnic society with only minor conflicts because of it, but a true multi-language culture may not be possible to create. Professor Peter Valdez claims that "language *is* culture." The clear implication is that separate language-speaking groups will always form separate cultures, and hence eventually want separate governments. George Will, writing in *Newsweek* (July 8, 1985), points out that language is the primary link between citizenship and a shared culture. "Immigrants, all of whom came here voluntarily, have a responsibility to reciprocate the nation's welcome by acquiring the language that is essential for citizenship" (78).

Children should not be denied the opportunity to succeed because of language difficulties. That is why they might be better off in intensive English language programs than in bilingual programs. No one in America should be forced to lose contact with their original culture. Mine is Italian, and it is a rich and valuable heritage. But neither should immigrants fail in their obligation to become a part of their new culture. America, too, as a varied multi-ethnic nation is rich and rewarding. I believe that all of us should be bilingual if we want to be well educated. But evidence would seem strongly to support the contention that our first language must be English if we want to be American.

In the following investigation, Julia Buchanan worked extensively with secondary sources. As a freshman planning to major in Mass Communications, she turned a critical eye on the media's role in reporting a major forest fire. "I was excited about what I found," she said. "It totally turned around my understanding of what happened."

Clearing the Smoke
Julia Buchanan

"A smoke blackened ruin." This is how *The Wall Street Journal* described Yellowstone Park following the fire of 1988 which reportedly "destroyed" one-half of the national forest. The American public was left with a vision of one of its favorite parks as a charred and sterile wasteland. According to Les Line, in his *Audubon* editorial "Etcetera," media coverage of this major ecological event was negative. During a total forty-seven minutes of television coverage by Tom Brokaw, Peter Jennings, and Dan Rather, the public was led to believe that the fire was an ecological disaster (4). In "Yellowstone Renewed," *U. S. News and World Report*, May 15, 1989, Michael Satchell reports that T.V. images and published reports angered the public (26). The media led us to believe Yellowstone Park was "a smoke blackened ruin," which led to harsh criticism of William Penn Moot, Park Service Director and the park's "let burn" policy. Only once did a report suggest that the fire may have some beneficial effects (Line 4).

In his article "Incineration of Yellowstone," *Audubon*, January, 1989, Ted Williams criticizes newspapers like *The New York Times* for reporting that one half of the park had been destroyed when actually only half that amount had been burned. The media failed to inform the public and left them with the impression that the destruction was total (76). Richard Conniff's investigation, "Yellowstone's 'rebirth' amid the Ashes," published in the September 1989 issue of the *Smithsonian*, also criticizes the media for exaggerating the scale of the fire, and for publishing deliberately distorted photographs. He claims that many of the photo journalists angled their cameras so that the pictures they took made Yellowstone look firebombed. They did not bother to explain that many of the trees had already fallen down in a destructive windstorm in 1984 (40). In his investigative article on the fire, "Yellowstone: the Great Fire of 1988" for *National Geographic*, February, 1989, David Jeffrey reports that the media led the public to believe fires are disgraceful, and result from negligence and stupidity on the part of the forest service (271).

Why all this criticism of the media? So they exaggerated a little? So the photographs pictured death and destruction? So Brokaw, Rather and Jennings chose to present a negative picture rather than leaving us with a glimmer of hope. What else might they have reported?

They could have reported the facts. The American public relies on the media for information. While many of us might accept some exaggeration, we expect journalists to do their homework. Although it is true that the National Park Service does have a "let burn" policy, the media failed to inform the public just what that policy means or why it was adopted. Given the opportunity to educate us, what information might have been reported?

First, the positive effects of fire on forests has been well established by scientists for the past century. A natural burn tends to stimulate forest growth and make meadows. Irregular fire burn patterns promote growth of diverse vegetation which in turn supports diverse animal life. Fire also clears out deadwood fallen under healthier trees, and because fires burn corridors through solid masses of trees, the risk of future fire spreading is actually reduced. Jeffrey quotes John Varley, Yellowstone's director of research, as saying that he looks forward to an increase in plant and animal species in the park over the next twenty years (258).

Ted Williams points out that evidence shows major fires every two hundred to four hundred years are natural, and those who know how to look understand the value of natural burn. "Many plant communities absolutely require it" (51). His reassurance that the burned meadows in Yellowstone would be recovered the following summer has been confirmed by many visitors who returned to the park during the summer of 1989. Satchell reports sightings of larkspur, delphinium, American bistort and other native wildflowers (25). According to Conniff, a year later meadows were green. Grizzlies, elk, bison, moose, bighorn, small mammals, bluebirds and sandhill cranes had returned. Insects had begun to recolonize. "It looks like there's nothing here, and then you wait round a while and things show up," Conniff reports (38).

A year after the fire, the American public is now being reassured by the media that the forest will be healthier and more biologically diverse (Satchell 24). Photographs of blooming wildflowers and new grass sprouting out of a charred landscape have helped us forget the negative and exaggerated newspaper and television reports which succeeded in convincing us that Yellowstone was indeed "a blackened ruin." A year after the fire, the Interior Departments' post fire review has found that the "let-burn" policy was sound and should remain unchanged (24). While photos taken in 1989 of elk grazing in a sunlit meadow may help the public forget the disastrous reports of the fire the year before, none of us should forgive the media for choosing to sensationalize and exaggerate a major ecological event. The media had the option of clearing the smoke by educating the public to the benefits of forest fire and a sound Park Service policy. They failed the test.

Lynette Lamb wrote the following essay for the Utne Reader, *a journal devoted to "alternative" views. Using both primary and secondary sources, Lamb investigates censorship that may be occurring out of sight of the general public.*

Censorship in Publishing

Lynette Lamb

Book censorship is not confined to small-town bonfires of *Catcher in the Rye*, nor does it necessarily begin only after a book is published. Many controversial books today never make it past the editor's desk. Critics contend that the current structure of the industry—with huge corporations pushing blockbuster bestsellers—has increasingly led to timidity among publishers and pervasive self-censorship among writers and editors.

Books written by marketable name authors have a better chance of being published today than do good books, claims Louise Armstrong in *The Women's Review of Books* (March 1987). She believes feminist writers have toned down their former "passion and intensity" in order to be accepted by female editors who fear their own credibility will be jeopardized should they appear too feminist. Women writers thus have difficulty finding publishers for their more radical work. Says agent Ellen Markson, who represents Andrea Dworkin, among others, "It is women who are censoring women and you can quote me on that."

A book that does make it off the press can still be censored—usually by a publisher who decides at the last minute that its business interests are threatened by the book's content. A prime example of this brand of censorship, writes Michael Moore in *Multinational Monitor* (Sept. 1987), was the destruction of all 20,000 copies of the first printing of *Katharine the Great: Katharine Graham and the Washington Post*.

In her 1980 book (which finally hit the bookstores in 1986 when it was republished by the National Press), author Deborah Davis contended that the *Washington Post* disseminated information helpful to certain U.S. administrations and had maintained close ties with the CIA. Although the book had already been chosen as a Literary Guild selection and touted by Publisher Harcourt Brace Jovanovich (HBJ) as a top nonfiction selection (and with the entire first printing already sold to eager bookstores), HBJ chose to yank it when *Washington Post* editor Ben Bradlee implied that its publication would put HBJ in the *Post's* bad graces. Like most publishers, HBJ relies on favorable reviews in powerful newspapers to help sell its books, so rather than risk incurring the *Post's* permanent wrath, HBJ chose to destroy the books.

Frightening as it is when two supposed upholders of the First Amendment conspire, as Moore put it, "to kill a book that one of them found em-

Reprinted from *Utne Reader*, Jan./Feb. 1988, Issue No. 25.

barrassing and the other found detrimental to his business interests,'' the *Washington Post* example is by no means unique.

Indeed, cases of business interests prevailing over freedom of the press are only likely to become more common in the U.S. as the book publishing industry becomes increasingly concentrated in the hands of a few owners. Ten large companies own the majority of the 2,500 publishing houses in this country, Moore points out, and most of these corporations also own banking, insurance, industrial, and defense-related subsidiaries.

In *Extra! The Newsletter of FAIR* (Fairness and Accuracy in Reporting, June 1987), Ben Bagdikian points out that just 26 corporations control half or more of *all* media (including book publishers, TV, radio, newspapers, and movie production companies)—down from 50 corporations in 1982. (This situation is chronicled in a new updated version of his important book, *The Media Monopoly*, Beacon Press.) Although this will undoubtedly prove profitable for the shrinking number of media moguls, it is highly dangerous to freedom of the press, says Bagdikian, adding, ''The safest way to ensure diversity of opinion is diverse ownership.''

Publishing's increasingly corporate mentality has changed the whole nature of the profession, says Ted Solotaroff in *The New Republic* (June 8, 1987). Once a world of small, privately owned houses supported by the classic books on their backlists, the publishing business today must rely on blockbuster bestsellers to support their fat ad budgets and high overheads.

As the old publishing companies are swallowed up by megacorporations and move further and further from their proud roots, says Solotaroff, publishing ''. . . works, thinks, and wills like any other big business. Its paramount concern is not the integrity of its product but the value of its share. . . .'' The result, says the author (who is a senior editor at Harper & Row), is an exploding number of self-help, cooking, romance, fad, celebrity, and other big mall-selling books and a dwindling number of riskier serious fiction and nonfiction books, especially those written by unknown authors. ''As the CEO and his number crunchers exert themselves, publishing decisions become more reckless and short-sighted,'' concludes Solotaroff.

The one piece of good news, says Solotaroff, is that serious books are still finding their way into print via alternative and university-based publishers still willing to take a chance on them.

Consumers Union is a nonprofit organization that investigates the quality of consumer goods and services. In the following study on the misuse of language in advertising and marketing, excerpted from Consumer Reports, *the writers search out details, look for contrasts and contradictions, use interviews, and compare both products and statistics.*

It's Natural! It's Organic! Or Is It?

Consumers Union

Langendorf Natural Lemon Flavored Creme Pie contains no cream. It does contain sodium propionate, certified food colors, sodium benzoate, and vegetable gum.

That's natural?

Yes indeed, says L. A. Cushman Jr., chairman of American Bakeries Co., the Chicago firm that owns Langendorf. The word "natural," he explains, modifies "lemon flavored," and the pie contains oil from lemon rinds. "The lemon flavor," Cushman states, "comes from natural lemon flavor as opposed to artificial lemon flavor, assuming there is such a thing as artificial lemon flavor."

Welcome to the world of natural foods.

You can eat your "natural" way from one end of the supermarket to the other. Make yourself a sandwich of *Kraft Cracker Barrel Natural Cheddar Cheese* on *Better Way Natural Whole Grain Wheat Nugget Bread* spread with *Autumn Natural Margarine.* Wash it down with *Anheuser-Busch Natural Light Beer* or *Rich-Life Natural Orange NutriPop.* Snack on any number of brands of "natural" potato chips and "natural" candy bars. And don't exclude your pet: Feed your dog *Gravy Train Dog Food With Natural Beef Flavor,* or, if it's a puppy, try *Blue Mountain Natural Style Puppy Food.*

The "natural" bandwagon doesn't end at the kitchen. You can bathe in *Batherapy Natural Mineral Bath* (sodium sesquicarbonate, isopropyl myristate, fragrance, D & C Green No. 5, D & C Yellow No. 10 among its ingredients), using *Queen Helene "All-Natural" Amino Peptide Shampoo* (propylene glycol, hydroxyethyl cellulose, methylparaben, D & C Red No. 3, D & C Brown No. 1) and *Organic Aid Natural Clear Soaps.* Then, if you're so inclined, you can apply *Naturade Conditioning Mascara with Natural Protein* (stearic acid, PVP, butylene glycol, sorbitan sesquioleate, triethanolamine, imidazolidinyl urea, methylparaben, propylparaben).

* * *

The word "natural" does not have to be synonymous with "ripoff." Over the years, the safety of many food additives has been questioned. And a consumer who reads labels carefully can in fact find some foods in supermarkets that have been processed without additives.

But the word "natural" does not guarantee that. All too often, as the above examples indicate, the word is used more as a key to higher profits. Often, it implies a health benefit that does not really exist.

Co-op News, the publication of the Berkeley Co-op, the nation's largest consumer-cooperative store chain, reported on "two 15-ounce cans of tomato sauce, available side-by-side" at one of its stores. One sauce, called *Health Valley*, claimed on its label to have "no citric acid, no sugars, no preservatives, no artificial colors or flavors." There were none of those ingredients in the Co-op's house brand, either, but their absence was hardly worth noting on the label, since canned tomato sauce almost never contains artificial colors or flavors and doesn't need preservatives after being heated in the canning process. The visible difference between the two products was price, not ingredients. The *Health Valley* tomato sauce was selling for 85 cents; the Co-op house brand, for only 29 cents.

One supermarket industry consultant estimates that 7 percent of all processed food products now sold are touted as "natural." And that could be just the beginning. A Federal Trade Commission report noted that 63 percent of people polled in a survey agreed with the statement, "Natural foods are more nutritious than other foods." Thirty-nine percent said they regularly buy food because it is "natural," and 47 percent said they are willing to pay 10 percent more for a food that is "natural."

According to those who have studied the trend, the consumer's desire for "natural" foods goes beyond the fear of specific chemicals. "There is a mistrust of technology," says Howard Moskowitz, a taste researcher and consultant to the food industry. "There is a movement afoot to return to simplicity in all aspects of life." A spokeswoman for Lever Bros., one of the nation's major food merchandisers, adds: " 'Natural' is a psychological thing of everyone wanting to get out of the industrial world."

Because consumers are acting out of such vague, undefined feelings, they aren't sure what they should be getting when they buy a product labeled "natural." William Wittenberg, president of Grandma's Food Inc., comments: "Manufacturers and marketers are making an attempt to appeal to a consumer who feels he should be eating something natural, but doesn't know why. I think the marketers of the country in effect mirror back to the people what they want to hear. People have to look to themselves for their own protection." Grandma's makes a *Whole Grain Date Filled Fruit 'n Oatmeal Bar* labeled "naturally Good Flavor." The ingredients include "artificial flavor."

"Natural" foods are not necessarily preferable nor, as we have seen, necessarily natural.

Consider "natural" potato chips. They are often cut thick from unpeeled potatoes, packaged without preservatives in heavy foil bags with fancy lettering, and sold at a premium price. Sometimes, such chips include "sea salt," a product whose advantage over conventional "land" salt has not been demonstrated. The packaging is intended to give the impression that "natural" potato chips are less of a junk food than regular chips. But nutritionally there is no difference. Both are made from the same food, the potato, and both have been processed so that they are high in salt and in calories.

Sometimes the "natural" products may have ingredients you'd prefer to avoid. *Quaker 100% Natural* cereal, for example, contains 24 percent sugar, a high percentage, considering it's not promoted as a sugared cereal. (*Kellogg's Corn Flakes* has 7.8 percent sugar.) Many similar "natural" granola-type cereals have oil added, giving them a much higher fat content than conventional cereals.

Taste researcher Moskowitz notes that food processors are "trying to signal to the consumer a sensory impact that can be called natural." Two of the most popular signals, says Moskowitz, are honey and coconut. But honey is just another sugar, with no significant nutrients other than calories . . . , and coconut is especially high in saturated fats.

While many processed foods are less nutritious than their fresh counterparts, processing can sometimes help foods: Freezing preserves nutrients that can be lost if fresh foods are not consumed quickly; pasteurization kills potentially dangerous bacteria in milk. Some additives are also both safe and useful. Sorbic acid, for instance, prevents the growth of potentially harmful molds in cheese and other products, and sodium benzoate has been used for more than 70 years to prevent the growth of microorganisms in acidic foods.

"Preservative" has become a dirty word, to judge from the number of "no preservative" labels on food products. Calcium propionate might sound terrible on a bread label, but this mildew-retarding substance occurs naturally in both raisins and Swiss cheese. "Bread without preservatives could well cost you more than bread with them," says Vernal S. Packard Jr., a University of Minnesota nutrition professor. "Without preservatives, the bread gets stale faster; it may go moldy with the production of hazardous aflatoxin. And already we in the United States return [to producers] 100 million pounds of bread each year—this in a world nagged by hunger and malnutrition."

Nor are all "natural" substances safe. Sassafras tea was banned by the U.S. Food and Drug Administration several years ago because it contains safrole, which has produced liver cancer in laboratory animals. Kelp, a seaweed that is becoming increasingly fashionable as a dietary supplement, can have a high arsenic content. Aflatoxin, produced by a mold that can grow on improperly stored peanuts, corn, and grains, is a known carcinogen.

To complicate matters, our palates have become attuned to many unnatural tastes. "We don't have receptors on our tongues that signal 'natural,' " says taste researcher Moskowitz. He points out, for instance, that a panel of consumers would almost certainly reject a natural lemonade "in favor of a lemonade scientifically designed to taste natural. If you put real lemon, sugar, and water together, people would reject it as harsh. They are used to flavors developed by flavor houses.'' Similarly, Moskowitz points out, many consumers say that for health reasons they prefer less salty food—but the results of various taste tests have contradicted this, too.

In the midst of all this confusion, it's not surprising that the food industry is having a promotional field day.

* * *

What can be done about such all-but-deceptive practices? One might suggest that the word ''natural'' is so vague as to be inherently deceptive, and therefore should not be available for promotional use. Indeed, the FTC staff suggested precisely that a few years ago but later backed away from the idea. The California legislature last year passed a weak bill defining the word ''organic,'' but decided that political realities argued against tackling the word ''natural.''

''If we had included the word 'natural' in the bill, it most likely would not have gotten out of the legislature,'' says one legislative staff member. ''When you've got large economic interests in certain areas, the tendency is to guard those interests very carefully.''

Under the revised FTC staff proposal, which had not been acted on by the full commission as we went to press, the word ''natural'' can be used if the product has undergone only minimal processing and doesn't have artificial ingredients. That would eliminate the outright frauds, as well as the labeling of such products as Lever Bros.' *Autumn Natural Margarine*, which obviously has been highly processed from its original vegetable-oil state. But the FTC proposal might run into difficulty in defining exactly what ''minimal processing'' means. And it would also allow some deceptive implications. For instance, a product containing honey might be called ''natural,'' while a food with refined sugar might not, thus implying that honey is superior to other sugars, which it is not.

A law incorporating similar regulations went into effect in Maine at the beginning of this year. If a product is to be labeled ''natural'' and sold in Maine, it must have undergone only minimal processing and have no additives, preservatives, or refined additions such as white flour and sugar.

So far, according to John Michael, the state legislator who sponsored the bill, food companies have largely ignored the law, but he expects the state to start issuing warnings this summer.

PART V

Writing About Ideas, Issues, and Values

The voice of the intellect is a soft one,
but it does not rest until it has gained a hearing.
Ultimately, after endless rebuffs, it succeeds.
This is one of the few points in which
one may be optimistic about
the future of mankind.

SIGMUND FREUD

Exploring

23

Classical Patterns of Thought

G ood old Aristotle. The more we need to confront the complexities and issues of our time, the more often we turn to ancient Greeks for advice.

From them we have inherited a number of invaluable tools for thinking about difficult problems, ways of organizing our thought processes and of inspecting ideas. It was Aristotle's notion that through close perception we could find order and pattern in the world. His work demonstrated that we must first learn to see a thing—a fact—as it really is. In itself, that was a radical concept for its time. But Aristotle went beyond facts. He demonstrated that by looking at relationships and categories, facts could lead to general principles.

Good writing and clear thinking, then, are united in the same way. We begin with intense perception, with learning how to see the thing, the detail. And then we learn to go beyond our senses—or rather to build upon them.

More and more, that which catches our attention should be a detail or fact illuminated by an idea or an idea incarnated in a fact. We must now further develop techniques that help us identify relationships and form judgments. And that takes us back to Aristotle again. From his work we've also inherited a number of strategies for accomplishing all of this: *comparison* and *contrast, classification, definition,* and *illustration.* Each of these, alone or in combination, provides a valuable method for exploring ideas in our minds—and then for organizing them in our essays.

If you haven't done this type of thing before, it may at first seem confusing. Be patient. Activities of the mind are not separate from your inner life. All truly valuable intellectual work grows from spiritual strength. The merit of the mind lies in its ability to adapt to new principles and new techniques, even when they're hard to come by. Remember that the goal is not the technique in itself, but the excitement, the nourishment the mind and soul derive from mastering deeper intellectual insights.

COMPARISON AND CONTRAST

To *compare* is to show similarities. To *contrast* is to show differences. Note that in both cases I've used the phrase *to show*. Because the use of comparison and contrast enables the writer to be specific, it has proved to be one of the most successful methods of writing about abstractions. But to use it in writing, you must first see it in your subject.

Do you want to understand the feminist movement? One way might be to compare it with other social revolutions, perhaps the effort of black Americans to achieve civil rights.

Comparison
Both women and blacks have been arbitrarily limited to certain occupations and social roles because of inherited characteristics: sex and color.

Both have been considered less intelligent than white males, and both at times have been denied the right to education.

Both have been "honored" for stereotyped qualities: blacks, for physical ability and cheerfulness; women, for virginity and motherhood. As a consequence, both blacks and women have often attempted to live up to the stereotype.

Aristotle said that to see relationships is one of the highest acts of human intelligence. By comparing, we draw together similar qualities from things or concepts that previously may have seemed dissimilar.

Contrast often proves equally instructive. Again consider the feminist and black movements for equal rights.

Contrast

Although often disagreeing on means, blacks have tended to support the goals of equal rights; women, however, have been divided, and some have even formed groups to oppose equal rights.

The black movement produced a charismatic leader in Martin Luther King, Jr., a single person who represented and expressed the highest ideals; the women's movement has tended to remain fragmented.

Pressure for change has always begun first among blacks and been followed shortly thereafter by women. (Is there a cause-and-effect relationship?)

Here's another example from an essay titled "Football Red and Baseball Green" by Murray Ross. By contrasting America's two principal outdoor sports, Ross hopes to reveal new insights into our understanding of ourselves.

Football, especially professional football, is the embodiment of a newer myth, one which in many respects is opposed to baseball's. The fundamental difference is that football is not a pastoral game; it is a heroic one. One way of seeing the difference between the two is by the juxtaposition of Babe Ruth and Jim Brown, both legendary players in their separate genres. Ruth, baseball's most powerful hitter, was a hero maternalized (his name), an epic figure destined for a second immortality as a candy bar. His image was impressive but comfortable and altogether human: round, dressed in a baggy uniform, with a schoolboy's cap and a bat which looked tiny next to him. His spindly legs supported a Santa sized torso, and this comic disproportion would increase when he was in motion. He ran delicately, with quick, very short steps, since he felt that stretching your stride slowed you down. This sort of superstition is typical of baseball players, and typical too is the way in which a personal quirk or mannerism mitigates their awesome skill and makes them poignant and vulnerable.

There was nothing funny about Jim Brown. His muscular and almost perfect physique was emphasized further by the uniform which armored him. Babe Ruth had a tough face, but boyish and innocent; Brown was an expressionless mask under the helmet. In action he seemed invincible, the embodiment of speed and power in an inflated human shape. One can describe Brown accurately only with superlatives, for as a player he was a kind of Superman, undisguised.

Brown and Ruth are caricatures, yet they represent their games. Baseball is part of a comic tradition which insists that its participants be humans, while football, in the heroic mode, asks that its players be more than that. Football converts men into gods, and suggests that magnificence and glory are as desirable as happiness.

In this excerpt, Ross focuses on specific players in baseball and football, looking at each in detail, then draws a general conclusion about the two sports from what he sees in their most famous players. Comparison and contrast, together or separately, then, can lead to insight. You'll recall that *contrast, opposition,* and *contradiction* are some of the qualities reporters seek out in any subject. The same could probably be said of a State Department analyst studying military spending in Bulgaria or a business executive studying market trends. Comparison and contrast are perceptual strategies that clarify, as the concept of male is clarified by female, and female by male.

CLASSIFICATION

To *classify* is to arrange persons, places, ideas—almost anything—in groups or categories according to certain common characteristics. The goal of classification is to understand the whole of something by understanding an arrangement of its parts.

Actually, classification is something you do almost every day without much conscious thought. When you trudge down to the laundromat to wash your clothes, you sort bright colors into one pile, white clothes into another, or you make a separate grouping for synthetic fibers and another for cottons. Whatever your categories, you do it because to mix them randomly might mean that some clothes would be ruined. The purpose determines the way you classify, and you can apply the same principle to complex questions and issues. A concept won't be "ruined" by mixing all the parts, but any attempt to understand it may be confused.

When we classify, then, we determine the qualities that any particular item or concept must have to fall within a particular *class.* The items in the class, selected according to purpose, constitute a *subclass.* If you decide to write a humorous essay on the sexual attractiveness of males to college females, you might come up with the following:

class: potential college lovers

subclass: party boys, jocks, fire eaters, brains, duds

On the other hand, if you wanted to write a serious essay on the same subject, your subclass would be quite different:

class: potential college lovers

subclass: those who are afraid of commitments; those who are chauvinistic; those who need mothers; those who possess maturity and sensitivity

A further step in classification occurs when you identify the distinguishing characteristics of any one item in the subclass:

subclass: those who possess maturity and sensitivity

distinguishing characteristics: respect for self, openness to the needs of others, spontaneity, numerous interests, sense of humor, creativity

But how does all this help in working with abstract subjects? First, it offers you a means of narrowing any broad subject to a more specific and manageable topic. Second, the classes or subclasses you arrive at may form various portions of your paper (in other words, all this helps organize the body of the essay).

In a work titled ''Propaganda Techniques in Today's Advertising,'' professional writer Ann McClintock uses classification to accomplish both these aims. McClintock begins by pointing out that propaganda is not simply something governments use to retain the loyalty of its citizens. Advertisers, she argues, bombard us daily with claims and persuasive techniques intended to sell us products. McClintock then divides the propaganda of advertising into seven categories: *Name Calling, Glittering Generalities, Transfer Techniques, Testimonials, Plain Folks, Card Stacking,* and *Bandwagoning.* Each category serves as a natural division for her essay. Here's how she writes about one of those classifications:

Testimonial   The testimonial is one of the advertisers' most-loved and most-used propaganda techniques. Similar to the transfer device, the testimonial uses the admiration people have for a celebrity to make the product shine more brightly—even though the celebrity is not an expert on the product being sold.

   Print and television ads offer a nonstop parade of testimonials: here's Cher for Holiday Spas; then Bruce Jenner touts orange juice; Cliff Robertson, Joan Rivers, and Burt Lancaster appear for various telephone services; Michael Jackson sings about Pepsi; American Express features a slew of well-known people with lesser-known faces who ask ''Do you know me?'' and then assure us that they never go anywhere without their American Express card. Testimonials can sell movies—read the movie reviewers' comments in the newspaper ads. They can sell books—see the blurbs by celebrities and critics on the backs of paperbacks.

   Political candidates—as well as their ad agencies—know the value of testimonials. Carroll O'Connor endorses Senator Ted Kennedy, and Robert Redford lends his star appeal to Gary Hart's campaign. Even controversial social issues are debated by celebrities. The nuclear freeze, for instance, stars Paul Newman for the pro side and Charlton Heston for the con.

As illogical as testimonials sometimes are (Michael Jackson, for instance, is a Jehovah's Witness who does not drink Pepsi), they are effective propaganda. We like the *person* so much that we like the *product* too.

For both writer and reader, the world is a swarm of images and conflicting messages. Dividing it into separate units or categories, then focusing on each category individually, allows us to concentrate our minds and further our understanding.

Classification can also serve as a method of introducing a subject. Here is how business major Sheri Martin introduced a paper on economic systems.

> The relationship between the economic system of a country and the amount of government regulation of that system depends upon five different organizational structures: communism, socialism, fascism, regulated capitalism (as in the United States), and pure capitalism. In a short paper of this nature, I cannot treat all of these. Instead, I will attempt to outline the contrasting functions of government in two seemingly similar systems: regulated capitalism and pure capitalism. I will try to show that those functions are actually as unlike as day and night.

Economics (a difficult, abstract subject) has been classified into five methods of organizing the economic structure of a society. Sheri then narrows her proposed topic to two of those structures. By attempting to *see* (intellectually) a subject's various subclasses according to a defined purpose, you can clarify the resulting order and begin the process of understanding. For both writer and reader, classification focuses perception.

DEFINITION

Classification may reduce a subject from a general concept to more specific categories, but unless we all agree on the meaning of those categories, they still may not be clear. You've probably all had the experience of arguing with someone, perhaps in a heated and emotional exchange, only to discover you were using the same word to mean different things.

Without definition, communication may not occur. *Capitalism,* for example, is still a general term. *Regulated capitalism* is a rather specialized term, one that may not be familiar to many readers. Here's how Sheri

Martin continued the second paragraph of her paper on economic systems.

> Capitalism is one of the oldest economic systems in the world. In essence, it is characterized by a free market with private ownership of production and means of distribution. When two tribal farmers in West Africa meet in a market to sell and exchange goods based on their own needs and desires, without regulation by any other authority, they are engaging in a primitive form of capitalism. But regulated capitalism is very different. It is characterized by private ownership and imposed government restrictions. The restrictions theoretically prevent any one person or company from dominating the free market or prevent monopolies, like utilities, from earning an unfair profit. By contrast, socialism means that the government not only regulates the market, it may actually own much of the production and means of distribution, retaining all profits for itself.

Sheri has used several conventional methods of defining. She has *described* the basic qualities of both systems. She has given a specific *illustration* of one system and an *example* of the other. And she has *contrasted* the second system to something it is not.

As senses shape experience, so words shape our thoughts. Failure to define words leads to faulty thinking. But we are dealing here with something more than mere definition of specialized terms (as important as that is). Definition is inherent in the very notion of understanding ideas in themselves. Concepts such as *liberalism, imagination, faith, human nature,* as well as *capitalism,* may require extended definition—the pursuit of meaning through a complete essay. Here's an extended definition of "The American Dream," originally published in *U.S. News & World Report* by Betty Anne Younglove.

The American Dream

Betty Anne Younglove

The lament for the death of the American dream grows ever louder. And although the verses may vary, the chorus is the same: The American dream is out of reach, unattainable.

Some of the verses I hear most often:

- Young families cannot afford a three-bedroom house in the suburbs because the prices or interest rates or taxes are too high.

Betty Anne Younglove, Houston Community College. Copyright Dec. 8, 1986, *U.S. News & World Report.*

- The average family cannot afford to send its sons and daughters to "a Harvard" because the cost is equivalent to the total family income before taxes; moreover, there is not enough money to send the kids to a prep school to insure they can get into "a Harvard" even if they can come up with the money.
- Why, oh why, can't the young people of today be guaranteed the dreams their parents had?

First, let us get this dream business—and business it now seems to be—straight. The word *dream* is not a synonym for *reality* or *promise*. It is closer to *hope* or *possibility* or even *vision*. The original American dream had only a little to do with material possessions and a lot to do with choices, beginnings and opportunity. Many of the original American dreamers wanted a new beginning, a place to choose what they wanted and a place to work for it. They did not see it as a guarantee of success but an opportunity to try.

The dream represented possibilities: Get your own land and clear it and work it; if nature cooperates, the work might pay off in material blessings. Or the dream represented the idea that any citizen with the minimum qualifications of age and years of citizenship could run for President even if he were born in a humble log cabin. He had no guarantee he would win, of course, no more than the man clearing his land was guaranteed a good crop.

The preamble to the Constitution does not promise happiness, only the right to pursue it.

This new elegy, however, seems to define the American dream as possessions and to declare that material things, power and money are our rights; we not only deserve them but maybe a free lunch as well.

Whatever verse we have been listening to in this new song about the dream, we should recognize it as nothing more than a siren song leading us with Pied Piper promises. Let's go back to the original idea—a tune we can whistle while we work to achieve the goal of our choice.

Younglove of course contrasts two definitions of the American dream. Her essay might have been extended further by adding more detailed illustrations of each version, or by contrasting both versions to the promises of the good life made by Marxist nations, or by quoting from others whose words from the past may have contributed to our perception of the American dream—from Abraham Lincoln or John F. Kennedy or Martin Luther King, Jr. In other words, by extending the concept of definition to its limits, the material available to you is almost inexhaustible. And each additional piece of information, in turn, extends our understanding of the subject.

Definition means clarification through precision; it means uncovering the nature or basic qualities of a concept. The need for definition, then, begins inside ourselves as we first approach a subject. Later, as we begin to write, the need becomes public, to communicate and explain what we have learned.

Illustration   **285**

ILLUSTRATION

The traditional rhetorical methods of exploring ideas, issues, and values can sometimes seem overly abstract. *Comparing* and *contrasting, classifying,* and *defining* may be brilliant exercises of the mind, but without concrete details, they often seem fuzzy to readers. When using such strategies in our papers, we can sometimes forget that *showing* is more immediately effective than *telling.* One way to enrich every classical strategy (indeed, it is a classical strategy in itself), is to illustrate our thinking with concrete examples, anecdotes, or specific evidence.

Here's an example from freshman Charles Bonnette. Charles is writing about individual responsibility—an abstract concept that he needs to illustrate if the reader is to fully understand.

> In the United States we have long abandoned personal responsibility in favor of placing that responsibility on others—on "society," or our "parents," or the "government." But in other countries, individual responsibility still counts. For example, when I was traveling with my parents in Spain last summer, we stayed at a small hotel in the mountains. Outside our window, a winding narrow road made a sharp turn, dropped sharply, then began to climb again. Road crews had dug a deep hole in the right lane just beyond the sharp turn. At night, a single warning lantern and sign on a barricade indicated that cars coming down the hill should pull into the left lane. The barricade was placed thirty feet or so from the hole. For three nights in a row I watched car after car, plus several motorcycles, roar down the hill, speed around the sharp turn, crash through the barricade and drop into the hole.
>
> In the United States, we would claim that the government was at fault. Not enough warning, only one lantern, find a lawyer and sue. But in Spain, the hotel workers and a few guests would help the driver pull out his car, straighten out the fender, wipe away the nose bleed, and wave goodby as the driver sped away. Then they would replace the barrier, re-light the lantern, and wait for the next accident. In Spain, it was clear that a driver assumed responsibility for his own actions. If he was going too fast to stop, that was not the government's fault. Not one driver seemed to feel that someone else should have done something to protect him or his car. No one even dreamed about suing someone else.

Charles uses a traditional strategy here. He first makes a generalization, then signals the use of an illustration to support or clarify the generalization with the words, *for example.* The example itself, in this case, uses *comparison and contrast* to illuminate the differences in the way two cultures might respond to a specific incident.

Professional writers especially rely on illustrations. In an essay on "College Pressures," William Zinsser first divides college pressure into four categories, then uses an anecdote, followed by personal examples, to illustrate one of those categories.

> Peer pressure and self-induced pressure are almost intertwined, and they begin almost at the beginning of freshman year.
>
> "I had a freshman student I'll call Linda," one dean told me, "who came in and said she was under terrible pressure because her roommate, Barbara, was much brighter and studied all the time. I couldn't tell her that Barbara had come in two hours earlier to say the same thing about Linda."
>
> The story is almost funny—except that it's not. It's symptomatic of all the pressures put together. When every student thinks every other student is working harder and doing better, the only solution is to study harder still. I see students going off to the library every night after dinner and coming back when it closes at midnight. I wish they could sometimes forget about their peers and go to a movie.

It should be clear that *illustration* is not a strategy that exists apart from other techniques. Using specific examples supports and clarifies other classical methods of thinking discussed in this chapter. Perhaps I can best illustrate that myself by offering a brief excerpt of an essay by Desmond Morris, called "Territorial Behavior." Morris argues that human beings have evolved as tribal animals. For millions of years our home base was a protected hunting territory. In general, his essay analyzes ways in which contemporary humans continue to act as tribal units—by forming small subgroups such as teenage gangs, college fraternities, political parties, and local clubs.

Morris begins by *defining* the concept of "territory." He then divides the concept into categories, an act of *classification.*

> A territory is a defended space. In the broadest sense here are three kinds of human territory: tribal, family and personal.

To explain each category, and to make it vivid for the reader, Morris then uses paragraph-long examples that *illustrate* by making a *comparison* of a modern human activity with more primitive "tribal" activities.

> Each of these modern pseudo-tribes sets up its own special kind of home base. In extreme cases non-members are totally excluded, in others they are allowed in as visitors with limited rights and under a control system of special rules. In many ways they are like miniature nations, with their own flags and emblems and their own border guards. The exclusive club has its own "customs barrier": the door-

man who checks your "passport" (your membership card) and prevents strangers from passing in unchallenged. There is a government: the club committee; and often special displays of the tribal elders: the photographs or portraits of previous officials on the walls. At the heart of the specialized territories there is a powerful feeling of security and importance, a sense of shared defense against the outside world. Much of the club chatter, both serious and joking, directs itself against the rottenness of everything outside the club boundaries—in that "other world" beyond the protected portals.

The effective use of *illustration* grows directly out of the earliest stages of the writing process. Training yourself to see details, to become aware of specifics, to use concretions—enriches and clarifies even the most abstract forms of thought and analysis.

SYNTHESIS AND THE WRITING PROCESS

Which of all the mental processes reviewed in this chapter is best? Which will be most important to you in student papers? Which will serve you well in a career? The answer is: all of them. Like other teachers of writing, I have divided these mental processes into separate strategies for the sake of discussion and clarity. It is easier to learn one method at a time. But in a very real sense, everything I've said for 287 pages is a distortion of the way the mind actually works. The experienced writer does not sit down and say to himself or herself, "Now I'm going to write a 'compare and contrast' article for *National Review*." Instead, the writer begins with a subject—with prison reform in California or the treatment of women in American literature. In the process of studying the subject, the writer uses not only the methods described in this chapter—*comparison* and *contrast, classification, definition, illustration*—but all other methods covered in this book. He or she looks for *who, what, where, why, when,* and *how;* for the human examples that will make the subject come alive and seem relevant; for *change, conflict, characterization;* and for possible leads that will make an imaginative introduction. The writer *evaluates* and *interprets.* Each of these alone or in combination may be used as part of a formal essay. Each is a means to an end—to explain a subject to an audience. *Synthesis* is the act of combining separate parts to form a whole. In writing, one does not so much "combine" as move through a process of back-and-forth interaction with all possible strategies, a testing of the subject against all the varying capacities of the mind.

But remember, in themselves, each of these methods is only that—

a method. Even when combined they do not constitute knowledge. For that you must turn to personal experience, interviews, and reading, where you will *use* such methods to seek out the facts, the details, the substance that lead to understanding. Vitality in writing comes from the immersion of your energies, from a commitment to the experience you are writing about. Ideas, issues, and values—abstractions—will be significant only insofar as you do experience them, only insofar as you make them concrete, feel them, care about them. The fully synthetic essay, then, draws together everything you are, everything you've learned; it is the whole process working together. Don't expect it to come easy. Starts and stops, confusion, and wasted paper are normal. This will be the most demanding work you've attempted. But persist. Take on the challenge. Commit the whole self, the whole mind. Begin the act of synthesizing all that you have now studied and practiced.

Here's an outline of steps you might want to take in approaching an idea, issue, or value and of the various methods that might be useful in preparing to write about it.

Exploration process	*Method*
1. Begin with an overview of the subject as a whole.	*Define* the terms of the concept with a dictionary. Use an encyclopedia or general article to explore the background if necessary. Consider various ways the subject can be *classified.* What are its major categories? How can you narrow the subject to one specific component or subclass that might be treated in a short essay?
2. Form a question or series of questions on the narrowed subject.	Further *define* the specific terms and components you plan to write about. If possible, use the techniques of *comparison* and *contrast* to focus your purpose more clearly and to form specific questions for inquiry.
3. Investigate for details. If possible, locate original sources to interview. Read several articles or a relevant chapter from a book.	Look for the 5 *W*'s and 4 *C*'s. Collect specific illustrations to make the subject as concrete as possible. *Interpret* and *evaluate* what you discover.

Chapter 26 will show how a professional writer has used many of these techniques in a formal essay, but it must be remembered that the *product* you'll see there evolved from a *process* much like the one described here.

Exercises

1. *Classify* one of the following items. Assume your purpose is to write a humorous essay.

> male chauvinists
> college professors
> TV advertisements for toilet paper
> fraternities or sororities
> roommates

2. *Classify* the same subject again with a serious purpose: to write an essay critical of the subject.

3. Although no *definition* may be totally adequate, consider the following. In what way is each satisfactory (if it is), and in what ways is it unsatisfactory? What methods of definition are used? What additional methods might extend the definition and make it more complete?

> a. Americans seem to live and breathe and function by paradox; but in nothing are we so paradoxical as in our passionate belief in our own myths. We truly believe ourselves to be natural-born mechanics and do-it-yourselfers. We spend our lives in motor cars, yet most of us—a great many of us at least—do not know enough about a car to look in the gas tank when the motor fails. Our lives as we live them would not function without electricity, but it is a rare man or woman who, when the power goes off, knows how to look for a burned-out fuse and replace it. We believe implicitly that we are the heirs of the pioneers; that we have inherited self-sufficiency and the ability to take care of ourselves, particularly in relation to nature. There isn't a man among us in ten thousand who knows how to butcher a cow or a pig and cut it up for eating, let alone a wild animal. By natural endowment, we are great rifle shots and great hunters—but when hunting season opens there is a slaughter of farm animals and humans by men and women who couldn't hit a real target if they could see it. Americans treasure the knowledge that they live close to nature, but fewer and fewer farmers feed more and more people; and as soon as we can afford to we eat out of cans, buy frozen TV dinners, and haunt the delicatessens. Affluence means moving to the suburbs, but the American suburbanite sees, if

anything, less of the country than the city apartment dweller with his window boxes and his African violets carefully tended under lights. In no country are more seeds and plants and equipment purchased, and less vegetables and flowers raised.

John Steinbeck, *America and Americans*

b. Being an artist means, not reckoning and counting, but ripening like the tree which does not force its sap but stands, confident in the storms of spring, without fear that after them may come no summer. It does come, but only to the patient, who are there as though eternity lay before them so unconcernedly still and wide. I learn it daily, learn it with pain to which I am grateful. Patience is everything.

Rainer Maria Rilke, *Letters to a Young Poet*

c. The term "concept" has a multitude of meanings. Most of us have used or applied it in a myriad of ways, and among these uses there may not be a great deal of obvious similarity. For example, "concept" is commonly used as a synonym for idea, as when we say, "Now he seems to have the concept," in reference to someone who has finally caught onto a message. Or we may talk of an abstract state of affairs, such as freedom, and call it a concept. On other occasions, a concept seems to be akin to a mental image, as in the case of trying to conceptualize (visualize) an unfamiliar object or event from a verbal description. Undoubtedly, each of these examples captures in part the meaning of "concept." But clearly, it would be difficult (or impossible) to formulate an unambiguous definition from them.

In experimental psychology the term "concept" has come to have a rather specialized meaning, which may not encompass all its various ordinary uses. Psychology is the scientific investigation of the behavior of organisms, which includes as a sub-area the study of how organisms (human beings and lower animals) learn and use concepts. In such an undertaking, explicitly, communicable definitions of terms are an absolute necessity. "Concept" is no exception.

As a working definition we may say that a concept exists whenever two or more distinguishable objects or events have been grouped or classified together and set apart from other objects on the basis of some common feature or property characteristic of each. Consider the class of "things" called dogs. Not all dogs are alike. We can easily tell our favorite Basset from the neighbor's Great Dane. Still all dogs have certain features in common and these serve as the basis for a conceptual grouping. Furthermore, the grouping is so familiar and so well defined that few of us have any difficulty calling a dog (even an unfamiliar dog) by that name when we encounter

one. There is then the concept "dog"; similarly, the class of all
things called "house" is a concept, and the class of things called
"religion."

Lyle E. Bourne, Jr., *Human Conceptual Behavior*

4. For a class project, choose a product all of you buy frequently
and compare it with a competing product. For example, you might *compare* and *contrast* hamburgers purchased at Burger King with those purchased at McDonald's. Before you begin, create a fairly balanced criteria
by which to make judgments. In the case of hamburger restaurants, for
example, you might set up such standards as service, cleanliness, quantity, taste, location, price, and so on. Divide up into teams and rate your
competing products according to each category. If possible, use specific
examples to *illustrate* your points. Finally, come to a conclusion based
on your list and determine which product to recommend. Compare your
evaluation to other teams in the class.

Exploring

24

The Analytical Mind

Whether Aristotle invented analysis is unclear. But Aristotle did use analysis with such success that—after its rediscovery in the Renaissance—it became the dominant thought pattern of the Western mind. To analyze means to divide a subject into parts for individual study, much as you would for classification. But where classification may stop with identifying and describing the parts, analysis proceeds to evaluate their relationship.

Here, in simple outline, is the analytic process.

Consider the subject as a whole, as an idea, argument, issue, or whatever in its full context. General definition is essential at this point.

Divide the subject into its various components as you would in classification (that is, as determined by your purpose).

Consider each part separately. If the subject is too large, this is when to narrow your focus and deal primarily with only one or two components (as Sheri Martin did in her essay in Chapter 23). Each component may need further definition.

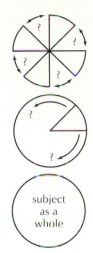

Evaluate the relationship of each part to every other part. The compare-and-contrast strategy will often prove helpful at this stage.

or

If you've narrowed your focus to a single component, consider how it relates to the subject as a whole.

Interpret your findings. What do you now know about the subject from having studied the parts and their relationships? (Students often omit this final phase, but analysis is of little value unless you draw the subject together again and form an overall assessment.)

Obviously, analysis incorporates other conventional methods: *classification, comparison* and *contrast,* and *definition.* By drawing them all together and by discovering relationships, you'll find that analysis becomes one of the single most important intellectual strategies you can learn. For further clarification, analysis is traditionally divided into two related but somewhat different approaches.

PROCESS ANALYSIS

If you wanted to understand relationships that are part of a chronological sequence, you could trace and evaluate the process. This text is an attempt to work with the process of writing. In preparing it, I first spent a number of years mulling over actual phases the mind goes through as it explores a subject, as words are put on paper for the first time, and as the mind reshapes and refines those words. I attempted to break down my own process into clear stages. I read about how others had described such stages in their writing. I attempted to see how each related in sequence. I have to admit that no new discovery resulted. *Exploring, drafting, organizing, revising,* and *editing* turned out to be a process long known by professional writers and many teachers of writing. But for me it was an invaluable insight. By identifying phases in the process and their relationship, the subject of writing as a whole seemed clarified. Analysis helped me understand why some methods of teaching writing might have disastrous consequences when taught out of sequence. It helped me see that the expository methods I'm discussing in this chapter are actually ways of looking at and thinking about a subject that can later become ways of organizing the same subject on paper. To analyze a process, then, is to explore the way the mind and the world works—in its actual sequence.

Here's an example from a book by John McPhee describing and narrating the simple process of turning fresh oranges into frozen concentrate.

> As the fruit starts to move along a concentrate plant's assembly line, it is first culled. In what some citrus people remember as "the old fresh-fruit days," before the Second World War, about forty per cent of all oranges grown in Florida were eliminated at packinghouses and dumped in fields. Florida milk tasted like orangeade. Now, with the exception of the split and rotten fruit, all of Florida's orange crop is used. Moving up a conveyor belt, oranges are scrubbed with detergent before they roll on into juicing machines. There are several kinds of juicing machines, and they are something to see. One is called the Brown Seven Hundred. Seven hundred oranges a minute go into it and are split and reamed on the same kind of rosettes that are in the centers of ordinary kitchen reamers. The rinds that come pelting out the bottom are integral halves, just like the rinds of oranges squeezed in a kitchen. Another machine is the Food Machinery Corporation's FMC In-line Extractor. It has a shining row of aluminum jaws, upper and lower, with shining aluminum teeth. When an orange tumbles in, the upper jaw comes crunching down on it while at the same time the orange is penetrated from below by a perforated steel tube. As the jaws crush the outside, the juice goes through the perforations in the tube and down into the plumbing of the concentrate plant. All in a second, the juice has been removed and the rind has been crushed and shredded beyond recognition.
>
> From either machine, the juice flows on into a thing called the finisher, where seeds, rag, and pulp are removed. The finisher has a big stainless steel screw that steadily drives the juice through a fine-mesh screen. From the finisher, it flows on into holding tanks.

In McPhee's *Oranges,* a relatively simple mechanical process is divided into each phase of the operation. The author traces the step-by-step process, using concrete detail to show us the oranges tumbling along the conveyor belt, almost as if we were watching a film. McPhee wants to help us understand the process. His intention is clearly not to instruct us in how to run such an operation, although by making the language more formal and directive, he could easily do so:

> First, cull all split and rotten fruit as it moves along the assembly belt. Second, scrub the oranges with detergent using spray-jet machinery. Third, insert the oranges into the Brown 700 De-Juicer. . . .

And so on. As in other types of writing, the purpose and audience help determine vocabulary, tone, and style. In either case, a relationship is illustrated by the natural narrative sequence of the process, first this, then this. A process analysis makes heavy use of transitions: *next, following, afterward, then, beyond this point, later, finally.*

But a process analysis can do much more than focus on simple sequential steps such as tying your shoes or making orange juice. It can give us insight into ideas and values. Here's a brief excerpt from sophomore Cray Steward's essay on "Romantic Love."

> Today we tend to see falling in love as a natural human right, and I would guess that most of us think of it also as a natural step toward marriage. There aren't many of us who would want to marry someone just for their money or their power. We want love, too. And we will marry people without money or power, without anything at all except love. But "sweep-me-off-my-feet" love is actually something new in human history. Marriage was once considered a property right that had little or no relation to love. As late as the Victorian period, marriage was something organized by families to preserve property, or even better to increase property, and to preserve blood lines. In the Western world, the bride was considered as belonging to her father, in the same way that a horse or good piece of furniture belonged to the father, and the father alone had the right to dispose of her. That's why in our marriage ceremony, we still ask the question, "who gives this woman?" at which point the father steps forward and says "I do." The ceremony is recognizing that the woman herself has no right to enter into marriage on her own without permission from the father. In fact, even a woman from a "good family" was not really very desirable if she didn't have some property to go with her. A beautiful lady who might be charming, loving, generous, and devoted was not enough in herself unless a dowry could be offered. Women were merely part of the exchange system concerned primarily with material values.
>
> According to Ernst Van Den Haag, in "Marriage vs. Love," our concept of romantic love originated in the Middle Ages. Romantic love was at first a poetic idea sung about by court entertainers who turned women into an ideal image of beauty and delicacy rather than see them as property. In these poems, knights would "fall in love" with a woman who was already married (already somebody else's property) and who was therefore unattainable. In such a way, their value to the knight could not be materialistic, but purely idealistic (30). The knights would do great deeds for their adored lady, such as slay dragons or set off in quest of some magic potion, but the knights did not expect to "win" their ladies because they were already possessed, and the lady was not expected to submit to expressions of love, although some did I guess. Instead, the two were united only by the bond of romantic love which was a new concept.

In *The Origins of Love*, Catherine Calloway states that idealized romance, which she terms a new "invention," led to two new developments in the way men and women saw their relationship to each other. . . .

Cray Steward's essay does not merely narrate a sequence of events. In fact, he moves back and forth between different types of human experience at different periods of history. But the overall pattern is clear by the third paragraph: in tracing the development of a new form of emotional bond between men and women, Steward hopes to explain the process by which we now believe in marrying for love rather than for property. By analyzing a contemporary value according to the historical process by which we arrived at that value, we discover more about who we are, and why we act and think as we do.

In addition to analyzing a process, analysis may also look at causes and effects. Where process concerns itself primarily with *how* something occurs, a cause-and-effect analysis concerns itself with *why* something occurs.

CAUSE-AND-EFFECT ANALYSIS

Whenever events occur in sequence, the possibility exists that one may have caused the other. But this type of potential relationship is fraught with danger. We must always distinguish between necessary factors and incidental factors. If X precedes Y, is it necessarily the *cause* of Y?

I have relatives, for example, who were living in Kansas when the first atomic bomb was dropped on Hiroshima, Japan. They heard the announcement on the radio and moments later the sky turned greenish black, the winds howled, and a tornado swept down upon them, barely missing their house. My relatives were convinced that what they were experiencing was caused by the atomic bomb. It was not an unnatural fear, nor was it an unnatural link for the mind to make. Tolstoy described how serfs on his estate believed that spring winds were caused by new buds on oak trees. Yet, in both cases, either a coincidence or an incidental relationship was incorrectly perceived as a cause. This type of fallacy has been so common throughout history that logicians have given it a fancy name—*post hoc, ergo propter hoc*. It simply means "after this, therefore because of this"—after my cat ate raw liver, she climbed a tree; therefore, my cat climbs trees because she eats raw liver. These examples may seem silly, but when a doctor is confronted with a symptom, a cause must be determined and the consequences of error could be fatal.

How then can we be reasonably sure of a cause-and-effect relationship? In the scientific laboratory, two rules have been devised as tests:

1. Without X there would be no Y.
2. Whenever we find X, we will find Y.

One or the other of these two conditions (some would say both) must be met for a cause to be considered reasonably certain. Yet in dealing with the complexities outside the laboratory, such a formula, valid as it may be, can lead to distortion and oversimplification. Without Hitler there might not have been World War II, but we cannot therefore say that Hitler was the sole cause of the war. Literally thousands of other factors played significant roles. Causal analysis, then, requires caution and a concern for finding both the *necessary factors* (as opposed to incidental ones) and a *sufficient number of factors* (as opposed to a single or simplistic one).

When anthropologist Margaret Mead, writing in 1977, asked "Can the American Family Survive?" she was fully aware of the danger of blaming a problem on a single cause.

> In recent years, various explanations have been suggested for the breakdown of family life.
>
> Blame has been placed on the vast movement of Americans from rural areas and small towns to the big cities and on the continual, restless surge of people from one part of the country to another, so that millions of families, living in the midst of strangers, lack any continuity in their life-style and any real support for their values and expectations.
>
> Others have emphasized the effects of unemployment and underemployment among Blacks and other minority groups, which make their families peculiarly vulnerable in life crises that are exacerbated by economic uncertainty. This is particularly the case where the policies of welfare agencies penalize the family that is poor but intact in favor of the single-parent family.
>
> There is also the generation gap, particularly acute today, when parents and their adolescent children experience the world in such very different ways. The world in which the parents grew up is vanishing, unknown to their children except by hearsay. The world into which adolescents are growing is in many ways unknown to both generations—and neither can help the other very much to understand it.

Then there is our obvious failure to provide for the children and young people whom we do not succeed in educating, who are in deep trouble and who may be totally abandoned. We have not come to grips with the problems of hard drugs. We allow the courts that deal with juveniles to become so overloaded that little of the social protection they were intended to provide is possible. We consistently underfund and understaff the institutions into which we cram children in need of re-education and physical and psychological rehabilitation, as if all that concerned us was to get them—and keep them—out of our sight.

Other kinds of explanations also have been offered.

There are many people who, knowing little about child development, have placed the principal blame on what they call "permissiveness"—on the relaxing of parental discipline to include the child as a small partner in the process of growing up. Those people say that children are "spoiled," that they lack "respect" for their parents or that they have not learned to obey the religious prohibitions that were taught to their parents, and that all the troubles plaguing family life have followed.

Women's Liberation, too, has come in for a share of the blame. It is said that in seeking self-fulfillment, women are neglecting their homes and children and are undermining men's authority and men's sense of responsibility. The collapse of the family is seen as the inevitable consequence.

Those who attribute the difficulties of troubled families to any single cause, whether or not it is related to reality, also tend to advocate panaceas, each of which—they say—should restore stability to the traditional family or, alternatively, supplant the family. Universal day care from birth, communal living, group marriage, contract marriage and open marriage all have their advocates.

Each such proposal fastens on some trouble point in the modern family—the lack of adequate facilities to care for the children of working mothers, for example, or marital infidelity, which, it is argued, would be eliminated by being institutionalized. Others, realizing the disastrous effects of poverty on family life, have advocated bringing the income of every family up to a level at which decent living is possible. Certainly this must be one of our immediate aims. But it is wholly unrealistic to suppose that all else that has gone wrong will automatically right itself if the one—but very complex—problem of poverty is eliminated.

Mead recognizes that complex issues and ideas almost always have complex causes. Her review of possible causes for the deterioration of traditional family life establishes the context for her own understanding of the problem, and as readers, we now know that simple cause-and-effect relationships will not be forthcoming, nor would they be accurate.

And we also know that identification of so many causes may force us to consider broader and more imaginative solutions than we had at first thought necessary.

If the first rule of cause-and-effect analysis is to avoid oversimplification, the second is to avoid settling for clichés and stereotypes. For example, it would be easy to say—and has been said—that girls do not enter the fields of physics and chemistry because they do not have analytical minds. But when Sheila Tobias studied the situation for her book, *Overcoming Math Anxiety,* here is what she found.

> Although fear of math is not a purely female phenomenon, girls tend to drop out of math sooner than boys, and adult women experience an aversion to math and math-related activities that is akin to anxiety. A 1972 survey of the amount of high school mathematics taken by incoming freshmen at Berkeley revealed that while 57 percent of the boys had taken four years of high school math, only 8 percent of the girls had had the same amount of preparation. Without four years of high school math, students at Berkeley, and at most other colleges and universities, are ineligible for the calculus sequence, unlikely to attempt chemistry or physics, and inadequately prepared for statistics and economics.
>
> Unable to elect these entry-level courses, the remaining 92 percent of the girls will be limited, presumably, to the career choices that are considered feminine: the humanities, guidance and counseling, elementary school teaching, foreign languages, and the fine arts.

Tobias has uncovered causes that challenge our biases and force us to reconsider the standard answers. Freshman Melinda Holt tried to do the same thing when she studied causes and effects of television on family life.

> But is it really that bad? Are we really all such sheep that we sit mindless in front of the tube letting the blue glow hypnotize us? In my family, the TV actually brought us *together,* and we didn't sit passively either. We talked to each other about what was happening. Sometimes we poked fun at banalities of situation comedies. Other times we laughed and argued with the newscasters. In other words, I think that in my family, the TV was more like a guest in our home who for an hour or so each evening drew us all together. We talked *to* the TV just as we talked to each other, and when we grew bored, we didn't sit around and flip channels; my dad would turn it off and all of us went our separate ways. Wagoner's idea that TV has "isolated us from each other and destroyed our abilities to act like social animals" (130), or that it has taken away time that would have been spent doing things like playing basketball with our fathers and baking cakes with our mothers, is simply not true in my household.

Watching television was the one time in the evening, other than dinner itself, when the whole family sat down together. It was no different than if we'd all got in the car and gone to the movies together (which by the way, is something I can never remember us doing).

Thus in my case, TV had the opposite effect usually attributed to it.

Like other forms of writing, cause-and-effect analysis requires you to provide concrete or specific evidence. Merely asserting a cause or an effect convinces no one. Examples, facts, personal experience, or logical argument are all essential. Melinda, of course, has only demonstrated that the effect of television on her family was positive. She has not yet proven that television has a positive effect on other families. To do that, she will have to broaden her study and find evidence that suggests whether her family is typical or whether it is the exception.

Cause-and-effect analysis, then, is a process of beginning with a whole problem, issue, or concept, dividing it into parts (according to your purpose), and then studying the cause-and-effect relationship of those parts. But such an analysis often requires you to gather supporting data, investigate other sources and authorities, and explore numerous possibilities to avoid oversimplifying.

 *Exercise*

For in-class discussion of *analysis,* consider the problem of "cheating in college." Begin by defining the problem. Then break it down into component parts (see pages 292–293). Decide which two parts might serve for an effective comparison-and-contrast essay, and what kind of insights you might gain. Consider which single part might be investigated for itself, and what insight might be derived. What kind of results could a "process analysis" lead to? What could a "cause-and-effect" analysis lead to? How could the 5 *W* method or the 4 *C* method play a role in your analysis?

Exploring

25

Creative Problem Solving

A fox lives in a den among the gnarled roots of an old oak. To the fox, the oak is a tunnel of dark columns and beams with dank smells. The lattice of branches overhead seems to have nothing to do with his world.

A crow lives in a nest at the top of the oak. To the crow, the old tree is an intricate layering of branches, twigs, and leaves—of light and shade constantly shifting. The crow knows nothing of the root system and the dark den at the base of the tree. It has nothing to do with the bright world of sky where more important activities take place.

And what of the oak? Is it a heavy, solid object that soars over one's head or is it something lacy, intricate, filled with open spaces, and sliding downward toward an insignificant connection with the earth below?

I came across this fine image in a book called *The View from the Oak,* by Judith and Herbert Kohl. The Kohls use the analogy to suggest that each of us lives within a narrow world of limited perspective. The truth of a matter tends to reflect not so much the thing itself as our own limitations. Aristotle himself was getting at this indirectly by arguing that to know something we must do more than merely see it. We must compare it or contrast it, classify it with other things of its kind, define it, or divide it and analyze its parts. All of these strategies are methods for better understanding the thing itself. But we have recently come to recognize that the human mind contains a potential for initiating other strategies that may help us focus on an issue, a value, an idea, or a problem with equally beneficial results.

CREATIVE PLAY

The goal is to discover a rational solution or a logical conception to a problem. The method is to use play, fantasy, intuition, or even what might be called irrational speculation.

If you've been attempting any of the journal exercises in this book, you've already involved yourself in a number of seemingly irrelevant acts of play. You may have invented song titles or made up stories or created absurd images. Hard as it may be to convince individuals trained to use logic on every problem, the type of play you've been asked to perform in your journal is not in fact irrelevant. Because play is pleasure in itself, it generates mental energy. Such pleasure is not dependent upon the purpose or outcome; it does not necessarily lead to anything. It may lead to nothing. Only the process is important—the process of relaxed and open play. Without play, without the willingness to suspend the conventional, we may be limited to the ordinary givens of life, to that which is already known and expected. Without play we may never discover the seemingly unimaginable—light bulbs, computers, laser surgery, or electronic music. We might never write a novel, organize a new basketball league in Alaska, or find a cure for cancer. Play may lead to nothing. Or it may lead to startlingly new insights. The only way to find out is to play. Either way, you'll enjoy it.

Studies in the creative process have found three types of play essential to creative problem solving.

1. The mental willingness to ignore the most fundamental laws of nature and man.
2. Play with words.
3. Play with metaphor and analogy.

The twentieth century tends to worship scientific expertise and rational objectivity. Yet when we do so, we accept and limit ourselves to a model of the world created by someone else. We limit ourselves to the view of the fox only, or the crow only, and fail to recognize that other perspectives may broaden our view of the truth. And we are unaware that the model of the world we so readily accept as rational was itself probably developed in an irrational way. In other words, by limiting ourselves to a rational model of any given problem or issue and by attempting to find solutions by using solely rational thought processes, we risk isolating our minds in a world of conventional logic and opinion. If we do not open our minds to ideas which defy common sense or which seem technically irrelevant, if we do not develop what Coleridge called the "willing suspension of disbelief," we are doomed to narrow vision and mediocre thought.

Yet it's difficult to teach anyone how to use intuition, how to detach one's self from problems or issues, how to feel empathy, even how to play imaginatively. One method, developed by William J. J. Gordon and a team of scientists, inventors, and psychologists, is called "synectics." The term derives from the Greek and means simply to join different and seemingly irrelevant parts. For our purposes, it will be easier to refer to the whole process as one of thinking or imagining through varying kinds of analogies.

Making analogies is a natural human act. The story of the fox and the crow is an example of the way analogies clarify and illustrate. But analogies can do more. They can help you discover the seemingly unimaginable, they can wipe away old problems with new and elegant solutions, they can provide insights into questions of value. Making analogies is a strategy for developing what is now called the "right side of the brain," the nonrational, intuitive, and creative side. Making analogies, then, can be a form of creative mental play that breaks through conventional mind-sets. The following material grows out of Gordon's report on synectics research of forty years ago and from other studies on the creative process.

DIRECT ANALOGY

A direct analogy is a comparison of similar or parallel qualities in two things that otherwise are distinctly different. Gordon describes how Alexander Graham Bell conceived of the telephone by considering how the bones of the human ear could be moved by a delicate membrane, and how thus, analogically, a piece of steel might be moved by a somewhat thicker membrane. And physicist George Gamow made discoveries about the play of force within an atomic nucleus by assuming that the material of the nucleus is built in the same way as any ordinary liquid. The coherence of the nucleus could then be understood in terms of a direct analogy to the surface tension in a droplet of water.

The richest source of direct analogy has proven to be the field of biology. We are most acquainted with the living, organic world about us. The blacksmith's bellows is clearly modeled on human or animal lungs. Sir March Isumbard Brunel is reported to have solved the problem of underwater construction by observing a shipworm constructing a tube for itself as it tunneled through wood. And Leonardo da Vinci's design for a flying machine evolved from studies of flights of birds. Leonardo is one of the best examples of a mind that used analogies for almost every new insight. Indeed, for him the earth itself was seen as a living organism, analogous to the human body. Here is what he wrote in his journal.

> We may say that the earth has a spirit of growth, and that its flesh is the soil; its bones are the successive strata of the rocks which form the mountains; its cartilage is the tufa stone; its blood the springs of its waters. The lake of blood that lies about the heart is the ocean. Its breathing is by the increase and decrease of the blood in its pulses, and even so in the heat of the world is the fire which is spread throughout the earth.

Direct analogies provide the opportunity to leap from the known to the unknown. They are the means by which we make the strange and impossible seem familiar and attainable.

PERSONAL ANALOGY

A personal analogy is more difficult to envision because it requires empathy. To make a personal analogy you must compare yourself to the problem, or, more figuratively, you must imaginatively project yourself *into* the problem. You must lose yourself, abandon your ego, and make a leap of the imagination. Artists are known for such ability. The Japanese painter, Hokusai, has written, "If you want to draw a bird, you must become a bird." And in one of Keats' letters he writes, "I looked out the window and saw a sparrow and I became the sparrow. I saw a piece of straw and I became the straw."

Scientists often work (or play) in the same way. Michael Faraday, the eighteenth-century discoverer of benzene, was equally involved in the study of electricity. Faraday is credited with developing the first dynamo and laying theoretical foundations for the classical field theory. To do so, he is said to have looked into the heart of the electrolyte "endeavoring to render the play of its atom visible" to his mental eye. He did not say, "I'm going to try to imagine what's going on here." He said instead, "I am a dancing molecule." He became the thing itself. And in so doing, he recognized the inner secrets of electrolysis. Einstein has said that this kind of "play" seems to be "the essential feature in productive thought."

Clearly detached observation and logical analysis are often necessary. At other times, objectivity must be abandoned in favor of empathetic involvement by personal analogy.

FANTASY ANALOGY

Sometimes we find our minds blocked by conventional thinking, by cynicism, or by the limits of language itself. We may even consciously deceive ourselves. "If it were possible to solve this problem," we may say, "it would have been solved years ago."

The solution may be to break through such a blockage with fantasy, because fantasy has no limits or conventions. We may find it helpful to imagine the problem in its most radical or idealistic form, to fantasize the most satisfying and elegant solution. What if people performed only as we wished, as loving, caring, tolerant individuals? What if we were not restricted by gravity? What would our view be if money were not a requirement for survival? In other words, we may need to imagine the *best* solution, temporarily disregarding all laws of nature, common sense, and experience. We must construct an ideal world in which an ideal solution is available.

To use Michael Faraday again as our example, Faraday had to cast away the common electrical terms of his era because he found that they limited and constricted his thinking. Only by fantasizing new concepts and terms—that is, by constructing an entirely new language—was his research free to go forward. Had he remained limited to conventional terminology, he could not have envisioned the possible solutions he was seeking.

SYMBOLIC ANALOGY

The final method is the most difficult. It requires you to compare the problem or issue to an abstract principle or to an objective image, to something that may be technically inaccurate, absurd, poetic, or pictorial. One of the more famous examples of this occurred when a nineteenth-century German chemist named Kekule solved the problem of the benzene molecule, which until then everyone had thought of as a chain of carbon atoms. The analogy of a chain, however, did not totally explain all of its actions. Kekule had been working on the problem with no success for months. Finally, exhausted from his studies, he is said to have sat slumped in his chair, half dozing, when suddenly he envisioned a snake swallowing its own tail. He realized immediately that the benzene molecule could only be a "ring" of six carbon atoms joined in a hexagon, not a "chain." The image of the snake served as a symbolic analogy for the solution to the problem.

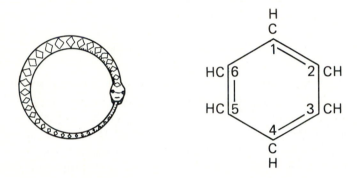

A similar story is told about James Clark Maxwell, who developed the theory of electromagnetic fields on a mathematical basis. He is said to have encountered blocks in his studies when logic, language, and math all failed to provide answers he needed. On each occasion he began to daydream, letting his imagination wonder over various mental images. And repeatedly his fantasy images served to symbolically illustrate solutions to problems that otherwise had no answer.

Unfortunately, symbolic analogies seem to occur only after you have already learned to relax and play with other types of analogies; that is, your mind has to be opened to the image. You can seldom call up such images on command. The process requires a willingness to allow your mind to wander, to dream. And it requires confidence in the imagination that such play may ultimately be constructive. Those who use symbolic analogies talk about them as occurring "complete," or all of a moment, coming in a rush, or revealing themselves with suddenness. What that probably means to the student is that you must learn to relax and play with other kinds of analogies first—personal, direct, and fantasy—if for no other reason than to maintain an open, creative imagination. Once you have trained yourself to trust your mind, to trust play as a mechanism for creativity, symbolic analogies seem to result naturally.

If we combine the left-brain models of detached observation (*comparing and contrasting, defining, classifying, illustration,* and *analysis*) with the intuitive right-brain models of creative play (*direct analogies, personal analogies, fantasy analogies,* and *symbolic analogies*), we have a full range of mental tools with which to approach complex problems, ideas, and values. Each of them alone, or in some combination, will provide you with strategies for approaching almost any type of issue you may ever be confronted with—strategies for thinking, for exploring, for discovering.

Exercises

Each of these exercises is intended to be undertaken with other members of your class.

1. To free the mind of its limitations, one must find ways to break through conventional images and expectations. The following illustrates how the mind can sometimes be trapped by conventional thought.

Connect all nine dots with no more than four straight lines and without lifting your pencil from the paper.

> •   •   •
>
> •   •   •
>
> •   •   •

2. America has too much grain. A small third-world country in a rugged mountainous area is suffering a severe drought and hundreds of thousands may starve. Airstrips are not large enough for grain to be transported by cargo plane. Rail and road travel is primitive. The government of the country is known to be corrupt, and the little grain that has been shipped in has been either hoarded or sold to other nearby countries. How can you deliver grain to the starving?

First, discuss the problem directly. Identify and agree on all aspects of it. Then explore direct analogies (including biological analogies) or fantasy analogies for a possible solution. Brainstorm any image, no matter how seemingly absurd. Remember that what *seems* irrelevant may lead to relevant solutions.

3. A religious sect in the Midwest believes that purity of body is next to godliness. Although in the past they allowed vaccinations for their children, they have recently prevented state health officials from

entering their homes and schools. A genuine threat of an epidemic from measles and other diseases is threatened. Some of the children may die. A state court has ruled that the sect has a right to uphold its religious values.

Analyze the problem to logically define each of its various aspects. Then use personal analogy to project yourself into a deeper understanding of the views of the sect. (What are you trying to protect? How can your values be justified? Why did you originally allow vaccinations to be given and why did you change? Explore your emotions honestly.)

Now consider the state's argument from your new perspective. Based on new insights, what kind of solution might be arrived at?

4. Your company is having financial difficulties. The president has ordered you to develop a product that will earn the company one billion dollars a year. Your research group is not concerned with how to sell such a product, only with developing it. Your only instructions are that it must be so unusual, so totally new, that the world can't resist.

First, explore possibilities. Be willing to ignore all limitations, including the laws of nature. Find the irresistible, needed product. Then find a way to make it. Use any kind of possible analogy to assist your team in inventing a working model.

5. Your state has recently changed its minimum drinking age to 21. Many of your fellow students argue that because they are old enough at 18 to drive, to serve in the armed forces, to vote, and to marry, they should be allowed to drink. Yet when beer was allowed, drunkenness was a serious problem in the residential halls and fraternity houses. Dances often deteriorated into fights. And alcoholism was a serious problem. Define the problem in logical terms. Find at least six rational solutions. Then explore various kinds of analogies—direct, personal, fantasy, symbolic. Force the analogies toward ever deeper connections, extending them as far as possible. In what ways do the analogies expand your understanding of the problem and of the differing solutions? Do they lead to any new solutions?

Journal Practice

Play

1. Begin practicing in your journal with simple similes:

   After the dance her eyes looked as heavy as oil on a rain puddle.

   I watched Charlie slip into the office like a senator on food stamps.

My aunt lived in clouds of fantasies. They floated around her like puffs from a Turkish water pipe.

2. Write an extended paragraph using one of the following to illustrate an idea or concept:

spinach soup	a contact lens	broken glass	a pimple
a scab	a spiral staircase	a deflated balloon	glue

3. Did you ever carry a lunch in a brown bag? Steve Martin has more interesting suggestions: line your pocket with vinyl so you can carry your favorite chip dip around all day, or equip your sport coat with a banana loader arranged so that by lowering an arm, a banana will drop into your hand. Can you come up with other possibilities? How about a recipe for folding soup so that it will fit inside an envelope? Invent precise and detailed instructions for at least one new way to carry your lunch.

4. How are a fish and a houseplant alike?

5. Authors have frequently written essays in which they compare themselves or their lives to another object. Anne Morrow Lindbergh compared her life to a special shell called a *channeled whelk*; Flaubert thought of himself as a bear; others have compared themselves both humorously and seriously to animals as bizarre as a friarbird and an oarfish. Compare your life to something from nature. Begin by describing the object or animal in detail. Then consider how you are like that object or animal. Extend the analogy and justify it with at least three reasons.

6. What are pickle flashers?
   Who are the oreos?
   How do bathtubs sing?
   Who broadcasts the mews?
   What is penguin terrorism?

Audience and Form

26

Shaping the Formal Essay

ormal essays have no prescribed form. Too bad. It would be so much easier if I could tell you to write first this, then that, or the other. But as in most other types of writing, *subject, audience, context*, and *purpose* must guide you. In writing about ideas, issues, or values, your purpose may be varied, but in one fashion or another, it will usually include the concept of explaining, of leading the reader toward some insight into the subject. Over the years, a number of traditions have evolved regarding how best to achieve that end. Many instructors will expect you to adhere fairly closely to them, at least in the beginning.

AUDIENCE AND CONTEXT

Formal essays may be written for national audiences in national magazines, they may take the form of specialized studies for scholarly journals, or they may be written—as they often are—for a college assignment.

Obviously, the needs and expectations of all those varying audiences will differ. It is exactly the differences you must keep in mind. Specialized terms and professional jargon may be satisfactory in many circumstances, whereas simple terms and careful definitions of abstract concepts may be the crux of your paper for another audience. *You* must be the one who asks yourself the needed questions: What experience does my audience have with the subject? What level of vocabulary can I expect my audience to recognize? What terms and concepts should I be sure to define? What, exactly, does my audience need to know?

A recognition of your audience also forces you to consider the tone of your paper. Tone was earlier defined as the attitude an author takes toward his or her material. Sarcasm may be effective in some cases. Anger or hostility may work in others. But for most essays, you will be expected to write in a straightforward, serious, and impartial tone. You should at least give the impression of objectivity. As Erich Fromm expressed it, "Objectivity does not mean detachment, it means respect; that is, the ability not to distort and falsify things, persons and oneself." A tone that shows "respect" will probably be the most convincing of all.

Finally, like tone, the voice you write in will be determined in part by audience and context. Some college instructors may want a strictly formal voice with complete absence of the personal "I." Others may feel the personal voice should be used in a paper dealing with values or in one that tries to persuade a reader to accept a certain argument. When context, however, is outside the college classroom, voice may be prescribed by a company's individual policy or by the journal to which you plan to submit your essay. Again, *you* are responsible for knowing your audience and making the determination in advance.

THE INTRODUCTION

As in earlier forms of writing, the imaginative lead may be an effective means of capturing your reader's attention while creating a sense of immediate involvement. Professional writers almost always use a lead. But a college essay may also require a formal introduction. Such an introduction may contain any or all of the following elements.

1. A general overview of the subject, usually in one or two sentences.

> The United States has been in the foreign-aid business since the end of World War II. Last year alone we spent more than $143 billion, supposedly in an attempt to help underdeveloped nations.

The overview presents the reader with a broad picture so that more focused details of the essay can be seen in perspective.

2. A brief review of the historical or cultural context.

> Since 1965 two national commissions have studied the effects on children of televised violence. Both commissions came to the same conclusion: Televised violence can teach, influence, and legitimatize antisocial behavior. The U.S. Surgeon General has presented testimony to the United States Senate that "the overwhelming consensus and the unanimous Scientific Advisory Committee's report indicate that televised violence, indeed, does have an adverse effect on certain members of our society. . . ." Yet ten years after the report NBC presented a prime-time film, *Born Innocent,* that depicted an explicit rape of a young girl with a broom handle. Three days later in San Francisco, three girls, ages 10 to 15, committed a similar attack on a nine-year-old child.

As no idea, issue, or value exists in a vacuum, the historical context prepares us to understand attitudes or events that influence the subject you plan to write on.

3. A definition of the concept that will be elaborated upon in the essay.

> In 1886, Thomas Henry Huxley defined education as "the instruction of the intellect in the laws of Nature, under which name I include not merely things and their forces, but men and their ways. . . ." Today, however, we define education as a process requiring compulsive attendance at an institution for twelve years. Only a fool believes that education means learning.

By beginning with a definition, you immediately begin to focus the subject.

4. A classification of the subject.

> There are two kinds of happiness. First is the happiness based on consumption and possession. The second, by contrast, is based on giving and sharing.

Classification directs the reader's attention to the specific categories or components you plan to discuss. The example given here also has the happy advantage of comparing and contrasting.

THE THESIS STATEMENT

A formal essay may also require a *thesis statement,* usually as the concluding sentence of the introduction. The concept sometimes sounds frightening, but it simply requires you to summarize the dominant idea of your findings in a single sentence. It should be a simple, unadorned statement of the argument you plan to support with evidence and reason. Traditionally, a thesis statement focuses and further restricts the subject, it states the purpose or direction of the paper in precise words, and, if possible, it indicates something about the writer's attitude toward the subject.

> The pollution problem in Lake Angelo can be solved only through the combined efforts of the city government and the Forystal Mining Company.

> *Subject of paper:* the pollution problem in Lake Angelo

> *Restriction of subject:* how the problem can be solved

> *Purpose of argument:* to demonstrate that a combined effort of two organizations can solve it

> *Attitude of writer:* This is the only way the problem can be solved.

In many ways the thesis statement is similar to a 5 W lead, except that instead of merely gathering together important facts, it shapes those facts and gives them a purpose or direction or meaning. A weak thesis statement will usually be caused by a failure to narrow the subject, by a failure to use precise language, by a failure to suggest a single dominating purpose to the paper, or by a sentence structure that is too complex and therefore confusing.

> *Subject too broad:* Pollution must be solved.

> *Imprecise language:* The pollution problem around here can be solved in a couple of good ways.

> *No clear purpose:* Lake Angelo is full of pollution from the Forystal Mining Company because of years of chemical dumping, even though the city has been aware of it.

> *Too complex:* Although it is now evident that only by working together can progress be made, the Forystal Mining Company, having spent 20 years dumping chemical waste in Lake Angelo without a sense of guilt, has been made recently aware of the bad public relations and wants to solve the problem, the same problem the city itself wants to solve, although to date conflicting proposals and bureaucratic bungling have prevented them from joining forces.

Here are four guidelines to keep in mind as you shape a thesis statement:

1. Use one or two simple declarative sentences.
2. Use language with precise denotations.

3. Narrow the subject to the single most important idea in your paper.
4. Clearly indicate the purpose or argument of the essay.

So far so good. But when should you write the thesis statement? Many argue that a thesis must be formulated *before* you begin a first draft. It may take several hours of thinking, writing, and rewriting. You have already studied your subject, asked questions, and narrowed your focus. You should now have at least a general idea of what you want to write about. Rather than begin randomly, however, formulate a thesis statement to help you organize before you write. This formulation forces you to identify the dominant argument or purpose. It forces you to shape your own attitudes toward that idea if you have not already done so. It forces you to be precise about what you want to say. This is the essence of what we mean when we say, "good thinking." Unless you put yourself through such a process, you may find your essay drifting off on irrelevant byways or surveying six ideas at once or beginning with attitude *A* and ending with argument *B*. The thesis statement is important to a reader, but even more important to the writer. It requires you to organize previously unorganized ideas.

On the other hand, not everyone's mind works alike. I have to confess I've seldom been able to write a thesis statement in advance of a first draft. I usually don't know what my argument is until I've reached my conclusion. And at times I've been fortunate to find new insights only because I allowed myself to follow an "irrelevant" byway. Although it will not be true for all, the effort to compose a thesis statement in advance may block creativity and inhibit the potential for discovering ideas in the course of the writing. So here's the result: If you don't form a thesis statement before the first draft, you *will* probably wander around and write a disorganized essay, and you *will* be envious of those who seem to have more structured minds. But if that's the kind of person you are, don't worry about it. Just don't submit your first draft (which you shouldn't be doing anyway). Use that draft as a time for exploration. Afterward, look over what you have written and force yourself at *that* point to identify your thesis. Write it up in a simple statement. Then reorganize and rewrite your essay to correspond to your newly perceived purpose. A thesis statement written after the first draft serves the same function as one written before the first draft. It defines and clarifies. It helps determine organization and gives a sense of direction to the essay. Only after years of frustration did I realize that the reader doesn't care *when* you organize, only *that* you organize.

> ## THE FORMAL INTRODUCTION
> Any combination of the following:
> —General overview of the subject
> —Review of the historical or cultural context
> —Definition of the basic concept
> —Classification of the subject
> Plus:
> —A thesis statement
> - Restriction to one narrow component
> - Purpose or argument made clear
> - Attitude of writer suggested
> - All in a simple focusing sentence or two

THE BODY OF THE ESSAY

Obviously, the rest of your paper will be shaped by subject and purpose. No single example can illustrate the variety of forms open to you, but the following essay by Warren Boroson, a New York writer and editor, demonstrates how some of the methods I've discussed can be combined into an interesting article that deals with an abstract concept. This essay first appeared in *Money*, which suggests the type of audience Boroson had to keep in mind as he wrote.

The Workaholic in You
Warren Boroson

Introduction classifies two types of people who work hard.

Thesis

Lots of Americans work hard and play hard. But some just work, either from the unquenchable love of it or from a compulsion beyond their control. Work lovers—the unquenchables—provide society with many leaders in business, politics, science and the arts. Those who overwork out of compulsion— the work addicts, or workaholics, of this world—are

Adapted from the June 1976 issue of *Money* Magazine by special permission; copyright © 1976 by Time, Inc., Magazine Company.

in trouble. Their addiction can lead to dead-end careers, to poor health, even to early death. They are so emotionally dependent on work that without it they start coming unglued. Though the purebred workaholic is rare, there is a little of him in almost everyone. It is well to know the warning signals and how to cope with them.

Contrast emphasized through example

Confusing workaholics with work lovers is a bit like confusing winos with oenophiles. Mark Twain was a work lover. In 1908, when he was nearly 73, he said he hadn't done a lick of work in over 50 years. Wrote Twain: "I have always been able to gain my living without doing any work; for the writing of books and magazine matter was always play, not work. I enjoyed it; it was merely billiards to me."

Contrast stressed again through analogy

Psychiatrist Carl Jung once said that the difference between the recondite prose of James Joyce and the poetry of Joyce's insane daughter was that he was diving and she was falling. The work lover is diving. He works hard and long by choice. When he wants to, he can stop without suffering acute withdrawal pains. When the work addict goes on vacation, however, it is not the natives but the tourists who are restless.

The work lover's work is also his play. The work addict's motives are mixed. In many cases, he is seeking the admiration of other people because he doesn't approve of himself. As Dr. Alan McLean, an IBM psychiatrist, points out, the healthiest people usually have various sources of satisfaction: they are lawyers, say, but they are also spouses, parents, friends, citizens, churchgoers, art lovers, stamp collectors, golfers and so forth. If such people lose their jobs, or if their work becomes less satisfying or its quality starts deteriorating, they have not lost their sole interest in life, the only prop to their self-esteem. Many compulsive workers, according to cardiologist Meyer Friedman of San Francisco, co-author of the bestselling book *Type A Behavior and Your Heart* (1974), "want status, and their status depends on what other people think of them." Eventually, many addicts manage to labor under the delusion that they are indispensable.

First major point analyzes underlying cause of problem.

In-text documentation

Specific illustrations

Guilt propels some workaholics. Several years ago, a theological seminary in the East had a problem with guilt-ridden students who kept working even when the school closed for vacations. To get them out, the school was finally forced to turn off the electricity and water and change all the locks during vacation periods.

Because of their diligence, work addicts in corporations tend to keep getting promoted; but a lack of imagination keeps them from reaching the top rungs. They make great salesmen and terrible corporation presidents. "Workaholics rarely become famous," says Dr. Frederic Flach, a New York psychiatrist who has treated many people with work problems.

Description of major consequence

"Because they lack creativity, they rarely make an original contribution to the welfare of mankind. They usually end up in upper-middle management, giving grief to everyone around them."

Analysis of experts

Continual work, Dr. Flach notes, "violates one of the basic rules of coming up with original solutions—to move into another area and let the problem simmer." He adds that one reason workaholics work ten to twelve hours a day is that "they are not good at finding ways to think about something in a new fashion." Work addicts, says Robert F. Medina, an industrial psychologist in Chicago, like "the sureness and safety of processing endless details. Creativity is a little too scary. It looks like idleness to them."

* * *

Second major point: effects of being a workaholic clarified by further classification

While work addicts work hard, they tend to die easily. Time and again, researchers have found that the compulsively hard-working person is particularly prone to heart disease in middle age. Dr. Friedman and his cardiologist co-author, Dr. Ray H. Rosenman, divide the world into two working types. Hard-driving people are classified as Type A and low-pressure people as Type B. Both types can become workaholics, but in different ways. The Type-A person is excessively ambitious and competitive, and frequently hostile; he feels pressured by deadlines. Cardiologists have found that he is two to three times as likely to have a premature heart attack as Type B, who is not so competitive and hard driving.

Type-B workaholics are civil service types who lose themselves in dull paperwork or other routine activities. Wayne Oates, a Louisville psychologist, thinks that a Type B work addict, unlike the individualistic Type A, tends to identify with the company he works for and "not have any selfhood of his own. The company is a flat earth to him. Everything beyond it is dragons and disaster."

*   *   *

Continued contrast between work lover and workaholic

Sometimes a work addict can persuade himself as well as other people that he is really a work lover, the way an alcoholic can persuade himself and others that he doesn't have a drinking problem because all he drinks is vintage cognac. Reading someone's basic motives can be difficult. But it's very likely that a work lover—unlike a work addict—has a job that offers freedom and diversity; he is well recognized and amply rewarded for his efforts. An obscure middle-aged heart surgeon or social reformer who works as hard as Dr. Denton Cooley or Ralph Nader is more likely to be a self-destructive work addict than those two men are. Nader scoffs at the notion that his ceaseless toil makes him a workaholic.

Notice integration of summary and quotation

"You wouldn't ask an Olympic swimmer or chess player why he works 20 hours a day," Nader says. People don't understand Nader "because we haven't a tradition which explains me."

Without being workaholics, most people experience the addict's symptoms from time to time. "Anyone who's been busy and active," says Dr. Flach, the New York psychiatrist, "has a tendency to get locked in, to become dependent on his work." Examples are

General description of various situations and examples that seem "workaholic" on surface . . .

accountants in March and April, salesclerks during the Christmas rush, air traffic controllers all the time. When they are no longer so busy, they may suffer from a mild version of "postpartum depression like women who have just given birth."

Some people work too long and hard at times because they fear being fired or are bucking for promotion or cannot do their jobs as well as they know they should. Other people sometimes lose themselves in work to escape emotional problems—the loss of a loved one, a financial setback or some other worry. They use work to keep from breaking down completely. Occupational therapy is, after all, one of the very best pain killers and tranquilizers.

. . . but contrast with true workaholic clarifies.

These people differ from chronic addicts in that once they have stopped working for a while, their pain begins to ebb, their spirits perk up, and they are back to normal. But someone who has been temporarily habituated to hard work would be best advised to unwind slowly. People who suddenly switch from hard work to idleness tend to develop a variety of physical and psychological illnesses, heart disease in particular. Social psychologist Jerome E. Singer of the National Research Council in Washington, D.C., mentions how people often die shortly after retiring from important posts.

*   *   *

Third major point: solution proposed

Jerome Singer recommends that hard-working people generally avoid making abrupt major changes in their work habits. People who work frenetically all year long may suffer if they suddenly flop down on a beach in Hawaii for a few weeks. Instead, Singer suggests that hard workers would be better off taking frequent short vacations or easing into long vacations by cutting down gradually on their work.

Example

Recognizing the value of vacations, many companies (General Motors, for one) now require all employees to take the vacations they are entitled to instead of accumulating them from year to year. Dr. Nicholas A. Pace, medical director of GM's New York executive offices, adds that employees who try not to take vacations "don't get brownie points any more. They're just looked upon as damn fools." But a vacation need not be long to be therapeutic. Dr. John P. McCann of the Life Extension Institute in New York, which gives physicals to executives, points out that for many people even a one-day vacation may constitute a refreshing change of pace.

Opinions of experts

The ideal vacation, in the opinion of Dr. Ari Kiev, a New York psychiatrist and author of *A Strategy for Handling Executive Stress* (1974), is a foil to a person's occupation. Someone who does close, detailed work all year long, like an accountant, might take up something less exacting, like sailing. (Says Dr. Howard Hess: "A Caribbean vacation is not the solution to everyone's problems. Just mine and yours.'') A person who sees in himself symptoms of workaholism should try developing interests outside of his job. Dr. Flach recommends returning to the hobbies of your adolescence—photography, stamp collecting or what have you. ''Your early interests,'' he believes, ''are perhaps the closest expression of you as a person.'' Wayne Oates suggests renewing old acquaintances, making new friends and reading books you don't have to read, like mysteries. It may be easier for those further along the path to addiction to switch to hobbies that, like work, have well-defined goals, such as woodworking or sports.

* * *

Specific illustrations

The incipient addict with the hard-driving personality of a Type A should consider slowing down the general pace of his life. Dr. Friedman, a Type A himself (complete with heart attack), deliberately began dressing informally. He spent lunch hours examining the stained glass windows in a nearby cathedral; he began rereading the seven parts of Marcel Proust's interminable *Remembrance of Things Past*. He now avoids cocktail parties: ''I found that all you do at them is shout, and no one cares whether you leave or stay.'' And he keeps away from ''people who readily bring out my free-floating hostility, because I've never been able to convince those sons of bitches about anything and they've never been able to convince me.''

Conclusion illustrates theme with irony

To get advice from other well-known people who are reputed to work very hard, I wrote Harold S. Geneen, president of ITT, actor Elliot Gould, film director Robert Altman, Governor Jerry Brown of California, and [cardiologist Dr. Michael] DeBakey, among others. A spokesman for ITT apologetically reported that Geneen could not reply because he had been very busy with management meetings recently and was out on the golf course. The others did not respond at all. Presumably they were too busy working.

This essay has obviously involved a good deal of investigation into primary and secondary sources. Such research into ''outside'' opinions is not a requirement for the typical formal essay. Yet I've found that few student writers have studied long enough, thought deeply enough, or known enough life experiences to sit down and write about an abstract idea, issue, or value off the top of their heads. Much of the bad writing in college occurs for the simple reason that the writer has nothing to say. If the body of even a short essay is to have substance, then, you might be best advised to investigate one or two sources at a minimum, if for no other reason than to stimulate your thinking on the subject.

THE CONCLUSION

As the conclusion is the last contact you'll have with a reader, you'll want to leave a strong impression. The following are some of the ways to *fail*:

> Don't have a conclusion at all; let the reader guess.
> Apologize for not having done better.
> Repeat everything you've said in the same words.
> Ignore the evidence in your own paper.
> End by saying, "In conclusion . . ."

But it's easier to say what you should not do than to clearly state what you should. A good conclusion grows naturally out of the argument or evidence of your paper. In that sense, every good conclusion is in some way original and cannot be demonstrated to you in advance. If you're not feeling very original, however, here are some tried and true methods you might consider.

1. Generalize on the significance of the evidence you've presented. Don't merely list all your points; rather, reflect on the meaning of them. Draw reasonable inferences from the overall pattern of information or ideas you've worked with.
2. If it is called for, offer a solution. Be modest and admit that it may not be the only answer, but at the same time, be firm and assert that it represents a good start toward resolving the issue.
3. Use an analogy.
4. Consider the consequences and suggest who may be affected or what the future will hold (but beware of overgeneralizations such as: "Humankind will destroy itself if . . .").
5. Use a striking quotation that reinforces your ideas but do not substitute the quotation for your own judgment. The final paragraph must still be written in your words and reflect your assessment. A quotation should be used only to add strength or support.

6. If the paper is long, make an emphatic restatement of your central idea. Don't, however, merely repeat your thesis statement word for word from the introduction.

No matter what method you use, base your final paragraph on the evidence presented in your essay. If possible, try to relate your conclusion to your opening, to some element of your lead, to your general introduction, to your thesis statement, or to your title. And be especially conscious of word order in the final sentence. A short, emphatic statement or an especially strong phrase will be most effective.

At this point you may be questioning the value of all this work. Just what does it have to do with you? With your interests in becoming an engineer or a dietician or a biologist? As surprising as it may sound, however, training in the formal patterns of perception and organization are proven methods of helping you discover and set forth *your* ideas. Such training demands that your mind engage all its resources in a self-disciplined effort at understanding not only the concrete world about you but also the ideas and values abstracted from that world. The ability to narrow a subject to a single quality, classify it, analyze it, and clarify it is one of the most valued abilities in any profession or career. Indeed, it is this type of self-disciplined intelligence that we most clearly associate with an educated man or woman.

If by this point you feel self-expression has become lost amid the jargon, the forms, and the various techniques, it may be good to remind yourself again that all of it is only a means to an end. "One must, of course, master technique," Pablo Casals has said, but "at the same time, one must not become enslaved by it. One must understand that the purpose of technique is to transmit the inner meaning, the message of the music."

Exercises

1. Consider the following thesis statements. In what way is each too broad for a 1,000-word essay? Suggest ways each could be rewritten to narrow the focus and make it more precise.

   a. Dumping chemicals is dangerous to human health.
   b. Blacks are still treated unjustly in America.
   c. The Supreme Court has ignored the wishes of the American people.
   d. Drug laws reflect the interests of drug companies.

2. Consider which of the following thesis statements are effective. Which would give the reader a clear indication of what to expect in the essay that follows? If you find one that is inadequate, identify the problem.

    a. Limited opportunities for entrance into medical schools cause pre-med students to cheat for the sake of higher grades.
    b. Television series on single-parent families create misleading myths.
    c. I believe there are six types of students in college today.
    d. Effective comedy requires an element of surprise and a sense of timing.
    e. The central idea of a paper can usually be expressed in a single sentence.
    f. Because of its cathartic effect, art can be a central tool in the treatment of mental illness.

3. Read one of the essays included at the end of this unit. Consider the following questions.

    a. What methods does the writer use to shape the introduction?
    b. How does the writer organize the body of the essay?
    c. What combination of formal methods is used in the body of the essay to clarify and explain?
    d. Is the conclusion effective? Can you identify any particular method discussed in this chapter as part of the conclusion, or is it unique to the particular way the writer has treated the subject?

4. What method of analysis have you used in studying the end-of-unit essay?

Journal Practice

Copying

A good conclusion often echoes the beginning of an essay by reminding the reader of the focus. Such a technique seems especially satisfying to a reader. It creates a sense of wholeness and completeness. The introduction and conclusion work together like bookends to support and contain the body of the argument.

    One way to get a feeling for how this is accomplished is to copy several introductions and conclusions by hand. Select some of the professional essays in this text or in a high-quality magazine such as *Atlantic* or *Harper's*. Copy introductory paragraphs, followed immediately by concluding paragraphs. Study the relationships, the techniques by which the authors echo introductions in their conclusions and, in those essays that present an argument or analysis, by which they integrate a forceful summation or judgment.

Here are the introductory and concluding paragraphs of a student essay by Sherry Shelly. Copy each paragraph into your journal and consider the various methods Sherry has used to pull them together.

Introduction

My father. Withered and silent, he looms before me.

This is the same image of the father I find in Richard Rodriguez's intellectual autobiography, *Hunger of Memory*. In a series of six essays, Rodriguez, a Mexican-American, takes a firm stand on affirmative action and bilingual education. He shares the effect formal education has had on his life. The pain and sadness of losing his past while gaining his education is conveyed to us as he progresses from elementary school to college. Although his father is mentioned scarcely throughout the essays, his presence is deeply felt. In a world where the English language is dominant, his Spanish-speaking father changes from a steady, confident man, to a silent, withdrawn man. Rodriguez's confidence in his father is shaken and the image the young boy once held for his father is shattered. The connection he feels to his father, one that goes back to his father's own youth, is forever lost.

Conclusion

Throughout *Hunger of Memory* Richard Rodriguez shares the changes he endured through formal education. These changes draw him away from his father as his father gives in to English, the alien language that enters his home and bears him down. While reaching out to better understand his father's life, Rodriguez comes to the recognition that this very English language which gave him success and fame in an English-speaking world separated him forever from one who, ironically, had encouraged him to learn it. I was moved by his need to share with his father. Losing the ability to touch and communicate with a person who affected such a great part of his life was something I could identify with, a loss I too have known. How odd that education which our parents so encourage is the culprit which distances us irrevocably from their world. I suspect that all of us must admire the courage it takes to look closely at one's life and relationships. There is, perhaps in all of us, a part of our past that is lost forever. Finding out what part, and why, is truly courageous.

Revising and Editing

27

The Challenge of Simplicity

Making the simple complicated is commonplace; making the complicated simple, awesomely simple, that's creativity.

MARVIN BELL

Theodore M. Bernstein, an editor of *The New York Times*, recounted the story of a plumber who cleaned drains with hydrochloric acid and wrote to a chemical research bureau inquiring about its safety. The bureau wrote back, "The efficacy of hydrochloric acid is indisputably established, but the corrosive residue is incompatible with metallic permanence." The plumber, impressed by such a response, thanked the bureau for its approval. Another letter arrived: "We cannot assume responsibility for the production of a toxic and noxious residue with hydrochloric acid. We beg leave to suggest to you the employment of an alternative procedure." More proud than ever, the plumber again expressed his appreciation. In desperation the bureau called in an older scientist, who wrote a third letter to the plumber: "Don't use hydrochloric acid. It eats the hell out of pipes."

© 1974 United Feature Syndicate, Inc.

JARGON

Jargon has its rightful place in the language: to communicate specialized concepts to other specialists. Every profession and occupation needs a specialized vocabulary. Linguists must talk of *deep structures;* mechanics need to discuss *carbon buildup;* government officials must consider *systems management.* Yet it is not just a matter of knowing your audience. Most audiences, even those trained in the specialties you may be writing about, usually prefer clear, concrete communication. Einstein was admired for his ability to write about scientific complexities with simplicity. Freud, who probably contributed more jargon to the twentieth century than any other individual, at least had the courtesy in his own writing to define his terms.

PRETENTIOUSNESS

The problem with jargon arises when we use it pretentiously for the sake of impressing rather than communicating or when it is used to obscure meaning, to hide ignorance through lack of precision. Yet all of us want others to think we are intelligent and wise. We seek praise and reputation. We sometimes believe that if our writing sounds obscure, others will think us profound. We may fear simplicity. Only dullards are simple. Those who are knowledgeable, we believe, impress us with their vocabulary. Why, all we need do is listen to our professors.

> . . . the most basic problems that arise in connection with knowledge utilization may be those that stem from the social and organizational character of educational institutions. . . . Public schools display a myriad of normative and other regulatory structures that promote predictability, as well as a host of adaptive mechanisms that reduce external uncertainties.

Quite impressive. But sad, nevertheless. Sad because this professor (of education, no less) is not honestly trying to inform us of anything. His real subject is himself. "Look at me," he says. "Just look at all the big words I know." And too often it happens to us all, especially when we begin to write formal prose about abstract issues or values. We shift to a serious tone, we adopt a pompous voice, and before the old computer even begins to warm up, we're writing as this student did.

> The choice of exogenous variables in relation to multicollinearity is contingent upon the derivations of certain multiple correlation coefficients.

Pretentiousness, affectation, overabstraction, circumlocution—the many names for such gobbledygook could fill a small dictionary. Those who admire language, those who respect it, have been railing for generations against the pseudointellectual misuse of it. Here is Sir Arthur Quiller-Couch writing in 1923:

> If your language be jargon, your intellect, if not your whole character, will almost certainly correspond. Where your mind should go straight, it will dodge: the difficulties it should approach with a fair front and grip with a firm hand it will be seeking to evade or circumvent. For the style is the man, and where a man's treasure is, there his heart, and his brain, and his writing will be also.

And a woman's too, we might add.

The product of writing is a social act. Like other social acts it imposes obligations. In the case of formal prose, our responsibility is to explain or set forth clearly so that the reader understands. The use of jargon or other outlandish abstraction becomes an evasion of that responsibility. That is why Quiller-Couch makes language a moral issue. The use of clear, straightforward prose means that you face up to your responsibilities, your obligation to communicate what you know.

Some of the most famous, or infamous, uses of language to avoid responsibility came from government officials during the Vietnam War. Generals described weapons that were intended to kill people as *antipersonnel devices. Protective reaction* was a military phrase meaning that we bombed "them" before they bombed "us." Concentration camps were termed *relocation centers.* Each of these is an example of a *euphemism,* that is, of a substitute for a straightforward, simple term. Certainly not all euphemisms are immoral. We call undertakers *morticians,* and we substitute *scoring* for *fornication;* we elevate janitors to *maintenance engineers,* and we promote old people to *senior citizens.* But euphemisms do lead us astray from reality in the same way that jargon obscures reality through inflated words.

CIRCUMLOCUTION

Unfortunately, we can sometimes lead ourselves astray just by using too many words, by circling about a subject without ever quite touching upon it. Here is a student example of *circumlocution*.

> The actualization of an objective decision to follow the rules was not something they really felt was something compelled by their hearts. Oftentimes, a person agrees with the legal legitimacy of something but it is against his ethical values to go ahead with it. Having been confronted with these postulates and their modifications or contingencies, it soon becomes difficult determining exactly what our response should be.

The consequence of inflated language is now apparent. When we substitute jargon, pretentious abstractions, euphemisms, and circumlocutions for precision, we run the risk of concealing our meaning—or lack of meaning—even from ourselves.

When Thoreau wrote his famous advice, "Simplify, simplify," he was speaking of our lives, but the advice applies no less to our writing. Most social issues and moral values are complex. To explain complexity in simple prose is not a fault; it is a mark of achievement. Yet few of us can sit down to the first draft and say, "Now I am going to write a coherent, simple sentence." What we can do is return to those first rough scribblings and ask, "Do I know what I'm trying to say?" and "Can the reader follow it?" Both questions are important. Unless you have discovered and fully explored your ideas, demanding exactness of yourself, all the tinkering in the world will fail to patch over your confusion. Once you feel confident that you do understand your own ideas, then you are obligated to question whether the reader can.

Your goal should be to find the simplest language possible while still conveying the seriousness and full weight of your intentions. Neither of the following examples would serve.

> The high-level government representative indulged in a special purchase of verdurous flora for a close relative.

> The guy got his mom some flowers.

The first is pretentious; the second sounds like Dick and Jane. Somewhere in the middle we might try:

> The senator bought roses for his mother.

Reprinted from "Masters of Babble" by permission of James P. Degnan.

If you have plowed your way through earlier chapters in this book on revising and editing, you should be fully prepared to handle the extra demands complex ideas may put upon your writing: Eliminate extra words; whenever possible, use concrete images instead of abstractions; trust the simple sentence; build paragraphs around a logical purpose; and so on. To simplify essentially means to be straightforward (avoiding circumlocutions and overblown abstractions) and to be exact (to convey a precise meaning, usually through concrete nouns or active verbs). But to that list of techniques, we must add an earlier concept: *honesty.* Not just honesty of perception, but honesty in the manner of presentation. Your goal should be to present what you know in your own voice as an expression of your imagination and intellect, avoiding the temptation to write as you think others are praised for writing—profoundly, elegantly—choosing instead to be responsible above all for clarity and precision.

Exercises

1. Consider the actual meaning of the following, and try writing a simple version for each.

   a. He established an objective and pursued the ultimate achievement of success with diligence.

      Example: *He set a goal and worked hard to achieve it.*

   b. From the director of the CIA: "I wish to restrict lateral input of outside retirees into positions that could be filled within our own ranks. Therefore, effective immediately, the further hiring of annuitants is prohibited."

   c. The neoclassical postulate of rationality and the concept of the entrepreneur as the profit-maximizing individual, should, I think, be replaced by a sociological analysis of the goals of the firm in relation to its nature as an organization within the sociopolitical system.

   d. "Thirdly, the aim [of this book] is not to set forth a list of abstract properties of human knowledge but to assist the reader in effecting a personal appropriation of the concrete, dynamic structure immanent and recurrently operative in his own cognitional activities. . . ."

   e. From a student paper: "Legalization of euthanasia is, retrospectively, a barbaric liability hung upon the corporate neck of civilized society today. It manifests our egocentrical natures and ignores our inherent rights constitutionalized in 1884.''

2. The following words and phrases have become the overused, empty, pretentious, or jargonish vocabulary found in almost everybody's writing. Find a simple word or phrase as a replacement for each.

utilize	in today's society
Example: *use*	Example: *today*
subject area	come in contact with
in the last analysis	in accordance with
fully recognize	absolutely essential
input/output	in the case of
the end result	in the field of
the final solution	factor
parameters	maturation
wholly justifiable	socioeconomic considerations
bottom line	delivery system
down the road	at this point in time

Readings

Bernard R. Kaplan is a freshman pre-law major. Consider how in the following essay he has combined such strategies as change, conflict, and consequence with definition and analysis.

A Prologue to Tragedy: Illiteracy in America

Bernard R. Kaplan

If the present trend continues, two out of three Americans will be functionally illiterate by the year 2000. According to Jonathan's Kozol's recent study, *Illiterate America* (1985), 25 million adult Americans cannot read a poison warning on a can of pesticide, a letter, a front page of a newspaper or even a street sign. An additional 35 million—many with high school diplomas—read just enough to get by. Individuals who can neither read nor write are dubbed *illiterate*. Those who can spell out letters but can't fill out an application or address an envelope without help are considered *functionally illiterate*.

Reprinted by permission of the author.

What does it mean to be illiterate? Imagine yourself waking up one morning in a train station in some remote area of China. You don't know exactly where you are or how you got there. You search for clues. Across from you an old man sits reading a newspaper printed with hundreds of ideograms that resemble numerous lines of bird tracks. Signs and posters hang from every wall, some with pictures and ideographs as wide as your hand. Pictures become your only clue to a meaning. You are hungry. You cannot read signs in the windows; you cannot read a menu. You join a crowd of people who stand shouting, their fingers knitting air as they point to the poster tacked to the wall, their voices agitated. You stand with your fists shoved into the pockets of your jacket with a sense of pain.

According to numerous estimates, nearly 60 million adults in America, one-third of the population, may be illiterate. In a country that once claimed 99.4 percent of all its citizens could read and write, these recent statistics are an alarming threat to both our citizenry and our democracy.

Schools get much of the blame. University professors point an accusing finger toward low standards in the secondary schools. High school teachers blame elementary teachers and elementary teachers blame parents who have turned their children on to television rather than on to books. But this is unfair according to Harold W. McGraw, Jr., chairman of McGraw-Hill: "The teaching of reading in schools is usually adequate . . . The problem is that an awful lot . . . just weren't turned on. They dropped out of school for lack of motivation . . ." (*Newsweek*, July 30, 1985).

Illiteracy costs the nation an estimated 20 billion dollars each year in unemployment, welfare, and accidents. *The New York Times,* August 19, 1982, reported that a feedlot worker destroyed a herd of prime beef cattle because he could not read the label on the bag. The nutritional substance he thought he was adding to the feed turned out to be poison. An industrial worker was killed because he could not read a warning sign. An anonymous male compared his inability to read to a form of twentieth-century leprosy: "Before you know it, you're being treated as a kid, as half what you used to be treated" (Kozol 151).

According to *The New York Times* (Sept. 9, 1985) the Federal Government spends one hundred million dollars yearly to address the needs of 60 million people. It has been estimated that nearly 5 billion dollars are needed just to keep even as 2.3 million additional illiterates surface each year. Adult Basic Education programs and U.S. military remedial programs for recruits serve thousands of illiterates. Thirty-three states have formed literacy councils to search for solutions. Volunteer organizations are on the rise. Volunteer Tom Critten has stated that Laubach Literacy Action provides 600 programs in 45 states, serving 50,000 illiterates. Many of America's largest companies offer remedial reading programs to their workers. In California, where 33% of all prisoners are illiterate, prisoners can work off one day of their sentence for each day of study (Kozol 22).

For those who can read and write, it is easy to dismiss illiteracy as someone else's problem; but illiteracy must be everyone's concern. The human price for illiteracy cannot be measured in dollars. Illiterate citizens cannot read leases; they cannot read insurance forms or deal with banking. They cannot read legal notices. They buy groceries at the local supermarket based on the pictures on the packaging. They cannot read a label or a menu or a telephone book. Illiterate citizens seldom vote. They cannot make intelligent decisions based on information gleaned from reading.

James Madison once wrote:

> A people who mean to be their own governors must arm themselves with the power knowledge gives. A popular government without popular information or the means of acquiring it is but a prologue to a farce or a tragedy, or perhaps both.

How long can a country continue to think of itself as a democracy when 60 million citizens are no longer their own governors but the governors of ignorance and shame, when the only power felt is the power of fear? Illiteracy in America may be a 20-billion-dollar problem, but who can measure the cost in human suffering and the cost to this nation's credibility as a democracy?

For a country founded on written principles, to discover that 2.3 million of its people cannot even begin to read and comprehend those principles is cause for alarm. Allowing the trend to continue can only undermine the heart's core of America—its wealth of active human intelligence.

Bruce Catton, one of America's best Civil War historians, won both the Pulitzer Prize and the National Book Award for his study, A Stillness at Appomattox. *The following essay, one of his most famous, is also one of the clearest examples of how the use of comparison and contrast can illuminate a subject.*

Grant and Lee:
A Study in Contrasts

Bruce Catton

When Ulysses S. Grant and Robert E. Lee met in the parlor of a modest house at Appomattox Court House, Virginia, on April 9, 1865, to work out the terms for the surrender of Lee's Army of Northern Virginia, a great chapter in American life came to a close, and a great new chapter began.

These men were bringing the Civil War to its virtual finish. To be sure, other armies had yet to surrender, and for a few days the fugitive Confederate government would struggle desperately and vainly, trying to find some way to go on living now that its chief support was gone. But in effect it was all over when Grant and Lee signed the papers. And the little room where they wrote out the terms was the scene of one of the poignant, dramatic contrasts in American history.

They were two strong men, these oddly different generals, and they represented the strengths of two conflicting currents that, through them, had come into final collision.

Back of Robert E. Lee was the notion that the old aristocratic concept might somehow survive and be dominant in American life.

Lee was tidewater Virginia, and in his background were family culture, and tradition . . . the age of chivalry transplanted to a New World which was making its own legends and its own myths. He embodied a way of life that had come down through the age of knighthood and the English country squire. America was a land that was beginning all over again, dedicated to nothing much more complicated than the rather hazy belief that all men had equal rights and should have an equal chance in the world. In such a land Lee stood for the feeling that it was somehow of advantage to human society to have a pronounced inequality in the social structure. There should be a leisure class, backed by ownership of land; in turn, society itself should be keyed to the land as the chief source of wealth and influence. It would bring forth (according to this ideal) a class of men with a strong sense of obligation to the community; men who lived not to gain advantage for themselves, but to meet the solemn obligations which had been laid on them by the very fact that they were privileged. From them the country would get its leadership; to them it could look for the higher values—of thought, of conduct, of personal deportment—to give it strength and virtue.

Lee embodied the noblest elements of this aristocratic ideal. Through him, the landed nobility justified itself. For four years, the Southern states had fought a desperate war to uphold the ideals for which Lee stood. In the end, it almost seemed as if the Confederacy fought for Lee; as if he himself was the Confederacy . . . the best thing that the way of life for which the Confederacy stood could ever have to offer. He had passed into legend before Appomattox. Thousands of tired, underfed, poorly clothed Confederate soldiers, long since past the simple enthusiasm of the early days of the struggle, somehow considered Lee the symbol of everything for which they had been willing to die. But they could not quite put this feeling into words. If the Lost Cause, sanctified by so much heroism and so many deaths, had a living justification, its justification was General Lee.

Grant, the son of a tanner on the Western frontier, was everything Lee was not. He had come up the hard way and embodied nothing in particular except the eternal toughness and sinewy fiber of the men who grew up beyond the mountains. He was one of a body of men who owed reverence and obeisance to no one, who were self-reliant to a fault, who cared hardly anything for the past but who had a sharp eye for the future.

These frontier men were the precise opposites of the tidewater aristocrats. Back of them, in the great surge that had taken people over the Alleghenies and into the opening Western country, there was a deep, implicit dissatisfaction with a past that had settled into grooves. They stood for democracy, not from any reasoned conclusion about the proper ordering of human society, but simply because they had grown up in the middle of democracy and knew how it worked. Their society might have privileges, but they would be privileges each man had won for himself. Forms and patterns meant nothing. No man was born to anything except perhaps to a chance to show how far he could rise. Life was competition.

Yet along with this feeling had come a deep sense of belonging to a national community. The Westerner, who developed a farm, opened a shop, or set up in business as a trader, could hope to prosper only as his own community prospered—and his community ran from the Atlantic to the Pacific and from Canada down to Mexico. If the land was settled, with towns and highways and accessible markets, he could better himself. He saw his fate in terms of the nation's own destiny. As its horizons expanded so did his. He had, in other words, an acute dollars-and-cents stake in the continued growth and development of his country.

And that, perhaps, is where the contrast between Grant and Lee becomes most striking. The Virginia aristocrat, inevitably, saw himself in relation to his own region. He lived in a static society which could endure almost anything except change. Instinctively, his first loyalty would go to the locality in which that society existed. He would fight to the limit of endurance to defend it, because in defending it he was defending everything that gave his own life its deepest meaning.

The Westerner, on the other hand, would fight with an equal tenacity for the broader concept of society. He fought so because everything he lived by was tied to growth, expansion, and a constantly widening horizon. What he lived by would survive or fall with the nation itself. He could not possibly stand by unmoved in the face of an attempt to destroy the Union. He would combat it with everything he had, because he could only see it as an effort to cut the ground out from under his feet.

So Grant and Lee were in complete contrast, representing two diametrically opposed elements in American life. Grant was the modern man emerging; beyond him, ready to come on the stage, was the great age of steel and machinery, of crowded cities and a restless burgeoning vitality. Lee might have ridden down from the old age of chivalry, lance in hand, silken banner fluttering over his head. Each man was the perfect champion of his cause, drawing both his strengths and his weaknesses from the people he led.

Yet it was not all contrast, after all. Different as they were—in background, in personality, in underlying aspiration—these two great soldiers had much in common. Under everything else, they were marvelous fighters. Furthermore, their fighting qualities were really very much alike.

Each man had, to begin with, the great virtue of utter tenacity and fidelity. Grant fought his way down the Mississippi Valley in spite of acute personal discouragement and profound military handicaps. Lee hung on in the trenches at Petersburg after hope itself had died. In each man there was an indomitable quality . . . the born fighter's refusal to give up as long as he can still remain on his feet and lift his two fists.

Daring and resourcefulness they had, too; the ability to think faster and move faster than the enemy. These were the qualities which gave Lee the dazzling campaigns of Second Manassas and Chancellorsville and won Vicksburg for Grant.

Lastly, and perhaps greatest of all, there was the ability, at the end, to turn quickly from war to peace once the fighting was over. Out of the way these two men behaved at Appomattox came the possibility of a peace of reconciliation. It was a possibility not wholly realized, in the years to come, but which did, in the end, help the two sections to become one nation again . . . after a war whose bitterness might have seemed to make such a reunion wholly impossible. No part of either man's life became him more than the part he played in their brief meeting in the McLean house at Appomattox. Their behavior there put all succeeding generations of Americans in their debt. Two great Americans, Grant and Lee—very different, yet under everything very much alike. Their encounter at Appomattox was one of the great moments of American history.

Marie Winn contributes regularly to The New York Times *and* The Village Voice, *but she is best known for her study,* The Plug-In Drug: Television, Children and Family, *from which the following excerpt is taken. Here, Winn uses contrasts and comparisons to write an extended definition of an addiction that never seems to satisfy.*

TV Addiction

Marie Winn

The word "addiction" is often used loosely and wryly in conversation. People will refer to themselves as "mystery book addicts" or "cookie addicts." E. B. White writes of his annual surge of interest in gardening: "We are hooked and are making an attempt to kick the habit." Yet nobody really believes that reading mysteries or ordering seeds by catalogue is serious enough to be compared with addictions to heroin or alcohol. The word "addiction" is here used jokingly to denote a tendency to overindulge in some pleasurable activity.

People often refer to being "hooked on TV." Does this, too, fall into the lighthearted category of cookie eating and other pleasures that people pursue with unusual intensity, or is there a kind of television viewing that falls into the more serious category of destructive addiction?

When we think about addiction to drugs or alcohol, we frequently focus on negative aspects, ignoring the pleasures that accompany drinking or drug-taking. And yet the essence of any serious addiction is a pursuit of pleasure, a search for a "high" that normal life does not supply. It is only the inability to function without the addictive substance that is dismaying, the dependence of the organism upon a certain experience and an increasing inability to function normally without it. Thus a person will take two or three drinks at the end of the day not merely for the pleasure drinking provides, but also because he "doesn't feel normal" without them.

An addict does not merely pursue a pleasurable experience and need to experience it in order to function normally. He needs to *repeat* it again and again. Something about that particular experience makes life without it less than complete. Other potentially pleasurable experiences are no longer possible, for under the spell of the addictive experience, his life is peculiarly distorted. The addict craves an experience and yet he is never really satisfied. The organism may be temporarily sated, but soon it begins to crave again.

Finally a serious addiction is distinguished from a harmless pursuit of pleasure by its distinctly destructive elements. A heroin addict, for instance, leads a damaged life: his increasing need for heroin in increasing doses prevents him from working, from maintaining relationships, from developing in human ways. Similarly an alcoholic's life is narrowed and dehumanized by his dependence on alcohol.

Let us consider television viewing in the light of the conditions that define serious addictions.

Not unlike drugs or alcohol, the television experience allows the participant to blot out the real world and enter into a pleasurable and passive mental state. The worries and anxieties of reality are as effectively deferred by becoming absorbed in a television program as by going on a "trip" induced by drugs or alcohol. And just as alcoholics are only inchoately aware of their addiction, feeling that they control their drinking more than they really do ("I can cut it out any time I want—I just like to have three or four drinks before dinner"), people similarly overestimate their control over television watching. Even as they put off other activities to spend hour after hour watching television, they feel they could easily resume living in a different, less passive style. But somehow or other while the television set is present in their homes, the click doesn't sound. With television pleasures available, those other experiences seem less attractive, more difficult somehow.

A heavy viewer (a college English instructor) observes: "I find television almost irresistible. When the set is on, I cannot ignore it. I can't turn it off. I feel sapped, will-less, enervated. As I reach out to turn off the set, the strength goes out of my arms. So I sit there for hours and hours."

The self-confessed television addict often feels he "ought" to do other things—but the fact that he doesn't read and doesn't plant his garden or sew or crochet or play games or have conversations means that those activities are no longer as desirable as television viewing. In a way a heavy viewer's life is as imbalanced by his television "habit" as a drug addict's or an alcoholic's. He is living in a holding pattern, as it were, passing up the activities that lead to growth or development or a sense of accomplishment. This is one reason people talk about their television viewing so ruefully, so apologetically. They are aware that it is an unproductive experience, that almost any other endeavor is more worthwhile by any human measure.

Finally it is the adverse effect of television viewing on the lives of so many people that defines it as a serious addiction. The television habit distorts the sense of time. It renders other experiences vague and curiously unreal while taking on a greater reality for itself. It weakens relationships by reducing and sometimes eliminating normal opportunities for talking, for communicating.

And yet television does not satisfy, else why would the viewer continue to watch hour after hour, day after day? "The measure of health," writes Lawrence Kubie, "is flexibility . . . and especially the freedom to cease when sated." But the television viewer can never be sated with his television experiences—they do not provide the true nourishment that satiation requires—and thus he finds that he cannot stop watching.

Vincent Ryan Ruggiero, Professor of Humanities at State University of New York at Delhi, is author of eight books on critical thinking. The following excerpt from The Art of Thinking *relies almost entirely on the use of illustration to bring clarity to a complex issue.*

Debating Moral Questions
Vincent Ryan Ruggiero

Nowhere is modern thinking more muddled than over the question of whether it is proper to debate moral issues. Many argue it is not, saying it is wrong to make "value judgments." This view is shallow. If such judgments were wrong, then ethics, philosophy, and theology would be unacceptable in a college curriculum—an idea that is obviously silly. As the following cases illustrate, it is impossible to avoid making value judgments.

Raoul Wallenberg was a young Swedish aristocrat. In 1944 he left the safety of his country and entered Budapest. Over the next year he outwitted the Nazis and saved as many as 100,000 Jews (he was not himself Jewish) from the death camps. In 1945 he was arrested by the Russians, charged with spying, and imprisoned in a Russian labor camp. He may still be alive there. Now, if we regard him as a hero—as there is excellent reason to do—we are making a value judgment. Yet if we regard him neutrally, as no different from anyone else, we are also making a value judgment. We are judging him to be neither hero nor villain, but average.

Consider another case. In late 1981 a 20-year-old mother left her three infant sons unattended in a garbage-strewn tenement in New York City. Police found them there, starving, the youngest child lodged between a mattress and a wall, covered with flies and cockroaches, the eldest playing on the second-floor window ledge. The police judged the mother negligent, and the court agreed. Was it wrong for them to judge? And if we refuse to judge, won't that refusal itself be a judgment in the mother's favor?

No matter how difficult it may be to judge such moral issues, we *must* judge them. Value judgment is the basis not only of our social code, but of our legal system. The quality of our laws is directly affected by the quality of our moral judgments. A society that judges blacks inferior is not likely to accord blacks equal treatment. A society that believes a woman's place is in the home is not likely to guarantee women equal employment opportunity.

Other people accept value judgments as long as they are made *within* a culture, and not about other cultures. Right and wrong, they believe, vary from one culture to another. It is true that an act frowned upon in one culture may be tolerated in another, but the degree of difference has often been grossly exaggerated. When we first encounter an unfamiliar moral view, we are inclined to focus on the difference so much that we miss the similarity.

For example, in medieval Europe animals were tried for crimes and often formally executed. In fact, cockroaches and other bugs were sometimes excommunicated from the church. Sounds absurd, doesn't it? But when we penetrate beneath the absurdity, we realize that the basic view—that some actions are reprehensible and ought to be punished—is not so strange. The core idea that a person bitten by, say, a dog, has been wronged and requires justice is very much the same. The only difference is our rejection of the idea that animals are responsible for their behavior.

Is it legitimate, then, for us to pass judgment on the moral standards of another culture? Yes, if we do so thoughtfully, and not just conclude that whatever differs from our view is necessarily wrong. We can judge, for example, a culture that treats women as property, or places less value on their lives than on the lives of men. Moreover, we can say a society is acting immorally by denying women their human rights. Consider the following cases.

In nineteenth-century Rio de Janeiro, Brazil, a theatrical producer shot and killed his wife because she insisted on taking a walk in the botanical gardens against his wishes. He was formally charged with her murder, but the judge dismissed the charge. The producer was carried through the streets in triumph. The moral perspective of his culture condoned the taking of a woman's life if she disobeyed her husband, even in a relatively small matter. A century later that perspective had changed little. In the same city, in 1976, a wealthy playboy, angry at his lover for flirting with others, fired four shots into her face at point-blank range, killing her. He was given a two-year suspended sentence in light of the fact that he had been "defending his honor."

Surely it is irresponsible for us to withhold judgment on the morality of these cases merely because they occurred in a different culture. It is obvious that in both cases the men's response, murder, was out of all proportion to the women's "offenses," and therefore demonstrated a wanton disregard for the women's human rights. Their response is thus properly judged immoral. And this judgment implies another—that the culture condoning such behavior is guilty of moral insensitivity.

Loren Eiseley was both scientist and humanist. His technical studies in anthropology are often as effectively written as his poetry and essays. In the following excerpt, from The Immense Journey, *Eiseley illustrates how an experienced writer blends various classical writing strategies. Description, comparison, definition, process analysis, and cause-and-effect analysis are all put to use.*

How Flowers Changed the World

Loren Eiseley

When the first simple flower bloomed on some raw upland late in the Dinosaur Age, it was wind pollinated, just like its early pine cone relatives. It was a very inconspicuous flower because it had not yet evolved the idea of using the surer attraction of birds and insects to achieve the transportation of pollen. It sowed its own pollen and received the pollen of other flowers by the simple vagaries of the wind. Many plants in regions where insect life is scant still follow this principle today. Nevertheless, the true flower—and the seed that it produced—was a profound innovation in the world of life.

In a way, this event parallels, in the plant world, what happened among animals. Consider the relative chance for survival of the exteriorly deposited egg of a fish in contrast with the fertilized egg of a mammal, carefully retained for months in the mother's body until the young animal (or human being) is developed to a point where it may survive. The biological wastage is less—and so it is with the flowering plants. The primitive spore, a single cell fertilized in the beginning by a swimming sperm, did not promote rapid distribution, and the young plant, moreover, had to struggle up from nothing. No one had left it any food except what it could get by its own unaided efforts.

By contrast, the true flowering plants (angiosperm itself means "encased seed") grew a seed in the heart of a flower, a seed whose development was initiated by a fertilizing pollen grain independent of outside moisture. But the seed, unlike the developing spore, is already a fully equipped *embryonic plant* packed in a little enclosed box stuffed full of nutritious food. Moreover, by featherdown attachments, as in dandelion or milkweed seed, it can be wafted upward on gusts and ride the wind for miles; or with hooks it can cling to a bear's or a rabbit's hide; or like some of the berries, it can be covered with a juicy, attractive fruit to lure birds, pass undigested through their intestinal tracts and be voided miles away.

The ramifications of this biological invention were endless. Plants traveled as they had never traveled before. They got into strange environments heretofore never entered by the old spore plants or stiff pine-cone-seed plants. The well-fed, carefully cherished little embryos raised their heads everywhere. Many of the older plants with more primitive reproductive mechanisms began to fade away under this unequal contest. They contracted their range into secluded environments. Some like the giant redwoods, lingered on as relics; many vanished entirely.

The world of the giants was a dying world. These fantastic little seeds skipping and hopping and flying about the woods and valleys brought with them an amazing adaptability. If our whole lives had not been spent in the midst of it, it would astound us. The old, stiff, sky-reaching wooden world had changed into something that glowed here and there with strange colors, put out queer, unheard-of fruits and little intricately carved seed cases, and, most important of all, produced concentrated foods in a way that the land had never seen before, or dreamed of back in the fish-eating, leaf-crunching days of the dinosaurs.

That food came from three sources, all produced by the reproductive system of the flowering plants. There were the tantalizing nectars and pollens intended to draw insects for pollenizing purposes, and which are responsible also for that wonderful jeweled creation, the hummingbird. There were the juicy and enticing fruits to attract larger animals, and in which tough-coated seeds were concealed, as in the tomato, for example. Then, as if this were not enough, there was the food in the actual seed itself, the food intended to nourish the embryo. All over the world, like hot corn in a popper, these incredible elaborations of the flowering plants kept exploding. In a movement that was almost instantaneous, geologically speaking, the angiosperms had taken over the world. Grass was beginning to cover the bare earth until, today, there are over six thousand species. All kinds of vines and bushes squirmed and writhed under new trees and flying seeds.

The explosion was having its effect on animal life also. Specialized groups of insects were arising to feed on the new sources of food and, incidentally and unknowingly, to pollinate the plant. The flowers bloomed and bloomed in ever larger and more spectacular varieties. Some were pale unearthly night flowers intended to lure moths in the evening twilight, some among the orchids even took the shape of female spiders in order to attract wandering males, some flamed redly in the light of noon or twinkled modestly in the meadow grasses. Intricate mechanisms splashed pollen on the breasts of hummingbirds, or stamped it on the bellies of black, grumbling bees droning assiduously from blossom to blossom. Honey ran, insects multiplied, and even the descendants of that toothed and ancient lizard-bird had become strangely altered. Equipped with prodding beaks instead of biting teeth they pecked the seeds and gobbled the insects that were really converted nectar.

PART VI

Analysis and Argumentation

In good speaking, should not the mind of the speaker know the truth of the matter about which he is to speak?

PLATO

Exploring

28

Critical Thinking

The winter sun had almost set and my office was growing dark when he knocked. I had been holding conferences with freshmen for several hours and their faces had begun to blur. He was a young black man who had just received his first *F* on a literature exam. He sat across the desk twisting the paper in his hands. "All you want us to do is repeat what you think," he began. "My ideas are just as good as yours."

Outside my window the lights came on in the gymnasium across the street. My wife would be expecting me home for dinner. I took a deep breath and tried to explain that his ideas might indeed be as valid as mine but that he must demonstrate their validity. He could not simply assert, as he had, that Robert Frost's poem, "Stopping by Woods on a Snowy Evening," dealt with a ghost. That might be true, I said, but he must point to specific evidence in the poem that would show me how he had come to such a conclusion.

"That's how I felt," he said. "That's what the poem made me feel."

I spent 15 minutes going over the poem with him. Where did he find evidence that the speaker of the poem was a ghost? Where did he find "church bells tolling for the dead"? (A line that did not appear in the poem.) His anger grew. My frustration increased. I was beginning to think all freshmen were alike. Finally, he blurted out, "All you honkies think you own the truth. Well, I got a different message than you did—I felt it, and that makes it true."

I was furious that race had been brought into the issue. It was a direct blow to my self-image. I handed back his exam and told him to leave. I even suggested several places he might take his truth. Afterward, I regretted my anger, but I knew that in both of us emotion had won out over reason.

The nature of truth has long presented us with one of our most complex intellectual challenges. Are all ideas equally true? Is there such a thing as truth at all? If so, how can we know it? If not, by what method can we determine even the probable truth of anything? Those who are most confident about the existence of something called Absolute Truth (a truth that is eternally undeniable and undebatable) usually depend on intuition and faith for their conviction. The problem is that Absolute Truth known through faith cannot be demonstrated to others. You either believe or you don't believe. By contrast, when we use *reason,* we ask that the truth of something be demonstrated through evidence or argument. In its simplest form, I might make a comparison with the concepts of *telling* and *showing* that have been emphasized in earlier chapters. You may *tell* me you perceive or possess the truth, but logic requires that you *show* me both the evidence and the method of reasoning you used to arrive at your conclusion.

Reason or logic, then, becomes a method of seeking probable truth through inference or interpretation of observable facts—something you began working with in earlier chapters. Before we pursue it further, however, we need to identify some of the problems that interfere with reasoning. The incident with my student reveals several. I was tired and quick to anger. I had begun to classify all freshmen as the same. He was convinced that all professors were the same and that racial bias had influenced my judgment. I felt that he must use logic to demonstrate the truth; he felt that emotion evoked by poetry contained its own truth. Both of us ended up *feeling* we were in the right. But sometimes feelings can be seriously wrong.

EMOTIONAL BLOCKS TO REASON

I recently spoke to an all-male audience of college students on the surprising growth of women's athletic abilities. Among dozens of other facts, I pointed out that 20 years ago in the 100-meter dash, the fastest woman in the world was 11.88 percent slower than the fastest man. By the end of 1985, this margin had been reduced to nine percent and was continuing to decrease as more women entered physical training earlier. In fact, the women's marathon record (26-mile run) is 2 hours, 24 minutes, 52 seconds—a mark that would have won every gold medal in the men's marathon at the Olympic games through 1956. In other words, all evidence tends to show that with better training and positive encouragement, women can and will close the gap on such male bastions as physical strength and endurance. My all-male audience responded with uncomfortable silence. Finally, one young man blurted out, "Well, women will never be able to play football!" The others in the room nodded in vigorous agreement and relief. The matter seemed to be settled. When we are emotionally committed to something, contradictory data are easily ignored.

What role does emotional bias or culturally trained attitudes play in each of the following statements?

1. The U.S. Congress refused to grant statehood to Utah until the Mormons ceased their immoral practice of polygamy.
2. Baby girls should be dressed in pink; boys, in blue.
3. From a United States senator: "The problem with trying to deal with the Soviets is that you can never trust them. Deceit and secrecy are part of their heritage—right back to the czars."
4. Do you know who won the Polish beauty contest? Who? No one.
5. A wife should be subordinate to her husband. As St. Paul writes in Ephesians 5:23–4, "Wives, submit yourselves unto your husbands . . . for the husband is the head of the family, even as Christ is the head of the church."
6. The proper way to cut your meat is to hold your fork in your left hand and your knife in your right hand. Cut off a single bite. Place your knife at the top of the plate. Shift your fork to your right hand and eat. Repeat the process for the next bite.

The emotional support we attach to our race, ethnic group, culture, or religion will often overpower the logic of mere reason. It seems normal in human nature to believe that *our* way of living makes sense, whereas others have funny habits. It seems normal to believe in our own superiority. The Indian word *Cheyenne* means "the people," a term that obviously suggests that other tribes, such as the Sioux and Blackfoot, were something less than people. Hitler manipulated just such an attitude to persuade a nation that Jews were an inferior "race" deserving barbaric treatment. Americans, too, are not immune. Racist attitudes separating blacks from whites or Chicanos from whites can cause people to act in ways that they would normally condemn in others. We create such strong stereotypes in our minds that when presented with facts to the contrary, we may tend to assume the facts are inaccurate and the stereotype true.

One example occurred during the Vietnam War. Day after day throughout the late 1960s and early 1970s, television reports and newspaper photos showed Vietnamese women crying over the dead bodies of their children, and husbands burdened with pain over the caskets of their wives. Yet many Americans insisted that Orientals did not value human life as we did. Even on the most everyday level we tend to see our city or neighborhood as better than others; we tend to believe that the way we eat or the clothing styles we wear are "normal." Once we become emotionally committed to our private or cultural truths, logical reasoning is blocked. Yet for some 2500 years, logic has been the primary method accepted by the Western world for determining truth. If we are to function successfully in such a world, we must recognize how emotion sways our thinking and affects our judgment.

INTELLECTUAL LAZINESS

Some problems to clear reasoning derive less from emotional blocks than from lazy thinking. We prefer simple ideas to complex ideas. Truth always seems more evident if we don't bother to consider details or consequences.

An *oversimplification* is caused when we fail to investigate an idea thoroughly. In 1988, for example, a Midwestern governor ran for reelection after more than one-third of the state's public school systems faced bankruptcy. Many schools had actually closed their doors. The governor campaigned on a banner of "no new taxes." He argued instead that because inflation was soaring, the state would collect more taxes anyway and the problem would take care of itself. The reasoning sounds clear. As inflation went up, people would spend more money to buy goods and thus pay more sales tax. The extra income would go to the schools. But the problem had been oversimplified. For one thing, the governor failed to explain that inflation would also drive up the cost of running the schools. In fact, school costs were already rising faster than inflation.

The oversimplification appealed to voters, however, and the governor was reelected.

Simplification may be a valuable approach to any subject if by simplifying we clarify. But when we *over*simplify we distort and mislead. Instead of telling the truth, we lie. Here are several types of oversimplifications that sound logical and convincing but ignore the complexities of human nature.

Faulty cause and effect

Alcoholism is caused by the availability of alcohol.

Rome fell after the introduction of Christianity; therefore, Rome fell because of Christianity.

Naturally, if alcohol did not exist, we would not have alcoholism, but the fact that it does exist does not make it the singular cause of the disease, because not everyone who drinks alcohol becomes an alcoholic. Nor does the fact that Christianity preceded the fall of Rome mean that it caused such a fall. In fact, the notion that "Rome fell" is itself an oversimplification.

Overgeneralizations

Democracy is the best form of government.
People on welfare are lazy.
Poor students are a result of poor teachers.

Overgeneralizations usually depend on a stated or implied *always, never, greatest, best,* or on other superlatives that claim a truth without exception. We can criticize the above examples by observing that for nations with no heritage of self-government, democracy may *not* be the best form of government, nor are *all* welfare recipients necessarily lazy, nor can *all* poor students blame their teachers. In each case, the writer should qualify his or her assertion: democracy is *often* the best form of government; *some* people on welfare are lazy; poor students *may* be a result of poor teaching.

Hasty conclusions

My friend scored 100 on an I.Q. exam. It's obvious his abilities are only average and he should become an auto mechanic.

I knew two girls who married in their sophomore year; the only reason a girl goes to college is to find a husband.

When a judgment is made too early in the reasoning process or before all evidence has been examined, it is called a *hasty conclusion.* An I.Q. of

100 indicates the score on a single type of examination. Your friend may be a creative genius in music or painting or sculpture, but none of those is tested on I.Q. exams. Nor can the marriages of two girls be considered adequate evidence to conclude that *all* girls seek marriage when they attend college.

Undefined abstractions

"Coke is it."
Sam Smith is neurotic.

But what exactly is *it*? Should Pepsi be considered a "not-it"? And what is *neurotic*? The term is often used to mean that someone acts in a way that seems "strange"—but strange according to whose standards? So many mental conditions have been grouped under "neurotic" that the American Psychological Association no longer recognizes the term as describing a meaningful medical condition. It seems to mean whatever we want it to mean. Without precise definition, the reader can rightly suspect that we don't really know what we're talking about.

Clear reasoning requires hard work, time, and careful attention to details. Some people are upset by complexity and leap at the first solution or easiest answer. But the successful writer builds an argument slowly, with arduous attention to word choice and concrete evidence. He or she works to clarify and simplify, not to oversimplify.

Consider the various types of oversimplifications you find in the following:

1. From the Hartford, Connecticut, sheriff: "Marijuana should never be legalized. Of twenty heroin addicts now in my jail, eighteen of them started on marijuana. That's 90 percent!"
2. Courtney Gibbs, Miss USA for 1988, ate Campbell's Tomato Soup when she was a little girl. Look at Courtney today!
3. Two hospital studies have shown that for pain other than headaches, Excedrin is more effective than aspirin.
4. Why, I would never promote fluoridation. Fluoridation was tried in Cleveland in 1843, and not *one* of those people who drank the water is alive today.
5. The Marines will make a man of you.
6. From a student paper: "The issue of interracial marriages is frequently judged by today's society. But times are changing and each generation should accept new ideas. When society is against a couple's marriage, they will have a closer

> bond of love between themselves. They won't argue as
> much. If all marriages were interracial, there wouldn't be
> any discrimination."
> 7. Without a college education, you can't find a good job.
> 8. If guns are outlawed, only outlaws will have guns.
> 9. The governor was reelected in 1988 because he oversimpli-
>   fied the school-tax issue.

FALSE MODES OF ARGUMENT

An argument is a course of reasoning aimed at swaying or influencing the audience to believe in the truth of something. Obviously, the various modes of arguing are many, but several methods can present particular problems in that they may seem to offer forceful reasoning while actually failing to demonstrate the truth they proclaim.

False Analogy

You've already studied analogies (Chapter 25) as a means of stimulating creative thinking. In logical reasoning, an analogy is a good way to show a relationship. Analogies lead a reader from something known to something unknown. If I tell you that learning to write is like learning to swim because both require practice and repetition, you may understand more about writing *if* you already know something about swimming. And my reasoning may be accurate if the likeness is close enough to make my conclusions "highly probable." But by definition, an analogy contains differences as well as similarities. If we decide that the differences are greater than the likenesses, we must call it a *false analogy*. A few years ago the Shell Oil Company ran a commercial on television that concluded with the analogy: "If Shell Oil Company can make such high-quality components for airplanes, think how good its gasoline must be." The problem, of course, is that even if Shell does build quality airplane parts, there is no guarantee that another branch of the same company, a thousand miles away, under different management, and pursuing a different manufacturing process in refining gasoline from oil, will also make a quality product. The only valid connection is the corporate name, not the quality of the product; therefore, the analogy is false.

Even when an analogy is successful in clarifying or explaining, it is still only a comparison. In itself, it does not *prove* anything.

Appeals to Authority

Calling upon authority can form an essential component to a sound argument. When you claim that elimination of all nuclear missiles will lessen the risk of war, an appeal to America's chief negotiator in Geneva may strengthen your argument. Most of us cannot be expected to understand the complexity of such topics. Citing someone who is recognized for extensive study of a subject, or for extensive experience, will often be more persuasive than logical argument alone.

On the other hand, a weak argument can be disguised, its falsity hidden, or its shaky reasoning overwhelmed by the use of a famous name. Citing Ronnie Milsap as one who supports elimination of all nuclear missiles should carry no weight. Milsap may be an authority in music but it's doubtful he knows more about disarmament than you or I. Beware also of the generalized citation: ''Religious leaders everywhere oppose nuclear arms,'' or ''Scientists tell us of the many dangers. . . . How many religious leaders? What kind? Which scientists? Where and when? And finally, always be suspicious of the appeal to authority for vague emotional reasons: ''John F. Kennedy believed in a world where each man was free to worship in his own way. Unless we abandon nuclear warheads, we will never live up to Kennedy's dream.''

Appeals to Emotion

A false appeal to authority is only one way of calling up emotions. During the presidency of Jimmy Carter, possession of the Panama Canal was returned by treaty to Panama. Arguments abounded that America had ''bought it,'' that American lives had been ''sacrificed'' in building it and operating it, that it constituted American territory and could not be ''given away.'' Appeals to loyalty, fear, religion, decency, family unity, and so on, seem to trigger automatic reactions in many people. A skilled writer or speaker can sway whole nations by such tactics, even though logic and evidence can demonstrate that the argument is false.

Misleading Statistics

In an age when presidents carry Gallup polls in their pockets to demonstrate the popularity of their policies, the danger of arguments founded on statistics needs to be especially noted. Because mathematics seems "scientific," we tend to be swayed by numbers, any kind of numbers, as if numbers in themselves always constituted proof. A college professor recently talked about how a committee he served on had reached a deadlock and could not decide whether to include a proposed course in the new curriculum. The professor broke the deadlock by announcing that 62 percent of the students favored such a course. The committee immediately voted its approval. Later, the professor admitted that the statistic was invented; yet it had exercised more influence than all the previous arguments.

Even if the statistic had been taken from a valid survey of student opinion, we would still need to know when the poll was taken, the size of the sampling (just how many students were actually questioned), the wording of the questionnaire, any biases it may have contained, and how the statistic was mathematically determined. Without such data, even valid statistics may be misleading. The American Medical Association, for example, has announced that the average American smokes a pack of cigarettes a day. But what exactly does average mean? If only two of your ten best friends smoked five packs of cigarettes apiece each day, the average for all your friends would be a pack a day, even though eight of them did not smoke at all.

Can such a statistic have the weight of proof? No. It *can* be offered as evidence, but it must always be evaluated as carefully as any other form of evidence or argument.

INDUCTIVE AND DEDUCTIVE REASONING

The heart of reasoning lies in clear relationships. A well-reasoned argument demonstrates how relationships are sound, whereas a weak argument either blurs relationships (as in appeals to emotion) or attempts to establish a questionable relationship (as in false analogies or the misuse of statistics). The surest kind of reasoning is usually considered *inductive:* moving from the specific to the general, from facts to a conclusion about the facts. A belief in the value of inductive reasoning is built into this book, which from the first page has argued that you must train yourself to see, to search out the concrete and specific details, to investigate, and then to draw inferences or to interpret your findings based solely on the evidence, evidence that a second observer can verify.

> William Shakespeare used more active verbs than passive verbs.
> John Donne used more active verbs than passive verbs.

Mark Twain used more active verbs than passive verbs.
Virginia Woolf used more active verbs than passive verbs.
Ralph Ellison used more active verbs than passive verbs.
Therefore, good writers use more active verbs than passive verbs.

Like all inductive reasoning, the connection between specific facts and the generalization may be proven wrong. Inductive reasoning does not guarantee truth. It works to establish a probable truth based on an accumulation of verifiable facts, observations, or experiences that form a clear relationship—a pattern—that seems to support a general conclusion.

Deductive reasoning works in the opposite manner. It reasons from the general to the specific, from broad abstractions to particular truths. In its simplest form, it includes three divisions of argument, which compose a *syllogism:* a proposition (called a major premise), a second proposition (called the minor premise), and then a conclusion deduced from the relationship.

All men are mortal.   (major premise)
John is a man.   (minor premise)
Therefore John is mortal. (conclusion, deduced from the relationship
                           between the major and minor premises)

The initial generalization must be either self-evident or of such a nature that we can agree on its truth without need for further evidence. The second, and any following premise in the chain, must be more specific and verifiable. If the conclusion illustrates a proper relationship between or among the premises, we can then claim that the conclusion is true.

But this pattern of argument can create problems.

All voters are good citizens.
John votes.
John is a good citizen.

Here all the requirements seem to have been met. We can say that this syllogism is valid insofar as it follows the prescribed form. Yet the conclusion is false. For it to be true, each step in the chain must be true, but the major premise or generalization in this case cannot be accepted as self-evident. All voters are not necessarily good citizens. A Mafia hit man is not a good citizen, even though he voted for George Bush. Therefore, the fact that John votes does not necessarily make him a good citizen.

Another danger occurs when the form of the syllogism is distorted in such a way that it makes the logical process look like nonsense.

All dogs have four legs.	All men have facial hair.
My cat has four legs.	My mother has a moustache.
Therefore my cat is a dog.	Therefore my mother is a man.

The complexity and subtlety of deductive reasoning are best left to a philosophy course. But you should be aware that a reasonable-sounding argument may not at all be reasonable. Each component of the argument and each relationship must be tested and held accountable in its own right for the conclusion to be true.

Consider the various problems found in the following arguments:

1. Seventy-one percent of all business transactions today occur over the telephone or via computers. Business people don't need to write letters anymore; therefore, colleges ought to cease requiring composition courses.

2. From a student paper: "To be a science fiction writer you have to be a little wacko, for the science portrayed in such works is usually fantastic and without a sound basis in fact."

3. King James of England said that as the monarch is the head of the state, democracy is demonstrably false. James argued that if you cut off the head of a body, the other organs cannot function, and the body dies. Similarly, if you cut off the head of a state, the state may flop around for a while, but it is due to perish in time or become an easy prey to its neighbors.

Emotional blocks, lazy thinking, syllogisms that seem logical but are not—the list begins to seem endless. Yet if we want to write clearly and persuasively, to think clearly and soundly, we need at least an elementary grounding in the all-too-human problems that interfere. Our hope must be that even if such problems cannot be eliminated, by knowing they exist we can triumph over them. Ultimately, a sensitive perception of facts, details, emotions, and ideas is not enough for the writer. The successful writer must also perceive reasonable relationships among those facts, details, emotions, and ideas.

Exercises

1. Because the emotional attachment to values learned through our family, our ethnic group, our social class, and our culture is so strong and so prevalent, politicians and advertisers often appeal directly to emo-

tions rather than to logic. Consider the type of emotion each of the following seeks to arouse. Why is it so powerful? Why wouldn't logic be better? Where does the illogic lie in each statement?

a. A vote for Governor Brown is a vote for freedom, integrity, and efficiency in government.

b. If he kissed you once, will he kiss you again? Take Certs, the breath mint, and be sure.

c. From an advertisement for 7-Up: "It's the same thing, only different."

d. From a speech by an individual running for city coroner: "I was born here and have lived here all my life. I went to Abraham Lincoln High School, and some of you probably still remember the home run I hit in the Medfield game."

e. A man running for state senator attacks his opponent: "Senator Hale has supported legislation that would encourage voter fraud. If elected, I promise to oppose any new attempt at instant voter registration."

f. In a 1939 *Saturday Evening Post*: "Thousands of physicians smoke Luckies."

2. The following paragraphs were written in freshman composition classes at one of the nation's largest universities. Evaluate each for its logical problems.

a. College is a beneficial experience to everyone who attends it. It is a start of a better life that gives a person an opportunity to pursue a meaningful and challenging career. A college graduate does not have to take a job he won't enjoy just for the purpose of money. College also enhances a person's personality in that one meets many different types of people with varying personalities. College also puts a person into a position of responsibility by making a person learn how to take care of himself.

b. Have you ever heard of a vice-president's taking over because the president was pregnant? Well, if a woman became president, there would be a good possibility that you would hear this. It would be kind of difficult for her to refrain from sexual intercourse with her husband for four years and then, if reelected, for four more years. It would seem apparent through the four or eight years she would become pregnant. After she had her baby, she would become the president again, but couldn't you picture the same thing happening again? Having the vice-president take her place and then her coming back would cause chaos because anything the vice-president passed that she disagreed with, she would try to change. So why don't we let women stay out of politics, so when she becomes pregnant she won't upset the whole diplomatic structure of the country?

c. You should not wear a watch if you are honestly concerned about your health. A survey was conducted by the American Heart Association to relate the incidence of heart attack to personal actions or qualities. It was found that people who wore watches had a higher rate of heart attacks than those who did not. Time is important to fast-paced, high-pressured people, where prompt-ness is a must to be successful. A high-pressured life-style also raises blood pressure, which leads to an increase in the chances of heart attack and slows the pace of life down to a new, healthier level.

d. The recent sexual revolution of our times has caused some tur-moil in our country; yet I'm a firm believer in premarital sex. Sex has been spoken of, in the past, only in harsh whispers or behind closed doors. This reluctance to discuss sex openly has caused certain people to lead sheltered lives and may also result in sexual inhibitions. Knowledge of one's body and that of the opposite sex brings about a greater feeling of sexual security. To acknowledge to your sexual partner the realities of how sex should be properly executed and to give them the freedom to explore brings about a better relationship. Knowledge has a ten-dency to take away the fears surrounding sexual intercourse. Fears of pregnancy are almost nonexistent with modern devices for birth control, for both men and women. Public awareness of these controls is also readily available. This relationship, having been established, will give proficiency in sexual intercourse with your future mate and provide the knowledge to inspire warmth and response in your mate through personal experiences.

3. Consider each of the following statements. Which contain de-ductive reasoning? Which lead to a valid conclusion?

a. The University of Southern California defeated Oregon State in football by 31 to 7. UCLA defeated that same Oregon State team by 14 to 7. The University of Southern California can obviously defeat UCLA.

b. All teen-agers have pimples. My sister has pimples. Therefore, my sister is a teenager.

c. A student should not be required to take classes he or she is not interested in when he or she gets to college. College students are legal adults and should be allowed to choose their own curriculum.

d. Most professors have Ph.D.'s. If all students were required to stay in college until they obtained a Ph.D., we would no longer need professors.

e. It is no longer important to have heroes in today's contemporary society. The last heroes we had, like Martin Luther King and John F. Kennedy, ended by getting shot.

4. Consider the following dialogue and determine its relationship to logical thinking. Does it express the limits of logic?

> Master Joshu was asked: "What is the ultimate principle of Zen Buddhism?"
> He replied: "The cypress tree in the courtyard."
> "You are talking," another monk said, "of an objective symbol."
> "No, I am not talking about an objective symbol."
> "Then what is the ultimate principle of Zen Buddhism?"
> "The cypress tree in the courtyard," answered Joshu again.

Exploring

29

Critical Reading

Pretend, for a moment, that you've just picked up an essay—an argument—on ethnic plurality in America. The author contends that when a black woman in Los Angeles desires to find her "roots" she is searching for something "that isn't there." He asserts that when a Polish-American in Chicago campaigns to save Polish neighborhoods, he is promoting group conformity. The author even argues that when a Mexican-American in Houston wants a bilingual school system, he is furthering inequality of the races.

Is the author right or wrong? How you respond to his arguments might range from enthusiastic support to hostility, depending on your own ethnic background. But can you separate your emotions from the argument in the essay? Can you evaluate it for logic and evidence? Can you determine its validity or find its fallacies through a fair and objective analysis?

Serious reading goes beyond entertainment. A chemist reads a scholarly journal to learn about a new discovery in organic neurology. An engineer reads about developments in architectural glass for sun control. A mother reads about a psychiatrist who claims children under five must be disciplined with physical punishment. How can any of them evaluate what they read except by considering it logically, analyzing its content, and judging its validity? Such a process requires *critical analysis*—a formal strategy that is both a method for perceiving and evaluating as well as a technique for writing. This chapter deals with analysis as a method that develops critical reading skills. The next chapter offers a traditional structure used for writing an analysis.

THE STRATEGY OF READING CRITICALLY

Analysis is a process in which you divide a subject into its various parts. By studying each of the parts and their relationship, you hope to understand more about the subject as a whole (see Chapter 24). But before you can actually analyze something you read, you must learn a particular method of reading that prepares you for each of the steps analysis will demand.

Understand the Content

The need to comprehend content sounds self-evident, but it is neither as easy nor as commonly accomplished as we might like to believe. Every college instructor is aware that perhaps one-fourth of the problems on essay exams can be traced to a student's failure to read or understand the question. Critical reading is a strategy—a method of approaching your reading so that you increase comprehension.

1. Underline key sentences and circle key words. Read each paragraph as a unit of thought. Look for the most important sentences and underline them, especially those that express the theme and the major points used to support the theme. Circle words used in special ways, words you don't know, or words repeated for emphasis.
2. Take notes in the margins. Try to summarize each major point in a few words directly beside the key sentence that makes the point. Try to use your own words for your summary. Being able to put an idea into your own words helps you understand and remember it. Number the notes in the margin so that at a glance you can tell how many major points the writer has made.
3. For every major word you don't know, use a dictionary. (Alas, how many times have you heard that commandment. But you live in a world of words. Ideas are expressed in words. If you don't know the language, you are a prisoner of ignorance.) Write

a brief definition in the margin by the word you've circled. Writing the definition helps you remember it.

4. Finally, once you've completed the reading, write a brief summary in your own words, *objectively* and *fairly* restating the author's theme, major points, and conclusion. (Do not interpret or make hasty judgments at this point.) Use your marginal notes to aid you in writing your summary. The summary helps draw together the author's ideas. Until you've written the summary, you may *think* you know what you've read but you can't be sure. The summary is excellent mental work for preparing to take an exam or to write a paper as well as to reinforce comprehension.

Evaluate the Content for Logic

Once you've objectively understood the content, you're in a good position to scrutinize the author's theme more critically. When you read about Japanese buying up American hotels and businesses, does the author appeal to your logic or to your emotions? Is more than one side of the issue presented? Are both sides given fair and equal treatment? Is the content based on opinion? Evidence? Logic? Are the Japanese presented as stereotypes? Is the author's argument based on overgeneralizations? Cultural or racial bias? Is the conclusion based on evidence or logical argument presented in the body of the work?

Here is where you'll want to challenge each major point separately, then compare each point to the others, then to the basic theme itself—all to determine logical relationships. If you've numbered each point in the margins, your work will proceed quickly.

Evaluate Yourself for Emotional Blocks

If you find you are easily convinced by the author's position, is it because you're already biased in favor of such ideas? If you are unconvinced, is it because you have a closed mind? In addition to considering the author, the audience, and the work, you must consider *your* relationship to it. If an author proposes a socialistic form of government for the United States, do you disagree because of fear of change? Or because of unexamined values and beliefs adopted from your parents? Is it possible you have misjudged the work because of a hasty conclusion? Or do the ideas sound perfectly logical to you because they conform to the values you want to believe in regardless of their logic? You cannot be sure you have considered your author's material fairly and objectively until you can be sure of your emotional biases.

Consider the Author and the Historical Context

Although it will not always be possible to find out who the author is or to discover what audience the work was originally intended for, every effort should be made to see the work in its original historical context.

1. Who is the author and what is his or her authority to speak on the subject? Sometimes the author's experience and credentials will be identified on the dust jacket or last page of a book. Articles in magazines may identify the author at the bottom of the title page or on the last page of the essay. In some cases, you'll need to do a little research. Almost all libraries contain reference books that identify authors and provide a guide to their backgrounds.

    Why do you need to know about the author? Because evaluation of source affects the worth of the information. A few years ago, for example, a book was published claiming to document an authentic account of cloning: An actual human being had been cloned from the cells of another human being and was alive and well. The author asserted that his story was true. But who was the author? He turned out to be a science fiction writer who had previously written fictional accounts of cloning. Could his claim for truth now be taken seriously? Perhaps. But his authority to document a scientific experiment of such magnitude had to be considered somewhat less reliable than had he been a noted scientist.

2. What is the historical context? Where and when was the work originally published, and who was the probable audience? No poem, essay, or book exists in a vacuum. It grows out of that complex relationship of *subject-audience-context-purpose.* The more you can know about each element, the better you can make reasonable judgments. Every era, for example, tends to promote its generally accepted assumptions. A writer may echo the values of his day or may attack them. Either way, an understanding of those cultural values would help you evaluate the argument. And if you can discover the audience or purpose for which a work is written, you can often understand why it takes the form it does, why it uses emotion or logic or a complex vocabulary or a simple vocabulary, and so on.

Reading and critical reading are different acts. Most reading is done for pleasure—a process of absorbing information without serious thought. But critical reading is an intense, concentrated form of evaluating what the author tells you. Here is an outline summary of the critical reading process.

UNDERSTAND THE CONTENT

- Underline key sentences; circle key words.
- Take notes in the margin.
- Use a dictionary.
- Write a brief summary of the main idea, major points, and conclusions.

EVALUATE THE CONTENT

- Look for logic; look for appeals to emotion.
- Look for both sides of an argument.
- Look for evidence, logical analysis, reasoning.
- Look for meaningful sources to support claims of fact. (If an author claims that 10,000 people died last year from wearing seat belts, where did he or she find this information? From U.S. Government research? Or from a pamphlet left on his or her doorstep by the "Freedom from Seat Belt Society"?)

EVALUATE YOURSELF

- Beware of your biases for and against certain ideas.
- Evaluate whether your reactions are caused by enculturated attitudes.
- Look for immediate denials or approvals; then evaluate whether you've made a hasty conclusion or reacted according to the cultural assumptions of your era.

CONSIDER THE AUTHOR AND HISTORICAL CONTEXT

- What is the author's authority to speak on a subject? (Personal experience? Scholarly study? Research?)
- What is the motive behind the author's essay? (Self-serving? Results of scientific inquiry? Propaganda?)
- Who was the original audience for the work? (Where was it first published? In a book? In a magazine? As a lecture?)
- What were the biases of the original audience?
- Do any elements in the historical period in which it was written explain elements of the work itself?

THE STRATEGY AT WORK

Here is how you might apply these guidelines to a specific reading.

Hidden Dangers in the Ethnic Revival

Orlando Patterson

Main thesis
emphasis upon
ethnic revival is
retreat from
traditional value
of equality

seemingly liberal,
actually reactionary

The ethnic revival sweeping the United States is <u>another example of this nation's retreat from its constitutional commitment to the ideal of equality</u>.

The fact that the movement has the strong support of many so-called liberals and minority activists makes it all the more insidious and disturbing. The harmless, if vain, search for ancestral roots and communal solidarity is the tip of an ideology that is <u>both</u> <u>reactionary and socially explosive.</u>

①Early ethnic
groups were
transitory;
actually aided
assimilation

The ethnic communities that developed in early 20th-century America were essentially transitory. They developed to buffer the economic and cultural shock of adjusting to a new host society. They were aids to assimilation, not barriers. And they succeeded.

What is remarkable about 20th-century America is the rapid rate of assimilation of immigrant groups into the mainstream of social life.

Chauvinism:
zealous and
belligerent
patriotism;
prejudiced devotion
to a cause

(Chauvinistic) intellectuals, by emphasizing those who remain "unmelted," shift the focus from the vast majority who assimilated to those few still remaining in ethnic neighborhoods, although the actual behavior of the majority of those remaining is in the direction of assimilation.

Examples of 1ˢᵗ
point:
– Jews becoming
assimilated
– black majority
wants
assimilation

The Jews, often regarded as among the most ideologically and socially cohesive of modern ethnic groups, exhibit increasing rates of out-marriage and secularism and tend more and more to live in non-Jewish neighborhoods. The same is true of all those of Eastern European origin. And despite the talk about black "soul" and separatism, every poll of the black

Ideology: body of doctrines or beliefs that guide an individual or group

Demagogue: leader who arouses emotion & prejudices

② *Ethnic revival is alliance between conservative demagogues and disenchanted intellectuals — basically ideological*

③ *Ideological rise of ethnicity is compensation for behavioral decline*

④ *Civil rights movement is another cause of revival — led to acceptance of chauvinism*

— but political chauvinism became a two-edged weapon

Example: Community control of neighborhoods first raised by blacks later used by whites to keep blacks out

community indicates that the great majority of blacks favor assimilation and would prefer to live in integrated neighborhoods.

This ethnic revival then is largely an ideological revival wrought by alienated and disenchanted intellectuals and activists in a dangerous alliance with conservative political demagogues. It is the *idea* of ethnicity that is being celebrated, in much the same way that the much talked-about religious revival is largely a commitment to the *idea* of religion.

It is an increasing of awareness about the need for roots. But the ideology has no content, for the roots are simply not there.

Paradoxically, the single most important factor accounting for the doctrinal revival of ethnicity is the behavioral decline of ethnicity. Doctrinal intensity is a reaction to, and a compensation for, the actual social indifference of ordinary, decent men and women who have other things on their minds.

Other factors account for the ideological revival of ethnicity. One of these is the climax of the black civil rights movement in the mid-1960s. To heal the low self-image created by centuries of racial discrimination, blacks felt obliged to glorify their race, history and culture.

The acceptance of black people's right to use ethnic chauvinism as a means of psycho-social liberation revived ethnicity in American political and popular intellectual life.

Soon conservative politicians and other leaders of the white backlash began to use the blacks' own weapon against them. A telling example of the way in which ethnicity became, for blacks, a viper biting its own tail, is the strange career of the principle of community control of neighborhoods.

It was black chauvinists who first made this demand during the 1960s under the mistaken belief that it was an effective means of social and economic independence. Today, the call for community control of schools and the ethnic integrity of neighborhoods comes no longer from blacks but from white reactionaries wishing to keep blacks out of their neighborhoods.

⑤ *Ethnic revival (a) damages social fabric*

Ethnic pluralism, however dressed up in liberal rhetoric, has no place whatever in a democratic society based on the humanistic ideals of our Judeo-Christian ethic. It is, first, socially divisive. However much the more liberal advocates of the revival may proclaim the contrary, the fact remains that the glorification of one's heritage and one's group always implies its superiority, its "chosenness" over all others.

(b) obscures real issues like poverty and racism

Second, the ethnic revival is a dangerous form of obfuscation. There are indeed many severe problems in our society but interpreting them in psychocultural terms immediately obscures the real issues such as poverty and unemployment in the midst of affluence, racism, sexism and environmental assault. These are tough issues requiring tough-minded and rational solutions as well as unswerving commitment to equality and human fraternity. We do not solve them by idle talk about "the twilight of authority" or by searching for largely fanciful roots.

Ethnicity: an → ethnic mentality (c) obscures common human heritage (d) supports concept of inequality

Ethnicity emphasizes the trivialities that distinguish us and obscures the overwhelming reality of our common genetic and human heritages as well as our common needs and hopes. By emphasizing differences, ethnicity lends itself to the conservative belief in the inevitability of inequality. It is no accident that the neoconservative thinkers have all hailed the revival.

Once again the vicious dogma "separate but equal" has resurfaced; only now it is phrased in the pseudo-liberal language of pluralism—we are plural but equal—and, even more tragically, it now has the sanction of misguided leaders and intellectuals of the very groups that hardly a few decades ago were savagely repressed and segregated in the name of this dogma.

⑥ *Ethnic revival is anti-individualistic; promotes conformism*

Profoundly anti-American in its anti-individualism, the ethnic revival celebrates diversity, not however of individuals but of the groups to which they belong. It is a sociological truism that the more cohesive an ethnic group, the more conformist or the more anti-individualistic are its members. Thus the call for a diversity of cohesive, tightly knit groups actually amounts to an assault on the deeply entrenched principle of individualism.

Ideology of ethnic pluralism is dangerous — shows parallels to fascist movement

The fact that the ethnic revival is largely ideological should not lead us to underestimate it. We know from the history of ethnic movements that ideology, under the right circumstances, can transform reality. European fascism was first and foremost an ideological movement, and, in a disturbing parallel with modern America, fascist ideology had its roots in the romantic revolt against the enlightenment—a revolt that, in its early phases, was generally liberal, very concerned with the social and human costs of "progress," and espoused the principle of ethnic pluralism.

Conclusion all humanists should support constitutional ideal of equality

The time has come when all genuine humanists who cherish the great ideal of the Constitution—that all human beings are created equal—must awake from their slumber and meet head on the challenge of the chauvinists.

At this point, several questions, perhaps even several challenges, to Orlando Patterson's argument may have arisen, but the first step in critical reading is to make sure we have objectively and fairly comprehended the author's ideas. We must suspend for the moment our questions and criticism. Now is the time for jotting down notes or summarizing the essay as a whole.

Here is how you might write a brief summary.

Orlando Patterson, in his essay "Hidden Dangers in the Ethnic Revival," argues that an emphasis upon ethnic pluralism is a retreat from the constitutional ideal of equality, "both reactionary and socially explosive." He contends that early ethnic groups were transitory. Today's revival of ethnicity comes from an alliance of conservative demagogues and disenchanted liberal intellectuals. Patterson contends that the decline of interest in things ethnic is actually the most important factor in an ethnic revival, although it was the climax of the black civil rights movement that brought about what he calls the acceptance of "ethnic chauvinism," which was then turned against blacks. Patterson asserts that ethnicity is "socially divisive": it obscures our common human heritage, is used by conservatives to support their belief in inequality, celebrates group conformity, and it is anti-individualistic. He sees many parallels to the ideological rise of fascism which, among other similarities, also supported ethnic plurality. Finally, he calls for humanists to support the constitutional ideal of equality.

Now we are ready to analyze the content. Analysis is a process of dividing the essay into its major parts, questioning each part for its logic and validity, and then evaluating the relationship of the parts to the whole. Here are the types of questions you would want to ask about Orlando Patterson's arguments. (Do not confuse this stage with the writing stage—that will come later.)

Major point 1: How did early ethnic groups actually aid assimilation? Is there statistical evidence to support Patterson's contention that a majority of blacks and other minorities want to be assimilated?

Major point 2: Is there any support for the assertion that the ethnic revival is an ideological movement? Does Patterson resort to name calling when he uses such terms as "alienated intellectuals" and "conservative demagogues"? And who, specifically, are these people? Patterson compares the belief in ethnic *ideas* with the belief in the *idea* of religion. Is this a good analogy? What is he getting at?

Major point 3: Isn't Patterson appealing to emotion when he speaks of "ordinary decent men and women" as having other things on their mind? If he is, does that in itself invalidate the argument that it is the *behavioral* decline in ethnic matters that caused the *ideological* rise?

Major point 4: Patterson observes that "ethnic chauvinism" was accepted as a means to "psycho-social liberation." Why all the big words? Is this a resort to jargon just to make us think his argument is highly intelligent, or is there some justification for his use of such terms? How effective is the analogy about the viper biting its own tail? What are the connotations of the analogy? Who are they aimed at?

Major point 5: The movement toward Patterson's main thesis seems to begin in these three paragraphs: Ethnic pluralism lends support to conservatives who believe in the "inevitability of inequality." Trace each step in the argument here. Is it well made? Are there gaps? How can these so-called conservatives make the leap from "differences" to "unequal"?

Major point 6: Are the phrase "profoundly anti-American" and the later analogy to fascism meant to be factually descriptive, are they appeals to emotions, or both?

Conclusion: The concluding sentence refers directly back to point 5, where Patterson stated, "By emphasizing differences, ethnicity lends itself to the conservative belief in the inevitability of inequality." But if conservatives do indeed believe in inequality, is it the same kind of inequality the Constitution was designed to overcome? Is it possible that two kinds of "equality" or "inequality" are being blurred here into a single point? And if they are, can an argument still have a probable truth even if there is a flaw in the method of arriving at the conclusion?

No analysis is complete at this point. You must still consider your emotional relationship to the argument as well as to the author and the historical context. Some of Patterson's ideas may seem convincing; some may seem illogical. They may even anger you. But to what extent are your feelings the result of your biases or of the cultural assumptions of your particular generation? Can reasons be found outside the reading itself that might help us to judge more temperately the overall worth of Patterson's argument?

That it was originally published in *The New York Times* may help establish part of the context. The *Times* is one of the world's major newspapers, read by both liberal and conservative intellectuals but usually considered to have a strong liberal slant. Many of Patterson's contentions would oppose the beliefs of liberal readers. He may be arguing that they are unwittingly playing into the hands of neoconservatives. But the timing is also important. By 1978, when the essay was published, the ethnic movement was at its peak. *Roots,* the story of a search for black identity, was both a best-selling book and a dramatic success as a TV series. Other ethnic groups—Poles, Chicanos—were increasing their own demands throughout the country. Perhaps Patterson felt that a heightened, even emotional rhetoric was needed to combat the swell of opinion.

But who is Patterson? The newspaper indicates, in a small box at the end of the essay, that he teaches sociology at Harvard. A quick check in the social and behavioral science volume of *American Men and Women of Science* (available in most libraries) gives us more information. Patterson was born in Jamaica and received a Ph.D. in sociology at the London School of Economics. He has held several postdoctoral fellowships and served as consultant both to the World Bank and to the prime minister of Jamaica. More importantly, his field of study is social change, and he has published widely on slavery and its social effects. Clearly, we're dealing with an expert on the subject, but one who disagrees with the trends of his time and with many other experts in the same field.

Having now considered the man and the historical context, having accounted for our prejudices, if any, and having scrutinized each part of the essay for logic and evidence, we can feel reasonably confident that an overall assessment can be made: What are the strong and weak points? Where is Patterson's argument most convincing? Where does this argument appear to fail and why? What is the ultimate value and worth of the essay in terms of the ideas it offers for consideration?

The critical voice is sometimes mistaken as a negative voice. Actually, to be critical means to discriminate with exactness. Hence a critical analysis must discriminate between good and bad. It praises as well as condemns. If we are exacting, we will usually discover that an author is seldom wholly right or wholly wrong. We will not slant our judgment to one side or the other, but toward fair and balanced understanding. The conclusion of a critical analysis should assess the work in its fullness.

By its nature the critical reading process is slow and methodical. It takes effort and self-discipline. But when objectivity is maintained, the close scrutiny of detail pursued, and relationships evaluated, it can lead to insight that is balanced, rewarding, and reasonable.

Exercises

1. Consider the following editorial that appeared in a college newspaper. In what ways are the arguments logical? Illogical? Does the author appeal to reason or emotion to support his position?

Alcohol Laws Won't Achieve Goal

Underdog Productions is sponsoring another dance in the Highsmith Center this weekend. This time, it's the "Cruis-o-matics," a well-known band which has played in many southeastern cities. UP is doing a good job—the word has it that they're pretty good—but if the turnout Friday night is anything like the "droves" who mobbed the Highsmith Center during the first dance this semester, they'd better plan to hold the next one in the gym.

Some have said one reason that first dance was a flop is because of the new alcohol laws. Of course, no one officially maintains that point of view, but given the facts, it's a logical conclusion.

By practically banning alcohol consumption on campus, the state has effectively closed off what was once a relatively safe way to party.

Forbidding someone under 21 to drink is a crock, anyway. An 18-year-old can get married, drive a car, cast a vote to help choose our leaders, beat up on his/her spouse, go to jail, be sent to Libya to fight and possibly die—all before he/she is 21 and legally able to buy a beer. Talk about a paradox.

In our opinion, the new law will make little difference in the long run. About the only end outlawing booze in the 1920s accomplished was making a select group of daring Mafia-type bootleggers very wealthy. Then, as now however, it was a handy hook for hapless politicians to grab.

Meanwhile, maybe the "Cruis-o-matics" will give UNCA students a chance to rock the Highsmith Center, even if cracking open a Bud Light is now illegal.

2. Study the following paper written by a freshman in a political science course. Because the essay was written in class, no opportunity was available for bringing in concrete evidence. Analyze it only for the logic and soundness of the argument.

We owe allegiance to the state, namely the United States of America, because we live here. We are part of the country. People can choose where they want to live and we have chosen to live here. The nation protects each person's individual liberties and thus demands certain duties from its people. Everyone has human rights—freedom of speech, religion, and the press. We can choose what area we want to live in and how we want to live our life. The list goes on and on. As our country gives us so much, we should be loyal to it.

In past years, many times when war was announced, that was it. A person's responsibility was now to the state and no one could take time to do what they wanted unless, of course, it was for the good of the war. When farmers fought during a war, their responsibility was often to themselves as well as to the state. They worked the land and it was theirs. The land was their life. They fought to protect it and to keep it free. People were impassioned during these wars to fight with all they had, in hopes that future generations would be free. It was an honor to go into battle and something that men and boys often looked forward to. There wasn't much of a question whether or not a person would go to war at that time, like there was during the Vietnam War—it was a person's privilege and responsibility.

Responsibilities that are greater than our responsibilities to the state are to yourself, your family and friends and your religion. You have to think of yourself because if you don't, no one else will. If you don't save yourself, you won't be any good to yourself or to anyone else. If your family and friends were killed, and you could have helped prevent it but didn't, what good would it be to be free? What would be the use of winning a war if you had nothing to live for?

A country grants each person certain civic rights that he possesses from the day he is born. It offers its citizens protection when they are away from it and privileges when they are at home. In turn, each citizen owes allegiance to his country. It is his duty to support his government, obey its laws, and defend his country.

Journal Practice

Use your journal to record reactions to your reading. Write whatever is important to you. Be honest. Record interesting facts, quotations, observations. Ask questions and attempt to answer them even if you find yourself stumbling around. Make maps, lists, webs, anything that involves you with the work and leads to a clearer understanding. Writing about your reading helps you absorb ideas.

In addition to keeping you alert as you read, recording your responses helps you remember. As you write, you begin the act of selecting; patterns emerge and fresh insights surface. Your reactions are sharpened and preserved.

Look up definitions for words you don't know. (In addition to some 32-odd journals kept during his lifetime, Walt Whitman filled 15 notebooks with words and definitions he wanted to remember.) If you are confused about a particularly difficult reading, talk your thoughts to the paper until your thinking clarifies. Copy passages that are difficult to understand. Sometimes what begins as confusion turns into startling insights. You may write pages of seemingly worthless meanderings before you experience the kind of illumination that becomes its own reward for all this effort—to see and understand for yourself just what it is you think and feel. You may also find that when it comes time to write a paper, you'll have much of your work already completed.

Drafting and the Discovery of Form

30

The Structure of Analysis and Argumentation

Some of your best arguments probably take place in the residence hall or sorority house late at night, or in a bar around the corner from the college. If you're like me, you enjoy a good debate. You like challenging flaws in your opponent's logic and the emotional heat that begins to build. You may find yourself holding opinions on numerous topics you've never investigated with any thoroughness. Perhaps you feel strongly about drug use or school prayer or abortion. And based on half-formed opinions, you may even come up with a decent, rational argument.

But almost all formal argument in college requires a more detached, reflective attitude, and most of the time it emerges from your reading rather than from oral debate. Your skill at analyzing and evaluating someone else's writing, as well as your ability to organize your counterargument, becomes an essential ingredient of the education process. That's because the world of scholarship is a print-centered culture. We trust the written word more than the spoken word, if for no other reason than because we can reflect upon a printed argument with more cool deliberation and objectivity. We can consider the very points of reasoning and evidence I've been talking about in previous chapters. We can more easily detect appeals to emotion or other fallacies. In turn, we write out our critiques and rebuttals (rather than enjoin our colleagues in bars late at night) for the same reason. The act of writing helps us clarify our thoughts and our argument for ourselves. And it gives others the chance to test our words and ideas against the highest standards. Written argument is thus a type of dialogue, an engagement of ideas between writer and reader, and if you write back, between reader and writer.

A good argument, of the type I'm describing here, requires both a good analysis and a thoughtful presentation of evidence and logic. To accomplish that, readers may expect you to follow a rather traditional form that has proven successful since Aristotle first began his studies on rhetoric. I'm going to describe that organization here and it may well sound as if I've fallen into my own trap: naming the ten elements of beauty or whatever. But there are no rules, only method. A conventional form is not like a glass bottle into which you pour the milk of your observations. It's more like a dance step. At first you may feel as if you're being asked to follow cut-out footprints pasted on the floor. Your movements may seem awkward. You may feel inhibited. But with practice and experience you'll find the organization is merely a mental guideline. You may continue to follow it mechanically and dully, or you may bring to it your own spirit and liveliness, investing it with style, grace, and originality.

THE FORMAL INTRODUCTION

In chapter 29 you needed an objective understanding of the essay by Orlando Patterson before you could analyze it. So, too, does your reader need an objective overview of a subject before you plunge into finer points of argument. A formal introduction usually includes three elements.

Name of Author and Work

Give the full name of the author and the essay or book you plan to discuss. (You'd be surprised at how many inexperienced writers forget to do this.)

Orlando Patterson, in his essay "Hidden Dangers in the Ethnic Revival," argues that . . .

According to Richard Poirier's "Learning from the Beatles" (*Partisan Review*, 1967) contemporary criticism fails to account for . . .

Martin Luther King's "Letter from Birmingham Jail" (April 16, 1963) is a major document explaining the nonviolent philosophy behind King's campaign for . . .

Each of these examples identifies author and title, then leads the reader toward the next step.

Characterization of the Whole

Although your audience may have read the work you are analyzing, you should not expect others to have memorized it or to have studied it as closely as you. You'll want to provide a brief summary of the article or book in its historical context. Knowledge about the author and his or her qualifications to speak—or about the cultural era out of which the work arose—can sometimes contribute to a general understanding. You may even want to note briefly the publishing history of a work if it is especially interesting or perhaps the reaction of critics when the work first appeared.

The summary itself is most important. No matter what your ultimate judgment, give fair hearing to the author at this point. Present his or her ideas accurately and without bias. As briefly as possible, give at least the basic theme and the author's conclusion. If the work is long and complicated, you may want to go into more detail and review some of the major points as well.

This combination of historical context and brief summary is common courtesy to the reader. It provides us with a context in which to follow your more detailed analysis. Here is how sophomore Ann Max introduced her subject, using a rather full characterization.

Identification of author and her credentials	Ellen Harris is a free-lance journalist and reviewer for such major publications as *The New Yorker* and *The New York Review of Books*. In 1988 she attacked the conventional understanding of the consumer as a victim of the sellers and the advertisers.
Overview of author's argument	
Title and source of publication	In "Women and the Myth of Consumerism," first published in *Advance* (June, 1989), Harris argues that the theory of the advertisers using depth psychology to convince women to buy a product is not only a false theory, but one that confuses cause and effect. The true purpose behind advertising, she claims, is merely
Summary of the essay	

Basic theme

capitalistic exploitation, which she finds normal and inoffensive in a capitalist society today. What does disturb her is that advertising creates images that reflect "women as they are forced by men in a sexist society to behave."

Judgment (must be supported later)

But her presentation is marred by her angry and bitter tone in the essay. *Advance* was a semirevolutionary magazine that grew out of the cultural upheaval of the

Historical context

early seventies. Harris obviously assumed that her readers already held anticapitalist, antisexist, anti-just-about-

Focusing thesis

everything attitudes. The result is interesting but contains serious oversimplifications and unsupported assumptions.

Ann Max took the time to find out about both the author and the magazine in which the author published. Ann summarizes the basic thesis, then moves toward a focusing of how she plans to criticize the work.

The Focusing (or Thesis) Sentence

If you plan to analyze an entire essay, you must first focus on how you propose to do it. If the subject is too complex to analyze the whole, then the focusing sentence should indicate how you've narrowed your subject. The reader also needs to move from the general overview of the work to the more specific argument you plan to take in your paper.

> Virginia Smith's essay is logical and effectively argued, but she fails to account for a great number of scientific studies that provide evidence on the other side of the issue. For example . . .

> Professor Harris's thesis is flawed by several dramatic breakdowns in clear reasoning. First . . .

> John Binder's book is especially important to the young person seeking direction and meaning to life. Perhaps his most important point is . . .

You might think of a formal introduction as following the same pattern used in the panoramic scene (described in Chapter 10). Begin with a broad overview that provides a general background; then move in closer, looking at major details—the theme and the conclusion; and finally, focus in (or narrow the subject) to the elements you find most important for analysis or argument.

ANALYSIS AND ARGUMENT

Much of your paper should present a detailed analysis of the single theme or major components of the work you have focused on.

1. *Describe* the specific portion of the work you plan to deal with. Your formal introduction gives only an overview. Here we need details. What is the major point the author is making? Use your own words to summarize. Back up your summary with a short but significant quotation.
2. *Analyze* the idea for its logic, its evidence, its soundness, and its relationship to other ideas.
3. *Interpret* your findings. Argue the soundness of the reasoning, or offer a counterargument with clear reasoning of your own.

Do not assume that your paper must follow the sequential organization of the original essay. Do not assume that you should discuss every argument in the original. In Chapter 29, I found six major elements in Orlando Patterson's essay on ethnic revival. For the sake of understanding Patterson's logic, I needed to question each point in my mind. But I would not want to write on each point. As in any other paper, the subject must be narrowed and only the most significant elements discussed. A formal critique on "Hidden Dangers in the Ethnic Revival" might focus on only one or two of Patterson's concepts. Your analysis will almost always seem more effective if you go into detail on a single but significant theme rather than attempt to discuss each phase of the original.

However, for each theme or argument that you do discuss, repeat the three steps listed here: *describe, analyze, interpret.* Be sure to include quotations and examples from the work itself to make your paper as concrete as possible—that is, to provide evidence that supports your own analysis. Here is an excerpt from freshman Tony Ludlum's critique of a single portion of John Locke's "Second Treatise of Civil Government." In a brief introduction, Tony narrowed his subject to the section of Locke's argument that deals with establishment of government. Then he began the body of his essay.

Description of the author's major point

After proposing that the natural condition of man is one of freedom and equality, Locke argues that freedom is limited by the "law of Nature" which is, as he defines it, "reason." This law teaches us that our liberty is not absolute. We may not, for example, kill or steal, unless it is to punish an offender of this law of Nature.

For the law of Nature would, as all other laws that concern men in this world, be in vain if there were nobody that in the state of Nature had a power to execute that law. . . . Locke then decides that in the perfect state of Nature, since all are equal, each of us has the right to prosecute the law, although punishment too must be guided by reason. Locke concludes this portion of his essay

Student integrates summary in his own words with selected quotations from the author.

by saying that it is not his intention to describe the "particulars of the law of Nature" but "it is certain there is such a law," one that is clearly understandable to rational creatures.

But is there? Apparently reasonable men in the eighteenth century believed there was. The Declaration of Independence mentions the same phrase. If a whole culture believed something to be true, maybe you can get away with such a statement so that there is not any need to go into detail or define it. But even if for the time being we suspend our twentieth-century doubts and accept such a law, how can it be so clear that Nature's law is reasonable? Or that it is so reasonable that it can be clearly "executed" by men even when it is not defined? However, Locke doesn't claim that the law is reasonable. He claims that the law *is* reason. I guess my problem with this is that I end up going in a circle: the law of nature is certain, the law is reason; if we are reasonable we will understand the law; if we are not reasonable we will supposedly not understand it nor even know that it is certain. Locke's use of the term cleverly says, in effect, if you believe me and accept what I say, you are a reasonable man, but if you don't accept what I say, or doubt my "certainty," you are unreasonable. Also since the rest of his argument in the essay depends upon this one concept, the reader is placed in a bind. Believe and you will be saved. Don't believe and you are not worth saving. For a reasonable man, this sounds like a strangely unreasonable argument.

Analysis begins by questioning—in this case, student focuses on a key term.

Student recognizes that historical factors may influence even reasoned belief.

Student focuses on logical relationships in author's argument.

Challenge to author's logic

Refutation and Rebuttal

A major element of the argumentative essay is the anticipation of those arguments or challenges that might be thrown back at you. By answering them in advance, you take away from your reader the opportunity for criticism. You also add further persuasion and force to your work by showing how thoughtful and careful you've been in building your argument. It suggests you have an informed perspective, a balanced rational view, which in itself gives additional force to your other contentions. Even if you can't absolve yourself of some inconsistency or potential flaw in your argument, it remains better to show your good faith and to admit it.

Here's how Greg Knopke, a business major, handled this part of his paper on economic losses caused by auto imports. (Greg has been arguing

that because 75,000 jobs may be lost due to Japanese imports and ro-
botics, government intervention and legislation is required.)

*First refutation given
fair hearing*

True, the purest form of Capitalism would lead us to
the conclusion that competition ought to be allowed full
reign and that those companies which are less efficient
should be allowed a peaceful death. All those unemployed
workers will eventually find other jobs in areas where

Student's rebuttal

America is more competitive. So the argument goes. But
what we are hearing here is only partly true. Seventy-five
thousand unemployed are not the only ones affected. For
every worker in the auto industry who loses his job,
Business Week (March 1987) estimates that three others in
subsidiary industry or in small business indirectly
supported by those workers will also lose their jobs. And
that army of 300,000 will require unemployment benefits
which you and I will pay. There will also be a loss of
local, state and federal taxes which will cause
retrenchment in everything from schools to road repair.
The social cost is too great to adhere to free-market
capitalism for its own sake.

Second refutation

Finally, one could also argue that government
intervention is only a short-term solution, that it will
merely forestall an eventual collapse of the auto industry.
And that the government will be required to pour more
and more subsidy, more and more tax dollars, into a lost

*Admission that argument
has truth to it*

cause. This is the strongest argument against my own
position. And I would say it will prove to be true unless
the government also initiates a limited partnership with

Student's rebuttal

the auto industry to insure that the subsidy is contingent
upon modernization and gradual retraining of workers.
The truth is that my argument for intervention is doomed
to failure without this additional commitment.

CONCLUSIONS

Conclusions are sometimes difficult to generalize on, for every good
conclusion flows naturally from the evidence or argument presented in
the body of the paper. But several important points about the conclusion
to a formal analysis can be made. Analysis is meaningful only when the
parts are joined together again with the whole. To have looked in detail
at a single theme or even at each major argument is not enough. You
must show your reader how it all relates to the whole.

Do the parts depend on rational arguments? On emotion or unclear
thinking? On an historical or cultural value? Where is the work sound
and meaningful? Where is it less effective?

As we noted earlier, the point of critical analysis is not to attack everything you read with a negative voice. The goal is to discriminate that which is valuable and that which is not, and then to persuade the reader to accept your reasoning. Although the examples I've given in this chapter have focused on weaknesses, a good critical argument may focus on strengths to which you add your own voice.

Finally, it is equally important that you take care that your conclusion does not reflect a personal bias, stereotype, or emotional argument of your own. Judgment must be based on reason and on critical thinking, not on personal opinions, such as "I don't like this book on cats because I don't like cats."

Here is how we might informally outline the structure of analysis and argument.

INTRODUCTION

- Name of author and work
- General overview of the subject, historical background, or summary of the argument
- Thesis (your position, focused and narrowed)

EVIDENCE

- Objective description of major point
- Detailed analysis of logic and relationships
- Interpretation followed by supportive argument or counter-argument
- Repetition of description, analysis, and interpretation if more than one major concept is covered
- Refutation and rebuttal

CONCLUSION

- Overall summary of findings
- Relationship of findings to the subject as a whole
- Critical assessment of the value, worth, or meaning of your findings, both negative and positive

---

Critical analysis does not guarantee you will discover the truth. Yet it can provide the concrete evidence that permits you to demonstrate (to *show*) you have used logical reasoning to arrive at a conclusion. Should your reasoning be faulty, the process also allows someone else to pinpoint precisely where you have erred. Thus analysis and argument is a method that permits verification by a second observer. In that sense, both you and the reader can feel more confident about the probable truths revealed by the process.

WRITING THE FIRST DRAFT

Did Tony Ludlum or Ann Max write a successful analysis in their first draft? The answer is simply no. For almost all of us, drafting remains a time of exploration, a time of crossing out and starting over. As E. M. Forster once said, "How do I know what I think until I see what I say?"

By studying the subject and taking notes before you begin to write (as described in Chapter 29) and by using the guideline described here as "the traditional structure of analysis and argument," your first draft might flow more simply and clearly than if you plunge in without preconceived direction. But for some students, obsessive concern with form will actually block ideas. The form must be thought of as a guideline only, not a God-given standard. Your personal experience with the subject, filtered now through reason, must still be the main focus as you face the blank page. You must be willing to follow new ideas as they occur, not force ideas to fit the form. Write the first draft as quickly as possible, absorbed in the subject. Use the form in the rewriting phase as a check against what you have written. For example, you may find you have failed to describe certain parts of the essay before you analyzed the detailed points. The formal guideline should remind you that your reader needs that description. Go back and work it in. In other words, use the drafting stage as you have in the past—to experiment and explore. Use the formal guideline to clarify and organize, either before or after the drafting, depending upon your personal needs. But do use it because the audience for critical writing will expect a clear and logical form.

Exercise

Study the following two essays for their logic and persuasive power. The first, by Carl Horn, is adapted from an article in a major southern newspaper. Horn, a lawyer, has served on the Jesse Helms for Senate steering committee. The second essay is by sophomore Carl C. Atworth, former president of a college Democrats for Action Club in New England. Which essay is more convincing? Do you find logical faults in either?

A Lack of Religious Values Threatens Our Religious Freedom

Our Declaration of Independence declares it "self-evident" that "[we] are endowed by [our] Creator with certain inalienable Rights." Today any such public affirmation of God's existence is greeted with embarrassment or disdain, at least by the "enlightened" elite.

In the preceding century, the greatest of all British jurists, William Blackstone, had written in his famous "Commentaries" that all laws were ultimately based on "the law of nature and of nature's God."

The first Congress—the same Congress that debated and proposed the First Amendment—where some civil libertarians find the strict and absolute separation of all things religious from all things public—not only retained the first legislative chaplains to pray and to provide spiritual counsel, but the day after proposing the First Amendment called on President Washington to proclaim "a day of publick thanksgiving and prayer, to be observed by acknowledging, with grateful hearts, the many favors of Almighty God."

Our second president, John Adams, went right to the bottom line: "Our Constitution was made only for a religious and a moral people," Adams said. "It is wholly inadequate for the government of any other."

Were Thomas Jefferson (who authored our Declaration of Independence), William Blackstone, George Washington, John Adams—and others of our Founding Fathers, who confirm their testimony—all wrong? Indeed, are our Pledge of Allegiance to "one nation under God" and our national motto ("In God We Trust") also unconstitutional? Are they, as groups like the American Civil Liberties Union and People for the American Way say, really violations of the separation of church and state?

Who is really out-of-step with "The American Way," Norman Lear and his telemarketed valueless hedonism, or those who continue to believe in God, country, family, and morality?

The fact is that we are having a modern, or post-modern, identity crisis—and there are two basic philosophies of life vying for dominance of our law, our politics, and what might be called our "public philosophy."

On the one hand, there is the Judeo-Christian world view that begins by affirming God's existence and, as Benjamin Franklin put it, that "God governs the affairs of men." If we believe in God, and trust in God, and believe that he "governs the affairs of men," we would be

By permission of Carl Horn.

foolish to ignore the ancient tradition, recorded in Holy Scripture, regarding what he requires of his creatures.

On the other hand there are the secularists—who do not so much deny God's existence as they pronounce it irrelevant. As the architects of the French Revolution believed, post-modern secularists think religion should be kept strictly private—except, of course, where religion can be used to advance the goals of socialism or Marxism. Morals, which are ultimately rooted in a religiously based world view, should likewise have no bearing on our public policy.

But, good remains good, and evil remains evil, however many Madison Avenue advertising campaigns may be purchased to convince us to the contrary. Solzhenitsyn is absolutely correct. If we do not stop yielding up our younger generation to atheism, freedom and prosperity as we have known it in America will be no more.

Carl Horn

Our Freedom Is Threatened by the Religious Right

"Good remains good, and evil remains evil," but Madison Avenue is attempting to persuade us otherwise. At least according to Carl Horn in "A Lack of Religious Values Threatens Our Freedom," an essay published in a major southern newspaper in February 1986. Mr. Horn argues that our country was founded by believers in God and that our Declaration of Independence and Constitution were authored by founders who upheld religious values. The problem, according to Mr. Horn, is that we're having a "post-modern identity crisis." Those who believe that God's existence is irrelevant are fighting against those who uphold Judeo-Christian traditions. But Mr. Horn's argument provides scanty proof for all this. Even if we personally believe that religious values are important to both the individual and the state of the nation—as I do—Mr. Horn offers only an appeal to patriotism and authority for support. And for his opponents, he offers only name calling and innuendo.

To support his contention that we are fundamentally a religious nation, Mr. Horn cites lines from the Declaration of Independence; he appeals to William Blackstone, a "famous" jurist of the 19th century; he observes the first Congress' request for a day of "publick thanksgiving and prayer"; and he cites our founding fathers: George Washington, Thomas Jefferson, John Adams, and Benjamin Franklin. He even points to our coinage ("In God We Trust") and to our Pledge of Allegiance. All this is a ringing roll-call of emotional appeal that we can hardly be unresponsive to. The evidence seems overwhelming, and most of us would probably concur. We do have a religious heritage. But Mr. Horn is not telling the whole story.

Citing William Blackstone's argument that laws are based on the "law of nature and of nature's God" has a good ring to it, but it is not supportable. It does not reflect a provable fact, only a cultural opinion which as I understand it grew out of the Enlightenment and which was supposed to have been widely held in the 18th and early 19th century. Had Mr. Horn cited a 12th century authority, he might have found one who argued that laws were based on the divine right of kings. And had he turned to the classical era, he would surely have found someone claiming all laws were based on Caesar's will. The problem with appeals to authority is that you can pick and choose the one most agreeable to your own mind-set.

Even his citation of patriots is flawed, because although Washington, Jefferson, Adams, and Franklin did believe in God, it was a type of God that would probably shock and horrify today's fundamentalist. Each was, to varying degrees, a believer in Deism, a type of religious philosophy that also grew out of the Enlightenment. Deism held that although God created the universe, He then retreated from any connection to or concern for it. The most famous metaphor for this was the watchmaker who constructs a watch, winds it up, and then leaves it to run according to its own mechanical laws—which is where Blackstone gets his argument about laws of nature (the mechanical clock ticking away) and of "nature's God" (the watchmaker, the creator of nature and of laws, but not the personal observer). In other words, although our founding fathers spoke strongly in favor of morality and God, their beliefs were not in a personal God of the type believed in by Christians, and they especially did not hold to any particular sectarian faith. Deism was not based on faith at all, but on reason, which helps explain the First Amendment's provision for separation of church and state. Jefferson and Franklin held beliefs that differed from the Puritan heritage of most of their countrymen, and they didn't want a common government dominated by any one sect of believers.

But there is another flaw in Mr. Horn's argument. Mr. Horn creates a dualistic world, black and white, with two great opposing forces. On the one hand is the Judeo-Christian heritage and all those founding fathers (the good guys who believe in God) and on the other hand are the "secularists," whom he associates with the French Revolution ("chop off their heads"), or with generally unnamed "elitists," "libertarians," and "hedonists" who either don't believe in God or who use religion to advance Marxism and Socialism.

A dualistic world itself is hard to accept, but the value of arguing for it is that it forces us to take sides. We certainly don't want to be on the side of evil, and if all those "secularists" and Marxists are evil, we want to be on the side of George Washington. But this is simply emotional innuendo and name calling. It begins in the second line of Mr. Horn's essay in which he says that today any public "affirmation of God's existence is greeted with embarrassment or disdain, at least by the 'enlightened' elite." Elitism is a bad word in America. And the use of quotation marks around enlightened shows what we all know—that those elitists out there aren't as enlightened as they think they are—whoever they are. Horn never identifies them except for Norman Lear, who he associates with "telemarketed valueless hedonism." As I understand, Norman Lear is a TV producer who founded a group called The American Way in an attempt to fight against the religious right. I don't know whether Mr. Lear is a hedonist, but apparently his connection to TV gives Mr. Horn the charge that Madison Avenue advertising is behind the attempt to turn our youth into atheists. No other evidence or support is provided. In other words, the argument seems to depend upon one *already* believing that Madison Avenue advertising is evil, or that one *already* knows for certain that Norman Lear is a hedonist, or that one *already* knows TV is valueless—or something. We have a charge, a little name calling, and nothing else.

By this time Mr. Horn's essay has degenerated into absurdity. Even if we grant, as I would, that our nation has a strong religious heritage, by the time we get to the proposition that modern secularists think "religion can be used to advance the goals of socialism or Marxism," we have spun off into another orbit. Marxism opposes religion. Marx called it "the opiate of the people." Most communist nations try to repress religion. How on earth can religion then be used to advance the cause of it? The answer is that it can't, but Mr. Horn has wanted to get in two more emotionally negative words: Marxism and socialism.

As a logical argument, this piece is so flawed it would be funny if it weren't also so successful and frightening as an emotional persuader, for that's exactly what it is—a minor masterpiece of emotional argument. First it oversimplifies the world into good and evil. On the side of good it enlists everything Americans hold dear from the Declaration of Independence to God, Ben Franklin, freedom, and even prosperity (the only thing missing is the Boy Scout Motto). On the side of evil it enlists hedonism, elitism, Marxists, Madison Avenue, telemarketing, socialism, and the French Revolution. This is an argument where connotation plays more importance than denotation, where patriotism is associated with religion, and where facts or evidence are ignored. And to me, that's the kind of argument that can be dangerous to our freedom because in its strong and effective appeal to emotion, it takes away our ability to think rationally. It takes away our freedom to make reasoned choices.

Carl C. Atworth

Readings

Charles Krauthammer is a Pulitzer Prize-winning columnist (1987) for the Washington Post Writers' Group and a regular contributor of opinion essays to Time, *where the following first appeared. Consider the various kinds of logical strategies he employs, as well as the way he presents and rebuts various alternative arguments. Does he commit any logical fallacies of his own?*

Pornography Through the Looking Glass
Charles Krauthammer

Television ushered in the new year by cracking what it breathlessly billed as "the last taboo": incest. Liberal Minneapolis celebrated by backtracking a couple of taboos and considering a ban on pornography. One would have thought that that particular hang-up had been overcome. But even though the ban voted by the Minneapolis city council was eventually vetoed by Mayor Donald Fraser, pornography is evidently a hang-up of considerable tenacity. And according to the proposed law it is more than that: it is a violation of civil rights.

Now that seems like a peculiar notion, but one has to read the proposed ordinance to see just how peculiar it is. The city council proposed banning "discrimination . . . based on race, color, creed, religion, ancestry, national origin, sex, including . . . pornography." What can that possibly mean? How can one discriminate based on pornography?

Anticipating such questions, the bill helpfully provides "special findings on pornography." If it ever passes (immediately after the mayor's veto proponents vowed to bring it up again), the findings are destined to be the most famous gifts from social science to law since footnote eleven of *Brown* vs. *Board of Education.** The *Brown* findings, however, were based on real empirical data. The Minneapolis findings are of a more metaphysical nature. They begin: "The council finds that pornography is central in creating and maintaining the civil inequality of the sexes." If that were true, then it would follow that where pornography is banned—as in the U.S. of 50 years ago or the Tehran of today—one should not expect to find civil inequality of the sexes. Next finding. "Pornography is a systematic practice of exploitation and subordination based on sex which differentially harms women." While it is true that some pornography subordinates women, some does not, and none is "systematic" or a "practice."

---

*The Supreme Court's 1954 ruling cited seven scholars to prove that separate-but-equal schooling harmed black children, and led one critic to complain that it thus needlessly gave ammunition to those who wished to see the *Brown* decision not as an expression of civilized truth but as a brand of sociology.

Outside the Minneapolis city council chambers, pornography means the traffic in obscenity. Inside, as in Alice's Wonderland, words will mean what the council wants them to mean.

The liberal mayor of Minneapolis was sympathetic with the proposal's aims, but vetoed it nonetheless. He found it too vague and ambiguous, a classic complaint against obscenity laws, old and new. In simpler times Justice Potter Stewart answered the question what is pornography with a succinct "I know it when I see it." But would even he know "subordination based on sex which differentially harms women" when he saw it? After all, the new dispensation seems to exclude homosexual pornography. And only embarrassment, not logic, would prevent including those weddings at which the bride is old-fashioned enough to vow "to love, honor and *obey.*"

The head of the Minneapolis Civil Liberties Union says, unkindly, that the ordinance "has no redeeming social value." That seems a bit harsh. Set aside for a moment the pseudo findings, the creative definitions, the ambiguities. The intent of the bill is to do away with the blight of pornography. What can be wrong with that?

A good question, and an important one. Over the decades it has spawned a fierce debate between a certain kind of conservative (usually called cultural conservative) on the one hand and civil libertarians on the other. The argument went like this. The conservative gave the intuitive case against pornography based on an overriding concern for, it now sounds almost too quaint to say, public morality. Pornography is an affront to decency; it coarsens society. As Susan Sontag, not a conservative, writing in defense of pornography says, it serves to "drive a wedge between one's existence as a full human being and one's existence as a sexual being." The ordinary person, of course, does not need a philosopher, conservative or otherwise, to tell him why he wants to run pornography out of his neighborhood. It cheapens and demeans. Even though he may occasionally be tempted by it, that temptation is almost invariably accompanied by a feeling of shame and a desire to shield his children from the fleshy come-ons of the magazine rack.

That may be so, say the civil libertarians, but it is irrelevant. Government has no business regulating morality. The First Amendment guarantees freedom of expression, and though you may prefer not to express yourself by dancing naked on a runway in a bar, some people do, and you have no business stopping them. Nor do you have any business trying to stop those who like to sit by the runway and imbibe this form of expression. It may not be *Swan Lake,* but the First Amendment does not hinge on judgments of artistic merit or even redeeming value.

Now this traditional debate over pornography is clear and comprehensible. It involves the clash of two important values: public morality vs. individual liberty. The conservative is prepared to admit that his restrictions curtail liberty, though a kind of liberty he does not think is particularly worth having. The civil libertarian admits that a price of liberty is that it stands to be misused, and that pornography may be one of those misuses; public morality may suffer, but freedom is more precious. Both sides agree, however, that one cannot have everything and may sometimes have to trade one political good for another.

Not the Minneapolis bill, and that is what made it so audacious—and perverse. It manages the amazing feat of restoring censorship, which after all is a form of coercion, while at the same time claiming not to restrict rights but to expand them. The logic is a bit tortuous. It finds that pornography promotes bigotry and fosters acts of aggression against women, both of which, in turn, "harm women's opportunities for equality of rights in employment, education, property rights, . . . contribute significantly to restricting women from full exercise of citizenship . . . and undermine women's equal exercise of rights to speech and action."

Apart from the questionable logical leaps required at every step of the syllogism, the more immediate question is: Why take this remote and improbable route to arrive at a point—banning pornography—that one can reach directly by citing the venerable argument that pornography damages the moral fiber of society? Why go from St. Paul to Minneapolis by way of Peking?

The answer is simple. As a rallying cry, public morality has no sex appeal; civil rights has. Use words like moral fiber and people think of Jerry Falwell. Use words like rights and they think of Thomas Jefferson. Use civil rights and they think of Martin Luther King Jr. Because civil rights is justly considered among the most sacred of political values, appropriating it for partisan advantage can be very useful. (The fiercest battle in the fight over affirmative action, for example, is over which side has rightful claim to the mantle of civil rights.) Convince people that censorship is really a right, and you can win them over. It won over the Minneapolis city council. And if to do so, you have to pretend that fewer rights are more, so be it.

Civil rights will not be the first political value to have its meaning reversed. The use of the term freedom to describe unfreedom goes back at least as far as Rousseau, who wrote, without irony, of an ideal republic in which men would be "forced to be free." In our day the word democracy is so beloved of tyrants that some have named their countries after it, as in the German Democratic Republic (a.k.a. East Germany). And from Beirut to San Salvador, every gang of political thugs makes sure to kneel at least five times a day in the direction of "peace." So why not abuse civil rights?

The virtue of calling a spade a spade is that when it is traded in, accountants can still make sense of the books. The virtue of calling political values by their real names is that when social policy is to be made, citizens can make sense of the choices. That used to be the case in the debate about pornography. If Minneapolis is any indication of where that debate is heading, it will not be the case for long.

That is a pity, because while it is easy to quarrel with the method of the Minneapolis ban, it is hard to quarrel with the motive. After a decade's experience with permissiveness, many Americans have become acutely aware that there is a worm in the apple of sexual liberation. That a community with a reputation for liberalism should decide that things have gone too far is not really news. The call for a pause in the frantic assault on the limits of decency (beyond which lies the terra cognita of what used to be taboos) is the quite natural expression of a profound disappointment with the reality, as opposed to the promise, of unrestricted freedom. There are pushes and pulls in the life of the national superego, and now there is a pulling—back. Many are prepared to make expression a bit less free in order to make their community a bit more whole, or, as skeptics might say, wholesome.

That is nothing to be ashamed of. So why disguise it as a campaign for civil rights? (True, liberals may be somewhat embarrassed to be found in bed with bluenoses, but the Minneapolis case is easily explained away as a one-issue marriage of convenience.) In an age when the most private of human activities is everywhere called by its most common name, why be so coy about giving censorship its proper name too?

Gloria Steinem is one of America's leading feminists. Founder of Ms. *magazine, she has published widely, including* Outrageous Acts *and* Everyday Rebellions, *from which the following essay is taken. Trace the logic of her argument here and the types of evidence offered. How does she go beyond the conventional reasons for women to work? Where is she most convincing? Does she challenge your own biases or require you to look at the situation in new ways?*

The Importance of Work

Gloria Steinem

Toward the end of the 1970s, the *Wall Street Journal* devoted an eight-part, front-page series to "the working woman"—that is, the influx of women into the paid-labor force—as the greatest change in American life since the Industrial Revolution.

Many women readers greeted both the news and the definition with cynicism. After all, women have always worked. If all the productive work of human maintenance that women do in the home were valued at its replacement cost, the gross national product of the United States would go up by 26 percent. It's just that we are now more likely than ever before to leave our poorly rewarded, low-security, high-risk job of homemaking (though we're still trying to explain that it's a perfectly good one and that the problem is male society's refusal both to do it and to give it an economic value) for more secure, independent, and better-paid jobs outside the home.

Obviously, the real work revolution won't come until all productive work is rewarded—including child rearing and other jobs done in the home—and men are integrated into so-called women's work as well as vice versa. But the radical change being touted by the *Journal* and other media is one part of that long integration process: the unprecedented flood of women into salaried jobs, that is, into the labor force as it has been male-defined and previously occupied by men. We are already more than 41 percent of it—the highest proportion in history. Given the fact that women also make up a whopping 69 percent of the "discouraged labor force" (that is, people who need jobs but don't get counted in the unemployment statistics because they've given up looking), plus an official female unemployment rate that is substantially higher than men's, it's clear that we could expand to become fully half of the national work force by 1990.

Faced with this determination of women to find a little independence and to be paid and honored for our work, experts have rushed to ask: "Why?" It's a question rarely directed at male workers. Their basic motivations of survival and personal satisfaction are taken for granted. Indeed, men are regarded as "odd" and therefore subjects for sociological study and journalistic reports only when they *don't* have work, even if they are rich and don't need jobs or are poor and can't find them. Nonetheless, pollsters and sociologists have gone to great expense to prove that women work outside the home because of dire financial need, or if we persist despite the presence of a wage-earning male, out of some desire to buy "little extras" for our families, or even out of good old-fashioned penis envy.

Job interviewers and even our own families may still ask salaried women the big "Why?" If we have small children at home or are in some job regarded as "men's work," the incidence of such questions increases. Condescending or accusatory versions of "What's a nice girl like you doing in a place like this?" have not disappeared from the workplace.

How do we answer these assumptions that we are "working" out of some pressing or peculiar need? Do we feel okay about arguing that it's as natural for us to have salaried jobs as for our husbands—whether or not we have young children at home? Can we enjoy strong career ambitions without worrying about being thought "unfeminine"? When we confront men's growing resentment of women competing in the work force (often in the form of such guilt-producing accusations as "You're taking men's jobs away" or "You're damaging your children"), do we simply state that a decent job is a basic human right for everybody?

I'm afraid the answer is often no. As individuals and as a movement, we tend to retreat into some version of a tactically questionable defense: "Womenworkbecausewehaveto." The phrase has become one word, one key on the typewriter—an economic form of the socially "feminine" stance of passivity and self-sacrifice. Under attack, we still tend to present ourselves as creatures of economic necessity and familial devotion. "Womenworkbecausewehaveto" has become the easiest thing to say.

Like most truisms, this one is easy to prove with statistics. Economic need *is* the most consistent work motive—for women as well as men. In 1976, for instance, 43 percent of all women in the paid-labor force were single, widowed, separated, or divorced, and working to support themselves and their dependents. An additional 21 percent were married to men who had earned less than ten thousand dollars in the previous year, the minimum then required to support a family of four. In fact, if you take men's pensions, stocks, real estate, and various forms of accumulated wealth into account, a good statistical case can be made that there are more women who "have" to work (that is, who have neither the accumulated wealth, nor husbands whose work or wealth can support them for the rest of their lives) than there are men with the same need. If we were going to ask one group "Do you really need this job?" we should ask men.

But the first weakness of the whole "have to work" defense is its deceptiveness. Anyone who has ever experienced dehumanized life on welfare or any other confidence-shaking dependency knows that a paid job may be preferable to the dole, even when the handout is coming from a family member. Yet the will and self-confidence to work on one's own can diminish as dependency and fear increase. That may explain why—contrary to the "have to" rationale— wives of men who earn less than three thousand dollars a year are actually *less* likely to be employed than wives whose husbands make ten thousand dollars a year or more.

Furthermore, the greatest proportion of employed wives is found among families with a total household income of twenty-five to fifty thousand dollars a year. This is the statistical underpinning used by some sociologists to prove that women's work is mainly important for boosting families into the middle or upper middle class. Thus, women's incomes are largely used for buying "luxuries" and "little extras": a neat double-whammy that renders us secondary within our families, and makes our jobs expendable in hard times. We may even go along with this interpretation (at least, up to the point of getting fired so a male can have our job). It preserves a husbandly ego-need to be seen as the primary breadwinner, and still allows us a safe "feminine" excuse for working.

But there are often rewards that we're not confessing. As noted in *The Two-Career Couple,* by Francine and Douglas Hall: "Women who hold jobs by choice, even blue-collar routine jobs, are more satisfied with their lives than are the full-time housewives."

In addition to personal satisfaction, there is also society's need for all its members' talents. Suppose that jobs were given out on only a "have to work" basis to both women and men—one job per household. It would be unthinkable to lose the unique abilities of, for instance, Eleanor Holmes Norton, the distinguished chair of the Equal Employment Opportunity Commission. But would we then be forced to question the important work of her husband, Edward Norton, who is also a distinguished lawyer? Since men earn more than twice as much as women on the average, the wife in most households would be more likely to give up her job. Does that mean the nation could do as well without millions of its nurses, teachers, and secretaries? Or that the rare man who earns less than his wife should give up his job?

It was this kind of waste of human talents on a society-wide scale that traumatized millions of unemployed or underemployed Americans during the

Depression. Then, a one-job-per-household rule seemed somewhat justified, yet the concept was used to displace women workers only, create intolerable dependencies, and waste female talent that the country needed. That Depression experience, plus the energy and example of women who were finally allowed to work during the manpower shortage created by World War II, led Congress to reinterpret the meaning of the country's full-employment goal in its Economic Act of 1946. Full employment was officially defined as "the employment of those who want to work, without regard to whether their employment is, by some definition, necessary. This goal applies equally to men and to women." Since bad economic times are again creating a resentment of employed women—as well as creating more need for women to be employed—we need such a goal more than ever. Women are again being caught in a tragic double bind: We are required to be strong and then punished for our strength.

Clearly, anything less than government and popular commitment to this 1946 definition of full employment will leave the less powerful groups, whoever they may be, in danger. Almost as important as the financial penalty paid by the powerless is the suffering that comes from being shut out of paid and recognized work. Without it, we lose much of our self-respect and our ability to prove that we are alive by making some difference in the world. That's just as true for the suburban woman as it is for the unemployed steel worker.

But it won't be easy to give up the passive defense of "weworkbecausewehaveto."

When a woman who is struggling to support her children and grandchildren on welfare sees her neighbor working as a waitress, even though that neighbor's husband has a job, she may feel resentful; and the waitress (of course, not the waitress's husband) may feel guilty. Yet unless we establish the obligation to provide a job for everyone who is willing and able to work, that welfare woman may herself be penalized by policies that give out only one public-service job per household. She and her daughter will have to make a painful and divisive decision about which of them gets that precious job, and the whole household will have to survive on only one salary.

A job as a human right is a principle that applies to men as well as women. But women have more cause to fight for it. The phenomenon of the "working woman" has been held responsible for everything from an increase in male impotence (which turned out, incidentally, to be attributable to medication for high blood pressure) to the rising cost of steak (which was due to high energy costs and beef import restrictions, not women's refusal to prepare the cheaper, slower-cooking cuts). Unless we see a job as part of every citizen's right to autonomy and personal fulfillment, we will continue to be vulnerable to someone else's idea of what "need" is, and whose "need" counts the most.

In many ways, women who do not have to work for simple survival, but who choose to do so nonetheless, are on the frontier of asserting this right for all women. Those with well-to-do husbands are dangerously easy for us to resent and put down. It's easier still to resent women from families of inherited wealth, even though men generally control and benefit from that wealth.

(There is no Rockefeller Sisters Fund, no J. P. Morgan & Daughters, and sons-in-law may be the ones who really sleep their way to power.) But to prevent a woman whose husband or father is wealthy from earning her own living, and from gaining the self-confidence that comes with that ability, is to keep her needful of that unearned power and less willing to disperse it. Moreover, it is to lose forever her unique talents.

Perhaps modern feminists have been guilty of a kind of reverse snobbism that keeps us from reaching out to the wives and daughters of wealthy men; yet it was exactly such women who refused the restrictions of class and financed the first wave of feminist revolution.

For most of us, however, "womenworkbecausewehaveto" is just true enough to be seductive as a personal defense.

If we use it without also staking out the larger human right to a job, however, we will never achieve that right. And we will always be subject to the false argument that independence for women is a luxury affordable only in good economic times. Alternatives to layoffs will not be explored, acceptable unemployment will always be used to frighten those with jobs into accepting low wages, and we will never remedy the real cost, both to families and to the country, of dependent women and a massive loss of talent.

Worst of all, we may never learn to find productive, honored work as a natural part of ourselves and as one of life's basic pleasures.

PART VII

Critiquing the Arts

The activity of art is based on the fact that a man receiving through his sense of hearing or sight another man's expression of feeling, is capable of experiencing the emotion which moved the man who expressed it.

LEO TOLSTOY

Exploring

31

Awareness of the Arts

Thomas Carlyle, one of the major nineteenth-century men of letters, once wrote that "the tragedy of life is not so much what men suffer, but rather what they miss." Unfortunately, what seems so often missing from our twentieth-century world is an appreciation of the arts. In a technological age where value seems determined by what can be measured and weighed or bought and sold, the intangible, the imaginative, the dreamlike, or what exists solely because of its beauty seems at best of secondary importance. But psychologist Carl Jung has pointed out that our overemphasis on rationality has resulted in a dangerous moral and spiritual disintegration.

It may sound odd at first to insist that feelings need to be developed and educated with as much attention as we give to the mind. Yet training that focuses exclusively on analysis of objective facts and on logic is training that educates the intellect while leaving emotional and moral development in a primitive state, rather like an athlete who concentrates his attention on developing a single set of muscles, his biceps, perhaps, until they bulge and ripple—all in grotesque proportion to the rest of his body. Through much of this book we have been exercising our perception in objective ways, attempting to hold back private emotions, to eliminate personal feelings. In dealing with fact and reason, that is the only way probable truth can be found. But there are other kinds of truths.

THE EDUCATION OF EMOTION

Over 300 years ago, Pascal wrote that "the heart has its reasons which reason cannot know." Most of us live most of our lives in a world dominated by emotion that we seldom understand: we fall in love, we pursue each other sexually, we hate, we are horrified by the evil we think we detect in others, we admire the nobleness in some, we weep at loss, and we celebrate—sometimes just because we are alive. It is exactly this chaos of emotion that logic teaches us to avoid. By contrast, the artist attempts to deal with it, not by avoiding it, but by giving it shape and form. All art is primarily an expression of feelings structured according to the private vision of the artist. This ordering of feeling is the key to the way art educates our emotions.

If it is good art, we share the emotion; we experience it as real. We can even experience feelings we might never encounter in our lives: the tragic fall of a great man, the sacrifices of idealistic lovers. Through such experiences we expand our potential for human sympathy. But we also have the opportunity to stand back from the feelings expressed by the artist—as we seldom do from our personal emotions. This standing back allows us to contemplate both our experience and the form of the artist's vision. Because the mind finds meaning only in form, not in chaos, it is the shaping of art that allows us to interpret the experience, to uncover its significance, to question whether it reveals some important truth about human nature. Art, then, not only communicates emotion; it translates feelings into ordered patterns that help us understand emotion—and thus our humanness.

TRAINING PERCEPTION

As is true of all knowledge, our understanding and appreciation of the arts begin with sensory perception. Above all else, art is a concrete medium. Although it may sometimes express "ideas," it does so first through forms that reach out to our sight, hearing, or sense of touch. We listen to a rock band, but we also physically feel the beat of the music. We look at shadows and texture on a bronze sculpture by Henry Moore, but we also touch the sweep of motion with our hands. We read flat symbols on a page in a novel, but our imagination transforms them

 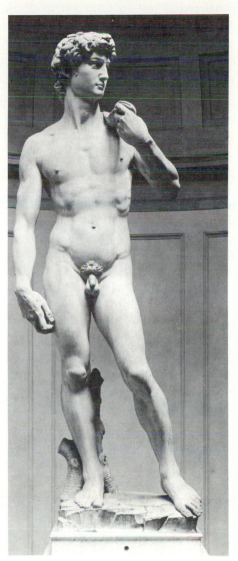

DONATELLO, <u>DAVID</u>. ALINARI/ART RESOURCE, NY　　　MICHELANGELO, <u>DAVID</u>. ALINARI/ART RESOURCE, NY

into visual images, sound images, smell images. In a novel like *The Red Badge of Courage*, Stephen Crane evokes every possible sense experience in order to involve us both physically and emotionally. Art *is* sensory experience.

　　Study the photos of the two famous works of sculpture above. You see them of course, but *what* do you see? Take your time. Slow down.

Both reach out to your sense of sight, but in different ways, for each artist has formed his material differently. Each is the product of an artist's interpretation of his experience and emotions—in one case, chiseled in stone, and in the other, cast in bronze. What do you see, and what different kinds of responses do you feel?

Here is how two students responded in their journals.

Student A

The statue on the right looks like a pretty athletic guy but the other one, to me, looks a little gay, it's probably by one of those fag artists who use tax dollars to promote gay rights. It turns my stomach if you want to know. The one on the right, however, has been working out and he looks ok.

Student B

My first reaction is to feel a little puzzled. I've seen pictures of Michelangelo's David before, and I think it probably distorts my reaction. He is probably beyond even the most ideal image of a man's body. Every muscular line is there, not overdone but perfectly carved. The face is serene, composed, confident, yet not arrogant, youthful but still masculine. His hands are incredibly large and heavy, weighted with power. The pose suggests great calmness and a lack of self-consciousness. He gazes into the future, to the next challenge. But Donatello's David is feminine. The hat (helmet?) looks like an Easter bonnet, the long curls flow over the *very* young boy's shoulders. The face has strength, but the lips are curved and full, like a girl's. In one sense the body is clearly pre-puberty: it lacks pubic hair, it's softer and less muscular, even though firm and beautiful in its own way. The pose is feminine, with one hip thrust out a little too much, the wrist curved in.

But he stands on the head of an angry Goliath. Sure. That's it. Donatello is showing us the young David, the shepherd boy who no one could expect to overcome a giant. He carries a sword almost as big as his body. It is the *contrast* that makes the point. Donatello is showing us a different kind of truth. David *was* an innocent young boy who played a lyre and tended sheep. He is the unexpected hero. He gazes down at what he's just done. He is absorbed in the act, not yet thinking about what is to come. On the other hand, Michelangelo's David is how we want our heroes to look. He is the god-like image we make of ourselves. He is the hero we created out of a young shepherd boy.

Student A fails to see anything with his senses and as a result he fails to feel or experience either work of art. He leaps to a conclusion based on an emotional reaction drawn from a stereotype rather than from the actual work in front of him. He expects art to come to him on his own terms. He expects it to match his preconceived images of—in this case—masculinity, and when the Donatello sculpture does not, he rejects it out of hand. But art does not necessarily confirm your own version of life. It may challenge you, defy you, even upset you. Good art almost always demands active involvement, an engagement of both intellect and imagination.

Student B has the advantage. She confesses that her first impression is confused, but she eventually becomes excited about both works of art because she sees details that lead her to understanding. She engages her perceptions fully, not just scanning the surface, but studying lines and forms of each figure. Various details *suggest* ways in which the art might be interpreted. By studying the "masculine" figure as well as the more "feminine" image, she recognizes that both may in fact be heroic. She does not limit her appreciation only to that which matches a Rambo-like stereotype of the hero. She explores each artist's vision in search of new aesthetic pleasure, new knowledge. She has perceived that it is the small details in art that communicate, and from the way the details are shaped and formed, she arrives at an interpretation.

FROM THE LITERAL TO THE SUGGESTIVE

All works of art begin with a literal, sensory experience. The first step in developing an increased appreciation of the arts is to become *sensi*tive to the actual picture or sound or shape the artist has created. The sense experience evokes our physical emotions. This is where feeling begins.

But a good work of art, through any number of techniques, may also suggest something larger than itself—may suggest something more than the literal sense experience. Doryphoros is literally a stone figure of man. It may suggest to us certain "heroic" or "godlike" qualities. No sign on the pedestal tells us we should see these attributes. We infer them from the shape of the stone. To put it another way, the details of the carving can be thought of as similar to the "facts" you have been searching for in other types of writing. From the facts you *infer* certain conclusions. The process of interpretation from objective facts or from artistic forms is almost identical, except that in art the forms may be ambiguous, and you may need to be more open-minded to various levels of suggestiveness.

Study the following poem by William Stafford. What do you see in it literally? What is the actual sense picture the poet draws for us in words? What type of feelings do the images evoke? And do any qualities of the poem suggest anything beyond the literal? Again, slow down. Take your time.

Traveling Through the Dark

Traveling through the dark I found a deer
dead on the edge of the Wilson River road.
It is usually best to roll them into the canyon:
that road is narrow; to swerve might make more dead.

By glow of the tail-light I stumbled back of the car
and stood by the heap, a doe, a recent killing;
she had stiffened already, almost cold.
I dragged her off; she was large in the belly.

My fingers touching her side brought me the reason—
her side was warm; her fawn lay there waiting,
alive, still, never to be born.
Beside that mountain road I hesitated.

The car aimed ahead its lowered parking lights;
under the hood purred the steady engine.
I stood in the glare of the warm exhaust turning red;
around our group I could hear the wilderness listen.

I thought hard for us all—my only swerving—
then pushed her over the edge into the river.

Here are two responses from student journals.

Student A

This poem doesn't seem to have much meaning. I don't get much out of it except that the deer got hit by his car and he threw it into the river, probably so the game warden wouldn't find it because it is against the law to kill a deer except during hunting season. The guy is probably afraid he will have to go to jail or pay a fine, and the people with him tell him to just hide it. I like poems that deal with emotion. This one just seems to tell a story.

Student B

It describes a scene where he has found a dead deer on a narrow river road. He stops his car and in the light from the tail lights he discovers that the deer is pregnant. By touching the doe's stomach, he can feel the live fawn inside but knows that it will never be born. For a moment he hesitates but knows that if he doesn't push the deer off the road into the river, another car might swerve to miss it and plunge into the river, killing the people. After thinking about all involved, he chooses human life and pushes the deer off the edge of the road.

So much is happening here that I don't know where to begin. It's like two kinds of death and two kinds of life are being considered. "I thought hard for us all—" he says. The doe is dead, but the fawn is alive. Life *inside* death. But someone else driving along the road might be killed. The wilderness listens for his answer. What kind of life will he choose? The pain is enormous, like why do you have to choose at all? Maybe the title sums it all up. He has been traveling through the dark on the side of the mountain. Also in a different way through his whole life. Now he is confronted with a choice that seems terrible to him, but he makes the choice—human life over animal life. The poem leaves me with an empty feeling, as if such choices should not have to be made.

Student A has found little of value in "Traveling Through the Dark" because he fails to see the literal image for what it is. He believes the car in the poem has struck the deer, but the first line clearly says that the speaker "found" a deer on the road. Later the student asserts that other people are with the speaker in the poem, but no such people exist.

The student even ignores or misses a central point: The doe contains a living fawn. Like the first student who observed the photos of sculpture, Student A has only scanned the surface. Because he sees no details, he sees nothing of significance and finds himself forced to "invent" a meaning. He speculates that the speaker in the poem may be avoiding the law to escape paying a fine. But the law is never mentioned in the poem, and the student offers no evidence that might support such an interpretation. This is not inference from fact, nor interpretation from sense details. It is guesswork. The result can only lead Student A to decide the poem lacks emotion. He has not worked from the literal to the suggestive. He has invented a poem and then invented an interpretation. No wonder he finds no feeling in it.

Student B, however, describes in detail the visual images, sound images, and touch images he sees in each line. He identifies the dilemma that actually exists by quoting the line, "I thought hard for us all." Having read the literal poem, the student goes on to contemplate the various ideas it suggests to him. First, he considers the paradox of life-in-death; second, he observes that we travel through life in darkness until confronted by such paradoxes; third, he questions why we should be faced with such choices at all. Throughout his comments, Student B continues to keep in mind the emotions stirred by such problems: pain, emptiness, terrible choices. Student B looks at the actual ordering of images, considers the feelings and questions they evoke, and allows the details to suggest several levels of significance we might find in the work.

THE HUMANISTIC HERITAGE

In both of these examples—responses to sculpture and poetry—the students who failed to exert effort, who failed to look and thus failed to feel, are left exactly where they began. They may be intelligent, but their intelligence remains limited to obvious surfaces. They do not question; they do not grow. Their lives are unchanged. They remain content to hibernate in their familiar caves, preferring only those experiences to which they are already accustomed and that demand nothing of their imagination.

The students who slowed down and looked intently at sense details, however, and who then allowed the details to suggest qualities of experience and emotion, found themselves contemplating aspects of human nature in terms that expanded their consciousness of life itself. The artist's vision presented them with a context for raising questions of values: Is it truth? Does it clarify an aspect of the human condition?

CHAGALL, <u>SELF-PORTRAIT WITH SEVEN FINGERS</u>. FOTO MARBURG/
ART RESOURCE, NY

Does it show the consequence of human choice and behavior? Do we
know more about ourselves than we did before? For these students,
intelligence and emotion interact. Through art, they discover a unity
between knowledge of fact and feeling about the fact. They participate
in the education of the whole person, not just the mind. As a result,
they find themselves linked to a great humanistic heritage, no longer
limited to an isolated narrow world of here and now, but joined in spirit
to ever-enlarging circles of human experience. Here is how Leo Tolstoy
expressed it.

> Art is a human activity consisting in this, that one man consciously
> by means of certain eternal signs, hands on to others feelings he has
> lived through, and that others are infected by these feelings and also
> experience them . . . it is a means of union among men joining them
> together in the same feelings, and indispensable for the life and
> progress towards well-being of individuals and of humanity.

The development of artistic appreciation begins then (as we began this
book and as we have begun each new unit) by urging you to seek out
the concrete details, the shapes and forms that they take, and by letting
them suggest to you both feelings and ideas.

INGRES, <u>NAPOLEON AS EMPEROR</u>. JOSSE/ART RESOURCE, NY

Journal Practice

1. Study the nineteenth-century portrait of Napoleon as Emperor of France on page 406. In your journal jot down your first general response and impression of the painting. Next, search out details, listing them in your journal. Look at each detail as closely as you would if you were going to write a character sketch. Study the various lines and suggested movements in the painting, the pose of the figure, the expressions of the face. Consider the staffs, the type of crown, the royal regalia, even the carpet. What is the artist trying to suggest about the emperor's character? Is the artist trying to associate Napoleon with any other historic figure? Could Napoleon ever have truly looked like this? Why not present us with a simple photographic likeness? After studying the details, what do you now know that expands or changes your first impression?

2. Following the same process, study Marc Chagall's "Self-Portrait with Seven Fingers" on page 405. Record initial thoughts and feelings in your notebook. Next, study the painting closely, recording the details and exaggerations you perceive: lines, shapes, facial expressions, posture, dress. Count the fingers. Consider the images in the background. When you've completed your study, explore thoughts and feelings about the painting in your journal. If the work seems distorted, can you suggest any reasons for it? What might the artist be trying to suggest about himself or about artists in general? What is more important here, the vision of the painter or the actual likeness of his self-portrait?

3. Compare the two portraits. What can you learn about two different visions of the world?

4. Here is a well-known poem by Ezra Pound. The simplicity of it may be deceiving. Read it slowly.

The River-Merchant's Wife: A Letter

While my hair was still cut straight across my forehead
I played about the front gate, pulling flowers.
You came by on bamboo stilts, playing horse,
You walked about my seat, playing with blue plums.
And we went on living in the village of Chokan:
Two small people, without dislike or suspicion.

At fourteen I married My Lord you.
I never laughed, being bashful.

Ezra Pound, *Personae*. Copyright 1926 by Ezra Pound. Reprinted by permission of New Directions.

Lowering my head, I looked at the wall.
Called to, a thousand times, I never looked back.

At fifteen I stopped scowling.
I desired my dust to be mingled with yours
Forever and forever and forever.
Why should I climb the look out?

At sixteen you departed,
You went into far Ku-to-yen, by the river of swirling eddies;
And you have been gone five months.
The monkeys make sorrowful noise overhead.

You dragged your feet when you went out.
By the gate now, the moss is grown, the different mosses,
Too deep to clear them away!
The leaves fall early this autumn, in wind.
The paired butterflies are already yellow with August
Over the grass in the West garden;
They hurt me. I grow older.
If you are coming down through the narrows of the river Kiang,
Please let me know beforehand,
And I will come out to meet you
      As far as Cho-fu-Sa.

In a few sentences record your initial response—what you think and feel on a first reading—in your journal. Don't try to be profound. Write simply and honestly.

Now copy the poem. Remember copying is a way of getting inside the words. It can sharpen your perception. When you've finished copying, check a dictionary for words and names you are unsure of. Then write about the literal scene, the images you respond to. Consider how the various sensory images build toward and contribute to the feeling achieved by the end. Describe that feeling. What ideas and values are suggested by the poem?

5. Telling stories is one of the most natural things people do. Stories can be as long as *War and Peace* or as short as a few paragraphs. Here's a short one by Ann Beattie that may at first surprise you with its brevity and simplicity.

Snow

Ann Beattie

I remember the cold night you brought in a pile of logs and a chipmunk
jumped off as you lowered your arms. "What do you think *you're* doing in
here?" you said, as it ran through the living room. It went through the library and stopped at the front door as though it knew the house well. This
would be difficult for anyone to believe, except perhaps as the subject of a
poem. Our first week in the house was spent scraping, finding some of the
house's secrets, like wallpaper underneath wallpaper. In the kitchen, a pattern of white-gold trellises supported purple grapes as big and round as Ping-
Pong balls. When we painted the walls yellow, I thought of the bits of grape
that remained underneath and imagined the vine popping through, the way
some plants can tenaciously push through anything. The day of the big
snow, when you had to shovel the walk and couldn't find your cap and
asked me how to wind a towel so that it would stay on your head—you, in
the white towel turban, like a crazy king of the snow. People liked the idea
of our being together, leaving the city for the country. So many people visited, and the fireplace made all of them want to tell amazing stories: the
child who happened to be standing on the right corner when the door of the
ice-cream truck came open and hundreds of Popsicles cascaded out; the man
standing on the beach, sand sparkling in the sun, one bit glinting more than
the rest, stooping to find a diamond ring. Did they talk about amazing things
because they thought we'd turn into one of them? Now I think they probably guessed it wouldn't work. It was as hopeless as giving a child a matched
cup and saucer. Remember the night, out on the lawn, knee-deep in snow,
chins pointed at the sky as the wind whirled down all that whiteness? It
seemed that the world had been turned upside down, and we were looking
into an enormous field of Queen Anne's lace. Later, headlights off, our car
was the first to ride through the newly fallen snow. The world outside the
car looked solarized.

You remember it differently. You remember that the cold settled in
stages, that a small curve of light was shaved from the moon night after
night, until you were no longer surprised the sky was black, that the chipmunk ran to hide in the dark, not simply to a door that led to its escape.
Our visitors told the same stories people always tell. One night, giving me a
lesson in storytelling, you said, "Any life will seem dramatic if you omit
mention of most of it."

This then, for drama: I drove back to that house not long ago. It was
April, and Allen had died. In spite of all the visitors, Allen, next door, had
been the good friend in bad times. I sat with his wife in their living room,

looking out the glass doors to the backyard, and there was Allen's pool, still covered with black plastic that had been stretched across it for winter. It had rained, and as the rain fell, the cover collected more and more water until it finally spilled onto the concrete. When I left that day, I drove past what had been our house. Three or four crocus were blooming in the front—just a few dots of white, no field of snow. I felt embarrassed for them. They couldn't compete.

This is a story, told the way you say stories should be told: Somebody grew up, fell in love, and spent a winter with her lover in the country. This, of course, is the barest outline, and futile to discuss. It's as pointless as throwing birdseed on the ground while snow still falls fast. Who expects small things to survive when even the largest get lost? People forget years and remember moments. Seconds and symbols are left to sum things up: the black shroud over the pool. Love, in its shortest form, becomes a word. What I remember about all that time is one winter. The snow. Even now, saying "snow," my lips move so that they kiss the air.

No mention has been made of the snowplow that seemed always to be there, scraping snow off our narrow road—an artery cleared, though neither of us could have said where the heart was.

a. Why does this story present only "moments" instead of a traditional narrative that might explain who the characters are, why they fell in love, and why they fell out of love?

b. Why does the author give two versions of the "story" in the first two paragraphs?

c. Since Allen seems to have had only a minor role in the lovers' story, why is a whole paragraph devoted to visiting his widow?

d. How does the imagery of the snow change and how might it suggest something about the relationship of the lovers?

e. Why doesn't the author tell us directly what the meaning of her experience was, rather than trying to evoke our emotions through sensory details?

Play

You are in the local bookstore rummaging through a pile of books on the after-Christmas sale table. You find the usual stuff—an already outdated Audubon calendar, *Jane Fonda's Workout Book*, several copies of *All I Really Need To Know I Learned in Kindergarten*, and *101 Uses for a Dead Cat*. But there, beneath a Tibetan cookbook, is a work you've been hearing a lot about, *If On a Winter's Night a Traveler*, by an Italian author. You take it to the counter, pay for it, and leave. At home, you settle down in your favorite chair, eager to read. You turn the pages almost lovingly—first the frontispiece, then the title page. You can hardly believe what you see. The name printed beneath the title is not that of an Italian author, but your own. Your breath quickens. You begin to tremble. How could your own work have been published without your knowing it? You can't even remember writing a novel. You tell yourself you're being duped by a friend or by your most desperate mother. You become angry, then calm again. You spend the entire night sitting up under a dull light, exhausted but exhilarated, reading your own story.

Write out the first chapter now in your journal. Let it flow. There are no rules. Just write what you see happening in your imagination. Begin with, "If on a winter's night a traveler. . . ."

Exploring

32

Literary Significance

There is creative writing, and there is creative reading.

RALPH WALDO EMERSON

As a sophomore in college I enrolled in a Victorian literature class. I was fascinated by my professor's enthusiasm for poetry and equally enthralled by his gymnastics. I remember how he once climbed upon a windowsill and sat precariously balanced, waving one arm and reading poems by Christina Rossetti. On another occasion he bounded up the center stairs of the classroom, reciting and acting out "The Charge of the Light Brigade." But the day I remember most clearly is the day I decided not to become an English major.

I had spent the night before looking over poems by Gerard Manley Hopkins. Although none of them made much sense to me, I pushed my way through half a dozen and went to class confident I had fulfilled the assignment. Then the lecture began. My professor perched himself cross-legged on a table and announced, quite to my discomfort, that the sweeping flight of a bird in Hopkins's "Windhover" was a symbol for Christ.

Image by image, line by line, he worked his way happily through the poem pointing out metaphors, subtle connotations, and historical allusions. By the end of the hour his face was red and puffed with pleasure while I sat crushed by my own inadequacies. I had seen no Christ symbol. Indeed, I wasn't even sure I had seen a bird. It was obvious that others "saw things" in poetry that I didn't.

Not until I began graduate studies seven years later did I return to English literature, knowing then that what had happened to me was not all that unusual with students. I had looked at Hopkins's poems, all right, but I had not really read—not for significance and insight. I had skimmed hurriedly in much the same way one glances through a newspaper, looking for information, willing to be entertained if that should happen, hoping the "meaning" would leap out at me. Admittedly I felt puzzled by strange language and odd sentences, but not so much that I was willing to reread. I had not even looked up in a dictionary the term *windhover*. How could I have known the poem was about a bird if I didn't know the title named the bird? Nor had I paid attention to the dedication, *To Christ Our Lord*, printed in bold italics directly under the title. After all, who reads dedications? The fact was I hadn't read at all.

The process of critical reading outlined earlier in Chapter 29 should give you the advantage over me. The strategy of reading described there is similar to the one you must use in reading for more than surface effects. Because a poem or novel or play may deal with so many complex levels (with emotion, fantasy, reality, myth, and alas yes, with symbols), we cannot outline the same straightforward steps we used for reading prose essays. Each work of art is unique, and each may present us with new demands. But we can illustrate a similar approach that at least introduces the essential concept of reading with an engaged imagination.

THE FIRST READING

Almost all art forms, and especially literary forms, must be experienced more than once. You should not expect to appreciate fully a poem or play or even a novel the first time you read it. A poem must be read many times. A play should be read at least twice, with parts of it several more times. And although a novel may be too long or your time too limited to read twice through, key sections will often require rereading. There is no escape from this fact: Art demands your participation, your committed involvement. Because art forms are often subtle or ambiguous, because they often work on more than one level of understanding, because indeed they are often obscure, you must be willing to *study* the work. The most serious mistake young people make about art is to believe it does not require at least as much study and attention as a good problem in geometry.

Here are nine primary steps to serious reading.

1. Read slowly. If you roller-skate through an art museum you won't see the paintings. Literature must be read at a slower pace than other forms of writing. Do not "speed-read" or skim. An author uses words as his or her basic tools. Every word counts for the author, as every color and line are meaningful for the painter. To feel the full effect, you must be conscious of words themselves; you must allow sounds, images, and connotations to set up reverberations. If you have been trained to look only for facts, you must slow down and be willing to experience feelings.

2. Read with pen in hand. Underline key phrases, key speeches by major figures, key statements by the narrator. Take notes on ideas or questions (do not trust your memory). Circle words used in special ways or repeated in significant patterns. Look up in the dictionary words you do not know or words you think you know but that seem to have special weight or placement—the author may be using them in new ways. *You cannot expect to understand literature if you do not know the meaning of the words.*

3. Be willing to read aloud. Words have sounds and sound is a sensory experience. Poetry, especially, needs to be listened to as well as read. Drama is by its nature a spoken medium. Even key passages from novels may become clear only when read aloud. James Joyce's *Finnegans Wake*, for example, looks like nonsense on the page; yet when listened to, its words become transformed into a hilarious, sensuous, flowing Irish brogue.

4. Begin each new novel, play, or poem without predetermined bias. If you decide in advance that all good art uses realistic settings and promotes your personal moral values, you close out the possibility of new experience. You do not have to, nor should you, enjoy every work of literature you read. But you should be willing to recognize that the imagination is limitless. No matter how comfortable you may be with certain traditional forms and ideas, a new form or experiment in writing may offer you as much or more imaginative pleasure than the old. A first reading is almost never the time to pronounce final judgment.

5. Ask silent questions of the material as you read. Do not read passively, waiting to be told the "meaning." Most authors will seldom pronounce a moral. Even if they do, a work of literature

is always more than its theme. Use the questions devised by reporters: *Who, What, Where, When, Why,* and *How.* You should usually be able to answer the first four questions after one reading—they form the surface of the work. *Why* and *How* may take more study—such questions probe the inner levels.

6. Look for those qualities that professional writers look for in real life: *conflict, contrast, contradiction,* and *characterization.* Most fiction and drama are built around one or all of these elements. Poetry, too, may use such devices, but in more subtle ways.

7. Keep a reading journal. Record first impressions, explore relationships, ask questions, write down quotations, copy whole passages that are difficult or aesthetically pleasing.

8. Look for rhythm, repetition, and pattern. Successful works of literature incorporate such structural devices in the language, in the dialogue, in the plot, in the characterization, and elsewhere. Pattern is form, and form is the shaping the artist gives to his or her experience. If you can identify the pattern and relate it to the content, you'll be on your way to insight.

9. Finally, do not force an interpretation. Because of the Western world's tradition of "interpreting" art, we often feel pressured to find instantaneous meaning: We search desperately for moralistic tags or simplistic messages or profound symbols. The truth is that a good work of literature comes to us by indirection, implication, suggestion, and feeling. The good author finds life too rich and complex for simplistic "messages." The good reader will wait patiently for understanding to grow out of various readings and rereadings. Keeping a reading notebook will help you explore the work and discover ideas.

The first reading must be thoughtful, but you must resist the temptation to plunge ahead with analysis. Read for the total feeling; read for an understanding of the work as a whole, before you return for more in-depth considerations.

Here is a very short story by Sherwood Anderson on which you might try applying some of these nine basic steps.

The Book of the Grotesque

Sherwood Anderson

The writer, an old man with a white mustache, had some difficulty in getting into bed. The windows of the house in which he lived were high and he wanted to look at the trees when he awoke in the morning. A carpenter came to fix the bed so that it would be on a level with the window.

Quite a fuss was made about the matter. The carpenter, who had been a soldier in the Civil War, came into the writer's room and sat down to talk of building a platform for the purpose of raising the bed. The writer had cigars lying about and the carpenter smoked.

For a time the two men talked of the raising of the bed and then they talked of other things. The soldier got on the subject of the war. The writer, in fact, led him to that subject. The carpenter had once been a prisoner in Andersonville prison and had lost a brother. The brother had died of starvation, and whenever the carpenter got upon that subject he cried. He, like the old writer, had a white mustache, and when he cried he puckered up his lips and the mustache bobbed up and down. The weeping old man with the cigar in his mouth was ludicrous. The plan the writer had for the raising of his bed was forgotten and later the carpenter did it in his own way and the writer, who was past sixty, had to help himself with a chair when he went to bed at night.

In his bed the writer rolled over on his side and lay quite still. For years he had been beset with notions concerning his heart. He was a hard smoker and his heart fluttered. The idea had got into his mind that he would some time die unexpectedly and always when he got into bed he thought of that. It did not alarm him. The effect in fact was quite a special thing and not easily explained. It made him more alive, there in bed, than at any other time. Perfectly still he lay and his body was old and not of much use any more, but something inside him was altogether young. He was like a pregnant woman, only that the thing inside him was not a baby but a youth. No, it wasn't a youth, it was a woman, young, and wearing a coat of mail like a knight. It is absurd, you see, to try to tell what was inside the old writer as he lay on his high bed and listened to the fluttering of his heart. The thing to get at is what the writer, or the young thing within the writer, was thinking about.

The old writer, like all of the people in the world, had got, during his long life, a great many notions in his head. He had once been quite handsome and a number of women had been in love with him. And then, of course, he had known people, many people, known them in a peculiarly intimate way that was different from the way in which you and I know people.

At least that is what the writer thought and the thought pleased him. Why quarrel with an old man concerning his thoughts?

In the bed the writer had a dream that was not a dream. As he grew somewhat sleepy but was still conscious, figures began to appear before his eyes. He imagined the young indescribable thing within himself was driving a long procession of figures before his eyes.

You see the interest in all this lies in the figures that went before the eyes of the writer. They were all grotesques. All of the men and women the writer had ever known had become grotesques.

The grotesques were not all horrible. Some were amusing, some almost beautiful, and one, a woman all drawn out of shape, hurt the old man by her grotesqueness. When she passed he made a noise like a small dog whimpering. Had you come into the room you might have supposed the old man had unpleasant dreams or perhaps indigestion.

For an hour the procession of grotesques passed before the eyes of the old man, and then, although it was a painful thing to do, he crept out of bed and began to write. Some one of the grotesques had made a deep impression on his mind and he wanted to describe it.

At his desk the writer worked for an hour. In the end he wrote a book which he called "The Book of the Grotesque." It was never published, but I saw it once and it made an indelible impression on my mind. The book had one central thought that is very strange and has always remained with me. By remembering it I have been able to understand many people and things that I was never able to understand before. The thought was involved but a simple statement of it would be something like this:

That in the beginning when the world was young there were a great many thoughts but no such thing as a truth. Man made the truths himself and each truth was a composite of a great many vague thoughts. All about in the world were the truths and they were all beautiful.

The old man had listed hundreds of the truths in his book. I will not try to tell you of all of them. There was the truth of virginity and the truth of passion, the truth of wealth and of poverty, of thrift and of profligacy, of carelessness and abandon. Hundreds and hundreds were the truths and they were all beautiful.

And then the people came along. Each as he appeared snatched up one of the truths and some who were quite strong snatched up a dozen of them.

It was the truths that made the people grotesques. The old man had quite an elaborate theory concerning the matter. It was his notion that the moment one of the people took one of the truths to himself, called it his truth, and tried to live his life by it, he became a grotesque and the truth he embraced became a falsehood.

You can see for yourself how the old man, who had spent all of his life writing and was filled with words, would write hundreds of pages concerning this matter. The subject would become so big in his mind that he himself would be in danger of becoming a grotesque. He didn't, I suppose, for the same reason that he never published the book. It was the young thing inside him that saved the old man.

Concerning the old carpenter who fixed the bed for the writer, I only mentioned him because he, like many of what are called very common people, became the nearest thing to what is understandable and lovable of all the grotesques in the writer's book.

BEGINNING WITH THE LITERAL

If you're like most of us, you've probably read Anderson's story too quickly. I point no finger of guilt here because in searching for a story to print as an example, I, too, read it hurriedly. "Ah," I said to myself, "here's a short, simple story with few complications. Just the thing for a brief example." Had you asked me about the story after my first reading, I probably would have said something like, "Well, it's about an old man who sees everyone as grotesque." But I would have felt uncomfortable in my answer. Something about my first reading left an ache about the old man, about something lost and something gained. Vague feelings I could not identify. My summary-type statement about the story would have seemed strangely inadequate for the feelings it aroused in me. Was there more to it than I had noticed? Had I really understood it at all? I began asking questions of myself, trying not to make hasty interpretations or judgments, but to *see* the literal level of the story.

Who	Who is the main character? The old man or the narrator? What is the role of the carpenter? What qualities about characterizing does Anderson use: physical details? actions? speech? background? others' responses? a self-created environment? And which are important in this particular story?
What	What actually happens in the story? Is there anything that could be called a plot? Is there a turning point or crisis? Any real conflict within the old man? With others? Any contrast between beliefs and actions? Is there a key scene where the action seems most revealing or important?
Where	Where does the story take place? A large city? A small town? Can we tell? Is it important? Does the old man's bedroom have any significance?
When	Do we know the time period in which the events occur? Should we ask when this particular event occurs during the old man's life? Would it make a difference?

Why	In some works, like *Hamlet*, the question "why" may be the central focus of the story: Why does Hamlet delay in killing his uncle? Is there a "why" in Sherwood Anderson's story? Does it relate to the old man? Or to the narrator?
How	How is the work put together? It may be too soon to answer this question. A second reading will probably be necessary to consider how each of the main elements relate—narrator, characters, plot, language, sense details, and so on.

Did I really ask myself such questions? Yes and no. Even after years of experience at reading literature, the questions hover in the back of my mind, although most of them have become more intuitive than conscious. For the beginning student, however, it seems to me that these questions do need to be consciously considered. Many will be rejected as inapplicable to any one particular work, but those that suggest possibilities must be followed up. And if you do not consciously work with such questions, chances are you'll forget some, perhaps the very ones that might have been most important.

The point is to understand the literal story. It makes no sense to pursue a "deeper" meaning if you haven't understood the surface. In Chapter 29, I encouraged you to write a brief summary after reading an essay. You may want to perform a similar act after reading a literary work. A poem, especially, cannot be dealt with intelligibly until you have understood its literal level. Writing a paraphrase—a type of summary in which you rephrase the sense of the work in your own words, not just generalizing from the whole, but holding fairly close to an image-by-image or stanza-by-stanza rewriting—is one of the oldest and most useful techniques for aiding comprehension. Ben Franklin, for example, taught himself to be a better writer by copying and then paraphrasing the thoughts of others.

You must remember, of course, that a paraphrase is not the poem or story. Your rephrasing only helps you understand the surface of the work. Many other levels must still be explored.

It's obviously time for a second reading. Let me urge you to turn back at this point and read "The Book of the Grotesque" one more time. If you didn't underline and take notes the first time, do so now, asking all the questions we've been considering.

CONTEMPLATING THE MAJOR ELEMENTS

The second reading is the real beginning of critical study. By the time you've finished a second reading of a poem you should have completed your paraphrase of it in your journal. A novel or short story is too long to consider writing a detailed paraphrase, but at the very least, you should have taken notes in the margins and in your notebook. Here is a reproduction of my own notes, exactly as I took them on my second reading of Anderson's story.

---

relationship {
Writer – old – young inside – "pregnant w/ (youth)"
carpenter — is he example of grotesque? How?
<u>Dream not a dream</u>? Key event?
  — the (young) in him drove grotesques before him
<u>Narrator's statement</u>
  — many thoughts, no truths
  — many made truths out of the thoughts
  — all were beautiful until adopted by
    individuals as their truths
  →) which <u>turned them into grotesques</u>
Writer in danger of becoming a grotesque
  — the (young) in him saves him
      ↳ 3rd tag of this idea
what is there about <u>the young</u> that saves the old man?
  — youth has innocence? No fixed truths?
  — open to experience?
<u>Relationship to truth</u> ??
  — are all truths beautiful until they
    become obsessions? My truth vs.
    your truth? Makes each of us
    grotesque

Your journal might look quite different. Yours might include webs, lists, definitions, questions, whole paragraphs detailing your observations, or even a whole paragraph copied word for word to catch the feeling and rhythms of the prose. You may have focused on different points or seen other important ideas that I missed. But from my notes you can tell that I was beginning to consider the major details. A scholar of literature might be sensitive to hundreds of different elements, but every beginning student should at least know the following.

Fiction

1. Almost all novels and short stories are written about characters, so *character* itself becomes the key quality to look for. Who is the major character? What is his or her basic quality: courage, innocence, pride, greed? Does the character change during the story? Is the character faced with conflict from external forces? From internal forces?

2. Who tells the story may be a key element in understanding both the character and the events. *Point of view* can come from the character's eyes, from a narrator, or from another character. Can you speculate on why the point of view would make any difference in the story?

3. Some fiction, but not all, has *plot.* A plot is more than just a series of events or actions; it also involves consideration of why such actions occur. What you need to consider most carefully is the relationship between the plot and the character. Does the character cause events to happen, or does the action bring about changes in the character?

Drama

1. Most plays are built around *character,* so the same basic element is our first consideration. But drama may also have specific types of characters that function in traditional ways. The main character is called a *protagonist.* A *foil* is a character who helps us understand the basic qualities of the main character, usually by exhibiting opposite traits.

2. As drama is constructed around the spoken voice, *dialogue* must be considered a prime element. Dialogue involves two or more speakers. In many plays, however, a character may talk aloud to himself in a *soliloquy.* The soliloquy tells us what the character is thinking about and may be a major clue to understanding ideas or actions expressed in the play.

3. Like fiction, plays usually have a plot, but the action or movement of drama is often formally divided into *acts* and *scenes.* The divisions may give insight into the way the author has shaped his

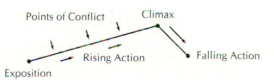

or her material. Even more important, many plays are traditionally built around a structure that moves from *exposition* (the situation at the opening), through *rising action* (a series of complications that increase tension) to the *climax* (a crucial moment for
the main character where his or her fate is often decided), and
a *falling action* (the final moments of the play where the new
situation is established as resolution to the drama).

Poetry

1. The poet has the widest range of options and, for that reason,
    may deserve the most concentrated attention. The most basic
    element of poetry is the language itself, the *words*. Every word
    counts. A good dictionary is mandatory. Both *denotation* and *con-
    notation* must be considered.
2. *Images* are the imaginative sense-pictures the poet creates with
    words. You must open yourself to seeing, hearing, touching, feel-
    ing, and tasting the images.
3. *Rhythms* of various kinds affect the experience of any one poem.
    A poet may use meter, the formal counting of stressed and un-
    stressed syllables; or the poet may achieve rhythm through such
    devices as parallel structure, line length, and even rhyme.
4. Most poets use *figurative language, metaphors, similes, analogies*, and
    symbols. In some way these elements may be the most difficult
    to analyze, but you must recognize that they are not exclusive
    to poetry and certainly nothing to be afraid of, for we use all of
    them every day in normal speech. A poet merely uses them with
    more precision and control.

A brief list like this cannot pretend to do justice to the many basic
elements, subtleties, and variations found in literature. Only a specialist
would recognize and appreciate them all. But you should be aware that
the artist does use such devices. Even though, on first reading, a good
story or poem may seem unified and indivisible, on a second or third
reading, with concentrated attention, you can begin to identify *how* the
writer has shaped such elements to form the total effect. Once you've
made that step, you are in a position to question how the parts relate.
In seeing relationships, you move toward the goal of serious reading:
an understanding or insight into the significance of the work.

MOVING TO THE SUGGESTIVE

After rereading, after questioning, after paraphrasing and recording
impressions in your journal, you should be ready to consider the work
on its suggestive levels. Indeed, by this point you've probably already

begun to interpret relationships and to see values in Sherwood Anderson's story that could not have been appreciated on the first reading. I, for one, was genuinely surprised at how much more complex and richly textured the story was than I first thought. After a second reading I could *not* say, "Here's a story about an old man who sees others as grotesque." Such a shallow response would be seriously inadequate.

How to see and interpret relationships, however, is not something that can be clearly illustrated in a text. A relationship is something that must be perceived inside your mind. It is an inner process for which we have no real mechanism of instruction. But we *can* identify two phases of the process that a good reader will work his or her way through when contemplating a work of art.

Searching for the Pattern

Even if the author provides a direct expression or generalized statement about the significance (as Anderson does), that expression or idea must be seen in relation to the characters, actions, and events. The reader must look for repetitions or variations of concepts, speeches, words, actions, feelings, or whatever. For example, you might consider why Anderson tags the word *young* three times in the story. Its repetition suggests that we should be considering its relationship to the "old" man and to his "truth." The story seems to center around those elements—hence we have the beginnings of a *pattern*. Only in looking at all the possible *connections* can you work toward an underlying significance.

Relating to the Emotion

All this effort will be wasted unless you can perceive a relationship of the parts to the whole, to the total experience of the work, and to the feelings it evokes. Students often complain that criticizing a poem or a story is destructive. And indeed, any critical approach that tears apart without joining together again may leave a negative impression. But the point of critical reading is not "to tear apart." When we read for significance, we study the details only to see their relationship to the whole. It is the total effect, *the feeling captured in form*, that we want to appreciate. The final step in serious reading, then, is to draw together all that we have seen and to consider its relationship to the human emotion the art expresses.

With a head full of feelings and ideas, a page full of notes, and a text underlined and marked, you're now ready to write. (You may even find that the relationships and questions explored in your reading journal have already presented you with a focused topic.) Only when you've engaged yourself in this type of thorough involvement with art can you expect to develop a written critique with any depth. The next chapter will discuss the actual job of getting it down on paper.

A SUMMARY OF BASIC STEPS IN READING FOR SIGNIFICANCE

Read Fiction, Drama, and Poetry More than Once
- Read first for the total experience of the work.
- Read slowly for the words, feelings, emotions, and ideas.
- Underline key passages, phrases, and words. Make marginal notes.
- Keep a reading notebook: copy, paraphrase, explore questions and ideas.
- Look up important words in the dictionary.
- In poetry and drama, especially, read aloud.
- Be open to new possibilities; do not reject that which cannot be understood instantly on first reading.

Ask Silent Questions
- Who, What, Where, When, Why, How?
- What is the conflict, contrast, contradiction?
- Is there a pattern? A design? A significant repetition?

Consider the Major Elements
- Study the character, his or her basic qualities, conflicts, and growth.
- Consider the actions, the movement, or plot.
- Always, always attend to the words themselves.

Contemplate the Relationships
- How do the parts relate to each other?
- How does the whole of it relate to the central feeling the work expresses?

Journal Practice

1. Read the following poem by Robert Hayden. Use the techniques discussed in this chapter. Read it once for the total impression, for the feeling. Then reread it aloud, slowly.

Those Winter Sundays

Sundays too my father got up early
and put his clothes on in the blueblack cold,
then with cracked hands that ached
from labor in the weekday weather made
banked fires blaze. No one ever thanked him.

I'd wake and hear the cold splintering, breaking.
When the rooms were warm, he'd call,
and slowly I would rise and dress,
fearing the chronic angers of that house,

Speaking indifferently to him,
who had driven out the cold
and polished my good shoes as well.
What did I know, what did I know
of love's austere and lonely offices?

Robert Hayden

a. Copy the poem thoughtfully in your reading journal, giving your full attention to each word, each image. Use a dictionary for any word you're unsure of. Consider both the denotation and connotation within the overall context.
b. Write a brief prose paraphrase (a retelling in your own words), moving almost line by line or stanza by stanza.
c. Consider some of the following questions.
    Which images (sensory pictures) in the poem contribute to its effect?
    What do you know about the speaker of the poem? About his feelings, his sensitivity, his present attitude, as well as his past experience?
    Is there any element of conflict in the poem? Is it important?
d. Now that you've studied the poem, can you draw together your various experiences with it? How would you describe the emotion the poet is trying to express? A poem does not need to have a "meaning" or a "moral." It may only communicate an experience. Which does this poem seem to present? What is its ultimate significance? Is it successful or does it fail? Consider the details

in the poem that would support your response to each of these
questions.

2. Here are two other poems you might want to read closely. Move
slowly through the steps that might apply to each poem. Do not rush
to judgment. Remember that it may take time for a poem to grow on
you.

A Blessing

Just off the highway to Rochester, Minnesota,
Twilight bounds softly forth on the grass.
And the eyes of those two Indian ponies
Darken with kindness.
They have come gladly out of the willows
To welcome my friend and me.
We step over the barbed wire into the pasture
Where they have been grazing all day, alone.
They ripple tensely, they can hardly contain their happiness
That we have come.
They bow shyly as wet swans. They love each other.
There is no loneliness like theirs.
At home once more,
They begin munching the young tufts of spring in the darkness.
I would like to hold the slenderer one in my arms,
For she has walked over to me
And nuzzled my left hand.
She is black and white,
Her mane falls wild on her forehead,
And the light breeze moves me to caress her long ear
That is delicate as the skin over a girl's wrist.
Suddenly I realize
That if I stepped out of my body I would break
Into blossom.

James Wright

in Just—

in Just—
spring   when the world is mud—
luscious the little
lame balloonman

whistles   far   and wee

and eddieandbill come
running from marbles and
piracies and it's
spring

when the world is puddle-wonderful

the queer
old balloonman whistles
far   and   wee
and bettyandisbel come dancing
from hop-scotch and jump-rope and

it's
spring
and
   the

      goat-footed

balloonMan   whistles
far
and
wee

e. e. cummings

3. The Parable of the Good Samaritan on page 428 is familiar to most readers. But consider it for its basic literary elements.

The Parable of the Good Samaritan

And Jesus said, A certain man went down from Jerusalem to Jericho, and fell among thieves, which stripped him of his raiment, and wounded him, and departed, leaving him half dead.

And by chance there came down a certain priest that way; and when he saw him, he passed by on the other side.

And likewise a Levite, when he was at the place, came and looked on him, and passed by on the other side.

But a certain Samaritan, as he journeyed, came where he was; and when he saw him, he had compassion on him,

And went to him, and bound up his wounds, pouring in oil and wine, and set him on his own beast, and brought him to an inn, and took care of him.

And on the morrow when he departed, he took out two pence, and gave them to the host, and said unto him, Take care of him: and whatsoever thou spendest more, when I come again, I will repay thee.

Which now of these three, thinkest thou, was neighbor unto him that fell among the thieves?

And he said, he that showed mercy on him. Then said Jesus unto him, Go, and do thou likewise.

New Testament, Luke 10:30–37.

a. Who is the major character?
b. What kind of conflict is involved?
c. Is there a pattern or repetition that helps suggest the theme or meaning of the parable? If you changed the story so that no repetition occurred, would it have the same meaning or impact?
d. If the story were told from a different point of view (from the Samaritan's or the victim's), what would be the effect on the overall meaning of the work?

Imitating

You've already learned that copying is one way you can help yourself become a better reader and writer. Now you're ready to go one step farther. Try deliberately imitating a passage by another author. Select a topic to write about that is completely different from the passage you're working with, but imitate the author's sentence structure, rhythms, and types of words. If the first sentence has ten words, you write approximately ten words. If the writer begins with a fragment, you begin with one, too. Match noun to noun, verb to verb, adjective to adjective—but let the rhythms carry you in new directions when your imagination is stimulated.

Writers imitate, not to write like someone else, but to discover all the possibilities open to them. Robert Louis Stevenson, Richard Yates, Somerset Maugham, and countless others have admitted this exercise helped them become better writers. Poet Dylan Thomas has told how he "wrote endless imitations . . . of anything [he] happened to be reading at the time: de Quincey, Blake, the Bible, Poe, Keats, Lawrence, and Shakespeare." Thomas confessed that it was "a mixed lot," but raised a question that any would-be writer must ask: "How can I learn the tricks of the trade unless I try to do them myself?"

You may not plan to become a professional writer, just as you may not plan to become a professional tennis player. But you can learn a lot about improving your forehand by imitating a tennis pro, and you can— with work and patience—improve your writing by imitating a successful author.

Here is the lead sentence from "The Magic Barrel," a short story by Bernard Malamud.

> Not long ago there lived in uptown New York, in a small, almost meager room, though crowded with books, Leo Finkle, a rabbinical student in Yeshiva University.

And here is how freshman Alice Reed imitated it.

> On the outskirts of Plain City, a small Mormon town just west of the Wasatch Mountains and nearly edging the great salt desert, lived Ordella Tippetts, a polygamist's wife who raised guineas and muscovy ducks.

Imitating is a way of freeing yourself to become the writer you want to be. You will become more proficient. As you play with language, you discover its structure and rhythms. You discover new words, and old words used in a new way. You absorb craft and technique, freeing yourself from safe monotonous patterns. You learn to take risks with language. By imitating, you teach yourself to write.

Try copying and then imitating any of the professional passages on pages 105–106 or 106–107.

Audience and Form

33

The Formal Critique

Until now I have discussed your audience as someone outside yourself, as a reader real or imagined, to whom you wanted to communicate. In studying art, however, you, too, form a part of the audience. First, you are audience to the creative work of someone else—to a symphony, a poem, a painting—before you are a writer about that work. Second, even though the paper you produce will be nominally addressed to a reader other than yourself, you'll find that during the actual process of writing, you continue to respond and react to the art. The writing process becomes a method of clarifying and discriminating for yourself, for your own understanding, not just for your imagined reader. In other words, writing about literature or music or art becomes in a genuine sense an exploration of your own experience, both emotional and intellectual. As the artist has given form to his or her feelings, so you must give form to yours, for your own benefit as well as the benefit of another reader.

THE OTHER READER

What does the audience for a formal critique want and expect? The concept of a *literary critique* does not include the notion of fixed form so much as the idea of a serious examination of a specific work of art, including an assessment of its value. The form is flexible, but your reader will expect more than just a "review," more than just a retelling of the plot. You'll be expected to use your analytical abilities to separate the work into its major components; to narrow your focus to the one or two elements you feel are most significant; and to look in detail at how they are constructed, how they relate, and how they work toward (or fail to work toward) the overall value of the work—toward the expression of feeling, meaning, significance, or whatever.

The best critique will not only analyze a portion of a work in some detail but will also communicate a sense of the feeling that a work imparts to a reader. For that reason it presents added complications. Your reader will probably expect you to use a personal voice yet retain an objective tone—that is, you must write in a natural way so that your feelings and human sympathies are not inhibited, but you must do so while scrutinizing the work with a critical eye. If you are too cold and analytical, you may lose the human feeling the art is primarily concerned with. If you become too personal, your own feelings may overshadow the story or poem. Keep this in mind: The experience and emotions you are to write about are the ones expressed by the art. If the art is successful, those feelings become your feelings, but the subject of your paper must be the play or the poem or the story—and how the artist has shaped his or her work in such a way that it evokes that feeling. The reader wants to know about the emotion rendered by the art, but the reader seldom cares whether the emotion reminds you of your grandfather or the time you visited Mississippi. This balancing act forces you to struggle with your feelings but to share them with the reader through an objective examination of the work itself.

THE CRITICAL PROCESS

Critical perception can be divided into four phases:

Description:	What do you see?
Analysis:	How is it put together?
Interpretation:	What does it mean?
Assessment:	What is its value or worth?

The four phases represent a logical progress you should follow, both in observing a work of art and in writing about it. First, look at the whole; then look more closely at the details; then interpret what you find; and, finally, form a judgment.

Many students mistakenly believe that if a story or a poem has been read by a class as a whole or even discussed in class, they need not guide the reader through each of these steps. Instead, they plunge immediately into analysis; or, worse, having completed the analysis in their minds, they plunge directly into interpretation. Even though the reader may have knowledge of the work being discussed, such abrupt leaps create a sense of disjointed confusion. You should not assume your reader has experienced the work as you have, even on the literal level. You have used your eyes; the reader has used his or hers. When studying a work of art and when writing about it, demand of yourself the discipline required to move the mind through each phase of the critical process.

THE FORMAL INTRODUCTION

The introduction to a formal critique must provide the reader with an essential overview before you consider the small details.

1. Name the author and the work.
2. Summarize the literal level—what the work is about as a whole.
3. Provide a focusing or narrowing of the subject. Describe or imply what specific element you plan to examine.
4. Give a general indication of the larger significance you plan to lead the reader toward.

Here is an example from a paper by Michelle Sheppard.

Provocative lead	His whole life had been a lie. Of all the characters John
Author and title	Ehle introduces in his novel *The Winter People*, only Gudger, the eldest son of the Wright clan, undergoes a complete
Student briefly summarizes the story as a whole	transformation. Set in the North Carolina mountains during the depression, *The Winter People* tells a story of the feuding Wright and Campbell clans in an atmosphere fraught with tension and mystery. The feud intensifies when Cole Campbell, father of Collie Wright's illegitimate son Jonathan, drowns in a creek on Collie's property. His
Begins to focus	death eventually brings about not only a truce between the clans but also Gudger's metamorphosis. In the beginning, Gudger sees himself as a bear: "A bear fights back. No lamb about him." But is he really strong and forceful, a
Subject narrows and significance suggested	power to be respected? Or is he a coward, a lamb in bear's clothing who does not know the truth about himself? And do these questions about Gudger suggest John Ehle's larger theme?

Although an introduction *can* be written without including a sentence that suggests the ultimate significance or judgment you plan to arrive at, by including it, you establish an element of interest at the beginning—you say, "Here, reader, is why this whole thing is important"—and you prepare the reader for your conclusion. In doing so, you will make the critique seem more unified and complete. Introductions often can't be written until you've completed your first draft. If you're like me, you'll need to explore ideas in a rough form before you can return and write a clear introduction of the kind I've presented here.

THE BODY OF THE CRITIQUE

Most of your essay should present a detailed analysis of the work or of the major elements of the work you have focused on. Each step of your discussion should repeat the analytic process:

1. *Describe* the specific element of the story or poem or play you plan to focus on. Use your own words to introduce your point; then provide a quotation, paraphrase, or description directly from the work.
2. *Analyze* that particular component. Show how the image works or what the character says or how the plot turns. This is the place for details.
3. *Interpret* your findings. Limit your interpretation to the single element you are dealing with, or show how it relates to other elements, but save your overall assessment for the end.

Repeat the three steps for each phase of the work you deal with: *describe, analyze, interpret.* Be sure to include quotations and examples from the work as evidence to support your ideas.

Here is Jim Havens, a freshman, writing about a long poem, "Stages on a Journey Westward," by James Wright. In his introduction, Jim has already narrowed his focus to the images in the poem that suggest death, and he has implied that the real subject of the poem is the dying of the American dream. In the body of his paper he looks in detail at each of the images.

| *Description of the literal level in student's own words* | In the first stage of Wright's work, he recalls the start of his trip westward by painting for the reader a scene of horses wandering into a barn to relax and eat. |

Reprinted by permission of James Havens.

Quotation to reinforce student's description

I began in Ohio
I still dream of home
Near Mansfield, enormous dobbins enter
    dark barns in autumn,
Where they can be lazy, where they can
    munch apples
Or sleep long.

Analysis begins—in this case by considering how individual words suggest a particular feeling.

But if we probe further in Wright's word choice, we discover a possible foreshadowing of death. A "dobbin" is a term that is used for old workhorses that are really no longer of use for labor, a horse that is ready for the glue factory. The use of the word *dark* itself suggests death. *Autumn* is the figurative season for dying. *Apples* are the biblical symbol that calls to mind the death of paradise for mortal man. Nothing at this point in the poem confirms this image of death. But as we move toward the next lines in the poem, the dark foreshadowing seems to continue.

Student admits that interpretation must await more evidence.

Description of literal level again: blend of paraphrase and quotation

Wright describes his memories of his father (or perhaps night dreams of his father) prowling, waiting in bread lines, wearing blue rags, leading a blind horse. He recalls how in 1932, "grimy with machinery," his father sang to him of a goosegirl while outside the house slag heaps were piled. In German folk tales the goosegirl was a Cinderella figure. Nineteen-thirty-two was the time of the Great Depression: poverty, hunger and degradation. The slag heap suggests the plight of the common worker. It was a pile of waste material that was separated during the smelting of iron. All of these negative images reinforce the foreshadowing of death we saw in the first lines. The suggestion is that the American dream of justice and individual dignity seemed to be coming to an end, as it surely must have seemed in 1932. Like the goosegirl story, the American dream was only a fairy tale.

Analysis of various images

Interpretation shows relationship of images to earlier points.

Transition; student will repeat same process for second stage of poem.

In the second stage of his journey, Wright moves further west, to Minnesota, where a series of new images build upon this theme of death. . . .

Jim Haven's interpretation might be disputed by another reader who saw no death images at all in the poem. But by demonstrating that a repetition (a pattern) of words and images suggests death or dying, Jim hopes to lead even the unconvinced reader to his conclusion. Does that mean his interpretation is "right" and someone else's is "wrong"? No. It means that an effective work of art may have several interpretations so long as each provides specific, concrete evidence from the work and so long as the overall context of the work supports it.

THE CONCLUSION

Because assessment is part of the critical process, you must arrive at a final judgment. Like all conclusions, yours must grow out of evidence and ideas you've developed in your paper. This is not the point to intrude with an irrelevant or personal opinion.

> I just didn't like this play because it was about sex and I don't like stories about sex.

If indeed the work has been poorly executed, your analysis should demonstrate it, and your conclusion should be strong, but it should be based on the argument you've presented.

> In *A Farewell to Arms*, Hemingway's hero hasn't really learned very much at all. If all the old values are no longer meaningful, we are left with the question, "How can I lead my life?" But Hemingway's vision is incomplete, for it fails to give us any answers. Hemingway implies, as I've tried to show, that values can be found in a return to sensations. But sensations are structureless, like a bunch of building blocks without any foundation. In terms of the current generation, *A Farewell to Arms* tells us what we already know, but it ends where it should begin.

If the poem or story or play has been successful, however, your conclusion should note it with equal forcefulness.

> The unity of the poem depends on the recurrence of light and dark images, to which Tennyson has given particular attention. Throughout the poem, the words *day* and *dark* have appeared again and again. The light and dark contrasts become symbolic of man's belief or doubt in God. They create a tension of opposites until they are brought together and seen as a balancing rather than a conflicting force. Tennyson's brilliance has been in leading us to see that faith swells not from "the light alone" but from the "darkness and the light."

A study of literature goes beyond merely increasing our appreciation of an art form. It increases our sensitivity to emotions and to the shades of human experience. It heightens our awareness of subtlety and ambiguity, of form and symbol, of line and color, of language itself. It develops our hearts and our minds.

THE STRUCTURE AS OUTLINE

Introduction
- Name of author and work
- Brief summary of the work as a whole
- Focusing sentence
- General indication of overall significance

Body
- Literal description of first major element or portion of the work
- Detailed analysis
- Interpretation
- Literal description of the second major development
- Detailed analysis
- Interpretation (including, if necessary, the relationship to the first major point)
- And so on

Conclusion
- Overall interpretation of the elements studied
- Relationship to the work as a whole
- Critical assessment of the value, worth, meaning, or significance of the work, both positive and negative

Exercise

Study the student critique that follows. In it, Diane Key, a sophomore biology major, has attempted to analyze Sherwood Anderson's story. The approach she has used is only one of many; you may have seen the story in a different light. But consider where Diane's effort is successful and where it might be strengthened.

Truth in the Grotesque

Analyze the components of Diane's introduction.

The title of a short story by Sherwood Anderson, "The Book of the Grotesque," appropriately depicts the overall significance of the story. At first glance, the plot seems bizarre. Anderson takes his readers through the story by introducing us to a writer, an old man past sixty. The writer employs the services of a carpenter to raise the writer's bed so that he can see out the window. As the writer lies in his elevated bed one night, many strange thoughts and feelings overtake him. Although the old man has a weak heart and would not be alarmed if death came to him in the near future, he feels at odds with death; he feels as if a youth or young woman lived within him. Even though awake, the writer experiences a dream or vision caused by the young thing inside his body. An hour-long procession of grotesque figures appears before the old man's eyes. Because he is a writer, the old man later writes a book describing his dream and its significance. The book contains hundreds of truths and describes how these truths can turn people into "grotesques." The narrator of the story foresees the possibility that the old man may also become grotesque if the old man becomes obsessed with his book, but the young thing inside him saves him from such an outcome.

Consider how Diane moves from concrete details to what they suggest and how they may relate to the larger theme.

Anderson puts a great deal of stress on the writer's age. Besides using the word *old* to describe him, Anderson indicates that he has a "white mustache," he has "some difficulty in getting into bed," he is "past sixty," "he would some time die unexpectedly," and "his body was old and not of much use any more." Old age suggests brittleness, conformity, death, and finality. In a sense, these words and images are like truths. A truth according to its dictionary definition is fact or actuality. A fact is rigid, incapable of being changed, and is clearly defined. A truth is an absolute—there is no gray between the black and white.

What traditional technique does Diane use here?

In conflict with the finality of his age, however, the writer senses a contrasting feeling:

> . . . something inside him was altogether young. He was like a pregnant woman, only that the thing inside him was not a baby but a youth. No, it wasn't a youth, it was a woman, young, and wearing a coat of mail like a knight.

The word *pregnant* holds special significance, as does the observation that the sensation felt like a young woman, someone capable of giving new life. We can even note that

Discuss how the student moves through description, analysis, and interpretation in this paragraph.

a coat of mail is *flexible armor*. These three concepts suggest birth, newness, and pliability. In fact, they are antonyms of the connotations of old age. Old age can be equated with rigidity and truth. Youth, on the other hand, is equated with flexibility, with that which is not absolute and can be changed. How does this all relate to the procession of grotesques that passes before the writer's eyes? It could be possible that as each person seizes a truth and tries to live his or her life according to its standards, he or she becomes cast into a mold that is unnatural and restricting. He or she is distorted into something other than human. "The grotesques were not all horrible. Some were amusing, some almost beautiful," states the narrator. But the grotesques are like the truths they embrace. Some of the grotesques are hideous when people try to live accordingly, like the truths of poverty and carelessness. Others are handsome, such as the truths of courage and thrift. The word *old*, therefore, suggests the inflexibility of "truth" and the "truth's" distortion of people. As the writer is old, he is in danger of becoming a grotesque, as his acquaintances have. But the old writer embodies the conflicting force of youth. "It was the young thing inside him that saved the old man."

One begins to wonder when the writer first realized the young force within himself. I feel that the old man's discovery began soon after the carpenter's visit. Here, again, words and images suggest that the carpenter aided the writer in seeing his vision of the grotesques and in finding the youth within him. By means of the carpenter, who is a builder, the old man's bed was raised. The carpenter brought the man's bed to the level of the window so the old man could see the tree, which might suggest life, growth, and youth, or, at the very least, something outside the confines of the old man's age. The carpenter is a grotesque himself because he is obsessed with the truth of war and death. Unknowingly, by serving as an example, the carpenter stimulates the old man to see the procession of grotesques later. This is not to say that the carpenter enlightened the writer. On the contrary, Anderson writes, "The plan the writer had for the raising of his bed was forgotten and later the carpenter did it in his own way and the writer, who was past sixty, had to help himself with a chair when he went to bed at night." It was the writer's plan to raise the bed and it was the writer who had to help himself. Active participation on the part of the writer was required if he was to recognize the youthful element in his life.

Did you see the carpenter's role as Diane does? If not, is her interpretation convincing?

Consider how Diane assesses the overall value of the story.

Perhaps Sherwood Anderson's story suggests that we should keep our youthful attitudes along with their flexibility. We should not be rigid and unbending; we

should not try to live our lives solely by a single truth. A
single truth, no matter how appealing, is always a
distortion. We must not accept only the black and white,
but live and experience the vast area of gray also. Yet there
is a danger of excess in following this vision too. Without
some kinds of truths, our lives would be meaningless.
What we need is to live somewhere between an unyielding
framework and total license. Sherwood Anderson's old
writer has found that middle ground and is all the more
human because of it.

Diane Key

Readings

Trinity

Pattiann Rogers

I wish something slow and gentle and good
Would happen to me, an easy and patient
And prolonged kind of happiness coming
In the same way evening comes to a wide-branched
Sycamore standing in an empty field; each branch,
Not succumbing, not taken, but feeling
Its entire existence a willing revolution of cells;
Even asleep, feeling a decision of gold spreading
Over its ragged back and motionless knots of seed,
Over every naked, vulnerable juncture; each leaf
Becoming a lavender shell, a stem-deep line
Of violet turning slowly and carefully to possess exactly
The pale and patient color of the sky coming.

I wish something that slow and that patient
Would come to me, maybe like the happiness
Growing when the lover's hand, easy on the thigh
Or easy on the breast, moves like late light moves
Over the branches of a sycamore, causing
A slow revolution of decision in the body;

Even asleep, feeling the spread of hazy coral
And ivory-grey rising through the legs and spine
To alter the belief behind the eyes; feeling the slow
Turn of wave after wave of acquiescence moving
From the inner throat to the radiance of a gold belly
To a bone-center of purple; an easy, slow-turning
Happiness of possession like that, prolonged.

I wish something that gentle and that careful
And that possessive would come to me. Death
might be that way if one knew how to wait for it;
If death came easily and slowly,
If death were good.

Abandoned Farmhouse

Ted Kooser

He was a big man, says the size of his shoes
on a pile of broken dishes by the house;
a tall man too, says the length of the bed
in an upstairs room; and a good, God-fearing man,
says the Bible with a broken back
on the floor below the window, dusty with sun;
but not a man for farming, say the fields
cluttered with boulders and the leaky barn.

A woman lived with him, says the bedroom wall
papered with lilacs and the kitchen shelves
covered with oilcloth, and they had a child,
says the sandbox made from a tractor tire.
Money was scarce, say the jars of plum preserves
and canned tomatoes sealed in the cellar hole.
And the winters cold, say the rags in the window frames.
It was lonely here, says the narrow country road.

Something went wrong, says the empty house
in the weed-choked yard. Stones in the fields
say he was not a farmer; the still-sealed jars
in the cellar say she left in a nervous haste.
And the child? Its toys are strewn in the yard
like branches after a storm—a rubber cow,

Reprinted from *Sure Signs: New and Selected Poems*, by Ted Kooser by permission of the University of Pittsburgh Press. © 1980 by Ted Kooser.

a rusty tractor with a broken plow,
a doll in overalls. Something went wrong, they say.

Marks

Linda Pastan

My husband gives me an A
for last night's supper,
an incomplete for my ironing,
a B plus in bed.

My son says I am average,
an average mother, but if
I put my mind to it
I could improve.
My daughter believes
in Pass/Fail and tells me
I pass. Wait 'til they learn
I'm dropping out.

What Were They Like?
(Questions and Answers)

Denise Levertov

1) Did the people of Viet Nam
   use lanterns of stone?
2) Did they hold ceremonies
   to reverence the opening of buds?
3) Were they inclined to rippling laughter?
4) Did they use bone and ivory,
   jade and silver, for ornament?
5) Had they an epic poem?
6) Did they distinguish between speech and singing?

1) Sir, their light hearts turned to stone.
   It is not remembered whether in gardens
   stone lanterns illumined pleasant ways.

2) Perhaps they gathered once to delight in blossom,
   but after the children were killed
   there were no more buds.
3) Sir, laughter is bitter to the burned mouth.
4) A dream ago, perhaps. Ornament is for joy.
   All the bones were charred.
5) It is not remembered. Remember,
   most were peasants; their life
   was in rice and bamboo.
   When peaceful clouds were reflected in the paddies
   and the water-buffalo stepped surely along terraces,
   maybe fathers told their sons old tales.
   When bombs smashed the mirrors there was time only
       to scream.
6) There is an echo yet, it is said,
   of their speech which was like a song.
   It is reported their singing resembled
   the flight of moths in moonlight.
   Who can say? It is silent now.

What To Say
When You're Depressed

Richard Chess

Instead of "my meal's cold"
Say "the ocean is the purest cold,
Even in Minnesota," and rather than calling
Night "my unlucky companion,"
Say "I purchased these
Handsome shoes on sale."
If the room is deserted, as it must be,
If the curtains billow with wind,
Call it "a gathering of close friends."
And if the lamp by which you measure
Your evenings is too bright or too dim
Say "our team is strong this year
And could go all the way."
"Our team is strong and the ocean
I purchased is the purest cold,"
You tell the close friends
You've collected, a poor man's hobby,

Over the years. But don't say
"A poor man's hobby," for if you say that
The glasses in the cabinet will rush
To say "we're empty,"
The windows, "through us you see
What's to be seen." If you can't say,
Before the candlelight tapering down,
"I love sailing with you
On nights like this," say nothing at all.
"We could go all the way
To Minnesota on this ship"
Would only make you happy
Which is more than you could bear.

The Ones Who Walk Away from Omelas

Ursula K. Le Guin

With a clamor of bells that set the swallows soaring, the Festival of Summer came to the city Omelas, bright-towered by the sea. The rigging of the boats in harbor sparkled with flags. In the streets between houses with red roofs and painted walls, between old moss-grown gardens and under avenues of trees, past great parks and public buildings, processions moved. Some were decorous: old people in long stiff robes of mauve and grey, grave master workmen, quiet, merry women carrying their babies and chatting as they walked. In other streets the music beat faster, a shimmering of gong and tambourine, and the people went dancing, the procession was a dance. Children dodged in and out, their high calls rising like the swallows' crossing flights over the music and the singing. All the processions wound towards the north side of the city, where on the great water-meadow called the Green Fields boys and girls, naked in the bright air, with mud-stained feet and ankles and long, lithe arms, exercised their restive horses before the race. The horses wore no gear at all but a halter without bit. Their manes were braided with streamers of silver, gold, and green. They flared their nostrils and pranced and boasted to one another; they were vastly excited, the horse being the only animal who has adopted our ceremonies as his own. Far off to the north and west the mountains stood up half encircling Omelas on her bay. The air of morning was so clear that the snow still crowning the Eighteen Peaks burned with white-gold fire across the miles of sunlit air, under the dark blue of the sky. There was just enough wind to make the banners that marked the racecourse snap and flutter now and then. In the silence of the broad green meadows one could hear the music winding through the city streets, farther and nearer and ever approaching, a cheerful faint sweetness of the air that from time to time trembled and gathered together and broke out into the great joyous clanging of the bells.

Joyous! How is one to tell about joy? How describe the citizens of Omelas?

They were not simple folk, you see, though they were happy. But we do not say the words of cheer much any more. All smiles have become archaic. Given a description such as this one tends to make certain assumptions. Given a description such as this one tends to look next for the King, mounted on a splendid stallion and surrounded by his noble knights, or perhaps in a golden litter borne by great-muscled slaves. But there was no king. They did not use swords, or keep slaves. They were not barbarians. I do not know the rules and laws of their society, but I suspect that they were singularly few. As they did without monarchy and slavery, so they also go on without the stock exchange, the advertisement, the secret police, and the bomb. Yet I repeat that these were not simple folk, not dulcet shepherds, noble savages, bland utopians. They were not less complex than us. The trouble is that we have a bad habit, encouraged by pedants and sophisticates, of considering happiness as something rather stupid. Only pain is intellectual, only evil interesting. This is the treason of the artist: a refusal to admit the banality of evil and the terrible boredom of pain. If you can't lick 'em, join 'em. If it hurts, repeat it. But to praise despair is to condemn delight, to embrace violence is to lose hold of everything else. We have almost lost hold; we can no longer describe a happy man, nor make any celebration of joy. How can I tell you about the people of Omelas? They were not naïve and happy children—though their children were, in fact, happy. They were mature, intelligent, passionate adults whose lives were not wretched. O miracle! but I wish I could describe it better. I wish I could convince you. Omelas sounds in my words like a city in a fairy tale, long ago and far away, once upon a time. Perhaps it would be best if you imagined it as your own fancy bids, assuming it will rise to the occasion, for certainly I cannot suit you all. For instance, how about technology? I think that there would be no cars or helicopters in and above the streets; this follows from the fact that the people of Omelas are happy people. Happiness is based on a just discrimination of what is necessary, what is neither necessary nor destructive, and what is destructive. In the middle category, however—that of the unnecessary but undestructive, that of comfort, luxury, exuberance, etc.—they could perfectly well have central heating, subway trains, washing machines, and all kinds of marvelous devices not yet invented here, floating light-sources, fuelless power, a cure for the common cold. Or they could have none of that: it doesn't matter. As you like it. I incline to think that people from towns up and down the coast have been coming in to Omelas during the last days before the Festival on very fast little trains and double-decker trams, and that the train station of Omelas is actually the handsomest building in town, though plainer than the magnificent Farmers' Market. But even granted trains, I fear that Omelas so far strikes some of you as goody-goody. Smiles, bells, parades, horses, bleh. If so, please add an orgy. If an orgy would help, don't hesitate. Let us not, however, have temples from which issue beautiful nude priests and priestesses already half in ecstasy and ready to copulate with any man or woman, lover or stranger, who desires union with the deep godhead of the blood, although that was my first idea. But really it would be better not to have any temples in Omelas—at least, not manned temples. Religion yes, clergy no. Surely the beautiful nudes can just wander about, offering themselves like divine soufflés to the hunger of the needy and the rapture of the flesh. Let them join the processions. Let tambourines be struck above the copulations, and the glory of desire be proclaimed upon the gongs, and (a not unimportant point) let the offspring of these delightful rituals be beloved and looked after by all. One thing I know there is none of in Omelas is guilt. But what else should there be? I thought at first there were no drugs, but that is puritanical. For those who like it, the faint insistent sweetness of *drooz* may perfume the ways of the city, *drooz* which first brings a great lightness and brilliance to the mind and limbs, and then after some hours a dreamy languor, and wonderful visions at last of the very arcana and inmost secrets of the Universe, as well as exciting the pleasure of sex beyond all belief; and it is not habit-forming. For more modest tastes I think there ought to be beer. What else, what else belongs in the joyous city? The sense of victory, surely, the celebration of courage. But as we did without clergy, let us do without soldiers. The joy built upon successful slaughter is not the right kind of joy; it will not do; it is fearful and it is trivial. A boundless and generous contentment, a magnanimous triumph felt not against some outer enemy but in communion with the finest and fairest in the souls of all men everywhere and the splendor of the world's summer: this is what swells the hearts of the people of Omelas, and the victory they celebrate is that of life. I really don't think many of them need to take *drooz*.

Most of the processions have reached the Green Fields by now. A marvelous smell of cooking goes forth from the red and blue tents of the provisioners. The faces of small children are amiably sticky; in the benign grey beard of a man a couple of crumbs of rich pastry are entangled. The youths and girls have mounted their horses and are beginning to group around the starting line of the course. An old woman, small, fat, and laughing, is passing out flowers from a basket, and tall young men wear her flowers in their shining hair. A child of nine or ten sits at the edge of the crowd, alone, playing on a wooden flute. People pause to listen, and they smile, but they do not speak to him, for he never ceases playing and never sees them, his dark eyes wholly rapt in the sweet, thin magic of the tune.

He finishes, and slowly lowers his hands holding the wooden flute.

As if that little private silence were the signal, all at once a trumpet sounds from the pavilion near the starting line: imperious, melancholy, piercing. The horses rear on their slender legs, and some of them neigh in answer. Sober-faced, the young riders stroke the horses' necks and soothe them, whispering, "Quiet, quiet, there my beauty, my hope. . . ." They begin to form in rank along the starting line. The crowds along the racecourse are like a field of grass and flowers in the wind. The Festival of Summer has begun.

Do you believe? Do you accept the festival, the city, the joy? No? Then let me describe one more thing.

In a basement under one of the beautiful public buildings of Omelas, or perhaps in the cellar of one of its spacious private homes, there is a room. It has one locked door, and no window. A little light seeps in dustily between cracks in the boards, secondhand from a cobwebbed window somewhere across the cellar. In one corner of the little room a couple of mops, with stiff, clotted, foul-smelling heads, stand near a rusty bucket. The floor is dirt, a little damp to the touch, as cellar dirt usually is. The room is about three paces long and two wide: a mere broom closet or disused tool room. In the room a child is sitting. It could be a boy or a girl. It looks about six, but actually is nearly ten. It is feeble-minded. Perhaps it was born defective, or perhaps it has become imbecile through fear, malnutrition, and neglect. It picks its nose and occasionally fumbles vaguely with its toes or genitals, as it sits hunched in the corner farthest from the bucket and the two mops. It is afraid of the mops. It finds them horrible. It shuts its eyes, but it knows the mops are still standing there; and the door is locked; and nobody will come. The door is always locked; and nobody ever comes, except that sometimes— the child has no understanding of time or interval—sometimes the door rattles terribly and opens, and a person, or several people, are there. One of them may come in and kick the child to make it stand up. The others never come close, but peer in at it with frightened, disgusted eyes. The food bowl and the water jug are hastily filled, the door is locked, the eyes disappear. The people at the door never say anything, but the child, who has not always lived in the tool room, and can remember sunlight and its mother's voice, sometimes speaks. "I will be good," it says. "Please let me out. I will be good!" They never answer. The child used to scream for help at night, and cry a good deal, but now it only makes a kind of whining, "eh-haa, eh-haa," and it speaks less and less often. It is so thin there are no calves to its legs; its belly protrudes; it lives on a half-bowl of corn meal and grease a day. It is naked. Its buttocks and thighs are a mass of festered sores, as it sits in its own excrement continually.

They all know it is there, all the people of Omelas. Some of them have come to see it, others are content merely to know it is there. They all know that it has to be there. Some of them understand why, and some do not, but all understand that their happiness, the beauty of their city, the tenderness of their friendships, the health of their children, the wisdom of their scholars, the skill of their makers, even the abundance of their harvest and the kindly weathers of their skies, depend wholly on this child's abominable misery.

This is usually explained to children when they are between eight and twelve, whenever they seem capable of understanding; and most of those who come to see the child are young people, though often enough an adult comes, or comes back, to see the child. No matter how well the matter has been explained to them, these young spectators are always shocked and sickened at the sight. They feel disgust, which they had thought themselves superior to. They feel anger, outrage, impotence, despite all the explanations. They would like to do something for the child. But there is nothing they can do. If the child were brought up into the sunlight out of that vile place, if it were cleaned and fed and comforted, that would be a good thing, indeed; but if it were done, in that day and hour all the prosperity and beauty and delight of Omelas would wither and be destroyed. Those are the terms. To exchange all the goodness and grace of every life in Omelas for that single, small improvement: to throw away the happiness of thousands for the chance of the happiness of one: that would be to let guilt within the walls indeed.

The terms are strict and absolute; there may not even be a kind word spoken to the child.

Often the young people go home in tears, or in a tearless rage, when they have seen the child and faced this terrible paradox. They may brood over it for weeks or years. But as time goes on they begin to realize that even if the child could be released, it would not get much good of its freedom: a little vague pleasure of warmth and food, no doubt, but little more. It is too degraded and imbecile to know any real joy. It has been afraid too long ever to be free of fear. Its habits are too uncouth for it to respond to humane treatment. Indeed, after so long it would probably be wretched without walls about it to protect it, and darkness for its eyes, and its own excrement to sit in. Their tears at the bitter injustice dry when they begin to perceive the terrible justice of reality, and to accept it. Yet it is their tears and anger, the trying of their generosity and the acceptance of their helplessness, which are perhaps the true source of the splendor of their lives. Theirs is no vapid, irresponsible happiness. They know that they, like the child, are not free. They know compassion. It is the existence of the child, and their knowledge of its existence, that makes possible the nobility of their architecture, the poignancy of their music, the profundity of their science. It is because of the child that they are so gentle with children. They know that if the wretched one were not there snivelling in the dark, the other one, the flute-player, could make no joyful music as the young riders line up in their beauty for the race in the sunlight of the first morning of summer.

Now do you believe in them? Are they not more credible? But there is one more thing to tell, and this is quite incredible.

At times one of the adolescent girls or boys who go to see the child does not go home to weep or rage, does not, in fact, go home at all. Sometimes also a man or woman much older falls silent for a day or two, and then leaves home. These people go out into the street, and walk down the street alone. They keep walking, and walk straight out of the city of Omelas, through the beautiful gates. They keep walking across the farmlands of Omelas. Each one goes alone, youth or girl, man or woman. Night falls; the traveler must pass down village streets, between the houses with yellow-lit windows, and on out into the darkness of the fields. Each alone, they go west or north, towards the mountains. They go on. They leave Omelas, they walk ahead into the darkness, and they do not come back. The place they go towards is a place even less imaginable to most of us than the city of happiness. I cannot describe it at all. It is possible that it does not exist. But they seem to know where they are going, the ones who walk away from Omelas.

PART VIII

Scholarly Research

Whether he is an archaeologist, chemist, or astronomer, at the heart the researcher's goal is very much the same. Basically, he looks for facts that interest him and then tries to arrange them in meaningful sequence. . . . He defines what happens, then figures out where, when, how, and why it happens. His adverbial search for cause and effect, for the basic ordering in things, is primal, compelling, and satisfying, quite apart from practical considerations.

JAMES H. AUSTIN

Exploring

34

The Preliminary Stages of Research

You came to college because you wanted to know something. You wanted to learn, to grow, to change. Maybe it's turned out to be more difficult than you thought. But here and there, in a biology class perhaps, or in your personal contacts with a professor or an advisor, you've found yourself challenged and excited. Perhaps you've had the opportunity to read philosophy or to explore new techniques in electronic music. Or your humanities instructor assigned you to write a library paper on medieval stained glass windows and you thought it would be boring but it turned out to be fascinating. Or after taking a course in accounting you've begun to doubt whether you really want to pursue it further. To your parents' grief, you've started thinking you might want to go into stage design.

Intellectual excitement stimulates personal growth. I suspect that's what undergraduate years are really all about. And one of the key ways such opportunity opens up for you is—of all things—through research, that old bugbear you may always have dreaded. Yet research is really the only way (other than personal experience) that we explore and discover new ideas and values. Research is the work of the mind. When approached with a lively spirit and a sense of inner order, it is an investment in intellectual growth and well-being. And because knowledge always moves from the known to the unknown, research in the undergraduate years is a way of helping you discover what is already known, so that you can spend the rest of your life, if you choose to do so, exploring the frontiers of knowledge.

Research need never be dull and tedious. Your personal interest and involvement may often be the only basis for pursuing it. A personal search emanates from your own questions: How can I overcome math anxiety? How can I help my alcoholic father? Do I really want to become a physical therapist? Is abortion the easy way out? A more objective search may be assigned in a particular class, such as Sociology 101, but usually you'll have a wide range of topics or avenues to follow: Is teenage suicide related to stress? Genetics? Cultural changes? Is it higher among bright students? Are incidents of suicide among youth rising or are reporting methods merely more accurate? Are there distinct differences in urban and rural levels of suicide? Racial differences? Gender differences?

The personal search may reach out toward a more extensive use of primary sources, such as interviews, letters, and phone calls; but like the more objective library search, it will require hours of solid reading in journals, magazines, and books. The differences may appear more in the final product (in tone or voice or the intended audience) than in method, because even the most seemingly intellectual research into the highest plane of ideas involves a commitment of the individual, of the self, of the personal "I."

RESEARCH AS INQUIRY

You may be asked to choose a topic suited to your personal interests or you may be asked to explore a subject related to some particular aspect of a course. Either way, you'll need to keep in mind that the whole of research is the asking of questions (and the search for answers).

Here are questions you need to start with. They ought to guide you from your earliest stages to the last sentence you revise.

1. What do I want to know? And why is it important?
2. What do I already know?
3. How do I find new information? Through interviews? Books? Field research?
4. How do I evaluate what I find? Is it accurate? True? Meaningful? Pertinent?
5. What have I learned? Is it significant? How is it related to the subject as a whole? Is it related to myself in any way?

Preparing a Work Schedule

Research cannot be rushed. Interviews must be arranged, books studied, notes gathered, outlines constructed, first drafts crossed out in favor of second and third drafts, citations recorded, and bibliographies suffered through. It all takes time, self-discipline, and planning. The first step is to organize a day-by-day schedule for yourself, as in the example on page 454.

You might need more or less time, depending on the length of the paper and on your personal working habits, but never underestimate the time it will take. A necessary book may turn up missing, information you've requested from a government agency may not arrive, or your roommate may use your most valuable note card for an ashtray. Build in time for the unexpected.

And build in time for relaxation. Numerous studies of the creative process show that most original ideas tend to appear in the mind when long periods of concentrated study are alternated with short periods of diversion and rest. Most documented cases of inspiration reveal that it seems to happen *between* intense work and play. No one knows why, but the unconscious elements of our mind need time to sort out and organize information. If your schedule is too tight or you find yourself working day and night, you may also find yourself overwhelmed by the material, unable to evaluate it and resorting to a so-called *cut-and-paste* product where ideas are merely strung together without thought. French scholar Jean Guitton has described the golden rule for intellectual work: "Tolerate neither half-work nor half-rest. Give yourself totally *or* withhold yourself absolutely. Never allow the two to overlap."

Psychologist Rollo May argues strongly that you must schedule one other element: *solitude*. The inner workings of the mind are a private thing. Students who surround themselves with stereo, television, and radio distract the mind from serious work. Rollo May asserts that we must teach ourselves the capacity for using solitude in constructive ways.

> It requires that we be able to retire from a world that is "too much with us," that we be able to be quiet, that we let the solitude work for us and in us. It is a characteristic of our time that many people are afraid of solitude: to be alone is a sign one is a social failure, for no one would be alone if he or she could help it. It often occurs to me that people living . . . amid the constant din of radio and TV . . . find it exceedingly difficult to let insights from unconscious depths break through. . . . [Yet] if we are to experience insights from our unconscious, we need to be able to give ourselves to solitude.

TENTATIVE WORK SCHEDULE

Days 1–3
Select a subject.
Evaluate what you already know.
Prepare a general question on what you want to learn.
Begin preliminary reading—an overview of the subject.
Narrow the subject based on overview.
Raise specific questions for specific inquiry.

Days 4–5
Locate topic in indexes, abstracts, and card catalog.
Select candidates for interviews.
Prepare a working bibliography.

Days 6–11
Investigate sources.
Gather data, ideas, facts, observations, and information.

Day 12
Organize notes.
Develop a specific focus or thesis to guide your writing.

Days 13–17
Begin drafting and revising, revising and drafting.

Days 18–19
Leave unscheduled days for the unexpected or to allow time
for cooling off before final editing.

Day 20
Prepare all bibliographic materials.

Day 21
Reread your last draft with critical eye.
Make final revisions, line-by-line editing.

Day 22
Prepare final typed draft and proofread. (If you have access to
a word processor, this stage can be accomplished with significantly greater ease.)

Day 23
Celebrate!

Conducting an Overview

Once you've outlined a tentative schedule, set to work immediately. Whether you've selected a subject or received an assigned subject as part of a class project, you'll need to obtain a general overview of the topic as a whole. You cannot plunge into research on educational innovations without knowing some background about, and history of, education. You cannot analyze a proposal for a guaranteed annual wage without knowing the cultural and economic context that has brought about such a proposal. Even if you already feel you have a background in the subject, you will need to verify your understanding of terms and concepts you plan to deal with.

Reference Tools

One of the primary goals is to seek information while wasting as little time as possible in the actual search. Reference works such as encyclopedias and dictionaries exist for exactly that purpose. They not only provide facts, statistics, definitions, biographical information, historical chronologies, and geographical data. They also often list the major sources for and authorities on a subject, saving you hours of random searching in the card catalog.

Encyclopedias

The *Encyclopaedia Britannica* is still probably the best single source for general information, especially for topics in the humanities and social sciences. Until 1974 the *Britannica* was arranged alphabetically with a final index volume. The newest edition provides a *Propaedia* (a single-volume introduction and outline of subjects), a *Micropaedia* (a ten-volume set of short, factual articles that serves as an index), and a *Macropaedia* (19 volumes of articles on most fields of knowledge). Of special value is the list of major sources that often follows each article in the *Macropaedia*. Be sure to make a list of such sources for later research.

The *Encyclopedia Americana* is less exhaustive but is in some ways a better general work on the sciences. Again, the list of sources at the end of articles is especially helpful. Volume 30 offers a comprehensive index and is a good place to begin a search.

Specialized encyclopedias in many ways provide even more technical coverage, as well as information on major authorities and sources. The *International Encyclopedia of the Social Sciences*, the *New Grove Dictionary of Music and Musicians*, and the *McGraw-Hill Encyclopedia of Science and Tech-*

nology are just a few of hundreds of examples. To determine whether your library has a specialized encyclopedia on your subject, consult the card catalog under your subject heading and look for the subdivision *Dictionaries*, where you'll find both encyclopedias and specialized dictionaries listed.

Dictionaries

As all subjects involve words and concepts, do not fail to obtain exact definitions. Any specialized term or jargon will probably need to be defined in your paper itself. Know the meanings *before* you begin your research, not after.

The American Heritage Dictionary of the English Language is one of the best desk-sized dictionaries. In addition to extensive definitions, it often provides connotations, synonyms, diagrams, photographs, and examples of how a word is used in a sentence.

Webster's Third New International Dictionary is even more exhaustive, but too large for most home use. You'll find it in almost every library. It seems especially strong in scientific and technical terms. (By the way, the name, *Webster's*, is not copyrighted and is used in the titles of many dictionaries. Do not confuse this major work with many of the smaller, less beneficial dictionaries.)

The Oxford English Dictionary is a multivolume work detailing the histories of words and can be particularly useful for understanding how the meaning of words may have changed over the years.

Again, specialized dictionaries are available in almost everything from ballet to physics. They may be essential to you for highly technical subjects.

Research and the Writer's Journal

You'll probably find that your journal is essential to you at this stage, and for some types of research, at every stage.

The journal can be used to record ideas and impressions during the overview process. It's an ideal place to keep track of references that spring up unexpectedly while checking a source. It offers you the chance to jot down questions as they occur to you. (Keep it near your bed for those late-night ideas that otherwise may fade away by morning.)

The working bibliography can be retained in your journal, with notes on books you couldn't locate and other books to return to later. If your research project is fairly short, you may want to go ahead and use the journal for note taking. Many writers divide journals into various sections to help them keep track of everything: one section for a working bibliography, another section for notes, another for interviews, and still another for ideas and explorations. Even if you use note cards for all official quotations and paraphrases, the journal remains the best place to explore ideas or questions as they come to you.

Sometimes, in coming across a single fact, you may be stimulated to write several pages. By writing spontaneously and informally, by trusting your imagination to explore possibilities, you'll not only retain better the facts you've uncovered, you will have simultaneously begun the process of assimilation and integration of concepts. You'll have a better feeling for your material, a clearer sense of what you know and what you need to know, and thus a firmer sense of direction. Finally, when you sit down to write the paper itself, you'll do so with more confidence. You may find that as much as 50 percent will already be drafted in the journal. In other words, the journal should remain integral to all your writing habits.

Focusing the Subject in Question Form

You cannot write a successful paper on World War II. You could not even do a satisfactory job on the role of women in World War II. You *might* be able to go into some detail on the role of women in the labor force during World War II *if* you were planning to write a master's thesis. But if you are considering a smaller research paper, you must find a single element of your subject that is appropriate both for the size of paper required and for the amount of research time available to you. Failure to narrow your topic may leave you awash in a sea of general information.

This is not the time to form an actual thesis statement that might lock you into an idea that can't be proved or into a subject on which information is unavailable. But it is the time to ask questions. All the different techniques you're familiar with should now come into play. Begin with the 5 *W*'s: *Who? What? Where? When?* and *Why?* Consider the 4 *C*'s of observation: *Change, Conflict* (or *Opposition*), *Consequence*, and *Characterization* (in the full sense of that term—*physical details, actions, speech, background, others' reactions*). And finally, recognize that all of the formal patterns of perception may also need to be included: *comparison* and *contrast, definition, classification, illustration,* and *analysis*.

That may seem like a lot to keep in your head at once, but you've already practiced using most of those techniques in earlier papers. What you'll need now is time—lots of it. You cannot rush this phase or postpone it. It may be the single most crucial step you perform in preparing to engage in effective research.

Here is how you might consider the subject of women's entrance into the labor force during World War II. Begin with a general approach that has some personal interest to you. Let's say that in this case you're curious about the origins of the current feminist movement. Perhaps you could begin with one or two broad questions: Did women's entrance into the wartime labor force create new expectations and demands from women? Did it bring about any change in male attitudes? A satisfactory start, but still too general. Even more focused questions must be found.

> Before the United States' entry into the war, what percentage of the work force consisted of women?
>
> What were men's and women's attitudes toward "working women" before the war?
>
> What percentage of women were working by the end of the war?
>
> Why did this movement occur?
>
> What kinds of jobs did women take?
>
> Was there any opposition to women's entry into male jobs at that time?
>
> Was the working woman viewed as a temporary wartime phenomenon? By women? By men?
>
> Was it a temporary phenomenon? Evidence?
>
> Can specific consequences be determined?
>
> What were men's and women's attitudes after the war?
>
> Did opposition arise against women who continued to work? Evidence?
>
> What kind of evidence would be satisfactory? Did women speak out? Were new labor laws passed?
>
> Where could such evidence be found?

This is only a small beginning. But notice already how raising questions about the subject has led to raising questions about evidence. If the initial subject is a poor one or too complex, such questions will begin to identify the dangers of pursuing it further. No need wasting several weeks on a topic if evidence is not available. Only by considering in advance the types of evidence you may need and where you may have to look to find it can you begin to be somewhat confident that your research will prove successful.

One final suggestion: Don't try all of this in your head. Sit down in a quiet location and write out questions as you think of them. Seeing the words on paper will stimulate more questions, and it will also help you begin early to find an order or pattern to your research. Related questions can be grouped. Questions that seem to lead nowhere can be struck out. Only by doing this will you be prepared for the next two steps in the process: finding and investigating sources of information.

LOCATING PRIMARY AND SECONDARY SOURCES

Because most students do not attempt to locate and use primary sources, you can often impress your reader by showing a little initiative and imagination. A letter to a congressman or a company president, a telephone call to a local journalist or director of a social agency may bring in unexpected and fresh information. An interview with the curator of the local art gallery or a scientist at a major university may provide new ideas as well as human interest. In your journal, make a list of the potential primary sources, and attempt to locate at least one or two if possible.

> authorities on the topic
> local or national organizations
> people involved in or affected by the issue
> letters, journals, diaries
> movies, television, records, radio
> original documents

A personal investigation may focus more on primary sources, but much of your effort will still occur in the library. Knowing that, some students head directly for the card catalog or the computer catalog. But the experienced researcher knows that other reference tools can be far more helpful at this early stage.

Indexes

Not all information can be found in books, especially if your topic deals with current issues and ideas. *Indexes* give author and subject listings of material found in magazines, journals, and newspapers. (A journal is usually published quarterly or biannually for a specific professional audience and tends to print technical or scholarly articles; *magazines* are usually published weekly or monthly and tend to print material aimed at the general reader.) Here are some of the most important indexes with which you should be familiar.

The New York Times Index is indispensable for research on people, events, and organizations in the news since 1951. It even offers a brief summary of the information contained in each article so that you can quickly determine whether you need to pursue it further.

The *Readers' Guide to Periodical Literature* lists articles published since 1900 in popular magazines like *Time, Redbook, Ladies' Home Journal*, and *Sports Illustrated*. Obviously, you probably won't find in-depth coverage in such sources. But *Readers' Guide* also lists many superior periodicals: *Atlantic, New Republic, Commonweal, Harper's*, and *National Review*. If you use this index selectively, you can often find excellent material, especially on current topics and problems.

For more technical or scholarly treatment, you'll need more specialized indexes. The *Applied Science and Technology Index* lists articles in highly specialized journals and may provide you with more depth on subjects like forestry, biology, chemistry, and the environment.

The *Business Periodicals Index* covers almost 300 different magazines and journals that deal with economics, finance management, and so on.

The *Humanities Index* will be the primary place to begin a study on the arts, literature, languages, music, and philosophy.

The *Social Sciences Index* provides author and subject headings for hundreds of magazines and scholarly journals in psychology, sociology, political science, and similar fields.

This list could continue for pages. Hundreds of specialized indexes list the works you may need to consult. You should probably begin your hunt for secondary sources in one of the general indexes, such as the *Humanities Index*, and then move toward more specialized indexes in your particular subject, such as the *Art Index*. Within an hour or so, you'll probably find a surprising amount of material impossible to locate through the card or computer catalog.

Bibliographies

A *bibliography* is merely a list of books on a given subject. If you can locate one on your topic, it may save you hours. If, for example, you were considering a study of the influence of black African writing on black American writers, you might begin with *Black African Literature in English Since 1952*. This one book would provide you with a list of books on African literature in English, a list of critical articles according to subject matter, a list of anthologies of black African writing, an alphabetical listing of black African authors publishing in English, and even a list of other bibliographies on the subject. You'll find specialized bibliographies on individuals, organizations, historical events, and individual topics. Some are *annotated*—that is, they offer brief comments on the contents and quality of each work they list.

Two places to look for bibliographies on your subject are the *Bibliographic Index* and the card or computer catalog under your subject with the subdivision *bibliography*: for example, *Women—Bibliography* or *Literature, Black—Bibliography*.

The Card Catalog and the Computer Catalog

Only now (after a preliminary search through indexes and bibliographies) should you turn to the card catalog for books. I make such a suggestion because too many students who begin their search at the card catalog never seem to get past it. No doubt, information from books will constitute a major portion of your research, but journals and magazine articles should not be omitted. By discovering what current material is being published in periodicals and by having studied the various classifications of books on the subject as listed in a bibliography, you are in a more credible position to make meaningful selections from the card catalog.

Books are listed in a card catalog (or in the newer on-line computer catalogs) in three ways: under author, under title, and under subject. If you've obtained some names of authorities from your previous overview of the subject, you will want to check their work under author headings. Otherwise, subject headings will group all works on a single topic, and you'll probably find it the most productive place to begin. But note that any topic may have several related subject headings. If your subject involves changing attitudes toward marijuana, don't look solely under the heading of marijuana. You would probably also want to try *drug abuse, drugs, drugs—laws and legislation*, and perhaps others. Give yourself several hours and be willing to explore.

In some libraries you may request a computer search of your subject. You will be charged for the search and may find it's not worth the cost, especially if your project can be more easily researched through a traditional card catalog. But for subjects that require government information, the use of statistical abstracts, specialized bibliographies, or technical research in medicine and law, the computerized data base may provide you with information you would never have located in any other way. Check with your reference librarian for the local cost and for advice about whether such service would be worthwhile for your particular topic.

The Reference Librarian

What if you can't determine other headings to look under? What if you don't know where the indexes are located? Or how to read some of the codes used in bibliographies? Fortunately, every major library has a *reference librarian*, an individual specially trained in locating the right index or bibliography and in helping you make the most productive use of the card catalog. Don't be shy. You need sources on your subject, and each library may have a different system for locating and organizing reference materials. You are not necessarily expected to know where to find such information or how to use it. Ask the reference librarian for help. That's what he or she gets paid for. The reference librarian may be your single best friend in any library.

PREPARING A WORKING BIBLIOGRAPHY

During this whole process of preliminary investigation, you'll want to compile a list of possible sources for your actual research. The list is called a *working bibliography* because it is indeed one from which you work. It will seldom be identical to the final bibliography you submit with your paper.

This preliminary list should have at least two to three times as many items as you expect to need. For every ten items on it, two may have been checked out by other students, one may be lost, one may have been stolen, and one will no doubt be at the bindery. Perhaps four will be found on the shelf. Of those, two may actually deal with your topic in a useful way. If you calculate that you will need 15 sources for your paper, then make a list of at least 30 to 45 entries. If you stop after the first 15, you'll only end up returning to the library a week later to begin the preliminary stage over again. Don't take chances or waste time. Be selective, of course, but be thorough.

Every researcher develops his or her own best method of working. If you're writing a fairly short paper, you may find it easiest to keep the working bibliography in a separate section of your journal. Some instructors, however, will want you to construct your working bibliography on 3- by 5-inch cards in the same format that later transfers to your final works-cited page. That has much to say for it. Time may be saved at the end. Other instructors may argue that because you don't know what you'll need at the end, your list at this point does not need to be formal, only complete. Later, when you decide to use a specific article or book, you can take time to fill out a formal bibliography card.

I tend to agree with the latter point of view. Your time might be better spent at this stage making judgments about the content of books and articles rather than worrying about the mechanics of a bibliography. An informal working list should probably look like the one below.

All this preliminary work may sometimes seem tedious and frustrating, but without it, your research phase will consist of random guesswork and hope work. Take the necessary time now to assure yourself that your actual investigation will be focused and productive.

Sample Working Bibliography

Name the index in case you must return to check entry.

Record name of author, title, name of magazine.

List full date and page numbers.

Record both volume number and page number for journals.

(For newspapers, the final numbers refer to page and column.)

Record call numbers for books.

> *Social Science Index*
>
> Frobes, Allyn, "The Disaster of CIA Involvement in Iran," *Harper's* (June, 83), 15-21.
>
> Greenbaum, R.A. "Who Really Controls Our Foreign Policy?" *Foreign Policy*, vol. 19, Sept. 1984, 101-117.
>
> "The Decline of American Influence in Iran," *N.Y. Times*, Sept. 19 [1978] 62-3.
>
> *Card Catalog*
>
> Lisko, Christopher, *A Ship of State Without a Captain*, N.Y.: Peabody Press, 1986 [328.13].

AN OUTLINE OF PRELIMINARY STEPS IN RESEARCH

1. Prepare a Work Schedule
   - Do not underestimate the time needed.
   - Build in unscheduled days for rest or to gain perspective on the topic.
2. Clarify and Define the Subject
   - Obtain an overview and historical background.
   - Check encyclopedias and dictionaries.
3. Narrow the Subject and Place in Question Form
   - Formulate your questions in impartial terms.
   - Consider kinds of evidence that will be needed.
4. Locate Primary and Secondary Sources
   - Consider potential organizations or authorities to contact for interviews.
   - Search indexes, bibliographies, and card catalog.
5. Prepare a Working Bibliography
   - Obtain two to three times as many sources as you think you'll need.
   - Write down all information available on each source in your journal.

Exercises

Here are several questions for class discussion.

1. Which section of the card or computer catalog (author, title, or subject) would you search to find the following books?

   a. An edition of Dickens' *Great Expectations*
   b. Criticism of *Great Expectations*
   c. General criticism of Dickens' work
   d. Dickens' letters
   e. Dickens' autobiography
   f. A biography of Dickens

2. How would you find an article on Richard Nixon published in *The New York Times*?

3. What is a specialized dictionary and what can it do for you besides define a word?

4. If you wanted a general overview of a topic, what reference book would you use?

5. To find material on social aspects of computer technology, what index would you check?

6. To find a list of critical articles on F. Scott Fitzgerald's *Tender Is the Night*, where might you turn?

7. What alternatives exist for locating citations on books rather than spending hours searching a card catalog?

8. If you can't find the material you're looking for, to whom should you turn?

Exploring

35

Thoughtful Note Taking

Once you learned to hold a pencil and scrawl your alphabet in shaky letters across the lined page. Each uncertain movement of the pencil was consciously made. Yet with time, the instrument in your hand and the words on the page became an extension of yourself. In the following chapters, detailed steps of formal note taking, outlining, and documenting may at first seem equally foreign and awkward. We all know it is not knowledge of such mechanics in itself that will bring the rewards of scholarship, yet with time the mechanics become second nature—like holding a pencil. Each technique becomes only another extension of yourself, freeing you for more concentrated attention to those qualities of intellectual endeavor that do bring satisfaction.

PRELIMINARY SKIMMING

A scholarly approach to a subject requires a selective approach. You'll not want to waste time reading unrelated material. Before sitting down to a 20-page essay, quickly study the opening paragraph and the conclusion. If you find nothing that points toward the narrowed questions you've posed for study, skim the remainder of the essay. Usually, this can be done by reading only the first and last sentences of each paragraph. If you find even a single idea that might be valuable, go back and read the whole more closely. Otherwise, in only a few minutes, you can determine that the essay has nothing of relevance and you can move on to something more important.

Skimming a book requires several additional steps. If you've already obtained an overview of your subject, you'll seldom need to read complete works; after all, you need specific information on only a narrow portion of a topic. Begin with the *table of contents*. Select from it those chapters that seem relevant, and skim each chapter in the same way you would a magazine article. Do not take notes until you are certain the chapter offers something worth your time. If none of the chapter titles seem pertinent, quickly read the *preface* and *introduction*. That's where most authors summarize their intentions, their basic thesis, and their approach to a subject. Finally, turn to the *index* at the back of the book. Search out several different headings or terms that relate to your specific topic, and check those individual pages. If nothing meaningful shows up, you've spent only a few minutes with a book that would have proved of little value in the first place. But if you find even a single potentially valuable idea, read the whole chapter in which it occurs. See the idea in the full context in which the author intended it. Then, if it proves useful, take notes.

Preliminary skimming allows you to investigate far more material than the average student, who checks out a few large books and reads them cover to cover. You will be able to research five times as much material with less effort and less wasted time.

THE PRELIMINARY REFERENCE LIST

If, after skimming an essay or book, you decide it will probably contain useful information or ideas on your topic, the first step—before you begin critical reading and certainly before you begin taking actual notes—is to create a bibliographic entry in your journal (for shorter papers or for personal search papers) or on a note card (for longer, more complex studies). You must train yourself to take this simple step first because no matter how good your intentions, generations of experience prove that students who jot down notes first may forget to record the full bibliographical data. The failure will not be apparent until you reach the final stage of writing your paper and suddenly find yourself needing a references-cited page. That's when your friends will see you at midnight pounding on the library door.

Don't take a chance. Write down all necessary information *before* you take a single note.

From the title page of a book, record the following:

1. Full name(s) of author(s) or editor(s) (last name first)
2. Full title of book, including subtitle (underlined)
3. Place of publication
4. Full name of publisher
5. Date of publication (Use the last date given because later printings may contain revised material or new page arrangements)
6. The library call number

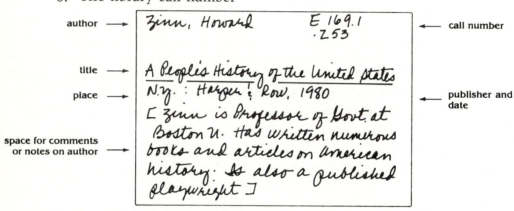

For an article from a magazine or journal, record the following:

1. Full name(s) of author(s) (last name first)
2. Title of the article (in quotation marks)
3. Full name of magazine (underlined)
4. Volume number (usually located on table of contents page)
5. Date of the magazine
6. Inclusive pages (for example, 125–152)

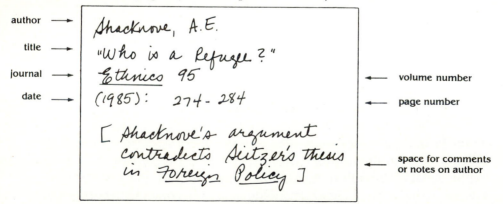

Although these two formats should serve for most sources, from time to time you'll encounter a source that creates special problems in both bibliographic and footnote entries. That's when you'll need to consult a *style manual*. Two of the most widely used are Kate L. Turabian's *A Manual for Writers of Term Papers, Theses, and Dissertations* and the *MLA Handbook for Writers of Research Papers*. Both offer dozens of variations on footnoting and bibliographic forms. Both are usually available in college bookstores or libraries.

CRITICAL READING

Once you've found material directly relevant to your narrowed topic, you'll want to apply all the mental steps of critical reading covered earlier in Chapter 29. Approach the material as objectively as possible. Attempt to understand the author's ideas on his or her terms. Know your own biases as best you can, and avoid making hasty judgments. Do take notes with careful evaluation of the content: Make an effort to discover who the author is and what his or her authority to speak on the subject might be; try to consider the historical and cultural context in which the work was written; and, most important, look for logic, look for appeals to emotion, look for evidence supported with valid sources, and look for sound reasoning.

NOTE TAKING: THE WRONG WAY

Learning how to take proper and meaningful notes requires more skill than young writers may first realize—and more effort. Here are three methods you'll want to avoid.

1. Do not copy an author's ideas word for word. A note that consists of nothing but a long quotation taken directly from a secondary source may give you the impression you're busy working hard—after all, it takes a long time to copy down a page of print in longhand. With few exceptions, however, you'll seldom need a page-long quotation from anyone. If you do, a photocopy machine can do it faster. But that leads to negative warning number two.

2. Do not photocopy passages from secondary sources as a *substitute* for taking a note. Photocopying machines are wonderful inventions. Yet they obviously do not *digest* or *contemplate* information

as you should be doing. The time saving may be dangerously misleading.

3. Perhaps equally wasteful is the method of avoiding all note taking by underlining important passages in books or marking them with slips of paper and trying to write the first draft by spreading a dozen books about you on desk and floor, turning from one to another and typing the paper as you go. Again, no assimilation or understanding of the material occurs. Such a writer is not really writing, only collating.

None of these methods will accomplish your purpose. No real thinking occurs. A machine can copy; the human brain has more potential. Unless you are summarizing or paraphrasing ideas in your own words, you are not really exerting intellectual effort; you are not grasping the meaning of ideas, evaluating, or interpreting. Note taking must be a thinking process, not merely a recording process. As your research progresses, you must continually reassess and refine your subject. You must be alert for areas of exploration that you might not have anticipated earlier. It may be possible that the direction established by your main question will prove unfruitful. New questions will almost always appear as you move from source to source. Unless you are actively engaged in thinking about the material, questioning the material, challenging the material *as* you take notes, you are not truly engaged in research at all.

NOTE TAKING: THE RIGHT WAY

Correct note taking involves a two-phase process. First comes the thinking phase. You must make repeated judgments about the worth and meaning of each idea you encounter. You must be involved in a constant process of evaluating the relationship of that idea or fact to all others you have uncovered. Train yourself to be highly selective. Take notes only on relevant ideas you have thought through or on your own ideas as they occur to you. Correct note taking should accompany intellectual activity, not overshadow it. If you find yourself recording piles of information, it may be a signal that you're depending too heavily on your sources and not assimilating or digesting material. Too many notes also have a way of pressuring you to use each and every one of them. All that effort expended on writing them down makes you feel guilty if they aren't used, whether they're needed or not. The first phase in note taking, then, involves the careful screening of information. You'll want to select only the most significant ideas for recording.

The second step involves the actual writing of the note on paper. Here, too, the most effective method requires experience, but it is one that can be more easily illustrated. Consider the following passage by Paul Zweig taken from a *Saturday Review* essay on heroes.

> Which is not to say that the contemporary world does not have its "heroes." For I doubt that human beings can live without some expanded ideal of behavior, some palpable image of the spaciousness of man. We want to know that our personal limitations are only a special case, that somewhere there is someone who can translate his words, thoughts, and beliefs into acts, even if we can't. Heroes in this sense represent a profoundly humanistic ideal.

Here are two different student notes taken during an in-class exercise.

Student A
Zweig believes that the contemporary world has its "heroes." He doubts that human beings can get along without some expanded ideal of behavior. All of us want to know that our personal limitations are special and that somewhere there will be someone else who can turn words, thoughts, and beliefs into acts. Heroes thus represent a profoundly humanistic ideal.

Student B
Heroes still seem necessary today according to Paul Zweig. Although each of us personally may feel small and limited, we require the knowledge that somewhere out there someone can put our ideals into action.

Student A has seemingly rephrased Zweig's material in his own words, but a closer look reveals a serious problem. Although a phrase or two have been omitted, the expression of ideas is almost identical to the original. Only a few minor words have been shifted out. The student thinks he has paraphrased correctly, but should this note end up in his final paper, it would be considered plagiarism. Student B, on the other hand, has succeeded in taking a valid note that is accurate to the sense of the original while actually *rephrasing* the ideas in her own words.

A *paraphrase* expresses the sense of a passage in your own terms. Technically, a paraphrase is a rewording of the *whole*. In practice, it may be handled like a summary: You may condense information or extract selected ideas, so long as you rephrase them. Any time you present information from another source, the words themselves must be yours, *or* the words must be enclosed in quotation marks. If the words are not in quotation marks and are as similar to the original material as Student A's example is, plagiarism will be charged.

Plagiarism involves the appropriation of someone else's words or ideas as your own. The sad thing is that plagiarism may be accidental. Students may believe that because they have changed a word or two, they have written a proper note. Or students may believe that because they have documented the material by saying, "Zweig believes. . . ," they have precluded plagiarism, no matter how close their phrasing is to the original. Ignorance, however, should not be an excuse. *Even when you give credit to the source in text or footnote, the words of a paraphrase must be yours.*

Fortunately, you can almost guarantee yourself a proper note (one that is not plagiarized), as well as an accurate note, by following a traditional procedure developed by generations of students and scholars. And although the doing requires concentrated effort, the method is surprisingly simple: *Do not look at the original material when writing your note.* Inexperienced writers tend to write their notes by keeping one finger in the book, pointing to the original sentences while writing the note with their other hand. Their eyes move back and forth between the two. But words printed in a book, especially words you've selected as important, have a way of psychologically dominating your own vocabulary. "How can I say it any better—or any differently?" you ask yourself. You may find yourself changing small, insubstantial words while retaining the author's principal phrases.

Instead, once you've chosen a passage as relevant to your study, *turn completely away from it.* Either close the book, turn the book upside down, or move your notepaper so that the book is out of your line of sight. Now write down the idea that struck you as important. This will set in motion a train of meaningful intellectual consequences. What you'll discover is that your brain is suddenly required to recall the idea. Without the direct influence of the author's words, your vocabulary will be all you can depend on. Psychological studies have repeatedly shown that unless you can say something in your own words, you cannot be certain of having understood it. Once you've phrased it for yourself, you not only know that the idea is understood, but you have also made it more permanently a part of you. Recall implants the idea in your memory. Finally, you have in a sense forced yourself to think through the idea in order to phrase it, and you're in a sounder position to evaluate it or to compare it to others. Ideas of your own are likely to develop. Relationships and interpretations become possible. In other words, by the simple act of turning away from the original to write down your note, you discipline your mind and demand that it deal with the idea on its own terms. You engage yourself in the actual process of what we call "study."

One final step remains. Once you've completed your note, you must turn back and check the accuracy of it with the original (see Chapter 38 for a full discussion of accuracy). Again, an important train of consequences is set in motion. In the act of checking for accuracy, you assure yourself that your understanding of the author's idea is correct. If your note is in error, you are in an immediate position to clarify the mistake. If the note is accurate to the *sense* of the original, you can proceed with your reading, confident that when the time comes for writing your paper, you will be able to include the author's information accurately, thoughtfully, in your own words—because it already *is* in your own words.

This process of successful note taking does not seem to come naturally to many of us. We must train ourselves, and the training is demanding. Turning away and writing an idea in your own words requires an incredible amount of concentration. You may constantly find yourself tempted to do it in the old way. What you are faced with is the question of means and ends. If your "ends," your goal, is nothing more than to slide through college and life with the least possible effort, the old method will serve you. But if you have higher goals, if training your mind is important to you, then the "means" begins with the first step. It cannot be leaped over. *Note taking must be a thinking process, not merely an act of recording.*

NOTE-CARD MECHANICS

Every individual tends to devise his or her own format for keeping notes, but the following points have generally proven essential.

1. If you're keeping notes in a journal, create a separate section for all notes and use a separate page for each source.
2. If you're using cards, I recommend 4- by 5-inch cards that allow more room for writing.
3. Write on one side of the page or one side of the card only.
4. Record only one idea, statistic, or fact on each card or page.
5. Always identify the source and page number(s).
6. For cards, write a brief generalization in the upper right or left corner to identify the contents of the card at a glance. For journals, write the generalization in the margins at the side of the note.

Since you should have already created a complete bibliographic entry, you need not repeat that information, but you must still take extraordinary care to label your notes accurately. The best advice is to write the author's last name and the page number first, before you take the note. Make it a habit and you'll never end up with a mystery note that provides an idea without a source or page reference.

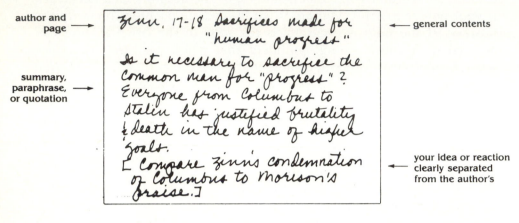

author and page →

summary, paraphrase, or quotation →

← general contents

← your idea or reaction clearly separated from the author's

Exercises

1. The following three paragraphs express fairly complex ideas. Write a paraphrase of each (or a summary-type paraphrase in which you select the most important elements to put in your own words). Use the techniques described in this chapter: (a) do not look at the original material when writing your note; (b) attempt to recall the most important elements of the idea and express them in your own words; (c) reread the original and check the author's expression against your own to determine whether your understanding is accurate and correct to the sense of the original.

> a. In theory, computers should be able to reflect an artist's sensibilities as validly as a brush and canvas; if the result seems banal or mechanical, it's the fault of the artist and not the medium. But can computer art convey the wealth of feelings that great art conveys? Can a program incorporate the quirks and flashes of inspiration that go into a masterpiece? And do the computer's immense capabilities somehow diminish the role played by the man at the controls? A similar question was raised during the early days of photography, when critics wondered how much of the final product was due to the nature of the camera and how much to the eye of the photographer. "Computer art is going through the same evolution as photography," says computer scientist Chuck Csuri of Ohio State University. "But when you look at the impact of photography today, it's absurd to question its artistic value."
>
> *Time* Magazine

b. The emphasis on equality within our social system has led to an almost dogmatic conviction that society can and must eradicate all differences between individuals. But a series of studies by Alexander Thomas, Stella Chess, and Herbert Birch has conclusively demonstrated what all mothers know: Babies are innately different. Infants only one to two weeks old possess clearly defined temperamental predispositions; they show measurable differences in activity levels, irritability, responsiveness, and general mood. In these studies, it was found that the key to a child's development over time lies in the interaction between the temperament of the caregiver and that of the child. An efficient, quick-moving parent, for example, may have to learn not to become exasperated with a daydreaming, dawdling offspring.

Diane McGuinness, Human Nature

c. In this final conception of conscience, Freud continued to be impressed with the importance of guilty fear and the internalized parent, but in addition he postulated that there is an internalized ideal of behavior by which we, our actual selves (our egos), judge our own behavior—and in our failures experience true guilt. Guilt, then, is a form of self-disappointment, a sense of anguish that we did not achieve our standards of what we ought to be. We have fallen short. We have somehow or other betrayed some internal sense of potential self. This is why guilt is the most internalized and personal of emotions. You-against-you allows no buffer, and no villains except yourself. Even when guilty fear is internalized, it is as if someone else were there. But guilt is like tearing apart our internal structure. This is why guilt is so painful to endure.

Willard Gaylin, The Atlantic

2. Make up three sample reference citations from the publication data provided below. The information is listed in a jumbled sequence, and, in some cases, more information is given than you'll actually need.

a. Holmes & Meier Publishers, New York
   473 pages
   Printed in Great Britain
   Eda Sagarra, author
   A Social History of Germany: 1648–1914
   copyright, 1977
   Library call number: 301.143 Sal8

b. Bruce E. Nickerson, author
   The Journal of American Folklore

Published for the American Folklore Society by the University of
    Texas Press
"Is There a Folk in the Factory?"
Vol. 87, April–June, 1974
pp. 133–140
Journal Editor, Barre Toelken

  c. "Opiate of the Masses"
March 8, 1965
Newsweek
Published weekly by Newsweek, Inc., Dayton, Ohio
Editor, Osborn Elliott
pp. 83–84

3. Consider the hypothetical research project described below. Following the description is a passage that offers ideas and information on the project. First, prepare a complete reference citation based on the data provided. Second, prepare one or two sample notes on which you select, summarize, or paraphrase relevant material. You should include only a few direct quotations. Your note cards must be both complete and accurate, but the notes themselves should be highly selective, with only one main idea per note. Be sure to choose only information directly relevant to your project.

Project:	You are researching natural childbirth and decide to investigate the early uses of anesthesia. You are specifically interested in why it became popular even though many doctors and clergy condemned its use. You discover the following passage in an essay on nineteenth-century attitudes toward childbirth.
Publication data:	"Temple and Sewer: Childbirth, Prudery, and Victoria Regina" by John Hawkins Miller in *The Victorian Family: Structure and Stresses* edited by Anthony S. Whol St. Martin's Press, New York, 1978
Relevant passage (pp. 24–25):	On 7 April 1853, Queen Victoria gave birth to her eighth child, Leopold, Duke of Albany. Present in the lying-in room with the Queen were Mrs Lilly (the Queen's monthly nurse), Mrs Innocent, and Dr John Snow. This nominally spiritual and immaculate trinity might well have helped the Queen to overcome her distaste for the 'animal' and 'unesthetic' aspects of childbirth so well-represented in

the confinements attended by Mrs Bangham and Sarah Gamp of Victorian fiction. During this confinement, moreover, the Queen did not have to endure the 'sacred pangs' of labour, for, as she wrote later, Dr Snow 'gave me the blessed Chloroform and the effect was soothing, quieting, and delightful beyond measure.' Her personal physician, Sir James Clark, wrote to James Young Simpson, the Edinburgh obstetrician who first used chloroform in midwifery, that the anaesthesia 'was not at any time given so strongly as to render the Queen insensible, and an ounce of chloroform was scarcely consumed during the whole time. Her Majesty was greatly pleased with the effect, and she certainly never has had a better recovery.'

While the Queen testified to the heavenly benison bestowed by the drug in relieving women of the ancient curse upon Eve (that 'in sorrow shall she bring forth'), there were members of the clergy who considered chloroform a 'decoy of Satan, apparently offering itself to bless women; but in the end, it will harden society, and rob God of the deep earnest cries which arise in time of trouble for help.' The more puritanical and abstemious also inveighed against chloroform because of its well-known intoxicating effects: 'To be insensible from whisky, gin, and brandy, and wine, and beer, and ether and chloroform, is to be what in the world is called Dead-drunk,' wrote Dr Meigs, in his *Obstetrics: The Science and the Art.* 'No reasoning—no argumentation is strong enough to point out the 9th part of a hair's discrimination between them.'

This debate was largely resolved by the women themselves—including the Queen, a lady not known for irreligion or drunkenness. It was the Queen, as Head of the Church, who effectively silenced the objections of religious leaders by legitimizing the use of anaesthesia through her own use of it in 1853, and again in 1857 for the birth of her last child. It has even been claimed by Elizabeth Longford that her 'greatest gift to her people was a refusal to accept pain in childbirth as woman's divinely appointed destiny.'

According to a story current at the time, many of the Queen's subjects were eager to learn of Her Majesty's reactions to the use of anaesthesia. John Snow, the anaesthetist, was besieged with requests from his patients for such information. One woman, to whom Snow was administering anaesthesia while she was in labour, refused to inhale any more chloroform until told exactly what the Queen had said when she was breathing it. Snow replied: 'Her Majesty asked no questions until she had breathed very much longer than you have; and if you will only go on in loyal imitation, I will tell you everything.' The woman obeyed, soon becoming oblivious of the Queen. By the time she regained consciousness, Dr Snow had left the hospital.

While we too may be curious about what the Queen said at the time, we do know that she heartily approved of the effects of the anaesthesia, and many of her subjects were persuaded, in loyal imitation, to demand it during their confinements. What was technically called 'intermittent chloroform analgesia,' became more commonly known as 'chloroform *à la Reine.*'

Discovering Form

36

Organizing Complex Material

As your research continues, you will usually reevaluate and reformulate your questions about the subject. Your insight will change and grow as unexpected ideas enter the picture. By the time you near the end of your project, you may feel overwhelmed with possibilities. How can it all be pulled together?

CATEGORIZING NOTES

Begin by reviewing and sorting your notes according to categories. Use the brief summaries you've jotted in the upper corner or in the margins as a guideline. All notes with similar or related ideas should be placed together. For example, a study of how superstition continues to influence our lives might be broken down into three groups: customs, ceremonies, and gestures. Or you might see other possibilities: fear, sexuality, and anger. The same topic might be organized around one of the 4 *C* methods: change, conflict, consequence, and characterization. Causes and effects—or comparisons and contrasts—might be grouped separately. Commonly mistaken views of superstitions might be sorted into one pile, whereas more accurate interpretations (that you've discovered) are collected in another. Or you might arrange note cards according to a historical sequence: the continuing evidence of superstition through the twentieth century. The possibilities are endless.

Unfortunately, no one can give you a simple formula. The subject itself, your powers of reasoning, and a little intuition must all interact. But the organizing is essential. Form may be "discovered" in the first-draft stage of personal writings, reports, and even expository essays. The research paper is decidedly different. Complex ideas, dozens of sources, conflicting views—the research paper *must* be organized before you begin the first draft. Indeed, as you think through your ideas and consider your material, change those questions you began with into a thesis.

© 1971 United Feature Syndicate, Inc.

THE THESIS

The concept of a *thesis statement* was introduced in Chapter 26. Essentially, it is a brief statement, usually in a single sentence, that summarizes the dominant idea of your findings. If you're not yet sure what the dominant idea is, all the more reason for pausing at this point and working on it. Indeed, you may not be able to sort those note cards at all until you have a clearly defined thesis. More than likely, however, you began to develop a thesis in your head while you were reading your sources—although you may not have called it such. You may simply have thought, "Here's a fascinating angle on the subject," or "Look at how all of these points are pulling together." Now's the time to shape those vague feelings into an exactly worded statement that will guide you in organizing your paper and eventually guide the reader in reading it.

1. Narrow your topic to the *single* most important element of your subject.
2. Start writing about the one or two significant points you've discovered about that element. Use your own voice. Don't worry about being formal or writing for an audience at this stage. This one's for you.
3. Be forceful. State what you know now in such a way that if someone asked you to prove it, you could begin offering evidence from that pile of note cards you've collected.
4. Get your attitude or opinion into it. If you think something is wrong, say so. If you think something needs to be changed, say so. Don't worry about bias; you can return later and make it sound more objective. At this point it's more important to get yourself involved with the subject.

And what if nothing happens? You stare at the page and you have all this information but nothing seems to shape up. Then try another tack. Pretend you're sitting in a bar with a group of friends interested in the same subject you've been studying. Someone asks you to tell them about it—only the catch is that the bar closes in 15 minutes. You have time only to summarize. Everyone looks at you, waiting. Start talking. Tell your friends about the most important ideas you've found. Talk out loud. Most of us are a lot more relaxed talking out loud than writing silently on paper. So talk. Your friends are waiting, and you've got to summarize what you now know as briefly as possible but as forcefully as possible. Try to find the three or five most important points. Then, if you can, narrow it to the one or two most important points. *Talk out loud.* Finally, grab a pencil and paper and write down in your journal the single most important point you've learned. Sometimes you may have to write down all five, but that's OK, too, because now you've got five ideas on paper and you can begin working on how to generalize about them in a single sentence.

All of this is only to suggest that although most of us think of the thesis as a formal (and perhaps somewhat inhibiting) statement, it is actually only a *means,* not an end in itself—a means of helping you come to precise understanding of your study before you begin to organize and write. Later, it may form a portion of your introduction and will serve the reader as a means of getting into the same ideas.

Here are some good and bad thesis statements. The bad ones are bad only because they couldn't help either the writer or the reader get a focus on what the material is about.

Effective thesis statement	*Weak thesis statement*
Professional basketball has been destroyed by the players' greed for million-dollar salaries.	Robert Frost writes poems that reveal some moral values. [*Which poems? Which moral values? And is that good or bad? What is the purpose of telling us?*]
During 1987 and 1988 Ronald Reagan's foreign policy was guided more by ideology than by pragmatism.	America needs energy. Socialism may be the answer, although it has not solved the problem in Europe. [*Where's the focus? Energy? Or socialism in Europe? How are they related?*]
America's health care costs are continuing to inflate because three special interest groups—the physicians, the politicians, and the insurance companies—are all making a profit. The patient is the only one who pays, and no change is in sight.	Today's society is composed of a phenomenon in which we find ourselves afraid to be individuals or to be willing to challenge the conformity imposed upon us. [*Too broad. Individualism and conformity are abstract subjects that need narrowing to specific components.*]

Notice that the last example of an effective thesis (in the left column) uses more than one sentence. Try as you might, sometimes you'll find that a complex subject needs two sentences or three or even a paragraph to state the thesis fully. The single-sentence ideal is not a holy commandment that can't be broken. The point is to design a statement that helps you organize your paper, not to terrorize yourself with a rule that can't possibly anticipate every situation. Make the thesis statement work for you; don't become its slave.

DEVELOPING A DESIGN

No one can predict at what stage in the process a design will begin to take shape. By this point, you may already have a solid feel for how you're going to organize. If not, here's a quick review of all the different possibilities.

1. As in narration and description, almost all organizations move from either the general to the specific or the specific to the gen-

eral, from most important to least important or from least important to most important (see Chapters 8 and 10 for a review).

2. An imaginative lead is effective for both reader and writer and can help the writer envision an organization. A provocative statement, a dramatic scene, a statement of contrast or conflict, a question, or a pileup of statistics that intrigue the reader—each can suggest a pattern for the rest of the paper to follow (see Chapters 20 and 21 for a review).

3. Definition, classification, comparison and contrast, illustration, process analysis, or cause-and-effect analysis may also give an almost automatic shape to the material (see Chapters 23 and 24).

Here is what you must remember: The methods you used to *see* your subject, whether sensory or intellectual, are almost always productive methods around which to design your paper. If to understand Confucianism you study the historical and cultural development of it, then it follows that a narrative presentation may be the most effective organization. But if you compare Confucianism with Christianity, it only makes sense that you will probably use one of the two contrast designs. And if you analyze the decline of Confucianism under the Communist Chinese rulers, then of necessity you must break the subject into parts and move step by step through each one, showing how each relates and whether or not there was cause and effect.

Before you move to the outline stage, take a few minutes and draw some visual designs—boxes, pyramids, circles, or whatever. Try to visualize the pattern your material may fit into. We are visually oriented creatures. Scientists tell us that some 90 percent of all information we gather comes through our eyes. The direction and organization of your paper may become more clear if you can design a visual statement of it—if you can *see* the pattern you're about to follow.

THE WORKING OUTLINE

Some instructors who want to make sure you've thought through your project may require you to submit a formal topic outline, as in this example.

> *Thesis Statement: The decision by Harry S Truman to drop the atom bomb on Japan was expedient but immoral.*
>   I. Summary of historical events leading up to Hiroshima
>   II. Truman uninformed of atomic experiments

    A. Secrecy under Roosevelt
    B. Truman puzzled by Stimson's account
  III. The alternatives as perceived by Joint Chiefs of Staff
    A. Invasion of Japan
    B. Public threat of invasion by all allies jointly
    C. Show of power with atomic bomb
  IV. How Truman made his decision
    A. Military considerations
    B. Political considerations
    C. Moral considerations
   V. Evaluation of his final decision
    A. Consequences in terms of military effectiveness
    B. Consequences in terms of political effectiveness
    C. Consequences in terms of human life
  VI. Overall assessment
    A. Politically and militarily correct
    B. Morally wrong
    C. The dilemma of choice

The assumption behind a conventional topic outline is that, at the very least, you will divide your subject into main ideas and subideas, as in the above example. Some writers may go further and fill in examples or perhaps even specific details and facts.

  I. Main idea
    A. Subidea
      1. Example
      2. Example
    B. Subidea
      1. Example
        a. Specific fact
        b. Specific statistic
        c. Specific quotation
      2. Example

How much detail you go into depends on your personal needs and methods of working. Some students are best advised to omit nothing: Only in such a way will gaps in information or logical flaws be revealed. Others work well from general subheadings or even from a casual outline that does not use roman numerals.

Wartime pressures, national debt, and rationing put pressure on Truman to end war.

The alliance between Russia and the West was weakening.

Chiang Kai-shek was more interested in consolidating his own gains in mainland China.

After Roosevelt's death, Truman discovered he was totally unprepared for all the complexity.

Stimson's information about a new secret weapon was more puzzling than helpful.

The Joint Chiefs of Staff presented Truman with several alternatives but could not agree among themselves.

And so on.

An outline is a working tool. Don't be afraid of it. Use your piles of note cards to shape each step. Be willing to revise several times. And recognize that no matter what method you use or how thorough you are, new ideas may still occur during the first draft that will cause you to break the pattern of your outline. After you finish the first draft, a second or third outline may be needed before you begin rewriting.

37

Drafting and Documenting

Y ou've conducted your interviews, read magazines and books, organized your ideas, and drawn up a design to follow. But certain components of a research paper tend to create problems you may not encounter in other forms of writing. The introduction, the handling of documentation, and the final organization of a works-cited page all require extra attention.

LEADS AND INTRODUCTIONS

Although a research paper may begin with a formal introduction, an imaginative lead always adds interest and spark. The two can sometimes be combined. Here's how a freshman nursing major drew together various elements from her research to organize an effectively unified lead and introduction.

An Undignified Death

Lead consists of three examples.

In New Freedom, Pennsylvania, George McGraw, a fifty-eight-year-old construction worker, rushed to the hospital after being involved in an automobile accident, was released because he appeared to only suffer from a scraped elbow. No X-rays were taken. On the way home, fragments of bone from a fractured neck and skull "sliced" into McGraw's brain and spinal cord, paralyzing him for life ("Auto").

In New York, a thirty-five-year-old printer who had been released from an emergency room with only painkillers for a stomach ache died at home with massive hemorrhaging of stomach ulcers ("Law").

In Dallas, an accident victim brought in "appearing" to be dead on arrival was ignored for several hours until he caught someone's attention when he coughed. The patient survived but because of delay in treatment he suffered severe brain damage ("Dead").

Formal introduction begins with general overview.

These three cases are almost insignificant when compared to the more than one million lives annually lost in crisis situations, with approximately sixty thousand of those being preventable deaths. These losses and tragedies are a result of mishandlings due to either inadequate emergency facilities or inadequate emergency treatment.

Historical context is established.

Fifteen years ago, the American Academy of General Practice listed a membership of 95,526 doctors, but today the list contains only 68,326 members (NBC). Although more and more doctors are turning to specialization, more and more people are turning to the emergency room for treatment. According to Scudder Winslow, M.D., and head of New York's Roosevelt Hospital Emergency Service, the emergency room has "simply become a substitute for the family doctor" because there are only a few general practitioners for people to turn to (216). Yet 90 percent of the seven thousand accredited hospitals in the United States provide emergency rooms that are poorly equipped and understaffed (NBC). This failure of hospitals and medical associations to deal with—or at times even to recognize—the emergency-room crisis has led to a frightening situation that shows no signs of early solution. As a future nurse, I'm vitally concerned.

Specific focus begins to take shape.

Thesis stated.

Terrie Clinger

Obviously, an introduction can take other shapes, but Terrie has followed a fairly conventional and traditionally successful method.

1. An imaginative lead (provocative statement, literary scene, contrast, question, quotation, and so on).
2. General overview of what the paper is about as a whole (in a sentence or two).
3. A brief summary of the background or historical context to orient the reader and establish the foundation for evidence that follows.

4. A focusing sentence (usually the thesis statement) that narrows the topic or presents the dominant idea that will be explored and supported by the body of the paper.

It might be misleading, however, to leave the impression that Terrie's introduction looked like this on a first draft. Actually, it went through hours of work and half a dozen thrown-away pages. For most of us, the introduction remains the most difficult element of any paper to write. In fact, some writers avoid it entirely until the rest of the first draft is complete. If the introduction becomes hopelessly bogged down, give it up. Go straight to the body of the paper. Begin with your first example or quotation and write as fast as possible. You can return later and decide how to introduce the whole. As Ezra Pound put it, "It doesn't matter which leg of your table you make first, so long as the table has four legs and will stand up solidly when you have finished it."

COMPOSING VERSUS COLLATING

I want to stress one final time that a first draft should be written as quickly as possible. You should see the subject with your mind's eye; concern yourself only with ideas; and save spelling, punctuation, correct usage, and all other necessary mechanics for later revisions. But research papers traditionally raise another problem. You'll find yourself concerned not only with your own ideas but also with those taken from others. You may be tempted to "sew together" your notes, moving slowly from one to the next and merely transcribing information from note card to paper, adding here and there a transition like *also* or *therefore*. Any personal understanding of the subject gained during research may be overwhelmed by all those facts gathered from authorities. You may find yourself repressing your own views and merely collating the views of your sources. It's at that point you'll need to call up again the whole purpose of research. You'll need to remind yourself that your imagination, memory, and reasoning must form a major part of your writing. All those notes and facts from others exist to support what you've discovered. They are never a substitute for your own insights.

PRELIMINARY DOCUMENTATION

A second problem—and one that used to be far more difficult when you were required to use footnotes—involves documentation of material taken from other sources. More and more disciplines now use a parenthetical form of documentation, with footnotes reserved only for additional commentary or for reference to additional sources that aren't directly cited in your paper.

The following guidelines are adapted from a system published in 1984 by The Modern Language Association. Your instructor may provide you with a different format, and other instructors in other fields (psychology, chemistry, engineering, and so on) may provide you with still other guidelines. Don't fight it. What may seem a lack of consistency is actually only a matter of knowing your audience and learning to adapt to varying expectations.

For research papers in most writing classes, you'll be expected to document sources in two ways. First, when a quotation or direct paraphrase is used, you must parenthetically identify your source at that point, directly in the text. The parenthetical information should be condensed enough not to interfere with reading the text, but full enough to refer the reader to complete bibliographic information provided at the end of your paper under the heading *Works Cited*. The intention of this new method is to simplify the process for both reader and writer. As you write your first draft all you need to do is insert in parentheses a brief note referring to your source. You should not worry at that time whether it fulfills the technical requirements of the MLA format. Just insert a note to yourself so that as you continue drafting and revising, the note remains with the material. Perhaps it will look something like this.

> Studies have shown that at some colleges up to 90% of so-called student athletes have not been graduating (Chron. for Higher Ed, Carroway 9). Even worse is the attitude of many coaches. The story is told of a Texas A&M coach who is supposed to have glanced over the report card of one of his basketball players who received four F's and one D. The coach reportedly commented, "Son, looks to me like you're spending too much time on one subject" (Will, Newsweek 84).

At this stage, parenthetical notes serve to help you clarify where you found the material. Later, you'll want those notes to conform to an approved format so that your reader can also identify your sources with ease. Obviously, it would be better if preliminary documentation was absolutely accurate. But in early drafting, perfecting your ideas is more important than perfecting your documentation. One way or another, when you reach a final revision, you'll still have to double-check each citation to assure conformity to proper style. As long as you have basic information from your source in early drafts, you can then edit it prior to final typing.

PARENTHETICAL CITATIONS

Once you've reached your final revision, you'll want to follow these essential principles approved by the Modern Language Association for correct parenthetical citations.

1. If you are citing a *complete* work, and if you use the author's name or the title of the work in your sentence, you need not provide any further information.

> Guitton encourages students to commit themselves to a life of the mind.

> *or*

> A Student's Guide to Intellectual <u>Work</u> encourages students to commit themselves to a life of the mind.

2. If you are citing a specific portion of a work, you have the option of including the author's name in the sentence or in the parenthetical reference along with the page numbers.

> William James has observed that any attempt to define the concept has proven illusive for it takes us into a discussion about "fundamental properties of matter" (33).

> *or*

> Attempting to define the concept has proven illusive for it takes us into a discussion about "fundamental properties of matter" (James 33).

I strongly recommend that the first time you use a *new* source in any paper, especially if quoting, you give the author's full name and, if possible, some identification of the author or the work you are citing. To do so gives a sense of authority and authenticity to the information. It may mean little to a reader if you write:

Campaigning for President "has a tendency to change one's sense of values" (Stevenson 198).

But it can be quite persuasive if you write:

Adlai Stevenson, Democratic presidential candidate in 1952 and 1956, has observed that campaigning for the presidency "has a tendency to change one's sense of values" (198).

The reader now knows that the source you're citing has authority. Your evidence is more convincing, and the quotation is attached to a real human being, not just to a bibliographical citation.

PUNCTUATION

To simplify the old question of where to place the punctuation mark, the MLA recommends that a parenthetical reference always be located *before* the period, as in the above examples.

But alas, as in all things in life, there is one exception. If you use a long "block" quotation (and any quotation longer than four or five lines should be indented and quoted in block form), the parenthetical reference occurs *after* the period.

Because of the Brandeis studies, SAT scores are now being called into question nationwide:

This does not suggest that the SAT itself discriminates, but rather that certain uses of the SAT by admissions officers at American colleges may be discriminatory. The use of cutoff scores, for example, quite likely discriminates against the poor and minorities, as does the use of the scores to compare students from different economic and cultural backgrounds. (Owen 32)

COMMON FORMS OF IN-TEXT REFERENCES

A work by a single author
Janovy writes lyrically about nature: "One can never get enough of a falling star" (174).

A work by two or more authors
Darrow and Hicks have studied the problem but conclude that generational distrust is normal (132–133).

or

Later research by a team of psychologists failed to support the data (Gibbons et al. 5).

[The Latin abbreviation, *et al.*, means *and others* and indicates that three or more authors are involved.]

Same author, different work
On the one hand, Heldman argues, "Painting is an act of life itself available to all who have the courage to risk failure" (<u>Memories</u> 44). But later she returns to her 1909 thesis that the artist's life is unavailable to the common man, no matter his degree of courage (Art 110).

[Shortened titles in parentheses clarify different sources. Another method would be to include titles in the text itself.]

But later in <u>Art as a Way of Knowing</u>, she returns to her 1909 thesis that the artist's life is unavailable to the common man no matter his degree of courage (110).

Works without an author
The pamphlet, <u>Judaism Under Siege,</u> claims that Israel is threatened by twenty million hostile neighbors (3).

or

The claim has been made that Israel is threatened by twenty million hostile neighbors (<u>Judaism</u> 3).

Literary works
With little money left from what he inherited from his father, George Webber goes to Europe where once more "the hoof and the wheel came down the streets of memory" (Wolfe, 328; ch. 17, bk. 4).

[Literary works may occur in numerous editions. The MLA recommends that in addition to page numbers, you indicate chapters, sections, and parts to help readers with different editions locate the reference. For poetry, plays, and biblical citations, omit page numbers altogether and indicate only acts, scenes, lines, or verses.]

> Hamlet's soliloquy, "To be, or not to be . . . ," provides our first interior view of his dilemma (3.1.56–89).

[The reference is to act 3, scene 1, lines 56–89 of *Hamlet*. The periods distinguish act from scene and line. An alternative version is to use Roman numerals for act and scene with Arabic numerals for line numbers: (III, i, 56–89).]

Magazines, newspapers, and journals

> The question of whether pilot and crew should abandon a hijacked jetliner seems to have convincing arguments on both sides ("Agony" 26).

[The shortened title of the article refers the reader to the list of Works Cited, where full documentation will occur: "Agony of Pan Am Flight 73." *Newsweek* 15 September 86: 21–26.]

THE WORKS-CITED LIST

Each parenthetical reference must be supported at the end of your paper with full documentation in the form of an alphabetical list of Works Cited. The list follows the body of your paper with continuous pagination. Here are some of the most common entries you may need to use.

Book by a single author
Page, Russell. The Education of a Gardener. New York: Random, 1983.

Book by two or more authors
Crews, Frederick, and Sandra Schor. The Borzoi Handbook for Writers. New York: Knopf, 1985.

Two or more books by same author
Rhys, Jean. After Leaving Mr. Mackenzie. New York: Harper, 1982.

———. Wide Sargasso Sea. New York: Norton, 1982.

Book with corporate authorship
United States Bureau of the Census. Statistical Abstract of the United States. 104th ed. Washington: GPO, 1983.

Book by an editor or compiler
Baumback, Jonathan, ed. Writers as Teachers, Teachers as Writers. New York: Holt, 1970.

Item in an anthology
Minot, Susan. "Hiding." The Pushcart Prize, IX: Best of the Small Presses. Ed. Bill Henderson. New York: Pushcart P, 1984. 31–42.

Introduction, preface, or afterword
Hughes, Ted. Foreword. The Journals of Sylvia Plath. Ed. Ted Hughes and Frances McCullough. New York: Dial, 1982.

Translation
Tolstoy, Leo. War and Peace. Trans. Constance Garnett. London: Pan, 1972.

Book with a title within its title
Stafford, William T. Melville's Billy Budd and the Critics. Belmont, Calif.: Wadsworth, 1968.

Miller, James E., ed. Whitman's "Song of Myself"—Origin, Growth, Meaning. New York: Dodd, 1964.

Article in journal with continuous pagination
Saxon, David S. "The Future of Liberal Arts: A Scientist's View." The Georgia Review 39 (1985): 586–600.

Article in journal that pages each issue separately
McCormick, Frank. "Donne, The Pope, and 'Holy Sonnets XIV.' " The CEA Critic 2 (1983): 23–24.

Parker, Wilson. "The American Century is Over." American Policy Quarterly 12.1 (1990): 55–61.

Article in weekly or biweekly periodical
Fise, Frederick. "Architecture and Post Modernism on the College Campus." Chronicle of Higher Education 24 Nov. 1983: 5–6.

Article in a monthly periodical
Meisler, Stanley. "Vienna's Anguished Artists Presaged the Brilliant City's Fate." Smithsonian Aug. 1986: 71–81.

Article from a newspaper
"New Developments in Star Wars." The Wall Street Journal 9 Oct. 1988: 1, B15.

Grist, Tony. "Jazz Returns to Charlotte." <u>Charlotte Observer</u> 21 Jan. 1990: 1, 23.

Review

Creek, G. S. "Nightgames." Rev. of <u>Burning Bright</u>, by Marianne Bridges. <u>Philadelphia Enquirer</u> 7 Feb. 1990, sec. 1: 47.

Editorial

"Perception vs. Reality." Editorial. <u>The Asheville Citizen</u> 16 Sept. 1986: 4.

Films, radio, and TV

<u>CBS Evening News with Dan Rather</u>. Writ. Dan Rather. Prod. Martin Holms. CBS. WSPA Spartanburg, South Carolina. 3 Jan. 1987.

Advertisement

Halston for Men. Advertisement. <u>The New Yorker.</u> 30 Oct 1989: 17.

Pamphlet

Students for Choice. <u>Abortion Rights.</u> Los Angeles: mimeograph, n.d.

Kline, Karen. <u>How Can I Know if I'm an Alcoholic?</u> Asheville, N.C.: Blue Ridge Mental Health Clinic, 1987.

Reference Book

"Fred Chappell." <u>Dictionary of Literary Biography. American Novelists since World War II.</u> 2nd. Series. Ed. James E. Kibler, Jr. Detroit: Bruccolic Clark, 1980. 6: 36–38.

"Gerontology." Encyclopaedia Britannica: Macropaedia. 1983 ed.

Interview

Grisley, Robert K. Personal Interview. 6 Sept. 1987.

Mikhail Gorbachev. Interview. <u>CBS Evening News with Dan Rather</u>. Malta. 3 Dec. 1989.

Lectures, Speeches, Addresses

Gilcrist, Pamela. "Modernism in Art and Literature." Humanities Lecture Series. Museum of Fine Arts. Boston, 10 Jan. 1990.

For additional references or special problems, check the 1984 edition of the *MLA Handbook for Writers of Research Papers*.

Revising and Editing

38

Self-Criticism

Writing about abstract ideas may be the most difficult of all types of writing. The problem is often that writers know precisely what they mean but fail to recognize that their words do not express their meaning. The reader, however, knows only what the words actually say; we can't look into the writer's mind. The old excuse, "I know what I meant," is never an excuse; writers are always responsible for verifying that their words express their intention. That verification occurs during both the revising and editing phases. It may involve the slow, thoughtful review of every word and sentence, not just once, but several times.

ACCURACY AND PRECISION

Several types of accuracy must be checked. Most important is the accuracy of summarized or quoted material. Not only is it a courtesy to the author you've read or the expert you've interviewed, but it is also one of the most unbreakable rules of intellectual work: *Thou shalt not misquote.* Every word inside a quotation must be accurate, and ideas rephrased in your own words must be accurate to the *sense* of the original.

Here is how one student writer expressed an idea he found in Charles W. Ferguson's book *Say It with Words*. I've placed Ferguson's original material to the left for you to compare.

Ferguson	**Student version**
No generalization is wholly true, as Disraeli reminds us, including this one, but you will find it of great practical use to husband verbs.	In a chapter called "Mind Your Verbs," Ferguson shows us just how long attention has been paid to verbs: "Disraeli reminds us . . . you will find it of great practical use to husband verbs." And Disraeli was a prime minister of England in 1868!

The error here is serious. The student believes he has quoted accurately because every word inside the quotation appears in the original. But both Ferguson and Disraeli have been misrepresented. Either from careless reading or in a careless transferral of reading notes to manuscript, the student has botched the whole idea. Ferguson is paraphrasing Disraeli as saying that "no generalization is wholly true." Ferguson offers no indication that Disraeli ever said a word about verbs.

Unfortunately, this type of thing happens all too frequently to all of us when we work under pressure. We read too quickly; we write the paper late at night, glance over it hurriedly for spelling errors, and submit it. Critical thinking, however, demands a slow, attentive concern, not only to ideas others have presented but also to the way you represent those ideas. Here is how another student described a portion of Kate Millett's work on *Sexual Politics*.

Millett	**Student version**
. . . it was the Renaissance which furnished the first applied theories of education for women. Alberti's *Della Famiglia* is fairly representative of these. The purpose of such minimal training as it recommends is merely an aesthetic and convenient docility.	Also Millett tells us that the education for women has risen as a sort of modern-day achievement of educating the lower levels of man to simply keep them content and satisfied. This is illustrated when Alberti said in *Della Famiglia*, "The purpose of such minimal training as it recommends is merely an aesthetic and convenient docility."

Like the previous student, this one attributes a portion of the author's ideas—this time, Kate Millett's—to someone she has referred to in her text. It was not Alberti who said, "The purpose of such minimal training. . . ." Those are Millett's words. But the first part of the student's summary is also inaccurate because the student has not looked closely at his own words and considered what they mean: ". . . education of women has risen as a sort of modern-day achievement *of educating the lower levels of man.* . . ." Not only does Kate Millett say no such thing, it makes no sense. How can the education of women be aimed at *educating* the lower levels of man? What the student probably means is that Millett believes the education of women in the Renaissance was aimed at *satisfying* the lower levels of man. The failure to find the precise word makes a parody of the original material.

Another type of imprecision shows up in this student's paper.

> The stock show champion was sired by a prize steer from Lyndon Johnson's ranch.

President Johnson would no doubt have been surprised that a steer could sire anything since, by definition, a steer is a castrated bull.

Accuracy and precision include historical ideas.

> . . . it was Abraham Lincoln who was elected on the promise of freeing the slaves.

Lincoln, of course, promised nothing of the kind and probably would not have been elected if he had. Such a historical inaccuracy casts a dark shadow over the paper as a whole. If a writer can make this kind of error, how can we trust his or her other information to be sound?

A final illustration appears in this freshman analysis of an essay on gun control.

> The First Amendment to the Constitution gives everyone the right to bear arms.

But it is the Second Amendment, not the First, that discusses the right to bear arms. Even the Second is not clear as to whether "everyone" has such a right. The precise wording of the amendment may refer only to the right to form a state militia. Did the student verify the number of the amendment or the actual wording? Obviously not.

Accuracy and precision in themselves seldom bring a writer praise; inaccuracy and imprecision will invariably bring condemnation.

OMISSIONS

From the writer's point of view, the omission of a portion of an argument or even a single word may be terribly difficult to spot. I've often found myself reading a sentence four times before discovering that I've left out something, a phrase or word I could swear was there in print the first three times I read the sentence. Because our mind *knows* what the sentence is supposed to say, it tends to fill in any blanks. Unfortunately, the reader cannot.

Here's a student example I received a few years ago.

> Pitcher advised the divorcing parents to explain divorce to the young child in the following manner: This method will help ease the negative impact of the divorce on the child. Pitcher's method provides divorcing parents with a format that will help minimize the effect of divorce on the child.

The *method* around which the passage focuses is strangely absent. After some questioning the student recognized she had omitted a whole page of handwritten material. As she typed her paper, two pages had apparently stuck together—a simple error that could happen to any of us. But what should *not* have happened is that the student failed to reread her paper. She knew what she had written, but she failed to verify what she had typed.

Here's a different kind of omission.

> Art is also a form of therapy. Participating in creative with other people helps some individuals replace the loss of objects and to express their feelings openly.

As it is impossible to participate in "creative," a word must be missing. Creative *activities*? Creative *efforts*? Creative *arts*? We don't know. Neither do we know what the mention of a "loss of objects" means. It may be possible for participation in creative activities to help people express their feelings. But how does it replace a loss of objects? It turns out that the student had read a pamphlet on various mental problems that art therapists claimed to treat. Somewhere in that pamphlet, an emotional condition was defined as arising out of a loss of "objects" that were of no particular worth, but that held symbolic value for the patient. The student failed to include that explanation. He knew in his mind what the phrase meant. After all, he had read the pamphlet. But he failed to consider that his audience had not. A definition or explanation for specialized concepts must occur on the page, not remain buried in the writer's mind. A single missing word can make nonsense of an otherwise valid argument.

HIDDEN ASSUMPTIONS

We may so thoroughly believe something that we fail to realize others do not, that others might consider our beliefs only an *assumption*. If you believe that all human beings have souls, for example, you may argue that because Bob and Maria are human beings, they obviously have souls. The logic of your argument is valid, as long as we all agree on that first premise. Indeed, many reasonable arguments *must* begin with assumptions because we can't possibly know everything. But if you present an argument based on an assumption without realizing that it is an assumption, you may find yourself being challenged.

After an essay in *Fortune* described the struggle between the Environmental Protection Agency and certain large industrialists in the Southwest, a student criticized the essay with the following argument.

> The author has attempted to make us believe that Schrieber, Danforth, Holman, and other factory owners are struggling over a principle involving individual rights. But how many times has that been the rallying cry for self-interest? The Southern states used a similar justification for breaking from the Union just because they didn't want to give up slaves. Actually, the real reason Schrieber and his kind are resisting efforts to clean up the air and water is simple. They are involved in big business. Money is more important than the environment. They have to answer to their stockholders, not to the trees.

The student seems to have presented a forceful argument. The final sentence seems especially strong. He tries to discredit both the author and the industrialists by arguing that their actions are based on self-interest. But what is the student's proof? Answer: *Those involved represent "big business."*

Something is missing. The proof rests on a hidden assumption that the student believes his readers share: All those connected with big business are greedy. Money, to such individuals, means more than the common good. Only if we agree with that *assumption* can we find the student's argument valid. If we question such generalities, however, we are in a position to challenge the argument as a whole. Are *all* big business men greedy? Do *all* value money over the welfare of the nation? For a writer, the danger of the hidden assumption is that you may believe you've erected a convincing and logical argument when, in actuality, you've omitted its very foundation. As a result, the whole of it may come tumbling down.

The solution to all these problems—inaccuracy, imprecision, omissions—is to read your paper with the same critical attitude you use when you read someone else's work. You must apply the same criteria of logic, clarity, and concern for detail to your own essay that you expect to find in another's. The process of self-criticism is demanding, time-consuming, and often frustrating. But as Rimbaud once said, ''Excellence costs less trouble than mediocrity.'' You can be sure that if you don't criticize your own work, your audience will. Better to be embarrassed in private than in public.

Exercise

Check each of the following passages—all written by students—for inaccuracy, imprecision, or vagueness due to apparent omissions or for other problems that would cause confusion for a reader.

a. The two doctors are father and son who displayed two very interesting sides about vitamin C. The father told me that for colds, he tries to consult the patient to drink clear liquids. But his son goes much farther and tries to prevent the cold in the first place. Because a cold averages three persons per year, we know that prevention is more vital than cure. The son tries to get his patients to take massive doses of vitamin C before it gets them.

b. John Locke was not very bright if he believed in Natural Law. All scientific evidence shows that there are physical laws, but it is only a form of ego trip to believe that your personal moral values are God-given and form some kind of Natural Law or Absolute Law. John Locke was obviously enculturated into believing that the attitudes of his time were right and all others wrong. As common sense tells us that all men are not created equal, Locke was merely providing an argument that can only be described as wish fulfillment.

c. Burglars are of two varieties, the professional and the amateur. Most thieves are only interested in the merchandise they have come to steal, not inflicting bodily harm. . . . Most criminals work no harder than necessary to what they want . . . it is far easier for them to abandon a house with good locks on all doors and windows and look for one less protected,'' according to *Safety Strategy* by Jack de Celle. And evidence shows that what they want is televisions, tape recorders, and other electrical equipment. This has probably always been true such equipment is easier to sell than say clothes.

d. Katherine Anne Porter was trying to relate war and epidemic in her essay *Pale Horse, Pale Rider*, with epidemic as the rider and war as the horse. The horse carries his rider around, allowing him to cover more territory quicker and easier. Epidemic is not caused by war but war by an epidemic. World War I was a sign of the direction man was heading toward. War, although dating back into the ancient times, is a forerunner of death. War shows all the deathly sides of human nature. It causes people to want to die, to give up their lives, their will to live. There is a close knitting parallel between war and epidemic.

Student Research Papers

The following student research papers provide two models. The first is a more informal, more personal essay in which the writer narrates the process of the search itself and describes how it relates to her life. The second paper is what is often called a "library paper," one that focuses on an abstract concept and that, in this case, is based solely on secondary research. Both are valid models of scholarship that pursue questions of value and seek out possible answers from a variety of sources.

Trish Breen was an adult commuter-student who had lived in England and Africa before entering college as a freshman. In "My Mount Fuji," Trish begins with an imaginative lead and includes numerous scenes and descriptions of individuals who influenced her search. Use of the first person, an informal style, and concrete details create the quality of a personal essay. Yet she has used nine sources, integrating books, magazine articles, and interviews to substantiate her findings.

1

Patricia Breen

Professor Wright

CH 121

8 Dec. 1987

My Mount Fuji

Early one Sunday morning, my husband, Mike, and I
ran fifteen miles, winding through Hendersonville to
Flat Rock, North Carolina, then crossing along Little
River Road to Kanuga and back home.   Fifteen miles is
only eleven miles short of a marathon, I thought, and we
had only stopped once at McCrary's to get a drink.   I
knew I could run a marathon, with a little more effort of
course.   But a marathon would be like running from home
to Asheville Mall the back way.   What a challenge!

Thoughts of running such a distance had wandered
through my mind ever since I read Dr. George Sheehan's
book, <u>Running and Being</u>.   If you can run five miles, he
believes you can run ten; if you can run ten, you can run
twenty.   You should be capable of doubling any distance
you can run with ease, but slowly.   He also states that
eighty percent of first time marathoners finish in over
four hours.   Time is not important--finishing is.

Breen 2

Early in October, my husband brought home a flyer
for a lecture, "Feeling Good 24 Hours a Day," by George
Sheehan, on October 25th, at the University of North
Carolina at Asheville campus. I marked the calendar and
looked forward to going.

The auditorium opened at 7:30 p.m. and we headed
for the front row seats. A slight man, five foot six
maybe, stood on stage, writing on a blackboard. His
freckled skin glowed beneath wispy gray hair. He looked
like someone who is outdoors a lot, but not at all like a
noted cardiologist.

When he stopped writing, he walked to the stage's
edge, jumped down, and sat on its lip, looking up towards
the entrance as people drifted in. My heart thumped.
What an opportunity! I left my seat and walked up to the
stage.

"Hi," he said, and I thought of the accuracy of the
phrase in his book which described him as having a nose
that covered one-third of his face, an overbite, and a
scrawny body.

Quivering, I told him I was a runner and wanted to
prepare for a marathon and needed his advice. He wanted
to know how long I had been running and how much I ran.

"I've been running since July, 1982," I replied,
"and now run from twenty-five to thirty-five miles a
week, depending on the weather."

"That's great. You're probably ready. Don't be
concerned with miles. Run for time. An hour out on the
roads at a time. Two hours or more for a long workout.
Do you enter races?" I shook my head no. "Racing is the
best way to get a good workout. Start with five
kilometers and work up. Give it all you've got and don't
worry if everyone passes you," he said laughing.

"One thing to watch for is eating enough. Women
who diet and run are looking for trouble. Dehydration
is another hazard. People enter the New York marathon
and collapse midway from dehydration. Drink water,
lots of it, before, during, and after running." He
placed his hands behind his head and leaned back.
"Don't overtrain. Running can get boring and it's
lonely. If you're injured, don't run. Take a week off.
Running should make you feel good."

The hall filled up and people stood behind me
clutching books to be autographed. I thanked him and
walked back to my seat. A smile settled on my face for
the next few hours. What a break!

After talking and listening to Dr. Sheehan, I
realized how little I knew about how my body functions.
On a rainy Sunday later that week, I pulled out all my
Runner's World copies and spread them out on the rug.
I spent several hours reading and found an important
article titled "Body Fluids" by Richard Pearce.

Breen 4

Pearce states that symptoms of dehydration are a
fast beating heart, tired heavy muscles which can
collapse, and skipping heart beats. As the resting
pulse quickens, clumsiness, fatigue, disorientation,
headaches, and nausea also occur. The brain cells
shrink slightly and mental disturbances result (46). I
wondered how many times I had come close to dehydrating.

According to Pearce, long distance runners can
lose up to one and a half gallons during a long run. But
if the runner constantly replaces the fluid by drinking
before, during, and after running, this can be avoided
(46). I had been drinking little before and during a
run, thinking incorrectly that I would have to stop to
urinate. Fluid is lost by breathing and sweating. If
fluid is not replaced while running, the body will draw
fluid from cell "compartments" and deplete body fluids
further (48).

From the book Improving Women's Running, by former
Olympic coach Bill Squires, I learned that water is the
best source of fluid replacement. The body absorbs
water more quickly than any other fluid and with no side
effects (148). Commercial drinks, such as Coke and
orange juice, are highly concentrated and draw fluid
from the cells which, in turn, causes diarrhea.
Dangerous amounts of body fluid are lost in this way.
Clear urine indicates enough fluid is being ingested to

Breen 5

replace what is lost (Pearce 48). Medical authorities
recommend drinking about thirty-eight ounces of water
two hours before a race, but advise runners to
experiment to determine what's best for them (Squires
149).

   I began wondering, too, if I might be harming my
body by not eating the right foods. I'd never been a
junk food addict. Still I wasn't sure just what I should
be eating to prepare for a marathon. A book titled Long
Distance Runner's Guide to Training and Racing by two
experienced runners, Ken Sparks and Garry Bjorklund,
provided me with the information I needed. According to
the authors, fats (which I had avoided), proteins, and
carbohydrates are essential nutrients (143). I had
thought protein was the primary source for energy when
running, but found that fats and carbohydrates are the
major fuels needed (161). I need to eat more bread,
whole grain cereals, pasta, and fresh fruits (154). I
learned too that the body needs a certain amount of fats
to act as carriers for vitamins A, D, E, and K (161).
However, the pre-race meal, eaten three or four hours
before the race to allow time for digestion, should be
bland and low in fat (158). I was in the habit of eating
too many carbohydrates only one or two hours before
running.

   I was also concerned about preventing injuries.

Breen 6

In his article on how to combine sports to prevent
injuries, John Howard offers some sound advice. John
Howard is not only a marathoner but also a two-time
winner of the Hawaii "Iron Man Triathlon," a grueling
contest consisting of a two-mile ocean swim, a hundred-
and-ten-mile bike race, plus a marathon. It goes
without saying that many runners, including me, follow
Howard's advice. After running for a year, I have never
had a debilitating injury.

    John Howard's premise is that "tendons, ligaments
and bones are often stressed because of inflexibility.
If athletes practice only their own craft without
working any of the other muscle groups, an imbalance
occurs" (64). He believes cycling allows runners to
increase their pulse rate and get an aerobic workout
equivalent to distance running. After an injury he
suffered running, Howard rode a stationary bike and
practiced a series of yoga asanas that counterstretched
muscles used in running and cycling. He found that by
using this regimen he was able to return to distance
running and resume his training schedule with no loss of
aerobic fitness (64). I felt reassured that my habit of
combining running, cycling, and yoga would help prevent
injury.

    Dane Freeman, a longtime friend of my husband, is
a thirty-eight-year-old runner with eight years

experience. I called him one evening and asked him for some tips on training methods. He suggested that we meet on Friday evening and run together.

The following Friday, I jogged up Highlands Avenue and saw Dane waiting on the corner. His sandy red hair fluttered as the wind whipped up the leaves on the sidewalk. He wore a black Adidas T-shirt, black nylon shorts, and red and white striped Adidas running shoes. Strong muscular legs supported his lean body. "Where you wanna run?" He had to yell so I could hear above the traffic.

"You lead the way. Just remember, I've questions to ask, so no six-minute miles," I said laughing.

We crossed North Main at the traffic light, ran past Winn Dixie and the high school, the post office, then uphill into the residential area of Laurel Park. It was getting dark and the street lamps lit up. I felt good. The brisk wind smacked my face.

"How many marathons have you run?" I shouted, trying to keep abreast of him so I could hear. I don't often talk and run, so my breathing was labored.

"Fifteen. Ran the first in '75 in Greenville. Did Boston and New York too," he said, turning his head to me. "Not so keen on marathons now. I've been racing middle distance this year."

"Why?"

"I've had too many injuries: ankle, achilles and chronic knee problems," he said. "I'm supposed to have surgery on my knees but keep putting it off."

"Why so many injuries? Do you run too many miles?"

"Yeah. I was running between eighty to a hundred miles a week and I started getting injuries. Dropped down to about sixty now. I've started speedwork, intervals. Wanna try some?"

"Okay. What do you do?"

"Jog slow for a quarter of a mile, then fast as you can for a quarter. Jog, run, jog, run. Stop, check your pulse. It should double, then slow down to one-twenty fairly quick. Shows you're working hard enough. Then start over. Intervals are supposed to build up stamina and increase speed. But you can't do this for too long. Too strenuous. Maybe once a week at the most. Dr. Sheehan calls interval work 'character builders.' You read Dr. Sheehan, don't you?" he asked.

What a question, I thought.

"Anyway," he continued, "intervals are anaerobic. You're actually training your muscles to work without oxygen for short periods of time."

The slow run was easy. I felt my pulse rise as I began to sprint. My breath rasped and my chest tightened. Dane had stopped ahead and had his hand up to his neck looking at his watch. I stopped, bent over, and let my hands scrape the dirt. "Pulse okay," I said, my

fingers touching my wrist as I counted the seconds on my
watch. "Let's try once more and then head home," I said,
feeling invigorated and a little light headed.

It was dark. The city clock on Main Street chimed
six-thirty. Perkins' Pancake House loomed ahead of us.
We stopped outside. I bent over again to get my breath;
a stitch gnawed at my side. "You okay?" Dane asked.

"I'm fine. Just pooped. That was super. Thanks
so much," I said.

"See ya," he yelled. I waved and sprinted across
North Main before the light changed. My legs felt
tight, a vein throbbed in my groin. Exertion, I
thought, nothing to worry about.

Later that night, I thumbed through the latest copy
of Runner's World and read Joe Henderson's article,
"Tips for the First-Time Marathoner." Joe Henderson, a
California marathoner, had teamed up with former
Olympic runner and current Running Circuit Clinic
Coach, Jeff Galloway, to produce a running plan for new
marathoners.

Galloway believes that working with hundreds of
marathoners on the circuit led him to change his
thinking on training for marathons. Weekly mileage
counting is unimportant and can be dangerous. It
encourages runners to run too many miles without rest
(67). A long run every two weeks, near marathon

distance, is best. He recommends a running schedule.
Run three to ten miles as fillers in between the long
run, rest two days a week to recuperate. He believes one
long run every two weeks is essential (68). Both
Galloway and Henderson are convinced that the biggest
cause of injury in long distance runners is running too
many miles without rest (69).

Later as I searched through Galloway's Book on
Running he reemphasized this key concept. According to
Galloway, "You increase your total mileage by
lengthening the long run, not by an accumulation of
daily increases" (119). He believes total weekly
mileage is an inefficient way to increase endurance and
is the main cause of injury among runners (118).

I placed my hands behind my head, thinking about my
marathon. I've now put my marathon on a pedestal and I'm
working toward it. I've set my goal as spring when the
season begins. If I could run fifteen miles without
doing any of the methods I've learned, I must be
reasonably fit.

A mountain climber dreams of conquering the
highest peak. Galloway quotes a Japanese proverb: "One
who climbs Mount Fuji once is wise, but one who climbs
it more than once is foolhardy" (Henderson 69). My
"Mount Fuji" is running a marathon. I want to run one
marathon.

During the last few months I've worked out a more
sensible schedule, running for time, a long run every
two weeks. I have always combined running, cycling, and
yoga, long before I read John Howard's article. Still
it reassures me to know he supports my activities. My
fitness program is sound. I've had good advice. I'm
drinking more fluids now and eating energy giving
carbohydrates, fresh vegetables, fruits, and grains.
I know I'll be fit enough. It won't be easy. It may take
four hours or more, but I'm going to run a marathon.

Running a marathon won't change my life much. It's
a personal challenge. No one except those close to me
will care or even know about it. But I know that I will
have scaled "Mount Fuji" alone. It will be me who leaves
the starting line and runs twenty-six-point-two miles,
and when I finish I'll know I can do anything I put my
mind to.

Breen 12

Works Cited

Freeman, Dane. Personal interview. 3 Nov. 1984.

Galloway, Jeff. Galloways' Book on Running. Bolinas,
        California: Shelter, 1984.

Henderson, Joe. "Tips for the First-Time Marathoner."
        Runner's World Oct. 1983: 67-70.

Howard, John. "Combining Sports Can Prevent Injuries
        While Providing Flexibility and Muscle
        Strength." Runner's World April 1983: 64.

Pearce, Richard. "Body Fluids." Runner's World April
        1983: 45-48.

Sheehan, George. Personal interview. 25 October
        1984.

----. Running and Being. New York: Warner, 1978.

Sparks, Ken, and Garry Bjorklund. Long Distance
        Runner's Guide to Training and Racing.
        Englewood Cliffs: Prentice, 1984.

Squires, Bill, and Raymond Krise. Improving Women's
        Running. Brattleboro, Vermont: Steven Greene
        P, 1983.

*Alan Neilson was a sophomore honors student planning to major in political sci-
ence when he became interested in several court trials in which "humanism" was
attacked. Alan set out to explore and define the concept in "Has the Devil Returned
as a Humanist?" He begins with a provocative lead, describes the controversy,
traces the historical meaning of the term, and analyzes its varying usage. Ultimately he finds that the concept is too complex for a simple definition, but he has
nonetheless gained a great deal of insight into it.*

1

Alan Neilson

Professor Barbara Downes

Owen Hall 211

13 April 1987

Has the Devil Returned as a Humanist?

Here is what Secular Humanists believe in:

1. Abortion on demand
2. Homosexuality as normal
3. Sexual freedom and pornography
4. Prostitution is okay
5. Free use of drugs as desired
6. Religious atheism and evolution
7. Child's rights over parents'

At least that's what Secular Humanists believe

according to Dr. Robert L. Simonds writing in a

newsletter published by the Biblical News Service (11).

Dr. Simonds also accuses Humanists of believing there is

no right or wrong, and that situational ethics is where

one judges how an action applies only to one's own

desires.

But it gets worse. Writing in the same newsletter,

Neilson 2

H. Edward Rowe of the Church League of America says that Humanists believe that while man is good, God is actually bad, and that the only salvation will be through science (11).

And worse. Evangelist James Kennedy says that Secular Humanism is a "godless, atheistic, evolutionary, amoral, collectivist, socialistic, communistic religion," and that it threatens our school children (Safire 6). That threat has been taken seriously as evidenced by several trials around the nation in which school boards have been sued for using textbooks that promote these kinds of horrible things through literature. Examples of works which may corrupt Christian children include Shakespeare's Macbeth (which portrays witchcraft), The Diary of Anne Frank (in which she says it is valuable to believe in religion but that it does not matter which one), and The Wizard of Oz (where courage can be acquired from something other than God). Even United States Senators have become frightened by the Humanist evil. In 1984 Senator Orrin Hatch of Utah wrote into a funding bill for magnet schools a provision that forbids the schools to teach courses on secular humanism. When Senator Hatch was later asked to define Humanism, he described it as courses on "soft stuff," such as personal values or life styles (Safire 6).

Who are these Humanists who many see as a threat to our traditional way of life? According to Corliss Lamont, one of the major proponents of Humanism, the list includes Socrates, Aristotle, and Sophocles, among the Greeks; Leonardo da Vinci and Michelangelo, from the Renaissance; Francis Bacon, Erasmus, and Montaigne, from the 16th century; Thomas Jefferson and Thomas Hobbes, from the Enlightenment; and among moderns, almost everyone who is anyone: Albert Einstein, Erich Fromm, Julian Huxley, Linus Pauling, E. M. Forster, Walter Lippmann, Thomas Mann, Jean-Paul Sartre, and so on (23)--not a crowd one would normally be ashamed to associate with.

Edwin Wilson, a former editor of The Humanist, argues that Humanism's "central concern is for man, his growth, fulfillment and creativity in the here and now" (15). Wilson claims that Humanists are not anti-God but rather pro-man in that they are concerned with his condition in this world rather than in an afterlife. Wilson contends that there is no conflict between Humanism and Christianity. Like religion itself, Wilson claims that Humanism even upholds "religious aspirations of faith, commitment, loyalty, hope and love" (15).

Which is it then? Does Humanism represent the worst the devil can do to us? Or is it some mild

Neilson 4

philosophy about the hopes and needs of mankind? Is it
by definition secular and anti-godly? Or is it a
substitute for more traditional forms of religion? Is
it something we ought to fear or embrace?

The problem in part seems to lie in its all-
inclusiveness. A glance at the table of contents in
a collection of essays called Being Human in a
Technological Age illustrates the difficulty. The
essays, each on some aspect of Humanism, cover physics,
philosophy, theology, history, technology, ideology,
utopia, the social sciences, and "Neo-Vedantism" (v).
Paul Kurtz, a professor of philosophy at the State
University of New York at Buffalo, has observed that
there are as many varieties of Humanism as there are
wines and cheeses (16), and they include Marxist,
Catholic, liberal, naturalist, and existentialist, to
name only a few. The Dutch Humanists are apparently
skeptical of "science" and regard it as a potential
destroyer of man (Wilson 16), yet some American
Humanists have proclaimed science as the primary
salvation of man (Kurtz 14). Some Humanists are
outspoken atheists; some are fervent Christians and
Jews. How can we understand something so broad and so
seemingly full of contradictions?

First, a brief overview of its origins would help.
Second, an analysis of its seemingly inherent

contradiction--secular vs. religious--would clarify.
And then, finally, we might arrive at a definition that
would help us understand.

Humanism seems traceable at least back to the
Greeks in Western culture, and to the Buddhist and
Confucian legacies of Eastern culture.   Lamont
identifies Protagoras in the 5th century BC as the most
notable early Humanist--notable for saying that "man
is the measure of all things."   But apparently for
challenging the conventional views about the gods,
Protagoras was banished from Athens and his works burnt
(31).   The actual term, Humanism, was first used in the
early 16th century to designate writers and scholars of
the European Renaissance (12).   Originally, the word
merely referred to a man of letters such as Erasmus, who
studied the texts of ancient Greeks and Romans (Mandrou
42).   What separated them from the other scholars of the
time was a focus on politics, morals, philosophy, and
art in pre-Christian civilizations.   Instead of
studying and commenting on the Bible or the early Church
fathers, they studied what were considered "secular"
works and authors: Aristotle, Livy, Sallust, and
Herodotus.   Robert Mandrou, a professor of history at
the University of Paris, writes that the early Humanists
were so stimulated by new and exciting ideas that "there
was no limit at all to their curiosity, to their hunger

for knowledge" (44). Their discoveries, along with the general discoveries of the era (in geography and astronomy especially) led them to apply their new critical method to the sacred books of the Church (46) -- not to challenge faith, but to correct the errors of medieval copyists, corrupt translations, and false interpretations.

> Erasmus explains very clearly his position,
> which must be that of every philologist: 'There
> is no danger that anyone will suddenly depart
> from Christ if he happens to hear that a passage
> has been found in the scriptures which an
> unskilled or drowsy copyist has corrupted.' (47)

But Mandrou reports that the procedure eventually called up questions about the Church's most fundamental traditions (47), and that in part, it was the quest for knowledge by the Humanists that broke up the Catholic Church at the end of the Medieval period.

Corliss Lamont claims that Renaissance Humanism was a revolt against the other-worldliness of the Church, a turning away from preoccupation with personal immortality. The ideal human being, he writes, was no longer the ascetic monk but the earthly-achiever, typified by Leonardo da Vinci (20). The early Humanists, wittingly or unwittingly, promoted a break from religious control of knowledge. Erasmus, Montaigne, Francis Bacon, and Thomas More all rejected

Christian supernaturalism (21). And the Church was
fully aware of the threat. When an Italian, Pietro
Pomponazzi, adopted the Aristotelian position and
challenged the concept of immortality and an afterlife,
he attempted to avoid offending the Church, but his book
was nonetheless banned by the Inquisition (22).

The early Humanists then were interested in man, in
the cultures he had created, in his hopes and
aspirations as well as his failures. From Aristotle
they learned to be critical of truth that could not be
demonstrated and proven by reason or evidence, and thus
they grew skeptical about religious teachings,
especially supernatural beliefs. This history of
seeking knowledge about man without reference to
religious beliefs clearly relates to the present
controversy in America. But it also relates to several
aspects of our very founding. Lamont claims that
individuals such as Thomas Jefferson and Thomas Paine
were intellectuals who inherited and passed on to us the
primary assumptions of Humanism. "No nation in the
world is more secular and this-worldly in its
predominant interests than America" (16). Much of our
national character is "fundamentally Humanist" and it
is typified in our Declaration of Independence which
proclaims that all men have the unalienable right to
"life, liberty and the pursuit of happiness" (17). These

Neilson 8

are human-centered goals, not religious goals. The
attitude appears again in our Constitution, which
Lamont argues could be a summary of the Humanist agenda:

> We the People of the United States, in order to
> form a more perfect Union, establish Justice,
> insure domestic tranquility, provide for the
> common defense, promote the general welfare, and
> secure the blessings of liberty to ourselves and
> our posterity . . . (18)

By establishing and promoting the general welfare of
human beings on this earth, and by clearly separating
church and state in the First Amendment, we have,
according to Humanist definition, created a Humanist
society--a secular society that although clearly not
forbidding religion, makes it a private matter
independent of our basic societal goals.

Does that mean Humanism is godless? Is Humanism
another word for atheism or communism? The answer isn't
simple. Humanism is clearly a secular movement away
from religious domination. And some philosophies that
derive from the Humanist heritage are clearly opposed to
a belief in God. Marxism is the best example. But
numerous atheistic Humanists are also fervent
democrats, firm supporters of freedom and human rights,
yet equally strong in their conviction that anything to
do with religion smacks of superstition. Such

individuals include Corliss Lamont, who is still
considered a primary spokesman for Humanism in America.
In other words, Humanism may easily lead to an anti-
religious stance. Its emphasis is on the here-and-now,
on promoting human welfare in this world, and on
denouncing anything that might suggest that man's
destiny can be affected by anything other than man's own
efforts and personal sense of responsibility (Kurtz 5).
But that does not seem to also mean that such a position
leads automatically to any particular political
stance. One might hold to an anti-religious Humanism, a
secular Humanism, and still be a patriotic Republican
from Indiana just as easily as a communist from
Bulgaria. Some forms of Humanism may be godless, but no
form of Humanism is automatically related to any
particular political position.

In fact, many of the most important and influential
Humanists have not rejected religion, and many believe
in God. The prime example would be the 18th century
deists, such as Jefferson, Franklin, and Adams (Lamont
24). The deists were essentially Humanists who
recognized that the churches "represented the <u>status
quo</u>" and that the improvement of social conditions
required reason and self-responsibility (Tribe 21).
They believed in a spiritual being whose presence was
found in nature and the physical universe, but who had

given man the responsibility for affecting his own
welfare.

Deism was not popular after the 18th century, yet
the impulse for reconciling Humanist beliefs with
spiritual needs persisted. Algernon Black observes
that the intelligent Humanist will "not fall into the
trap of believing that man is the supreme power, the
highest form of life in existence" (73). Man may be the
highest form currently identifiable, but we know also
that the universe does not revolve around us and gives no
evidence of being created for us. Black argues that man
cannot live without hope and faith. And of the two, he
says, faith is the more important.

> It is a call to commitment, a readiness to strive,
> sacrifice, stake a life on an outcome and a
> fulfillment. To have faith is to have a sense of
> values worth living for; to try to be faithful to
> an ideal or a vision of possibility. (76)

The religious Humanist, then, works "to free faith and
devotion from the dogmas of theistic theologies and
supernaturalist psychologies" (Schneider 65). Or in
other words, to free the human need for spiritual values
from the control of organized religion.

Lamont stresses that "in so far as Christian
teachings stressed good works and moral achievement
rather than ritual, ceremony and salvation, it leads

toward Humanism" (54).   In America, the American

Humanist Association is an outgrowth of the Unitarian

religion (Wilson 16), as is the parallel movement called

"Religious Humanism" (Lamont 53).   In his work, <u>The</u>

<u>Philosophy of Humanism</u>, Lamont writes about how in 1923

three Unitarian ministers and two college professors

organized a movement that led to a "Humanist Manifesto"

(48-60).   The resulting document is one of the principal

focal points of fundamentalist and evangelical

attacks.   It claims that Humanism is without question a

religion because it strives to realize the highest

values of life.   The authors listed fifteen basic

beliefs, among which are the following:

> *The universe was not created but merely exists.
>
> *The supernatural does not exist.
>
> *Religion must formulate its hopes and plans in
> the light of a scientific spirit.
>
> *Religion consists of those actions and thoughts
> which are humanly significant (there is no
> distinction between the secular and the sacred).
>
> *The goal of life is the full realization of
> 'human personality.' (Lamont 285-289)

Jacques Maritain, one of the contemporary

proponents of Catholic Humanism, argues that the

interest in a religious form of Humanism after World War

I occurred at least in part as a reaction to the appeal of

Neilson 12

Communism, and that a reference in the Humanist
Manifesto to "socialism" as the form of government most
likely to promote the human good is the primary
evidence. The Humanist Manifesto would therefore be
better understood as a counterpart to a Communist
Manifesto--religious Humanism's alternative to the
most extreme form of secular Humanism (27-32).

But there have been many other calls for a
religious Humanism. Jacques Maritain in 1938 argued
that we should guard against defining Humanism "by
exclusion to all reference of the superhuman and by a
denial of all transcendence" (xii). Maritain argues
that "secular Humanism is part of Christian impulses
gone astray" (xvi) and that we need a new Humanism which
"does not worship man, but has a real and effective
respect for human dignity and for the rights of human
personality. . . ." (xvi-xvii). But Maritain suggests
a version "rooted . . . in incarnation" (65)--that is,
in fairly traditional Catholic theology.

In the 1960s Julian Huxley was calling for a
"religious affirmation of something new," a single
religious system that would replace the many
conflicting systems that currently compete for the
spirit of man (41). This new religion, he indicated,
would be a "spiritual ecology" in which man's relations
to all things were accounted for.

Humanism would seem to be an unlikely candidate for a "religion," yet it would equally seem in the eyes of many to be fully compatible with sanctity, with a religious spirit. It is not difficult to argue that the need for man to use his reason and imagination as ways of reaching his fullest potential is nothing more than using that which a creator gave to man for his expected use. By contrast, atheism would seem to have about it a negative quality--an absolute certainty that makes it somewhat opposite to Humanism, which tends in most cases to be portrayed as optimistic and open to doubt, open to scrutiny. Yet William Safire describes secular Humanists as "atheists who try to do good without believing in God" (6).

A definition with any precision, then, grows more and more unlikely. H. J. Blackman objects to adding any adjective to the word. "Ethical," "scientific," "religious"--each "mutilates the concept by limiting it to some single aspect of human life" (35). By contrast, Horace L. Friess, a professor of philosophy and religion at Columbia University, believes it is acceptable to have a variety of definitions. Each contributes to the whole, and each complements the other (44).

What we seem to be left with, then, is a definition in its most general sense. Humanism seems to be nothing

Neilson 14

more and nothing less than a concern for the human
condition. It attempts to find "a coherent answer" to
the question of human existence, and it tends to stress
self-understanding and self-responsibility (Van Praag
42-45). Although some extremist versions of it are
housed in totalitarian governments, the norm would seem
to "aim at an open society characterized by freedom of
opinion" (Van Praag 45) and typified by the United
States and Western Europe. A belief in Humanism does
not necessarily exclude God, but it does make man
responsible to himself, to others, and to society,
instead of to God--or in addition to God. "In general,
we can define Humanism as a perceptive loyalty to man and
a generous caring for him" (Friess 42).

It is understandable why some fundamentalist
church leaders are opposed to it. Yet to say that
Humanists are abortionists, communists, homosexuals,
free-lovers, pimps, and drug users is absurd. The devil
has not returned as a Humanist. Evangelical ministers
are misusing the term as a modern substitute for evil in
all its forms. Whether they like it or not, Western
civilization is now a thoroughly Humanistic culture.
Our heritage from the Greeks and the Renaissance,
through the Enlightenment and its fulfillment in the
American Constitution, is irreversible. Sophocles
wrote that "many are the wonders of the world/And none so
wonderful as Man." We need not be afraid of ourselves.

Neilson 15

Works Cited

Blackman, H. J. "A Definition of Humanism." The
     Humanist Alternative: Some Definitions of
     Humanism. Ed. Paul Kurtz. New York:
     Prometheus, 1973. 35-37.

Brochert, Donald M., and David Steward, ed. Being Human
     in a Technological Age. Athens: Ohio U P, 1979.

Friess, Horace. "Humanists' Responsibilities." The
     Humanist Alternative: Some Definitions of
     Humanism. Ed. Paul Kurtz. New York:
     Prometheus, 1973. 41-42.

Huxley, Julian. The Humanist Frame. New York: Harper,
     1961.

Kurtz, Paul, ed. The Humanist Alternative: Some
     Definitions of Humanism. New York: Prometheus,
     1973.

Lamont, Corliss. The Philosophy of Humanism. 5th
     edition. New York: Frederick Ungar, 1965.

Mandrou, Robert. From Humanism to Science: 1480-1700.
     Atlantic Highlands, NJ: Humanistic Press, 1979.

Maritain, Jacques. True Humanism. Trans. M. R.
     Adamson. London: Centenary Press, 1941.

Neilson 16

Rowe, H. Edward. "New Age Globalism." <u>Biblical News</u>
      <u>Service</u>. June 1984: 11.

Safire, William. "On Language: Secs Appeal." <u>New York</u>
      <u>Times Magazine</u> 26 Jan. 1986: 6-8.

Schneider, Herbert W. "Religious Humanism." <u>The</u>
      <u>Humanist Alternative: Some Definitions of</u>
      <u>Humanism</u>. Ed. Paul Kurtz. New York:
      Prometheus, 1973. 65-66.

Simonds, Robert L. "Christian Ethics Vs. Relativism."
      <u>Biblical News Service</u>. June 1984: 11.

Tribe, David. "Our Freethought Heritage: The Humanist
      and Ethical Movement." <u>The Humanist</u>
      <u>Alternative: Some Definitions of</u> Humanism. Ed.
      Paul Kurtz. New York: Prometheus, 1973. 20-30.

Van Praag, J. P. "What Is Humanism?" <u>The Humanist</u>
      <u>Alternative: Some Definitions of</u> Humanism. Ed.
      Paul Kurtz. New York: Prometheus, 1973. 43-48.

Wilson, Edwin. "Humanism's Many Dimensions." <u>The</u>
      <u>Humanist Alternative: Some Definitions of</u>
      <u>Humanism</u>. Ed. Paul Kurtz. New York:
      Prometheus, 1973. 15-19.

Suggested Writing Projects and Editorial Checklists

Suggested writing projects for each of the different types of papers discussed in *From Sight to Insight* are gathered here. Your instructor may assign one of them at any time—before, during, or after the work undertaken in a particular unit. Naturally these are only suggestions. You may have alternative projects you'd like to pursue, but if so, be sure you seek your instructor's approval.

Following each suggested writing project, you'll find a checklist to remind you of various elements you need to consider as you revise and edit your final draft. Your instructor may also want you to engage in *peer editing*, in which case the checklists can be adapted by simply replacing the personal pronoun "I" with a noun, "the writer," and occasionally with the pronouns "his" or "her."

PEER EDITING

If you haven't been involved in peer editing before, you should understand that it's part of the verification process. Once your paper is complete, you will read it critically to see if it satisfies you, to see if it accomplishes whatever purpose you had in mind. This is a valuable and needed private assessment of your work. But of course it must ultimately be shared with others. Only when an audience has read and reacted to your paper will you know whether you've succeeded. Peer editing is the stage where you turn to other readers who will approach your work with fresh insights and clear eyes. They can help you discover the strengths and flaws. They become a sort of sounding board. You might not agree with their comments or suggestions, but their reactions should encourage you to rethink what and how you have written.

And, of course, turnabout is fair play. You may be called on to act as editor for someone else's paper. Responding to another student's writing may at first make you feel uncomfortable. What is your role? How do you respond without creating hurt feelings? How can you possibly make suggestions to another student when you don't have all the answers?

As a peer editor, your responsibility is to respond with honesty and fairness. To do that, you must read the paper closely (with attention to detail) and sensitively (attempting to share the writer's desire to communicate some special idea, feeling, or insight). Here are some suggestions that may help:

1. Adapt an appropriate checklist from the following pages to serve as a guideline for critiquing. As an alternative, your instructor may wish you to create a checklist of your own as a class project.
2. Before you begin to write comments on the paper you've been asked to read, scan the entire paper quickly until you have a grasp of what is being written about and why. Remember that *subject, audience, context,* and *purpose* will always affect your judgment. A particular phrase or tone that seems appropriate for one paper may be inappropriate for another. You'll need to have a sense of the whole before you can be sure.

    Of course, if you can't determine what the focus is, or the intended audience, context, or purpose, you'll want to let the writer know. You won't be able to help the writer with small details until the larger directions are clear.
3. After getting a sense of the whole, reread the paper looking for and responding to specific points on your checklist. But don't limit yourself to the checklist. Strengths and weaknesses of any kind should be noted. Be honest and direct. General comments like ''good'' or ''weak'' leave the writer guessing: ''Good what?'' ''Weak what?''

    Instead of using judgmental words, specific written descriptions will be more valuable: ''I can see Bulldog Schmidt clearly.''

Or, "You've repeated the word *really* three times in this paragraph." Or ask questions: "Can you replace this passive verb?"

4. Finally, provide your writer with a brief overall summary of your response to the whole writing effort. Emphasize the best points and conclude with general recommendations.

PART I   WRITING FROM EXPERIENCE

Suggested Writing Projects

Unless your instructor suggests a different audience, any of the following exercises could be written for an audience of your peers, classmates or friends who would have a natural interest in sharing with you an experience from your life. But a word of caution: The beginning writer often wants to deal immediately with profound emotion. The result may be a melodramatic outburst ("I'm lonely, lonely!") that leaves the reader embarrassed. A professional writer knows that emotions are stimulated by real qualities in the world. To share experience with a reader, the writer must imaginatively portray the specific thing or event that inspires the original feeling. Begin small. Do not try to write about large emotions until you can first handle a simple but genuine experience arising from a simple cause.

1. Write an essay on an object owned and valued by you or some member of your family. For example, your mother may own a wicker basket brought from Italy by her great-grandmother in 1822. Your brother might think his collection of arrowheads is the most magical thing in his life. Your father may have a battered trumpet he played in the University of Minnesota marching band. Your job is to look at the object, perceive it physically (sight, smell, touch, taste, sound), and write about its history and meaning. Allow the detailed focus on the object to stimulate your imagination and lead you to an understanding about its emotional or personal significance.

2. Recall a particularly good experience in your life caused by a simple event (perhaps the night you and three friends camped out on a beach in Oregon or a summer afternoon you and your mother went shopping). Look in detail at all the sensuous elements that return to your memory. Re-create the experience in such a way that a reader can see it, hear it, and feel what you felt. Avoid generalizations except at the end, where you may want to reflect on the significance of the event, no matter how small.

3. Write an essay about a direct confrontation or painful experience you've had with someone who had an important influence on shaping your life. Call up the event in your memory and look at each of the details. Do you remember the smell of perfume on your Aunt Augustine's wrist? The way your math teacher's belly hung over his belt? The tone of voice of the parish priest as he told you he did not think the priesthood was right for you? Although it may be necessary to give background information, keep your essay focused on the primary moment. Share all the details with your reader. At the end, briefly consider in broader terms the effect and meaning such an experience had on your life.

Editorial Checklist

_____ 1. Have I included sensory details?
_____ sight (especially light) _____ touch _____ smell
_____ sound _____ taste

_____ 2. Have I used concrete, specific words and images to help my reader see?

_____ 3. Have I observed honestly with my own powers of observation?

_____ 4. Have I been faithful to my experience?

_____ 5. Have I eliminated all clichés? Both in language and perception?

_____ 6. Have I identified my audience? And considered their needs?

_____ 7. Have I adopted the most natural voice possible for that specific audience?

_____ 8. Have I searched for the right words instead of trying to get by with half-right words?

_____ 9. Have I double-checked for connotations? Have I overwritten just to impress?

_____ 10. Have I edited out every unnecessary word? Have I used ten where five would do?

_____ 11. Have I told what is instead of what isn't?

_____ 12. Have I eliminated unnecessary *who's, which's,* and *that's?*

_____ 13. Have I used strong nouns? Concrete nouns?

_____ 14. Have I used adjectives and adverbs selectively?

_____ 15. Have I cared enough to rewrite and edit until I feel I've achieved the best polished prose possible at this time?

_____ 16. Have I proofread and made corrections in ink?

PART II WRITING ABOUT PEOPLE AND PLACES

Suggested Writing Projects

Any of the following could be written for an audience of your peers, classmates or friends who might have a natural interest in sharing with you an experience from your life.

1. Write an essay in which you describe the character of someone who has had a special influence on your life. Avoid writing about your latest girlfriend or boyfriend; choose instead a relative, a teacher, neighbor, or lifelong friend. Focus on no more than two or three events in which you show your reader special qualities of the character. Narrate events according to a determined sequence; focus your description on selected details of action, physical qualities, speech, background, or environment the character has created around himself or herself. By the end of the essay, the reader should know the character so well that you will have little need to generalize upon what the person is like.

2. Write an essay that reveals character primarily through action or dialogue. You'll still need to describe the character with sense details, but actions, gestures, or speech will be the primary means by which the reader comes to understand inner qualities. Perhaps you have a roommate who always says he's going to get up at 6 A.M. to do his homework, but who inevitably sleeps in until 10 or even noon, then complains to others that it was your fault for not waking him. Or perhaps your mother stores groceries in her cabinets by alphabetical order: noodles followed by pancake mix followed by rice—and it drives you crazy. Or your neighbor talks only about his son's high school football record, even though his son graduated from high school more than 25 years ago. Focus on one or two scenes in which you reveal character through actions or speech. Include all the elements of scene.

3. Write an essay about a special place: the attic of your grandmother's farmhouse, a treehouse you and your father built together, or a dark crawl space behind the furnace in an old apartment building. (Were you hiding from the crazy lady in apartment 3?) Help your reader see it by using all the elements of scene. Why was it important to you? Can you find specific details of memory that will draw your reader into the experience? Did something happen there that made it special or that eventually changed its value? Describe the place and narrate one or two events that make your memory of it special.

Editorial Checklist

_____   1.   Have I included concrete images? Avoided unnecessary abstractions?

_____   2.   Have I observed honestly with my senses?

_____   3.   Have I used a natural voice?

_____   4.   Have I double-checked for connotations?

_____   5.   Have I organized descriptive passages from specific to general or from general to specific?

_____   6.   Have I organized narrative passages in an effective sequence?

_____   7.   Have I included major elements of characterization?
_____ physical description _____ actions _____ speech
_____ self-created environment _____ background _____ others'
reactions

_____   8.   Have I organized my essay around the basic elements of scene?
_____ light _____ time _____ place _____ character
_____ purpose _____ five senses

_____   9.   Have I edited out every unnecessary word?

_____ 10.   Have I eliminated unnecessary *who's, which's, there's,* and *that's?*

_____ 11.   Have I used strong nouns? Concrete nouns?

_____ 12.   Have I used adjectives and adverbs selectively?

_____ 13.   Have I used strong verbs in 50 percent of my sentences?

_____ 14.   Have I proofread and made corrections in ink?

PART III   OBJECTIVE REPORTING

Suggested Writing Projects

Assume you are writing one of the following projects for your student newspaper or for a newsletter that circulates among employees where you work. Even though your report must be objective, it should still use specific details selected from sense observations, especially dialogue and description. It might effectively incorporate a full scene. Brief characterization of those who are interviewed, as well as characterization of the whole situation, is almost always valuable.

1. Write an objective report on one of the following topics or on a topic your instructor approves of.

    tuition increases
    drugs on campus or on the job
    advancement opportunities for minorities at your place of work
    campus security
    sexual harassment by professors or employers
    class attendance regulations
    bookstore profits
    your college policy on athletics and grades
    parking problems

You might want to organize your essay into three parts: First, introduce the subject by characterizing the main elements as specifically and factually as possible; second, describe an interview held with someone directly involved in or affected by the subject (provide that person's opinions and any facts he or she can offer); and third, write a concluding paragraph in which you draw reasonable inferences based on your total findings. In all cases, try to hold back your personal views or emotions about the subject.

2. Write an essay in which you look at an event or issue by focusing on aspects of change, contrast, or consequences. Consider the latest changes in general education requirements, the opening of a new residence hall, conflicts in work rules, or new policies affecting financial aid. Gather as much factual information as possible from observation and interviews. (If you obtain more than one interview, you may want to devote separate paragraphs to each, a simple way of keeping your sources clearly identified for the reader.) Much of the information you gather in interviews can be summarized in your own words. Quotations should be reserved for the most significant statements. Maintain an objective attitude throughout your report.

Editorial Checklist

_____ 1. Have I investigated my subject for
_____ change? _____ contrast? _____ consequences _____
_____ characterization?

_____ 2. If I have characterized an aspect of my subject, have I included
_____ actions? _____ physical description? _____ background?
_____ others' reactions? _____ speech? _____ environment?

_____ 3 Have I looked for objective facts as distinct from opinions or
inferences?

_____ 4. If I have interviewed others, have I considered whether the
information provided was fact, inference, or opinion?

_____ 5. Have I opened my report with a 5 W lead that includes *who,
what, where, when,* and *why?*

_____ 6. Have I attempted to organize from most important to least
important?

_____ 7. Have I written a conclusion that summarizes or generalizes
upon my findings?

_____ 8. Have I integrated quotations with summaries?

_____ 9. Have I eliminated unnecessary words? Found the action in
every sentence and, if necessary, rebuilt the sentence around
the verb?

_____ 10. Have I prepared a professional-looking manuscript?

_____ 11. Have I proofread and made corrections in ink?

PART IV THE EXTENDED INVESTIGATION

Suggested Writing Projects

Extended investigations may be written for any number of audiences: for a company president investigating a new market for company products, for a U.S. congressman who needs information on complicated legislation, for a newspaper or magazine feature, or for an audience of scholars who share a common interest in a particular field of study. If your instructor does not identify an audience, be sure you select an appropriate reader before you begin. A number of my students have taken this assignment seriously and have targeted a specific group of individuals they hoped to influence. Several have published their essays in the student newspaper. One presented her work to the city council, which enacted local legislation as a consequence. Others have brought about changes in student life by encouraging student government to act on their findings.

Write an essay in which you investigate a narrowed subject that involves controversy. Choose a topic that offers the opportunity for personal observation, interviews (if possible), and access to primary and secondary sources. For example, you might want to investigate an institution (an institution includes buildings, customs, regulations, people, goals, activities, and much, much more). Your college, the local government, a nearby hospital, a library, or your place of employment might grant you access if you have focused your inquiry on a specific concern—the latest conflicts between fraternity houses and the community, the effectiveness of an urban jobs program, the entrance procedures at a hospital emergency room, the increasing theft of books and magazines from the open stacks.

The following suggestions may help:

1. Narrow the focus from a general topic to major categories to one category and its specific components.
2. Design a series of questions using the various strategies for inquiry listed on page 210.
3. Investigate your sources. Use your powers of observation; talk to people involved; search out primary and secondary sources.
4. As you investigate, evaluate your sources, evaluate the evidence, and interpret your findings (but avoid hasty conclusions that support your own bias).
5. As you conduct your investigation, keep an eye open for imaginative leads—a good quotation, a fascinating scene, and so on. Write down at least half a dozen or more so that you can choose the best.
6. When you're ready to begin drafting, consider various visual designs that might help you organize. Attempt to coordinate your lead with your organization.

Editorial Checklist

_____   1.   Have I focused on a single, specific component of my subject?

_____   2.   Have I investigated *who, what, where, when,* and *why?*

_____   3.   Have I looked for change, contrast, or significant consequences?

_____   4.   Have I looked for those qualities that characterize a subject?

_____   5.   Have I looked for and used both primary and secondary sources?

_____   6.   Have I evaluated the worth of each source and the facts or opinions provided?

_____   7.   Have I tried to find a pattern or relationship in the evidence that could lead to a reasonable interpretation?

_____   8.   Have I accepted only surface answers or have I pressed for deeper insights?

_____   9.   Have I provided full in-text documentation of all sources and their authority to speak on the subject?

_____   10.   Have I used an imaginative lead?

_____   11.   Have I organized my report around some evident design?

_____   12.   If I've used quotations, have I integrated them into my text?

_____   13.   Have I checked each paragraph for unity and logical purpose?

_____   14.   Have I read aloud and listened to the rhythms of my sentences?

_____   15.   Have I omitted unnecessary words and used strong verbs?

_____   16.   Have I proofread and made corrections in ink?

PART V   WRITING ABOUT IDEAS, ISSUES, AND VALUES

Suggested Writing Projects

Identify a specific audience for your project. Because essays on ideas and issues are one of the most common college assignments, you may want to write this one for students who share your intellectual interests or concerns. Be sure you take into account the type of vocabulary and tone your audience will expect. Identify how much the audience may already know about the subject. And consider whether you should use the personal "I" or a strictly objective third-person voice.

1. Select a subject about which you feel a personal concern, such as nuclear power, religious freedom, environmentalism, gay rights, America's trade position, single parents, or the quality of public education.

2. Consider types of questions that might help you focus your purpose more clearly: *Who* is affected? *Who* is responsible? *Why* are people concerned? *What* are the causes? *Why* has it happened? And so on.

3. With such questions in mind, consider whether *comparison* and *contrast* might be an appropriate strategy to help you focus and organize. Another method might be to *classify* the various categories of your subject according to the purpose you have for studying it.

4. Select a single component to write about. You may find it helpful to begin by preparing an extended *definition* of at least a paragraph.

5. If your subject concerns a problem (and most subjects do), give yourself the opportunity to play with possible solutions. Consider *direct analogies, personal analogies,* and *fantasy analogies.* Let yourself go. Allow your imagination to break free of all conventions and all previously suggested solutions. Take a risk with irrational possibilities and explore them seriously. Even if you come up with no dramatically new answers, this exercise may give you fresh points of view on the topic.

Editorial Checklist

 _____   1. Have I explored all the different strategies of perception to gain insight into my subject?
      __ who? what? where? why? when?
      __ change? conflict? consequences? characterization?
      __ comparison and contrast?
      __ classification?
      __ definition?
      __ illustration?
      __ analysis?
      __ creative analogies?

 _____   2. Have I narrowed my subject?

 _____   3. Have I attempted to make abstractions as concrete as possible?

 _____   4. Have I investigated primary or secondary sources?

 _____   5. Have I distinguished between objective facts and inferences or opinions?

 _____   6. Have I looked for relationships?

 _____   7. Does my introduction provide a general overview? a brief historical or cultural context? a definition? a classification of the subject?

 _____   8. Have I provided a focusing or thesis sentence that narrows the subject? Indicates the purpose? Suggests my attitude?

 _____   9. Have I designed each paragraph to effectively emphasize my purpose?

 _____ 10. Have I read aloud and listened to the rhythms?

 _____ 11. Have I eliminated unnecessary words and used active verbs?

 _____ 12. Have I proofread and made corrections in ink?

PART VI ANALYSIS AND ARGUMENTATION

Suggested Writing Projects

The audience for critical analysis and argumentation may vary from a single instructor in a class to a mass audience (with diverse backgrounds and points of view) that for some reason shares a common interest in the particular subject you're writing about. To choose the subject is in a sense to choose the audience. If you plan to analyze an essay on the historical accuracy of Shakespeare's Henry V, *you've narrowed your audience to a select group of students and scholars. If you plan to critique and argue against an article that appeared recently in your city newspaper calling for reduced funding for higher education, you've broadened your audience to all state and local taxpayers. In any case, as for any other writing project, you must consider the character of the audience before you begin the first draft. Will you be arguing against a commonly held assumption? How much background does your audience have on the subject? Are your readers' emotions going to interfere with your presentation of logic and reason? What tone will be most persuasive?*

1. Select one of the essays at the end of this unit for detailed analysis. Support or defend the writer's views with reasons of your own.
2. Find an editorial or opinion column in your student newspaper and critique the logic. If your reasoning differs from the author's, defend your position with logic and evidence.
3. *Time* and *Newsweek* run argumentative essays every week on contemporary topics. Choose one that angers you and write an essay in which you demonstrate with reason that the author is wrong about the issue.
4. Select one of the following topics. Find two sources and critique the reasoning found in both. If the sources disagree, come to a conclusion in which you clearly identify the most effective argument.

    nuclear waste dumps
    abortion rights
    teaching creationism in the schools
    date rape
    censoring record albums
    affirmative action in employment
    animal rights

Editorial Checklist

_____   1.   Have I written a complete, formal introduction, including
                 _____ name of author _____ title of work _____ general overview
                 of subject _____ a focusing (or thesis) sentence?

_____   2.   Does the body of my paper provide an objective description of
                 each major point as well as analysis and interpretation?

_____   3.   Does my conclusion interpret my overall findings and show the
                 relationship of my findings to the subject as a whole?

_____   4.   Have I assessed both the positive and negative values of the
                 work?

_____   5.   Have I made any effort to investigate the author's authority to
                 speak on the subject?

_____   6.   Have I evaluated my biases and tried to prevent them from
                 intruding into my argument?

_____   7.   Have I included refutation or rebuttal?

_____   8.   In rewriting, have I kept the needs of my audience in mind?

_____   9.   Have I eliminated unnecessary words and used active verbs?

_____   10.   Have I proofread and made corrections in ink?

PART VII   CRITIQUING THE ARTS

Suggested Writing Projects

The audience for the arts is almost always small. Yet it is one of the most sensitive and critically perceptive audiences you'll ever face. An analysis of a work of literature, of a film, or of a theatrical performance must take into account that your reader may have come away from the same work with a totally different experience than you did. Your job is to assume that the reader may have read the same book or looked at the same painting but that each of you brought to bear on it different backgrounds and different levels of sensitivity. Your attention to detail is therefore essential. Only with solid evidence and careful reasoning will you persuade.

1. Select one of the poems or stories in this unit to analyze and interpret. Focus on a single element of the work to discuss and trace its development. What is the relationship of the element you've selected to the significance of the whole? To the emotional effect of the work?

2. If you had a different interpretation of Sherwood Anderson's "Book of the Grotesque" (p. 416) than the one found in Diane Key's essay (p. 437), write a paper in which you analyze the story in your own terms. Show where Diane's interpretation may be weak or misleading.

3. Compare two poems with different subjects and themes but which seem to use similar styles, such as Richard Chess's "What To Say When You're Depressed" (p. 442) and Linda Pastan's "Marks" (p. 441). These poems seem to almost defy traditional views of poetry. Where are the rhythms and rhymes? Where are the elevated subjects such as love or heroism? Are these poems really poems?

Editorial Checklist

_____   1.   Have I looked at the literal level of the work—the sensory level—and let myself respond to it?

_____   2.   Have I studied the work before writing about it?
_____ taken notes? _____ defined key words? _____ read it aloud?

read it more than once, if possible?

_____   3.   Have I asked silent questions? *Who, what, where, when, why,* and *how?*

_____   4.   Have I looked for contrast, conflict, and characterization?

_____   5.   Have I looked for patterns and relationships?

_____   6.   Have I named the author and the work in my introduction?

_____   7.   Have I provided a *brief* summary of what the work is about as a whole?

_____   8.   Have I focused on one element or theme?

_____   9.   Have I described, analyzed, and interpreted that element or theme?

_____   10.   Have I come to a conclusion that shows a relationship to the whole? That assesses the value, worth, or significance? Both positive and negative?

_____   11.   Have I read my work aloud for rhythm and emphasis?

_____   12.   Have I edited for unnecessary words and strong verbs?

_____   13.   Have I proofread and made corrections in ink?

PART VIII   SCHOLARLY RESEARCH

Suggested Writing Projects

Almost everyone in a professional activity, from lawyers and doctors to scientists and journalists, engages in research, and the audience may vary widely, depending on purpose. But let's face it, the type of research paper you'll be expected to write in college usually has an audience of one—the instructor who assigns it. That means you'd do best to know well in advance what the instructor expects in terms of length, number of sources, style, tone, and level of intellectual depth.

Your instructor may want you to first prepare a "query." A query is a formal letter to a publisher or editor (in this case, to your instructor) detailing the type of research you propose to engage in and what you propose to accomplish. Indicate the purpose of your study and why it may be an important topic.

If you haven't yet selected a subject, here are some very broad suggestions.

recycling garbage	apartheid
alcoholism in college	billboards on national highways
values in Whitman's poetry	acid rain
AIDS epidemic	organic foods
Mark Twain's attack on religion	illiteracy in America
greenhouse effect	advertising on TV
animal rights	athletics and academics

Editorial Checklist

_____   1.   Have I used an imaginative lead? Does it truly lead into the basic theme of the paper?

_____   2.   Does my introduction provide a general overview of the subject in a few brief sentences?

_____   3.   Does my introduction provide historical or cultural context when necessary?

_____   4.   Does my introduction clearly focus the reader's attention toward a narrow aspect of the subject? (Is there a thesis?)

_____   5.   Is the body of the paper organized around a pattern? _____ from least to most important? _____ around contrasting views? _____ according to a narrative sequence? _____ according to a logical argument?

_____   6.   Have I used concrete details or sensory images to help my reader see?

_____   7.   Have I used strong nouns and active verbs?

_____   8.   Have I read aloud and listened to the rhythms?

_____   9.   Have I avoided pretentious language, jargon, circumlocutions?

_____   10.   Have I evaluated and eliminated my own bias whenever possible?

_____   11.   Have I avoided arguments that depend on emotion or stereotypes?

_____   12.   Have I avoided oversimplifications, overgeneralizations, undefined abstractions? false analogies?

_____   13.   Have I double-checked quotations, statistics, and dates for accuracy?

_____   14.   Have I double-checked all references cited for accuracy?

_____   15.   Is the works-cited page accurate down to the last period?

_____   16.   Have I proofread and corrected in ink?

Index